Instructor's Manual with Solutions Manual

Principles of Macroeconomics

SIXTH EDITION

N. Gregory Mankiw
Harvard University

Linda S. Ghent
Eastern Illinois University

SOUTH-WESTERN
CENGAGE Learning

Australia • Brazil • Japan • Korea • Mexico • Singapore • Spain • United Kingdom • United States

SOUTH-WESTERN
CENGAGE Learning™

For product information and technology assistance, contact us at **Cengage Learning Academic Resource Center, 1-800-423-0563**.

For permission to use material from this text or product, submit all requests online at **www.cengage.com/permissions**. Further permissions questions can be emailed to **permissionrequest@cengage.com**.

ISBN-13: 978-0-538-46832-9
ISBN-10: 0-538-46832-7

South-Western Cengage Learning
5191 Natorp Boulevard
Mason, OH 45040
USA

Cengage Learning is a leading provider of customized learning solutions with office locations around the globe, including Singapore, the United Kingdom, Australia, Mexico, Brazil, and Japan. Locate your local office at: **international.cengage.com/region**.

Cengage Learning products are represented in Canada by Nelson Education, Ltd.

For your course and learning solutions, visit **www.cengage.com**.

Purchase any of our products at your local college store or at our preferred online store **www.CengageBrain.com**.

Printed in the United States of America
1 2 3 4 5 6 7   14 13 12 11

Preface

The instructor's material that accompanies the five versions of Mankiw's *Principles of Economics, Sixth Edition* textbooks address the needs of both novice and experienced instructors. To meet the needs of these two groups, this *Instructor's Manual with Solutions Manual* comprises both chapter outlines and teaching tips as well as solutions to all of the questions and problems found in the textbook.

Linda Ghent of Eastern Illinois University prepared the main portion of each chapter including a synopsis of what is new in this edition compared to the third edition. Her work for each chapter also includes a list of learning objectives and key points. These items are followed by detailed chapter outlines that focus on the content found in the textbook. Helpful tips and icons occasionally interrupt these outlines. The bomb icon (Warnings) indicates areas where students may have particular difficulty with the material. The light bulb icon (Bright Ideas) offers ideas for presenting the material in a new or more thoughtful way. Also included in each chapter of the *Instructor's Manual* are classroom activities developed in part by Charles Stull of Kalamazoo College. Each activity provides important details to assist in planning as well as clear instructions for leading the activity. Recommended "Points for Discussion" connect the activity to the relevant economic concepts discussed in the chapter.

Using these resources, an instructor can quickly review the chapter learning objectives and chapter summaries to make sure their lecture notes cover everything in the text chapter. In addition, the chapter outlines are designed as a base for creating lecture notes for novice instructors. They may also be used as a complete set of notes for more experienced instructors. Therefore, this supplement is also available electronically from the product support Web site.

For queries and grading, the *Instructor's Manual* contains solutions to exercises from the textbook. Dean Croushore (University of Richmond) prepared many of the solutions for the "Quick Quizzes," "Questions for Review," and "Problems and Applications" found in the textbook.

Comparative Table of Contents

Contents

1 TEN PRINCIPLES OF ECONOMICS

WHAT'S NEW IN THE SIXTH EDITION:

There is a new *Case Study* on "The Incentive Effects of Gasoline Prices." Principle 10 on the Short-Run Trade-off Between Inflation and Unemployment has been updated to reflect changes in the economy in 2008–2009 and some of the response from the Obama administration.

LEARNING OBJECTIVES:

By the end of this chapter, students should understand:

➤ that economics is about the allocation of scarce resources.

➤ that individuals face trade-offs.

➤ the meaning of opportunity cost.

➤ how to use marginal reasoning when making decisions.

➤ how incentives affect people's behavior.

➤ why trade among people or nations can be good for everyone.

➤ why markets are a good, but not perfect, way to allocate resources.

➤ what determines some trends in the overall economy.

CONTEXT AND PURPOSE:

Chapter 1 is the first chapter in a three-chapter section that serves as the introduction to the text. Chapter 1 introduces ten fundamental principles on which the study of economics is based. In a broad sense, the rest of the text is an elaboration on these ten principles. Chapter 2 will develop how economists approach problems while Chapter 3 will explain how individuals and countries gain from trade.

The purpose of Chapter 1 is to lay out ten economic principles that will serve as building blocks for the rest of the text. The ten principles can be grouped into three categories: how people make decisions, how people interact, and how the economy works as a whole. Throughout the text, references will be made repeatedly to these ten principles.

1

KEY POINTS:

- The fundamental lessons about individual decisionmaking are that people face trade-offs among alternative goals, that the cost of any action is measured in terms of forgone opportunities, that rational people make decisions by comparing marginal costs and marginal benefits, and that people change their behavior in response to the incentives they face.

- The fundamental lessons about interactions among people are that trade and interdependence can be mutually beneficial, that markets are usually a good way of coordinating economic activity among people, and that the government can potentially improve market outcomes by remeding a market failure or by promoting greater economic equality.

- The fundamental lessons about the economy as a whole are that productivity is the ultimate source of living standards, that growth in the quantity of money is the ultimate source of inflation, and that society faces a short-run trade-off between inflation and unemployment.

CHAPTER OUTLINE:

I. Introduction

> Begin by pointing out that economics is a subject that students must confront in their daily lives. Point out that they already spend a great deal of their time thinking about economic issues: changes in prices, buying decisions, use of their time, concerns about employment, etc.

A. The word "economy" comes from the Greek word *oikonomos* meaning "one who manages a household."

B. This makes some sense because in the economy we are faced with many decisions (just as a household is).

C. Fundamental economic problem: resources are scarce.

> You will want to start the semester by explaining to students that part of learning economics is understanding a new vocabulary. Economists generally use very precise (and sometimes different) definitions for words that are commonly used outside of the economics discipline. Therefore, it will be helpful to students if you follow the definitions provided in the text as much as possible.

D. Definition of **scarcity: the limited nature of society's resources.**

E. Definition of **economics: the study of how society manages its scarce resources.**

> Because most college freshmen and sophomores have limited experiences with viewing the world from a cause-and-effect perspective, do not underestimate how challenging these principles will be for the student.

As you discuss the ten principles, make sure that students realize that it is okay if they do not grasp each of the concepts completely or find each of the arguments fully convincing. These ideas will be explored more completely throughout the text.

II. How People Make Decisions

Table 1

A. Principle #1: People Face Trade-offs

   1. "There ain't no such thing as a free lunch." Making decisions requires trading one goal for another.

   2. Examples include how students spend their time, how a family decides to spend its income, how the U.S. government spends tax dollars, and how regulations may protect the environment at a cost to firm owners.

   3. An important trade-off that society faces is the trade-off between efficiency and equality.

      a. Definition of **efficiency: the property of society getting the maximum benefits from its scarce resources.**

      b. Definition of **equality: the property of distributing economic prosperity uniformly among the members of society.**

      c. For example, tax dollars paid by wealthy Americans and then distributed to those less fortunate may improve equality but lower the return to hard work and therefore reduce the level of output produced by our resources.

      d. This implies that the cost of this increased equality is a reduction in the efficient use of our resources.

   4. Recognizing that trade-offs exist does not indicate what decisions should or will be made.

B. Principle #2: The Cost of Something Is What You Give Up to Get It

   1. Making decisions requires individuals to consider the benefits and costs of some action.

   2. What are the costs of going to college?

      a. We cannot count room and board (at least all of the cost) because the student would have to pay for food and shelter even if he was not in school.

      b. We would want to count the value of the student's time because he could be working for pay instead of attending classes and studying.

   3. Definition of **opportunity cost: whatever must be given up in order to obtain some item.**

> One of the hardest ideas for students to grasp is that "free" things are not truly free. Thus, you will need to provide students with numerous examples of such "free" things with hidden costs, especially the value of time. Suggested examples include the time students spend waiting in line for "free" sporting event tickets at their universities, time spent relaxing in the sun outside their residence halls, or dinner in a restaurant with their parents.

C. Principle #3: Rational People Think at the Margin

1. Economists generally assume that people are rational.

   a. Definition of **rational**: **systematically and purposefully doing the best you can to achieve your objectives.**

   b. Consumers want to purchase the goods and services that allow them the greatest level of satisfaction given their incomes and the prices they face.

   c. Firm managers want to produce the level of output that maximizes the profits the firms earn.

2. Many decisions in life involve incremental decisions: Should I remain in school this semester? Should I take another course this semester? Should I study another hour for tomorrow's exam?

   a. Definition of **marginal change**: **a small incremental adjustment to a plan of action.**

   b. Example: Suppose that flying a 200-seat plane across the country costs the airline $100,000, which means that the average cost of each seat is $500. Suppose that the plane is minutes from departure and a passenger is willing to pay $300 for a seat. Should the airline sell the seat for $300? In this case, the marginal cost of an additional passenger is very small.

   c. Another example: Why is water so cheap while diamonds are expensive? The marginal benefit of a good depends on how many units a person already has. Because water is plentiful, the marginal benefit of an additional cup is small. Because diamonds are rare, the marginal benefit of an extra diamond is high.

3. A rational decision maker takes an action if and only if the marginal benefit is at least as large as the marginal cost.

D. Principle #4: People Respond to Incentives

1. Definition of **incentive**: **something that induces a person to act.**

2. Because rational people make decisions by weighing costs and benefits, their decisions may change in response to incentives.

   a. When the price of a good rises, consumers will buy less of it because its cost has risen.

   b. When the price of a good rises, producers will allocate more resources to the production of the good because the benefit from producing the good has risen.

3. Many public policies change the costs and benefits that people face. Sometimes policymakers fail to understand how policies alter incentives and behavior and a policy may lead to unintended consequences.

4. Example: Seat belt laws increase the use of seat belts but lower the incentives of individuals to drive safely. This leads to an increase in the number of car accidents. This also leads to an increased risk for pedestrians.

5. *Case Study: The Incentive Effects of Gasoline Prices*

6. *In the News: Incentive Pay: Where the Buses Run on Time*

   a. Most bus drivers in Chile are paid per passenger rather than per hour, giving them an incentive to more quickly run their routes to pick up as many passengers as possible.

   b. This is an article from Slate.com that discusses how this type of incentive increases the likelihood that the buses run on time.

The Terminal, Chapter 10. This three-minute clips shows Tom Hanks as Viktor Navorski, who is forced to live in JFK Airport because he has no valid passport to enter the United States. Over time, Victor becomes hungry and desperate. He eventually figures out that he can gather luggage carts and return them for a quarter each. After the clip, discuss with your students why Victor is willing to do this while other people leave the carts lying around.

If you include any incentive-based criteria on your syllabus, discuss it now. For example, if you reward class attendance (or penalize students who do not attend class), explain to students how this change in the marginal benefit of attending class (or marginal cost of missing class) can be expected to alter their behavior.

III. How People Interact

A. Principle #5: Trade Can Make Everyone Better Off

1. Trade is not like a sports contest, where one side gains and the other side loses.

2. Consider trade that takes place inside your home. Your family is likely to be involved in trade with other families on a daily basis. Most families do not build their own homes, make their own clothes, or grow their own food.

3. Countries benefit from trading with one another as well.

4. Trade allows for specialization in products that countries (or families) can do best.

Activity 1—Getting Dressed in the Global Economy

Type: In-class assignment
Topics: Specialization, interdependence, self-interest, consumer choice, international trade
Materials needed: None
Time: 20 minutes
Class limitations: Works in any class size

Purpose
The advantages of specialization and division of labor are very clear in this example. The worldwide links of the modern economy are also illustrated. We depend on thousands of people we don't know, won't see, and don't think of in order to get dressed each morning. Self-interest follows naturally from interdependence. Wages, profits, and rents give people the incentive to perform these varied tasks. We depend on them to clothe us and they depend on our purchases for their incomes.

Instructions
Ask the class to answer the following questions. Give them time to write an answer to each question, then discuss their answers before moving on to the next question. The first question can be answered with a brief phrase. The second question is the core of the assignment and takes several minutes. Ask them to list as many categories of workers as possible. The third question introduces demand concepts; most of the determinants of demand can be introduced during this discussion. For the fourth question, ask the class to look at the country-of-origin tags sewn in their garments.

1. Where did your clothes come from?
2. Who worked to produce your clothes?
3. What things do you consider when buying a garment?
4. Where were your clothes produced (what countries)?

Common Answers and Points for Discussion
1. Where did your clothes come from?

There are many possible ways to answer, but many students will say "the mall" or another retail outlet. Some may say "a factory," "a sweatshop," or "a foreign country."

Mention the importance of markets here (this can be emphasized by asking, "Is anyone wearing something made by themselves, a friend, or a relative?") and discuss distribution versus production.

2. Who worked to produce your clothes?

There is no end to the possible answers; garment and textile workers are obvious but most students will also list workers dealing with raw materials, transportation, management, design, or machinery. Some may think more broadly to investors, road crews, bankers, engineers, or accountants.

3. What things do you consider when buying a garment?

Most answers focus on preferences (fit, style, quality, color). Price is cited less frequently. Ask about the importance of price until someone volunteers that income is important. Prices of substitute goods should also be discussed. Expectations of price changes may also be mentioned.

4. Where were your clothes produced (what countries)?

A large number of countries will be represented, even in small classes. Asia is always well represented. Latin American and European goods appear in smaller numbers. African products are conspicuously absent.

B. Principle #6: Markets Are Usually a Good Way to Organize Economic Activity

   1. Many countries that once had centrally planned economies have abandoned this system and are trying to develop market economies.

   2. Definition of **market economy: an economy that allocates resources through the decentralized decisions of many firms and households as they interact in markets for goods and services.**

   3. Market prices reflect both the value of a product to consumers and the cost of the resources used to produce it.

Explain to students that when households and firms do what is best for themselves, they often end up doing what is best for society, as if guided by market forces—or an invisible hand. Spend some time and emphasize the magic of the market. Use numerous examples to show students that the market most often allocates resources to their highest valued use.

   4. When a government interferes in a market and prevents price from adjusting, household and firm decisions become distorted.

   5. Centrally planned economies failed because they did not allow the market to work.

   6. *FYI: Adam Smith and the Invisible Hand*

      a. Adam Smith's 1776 work suggested that although individuals are motivated by self-interest, an invisible hand guides this self-interest into promoting society's economic well-being.

      b. Smith's insights are at the center of modern economics and will be analyzed more fully in the chapters to come.

C. Principle #7: Governments Can Sometimes Improve Market Outcomes

   1. The invisible hand will only work if the government enforces property rights.

      a. Definition of **property rights: the ability of an individual to own and exercise control over scarce resources.**

   2. There are two broad reasons for the government to interfere with the economy: the promotion of efficiency and equality.

   3. Government policy can improve efficiency when there is market failure.

      a. Definition of **market failure: a situation in which a market left on its own fails to allocate resources efficiently**.

    4. Examples of Market Failure

      a. Definition of **externality: the impact of one person's actions on the well-being of a bystander.**

      b. Definition of **market power: the ability of a single economic actor (or small group of actors) to have a substantial influence on market prices.**

      c. Because a market economy rewards people for their ability to produce things that other people are willing to pay for, there will be an unequal distribution of economic well-being.

    5. Note that the principle states that the government *can* improve market outcomes. This is not saying that the government always *does* improve market outcomes.

IV. How the Economy as a Whole Works

  A. Principle #8: A Country's Standard of Living Depends on Its Ability to Produce Goods and Services

    1. Differences in living standards from one country to another are quite large.

    2. Changes in living standards over time are also great.

    3. The explanation for differences in living standards lies in differences in productivity.

    4. Definition of **productivity: the quantity of goods and services produced from each unit of labor input.**

    5. High productivity implies a high standard of living.

    6. Thus, policymakers must understand the impact of any policy on our ability to produce goods and services.

    7. *In the News: Why You Should Study Economics*

      a. Training in economics helps us to understand fallacies and to anticipate unintended consequences.

      b. This is an excerpt from a commencement address by Robert D. McTeer, Jr., the former President of the Federal Reserve Bank of Dallas and describes why students should study economics.

  B. Principle #9: Prices Rise When the Government Prints Too Much Money

    1. Definition of **inflation: an increase in the overall level of prices in the economy.**

    2. When the government creates a large amount of money, the value of money falls, leading to price increases.

3. Examples: Germany after World War I (in the early 1920s) and the United States in the 1970s.

C. Principle #10: Society Faces a Short-Run Trade-off between Inflation and Unemployment

1. Most economists believe that the short-run effect of a monetary injection is lower unemployment and higher prices.

   a. An increase in the amount of money in the economy stimulates spending and increases the quantity of goods and services sold in the economy. The increase in the quantity of goods and services sold will cause firms to hire additional workers.

   b. An increase in the demand for goods and services leads to higher prices over time.

2. The short-run trade-off between inflation and unemployment plays a key role in the analysis of the business cycle.

3. Definition of **business cycle: fluctuations in economic activity, such as employment and production.**

4. Policymakers can exploit this trade-off by using various policy instruments, but the extent and desirability of these interventions is a subject of continuing debate.

5. This debate heated up during the early years of Obama's presidency. The severe downturn in the economy led policymakers to try to stimulate demand, but some feared that the end result would be inflation.

6. *FYI: How to Read this Book*

   a. Economics is very useful to understand, but it can be a difficult subject to grasp.

   b. There are nine tips to make reading and understanding the material in the book easier.

      i. Read before class.

      ii. Summarize, don't highlight.

      iii. Test yourself. At the end of each section of the text, you will find a "Quick Quiz." Answers to these "Quick Quizzes" can be found in the back of the textbook.

      iv. Practice, practice, practice.

      v. Go online.

      vi. Study in groups.

      vii. Teach someone.

      viii. Don't skip real-world examples.

      ix. Apply economic thinking to your daily life.

Activity 2—So Many Things to Do, So Little Time

Type:	In-class assignment
Topics:	Trade-offs, opportunity cost, thinking at the margin, incentives
Materials needed:	None
Time:	10 minutes
Class limitations:	Works in any class size

Give students a list of activities with corresponding time requirements: sleep, 8 hours; sleep, 6 hours; eat breakfast, 30 minutes; ride a bike, 1 hour; go hiking, 2 hours; study, 3 hours; study, 2 hours; go to class, 4 hours; go to class, 6 hours; watch TV, 2 hours; watch TV, 6 hours; take a nap, 1 hour; work, 8 hours; work, 4 hours; etc.

Make sure that there are many choices and that there are many pleasurable experiences—too much for a 24-hour period.

Ask students which Principles of Economics this activity illustrates.

If they do not say 1, 2, 3, and 4, help them see that this exercise has trade-offs in the choices they make, that each choice has an opportunity cost, that deciding whether or not to sleep 4 more hours may depend on whether you have already slept for 6, and that choices may be influenced by the incentives the student faces. For example, a student who is about to be placed on academic probation has an incentive to study harder.

SOLUTIONS TO TEXT PROBLEMS:

Quick Quizzes

1. There are many possible answers.

2. A country is better off by trading because trade allows more to be produced through specialization. Markets allow the "invisible hand" to guide self-interested individuals into promoting economic well-being. Economists believe that governments should enforce property rights and can improve on market outcomes when market failure occurs. Two common examples of market failures are market power and externalities.

3. The three principles that describe how the economy as a whole works are: (1) a country's standard of living depends on its ability to produce goods and services; (2) prices rise when the government prints too much money; and (3) society faces a short-run trade-off between inflation and unemployment. A country's standard of living depends largely on the productivity of its workers, which in turn depends on the education of its workers and the access its workers have to the necessary tools and technology. Prices rise when the government prints too much money because more money in circulation reduces the value of money, causing inflation. Society faces a short-run trade-off between inflation and unemployment that is only temporary. Policymakers have some short-term ability to exploit this relationship using various policy instruments.

Questions for Review

1. Examples of trade-offs include time trade-offs (such as studying one subject over another or studying at all compared to engaging in social activities) and spending trade-offs (such as whether to use your last 15 dollars to purchase a pizza or to buy a study guide for that tough economics course).

2. The opportunity cost of seeing a movie includes the monetary cost of admission plus the time cost of going to the theater and attending the show. The time cost depends on your next best use of that time; if it is staying home and watching TV, the time cost may be small, but if it is working an extra three hours at your job, the time cost is the money you could have earned.

3. The marginal benefit of a glass of water depends on your circumstances. If you have just run a marathon or you have been walking in the desert sun for three hours, the marginal benefit is very high. But if you have been drinking a lot of liquids recently, the marginal benefit is quite low. The point is that even the necessities of life, like water, do not always have large marginal benefits.

4. Policymakers need to think about incentives so they can understand how people will respond to the policies they put in place. The text's example of seat belt laws shows that policy actions can have unintended consequences. If incentives matter a lot, they may lead to a very different type of policy; for example, some economists have suggested putting knives in steering columns so that people will drive much more carefully! While this suggestion is silly, it highlights the importance of incentives.

5. Trade among countries is not a game with some losers and some winners because trade can make everyone better off. By allowing specialization, trade between people and trade between countries can improve everyone's welfare.

6. The "invisible hand" of the marketplace represents the idea that even though individuals and firms are all acting in their own self-interest, prices and the marketplace guide them to do what is good for society as a whole.

7. The two main causes of market failure are externalities and market power. An externality is the impact of one person's actions on the well-being of a bystander, such as from pollution or the creation of knowledge. Market power refers to the ability of a single person (or small group of people) to unduly influence market prices, such as in a town with only one well or only one cable television company. In addition, a market economy also leads to an unequal distribution of income.

8. Productivity is important because a country's standard of living depends on its ability to produce goods and services. The greater a country's productivity (the amount of goods and services produced from each hour of a worker's time), the greater its standard of living will be.

9. Inflation is an increase in the overall level of prices in the economy. Inflation is caused by increases in the quantity of a nation's money.

10. Inflation and unemployment are negatively related in the short run. Thus, reducing inflation entails costs to society in the form of higher unemployment in the short run.

Problems and Applications

1. a. A family deciding whether to buy a new car faces a trade-off between the cost of the car and other things they might want to buy. For example, buying the car might mean they must give up going on vacation for the next two years. So the real cost of the car is the family's opportunity cost in terms of what they must give up.

    b.   For a member of Congress deciding whether to increase spending on national parks, the trade-off is between parks and other spending items or tax cuts. If more money goes into the park system, that may mean less spending on national defense or on the police force. Or instead of spending more money on the park system, taxes could be reduced.

    c.   When a company president decides whether to open a new factory, the decision is based on whether the new factory will increase the firm's profits compared to other alternatives. For example, the company could upgrade existing equipment or expand existing factories. The bottom line is: Which method of expanding production will increase profit the most?

    d.   In deciding how much to prepare for class, a professor faces a trade-off between the value of improving the quality of the lecture compared to other things she could do with her time, such as working on additional research or enjoying some leisure time.

    e.   In deciding whether to go to graduate school, the student faces a trade-off between his possible earnings with a bachelor's degree and the benefits of an increased education (such as higher future earnings and greater knowledge).

2. When the benefits of something are psychological, such as going on a vacation, it is not easy to compare benefits to costs to determine if it is worth doing. But there are two ways to think about the benefits. One is to compare the vacation with what you would do in its place. If you did not go on vacation, would you buy something like a new set of golf clubs? Then you can decide if you would rather have the new clubs or the vacation. A second way is to think about how hard you had to work to earn the money to pay for the vacation. You can then decide if the psychological benefits of the vacation were worth the psychological cost of working.

3. If you are thinking of going skiing instead of working at your part-time job, the cost of skiing includes its monetary and time costs, which includes the opportunity cost of the wages you are giving up by not working. If the choice is between skiing and going to the library to study, then the cost of skiing is its monetary and time costs including the cost of possibly earning lower grades in your courses.

4. If you spend $100 now instead of saving it for a year and earning 5 percent interest, you are giving up the opportunity to spend $105 one year from now.

5. The fact that you have already sunk $5 million is not relevant to your decision anymore, because that money is gone. What matters now is the chance to earn profits at the margin. If you spend another $1 million and can generate sales of $3 million, you'll earn $2 million in marginal profit, so you should do so. You are right to think that the project has lost a total of $3 million ($6 million in costs and only $3 million in revenue) and you should not have started it. However, if you do not spend the additional $1 million, you will not have any sales and your losses will be $5 million. So what matters here is trying to minimize your loss. In fact, you would pay up to $3 million to complete development; any more than that, and you will not be increasing profit at the margin.

6. a.   The provision of Social Security benefits lowers an individual's incentive to save for retirement. The benefits provide some level of income to the individual when she retires. This means that the individual is not entirely dependent on savings to support consumption through the years in retirement.

    b.   Since a person gets fewer after-tax Social Security benefits the greater her earnings are, there is an incentive not to work (or not work as much) after age 65. The more you work, the lower your after-tax Social Security benefits will be. Thus, the taxation of Social Security benefits discourages work effort after age 65.

7. a. When welfare recipients have their benefits cut off after two years, they have a greater incentive to find jobs than if their benefits were to last forever.

    b. The loss of benefits means that someone who cannot find a job will get no income at all, so the distribution of income will become less equal. But the economy will be more efficient, because welfare recipients have a greater incentive to find jobs. Thus, the change in the law is one that increases efficiency but reduces equality.

8. By specializing in each task, you and your roommate can finish the chores more quickly. If you divided each task equally, it would take you more time to cook than it would take your roommate, and it would take him more time to clean than it would take you. By specializing, you reduce the total time spent on chores.

   Similarly, countries can specialize and trade, making both better off. For example, suppose it takes Spanish workers less time to make clothes than it takes French workers, and French workers can make wine more efficiently than Spanish workers can. Then Spain and France can both benefit if Spanish workers produce all the clothes and French workers produce all the wine, and they engage in trade between the two goods.

9. a. Efficiency: The market failure comes from the market power of the cable TV firm.

    b. Equity

    c. Efficiency: An externality arises because secondhand smoke harms nonsmokers.

    d. Efficiency: The market failure occurs because of Standard Oil's market power.

    e. Equity

    f. Efficiency: There is an externality because of accidents caused by drunk drivers.

10. a. If everyone were guaranteed the best healthcare possible, much more of our nation's output would be devoted to medical care than is now the case. Would that be efficient? If you believe that doctors have market power and restrict health care to keep their incomes high, you might think efficiency would increase by providing more healthcare. But more likely, if the government mandated increased spending on healthcare, the economy would be less efficient because it would give people more healthcare than they would choose to pay for. From the point of view of equality, if poor people are less likely to have adequate healthcare, providing more health care would represent an improvement. Each person would have a more even slice of the economic pie, though the pie would consist of more healthcare and less of other goods.

    b. When workers are laid off, equality considerations argue for the unemployment benefits system to provide them with some income until they can find new jobs. After all, no one plans to be laid off, so unemployment benefits are a form of insurance. But there is an efficiency problem—why work if you can get income for doing nothing? The economy is not operating efficiently if people remain unemployed for a long time, and unemployment benefits encourage unemployment. Thus, there is a trade-off between equality and efficiency. The more generous unemployment benefits are, the less income is lost by an unemployed person, but the more that person is encouraged to remain unemployed. So greater equality reduces efficiency.

11. Because average income in the United States has roughly doubled every 35 years, we are likely to have a better standard of living than our parents, and a much better standard of living than our

grandparents. This is mainly the result of increased productivity, so that an hour of work produces more goods and services than it used to. Thus, incomes have continuously risen over time, as has the standard of living.

12. If Americans save more and it leads to more spending on factories, there will be an increase in production and productivity, because the same number of workers will have more equipment to work with. The benefits from higher productivity will go to both the workers, who will get paid more because they are producing more, and the factory owners, who will get a return on their investments. There is no such thing as a free lunch, however, because when people save more, they are giving up spending. They get higher incomes at the cost of buying fewer goods.

13. a.   Both of these goals are intended to improve equality. However, reducing the cost of healthcare will lead to greater consumption of healthcare and less consumption of other goods. This reduces efficiency.

    b.   It is possible that some reforms will alter the production of healthcare, making more efficient use of the resources in that sector.

    c.   Providing some individuals with subsidized health insurance (by taxing households with higher incomes) reduces the incentive to work. This will lower productivity.

14. When governments print money, they impose a "tax" on anyone who is holding money, because the value of money is decreased.

15. To make an intelligent decision about whether to reduce inflation, a policymaker would need to know what causes inflation and unemployment, as well as what determines the trade-off between them. This means that the policymaker needs to understand how households and firms will adjust to a decrease in the money supply. How much will spending decline? How much will firms lower output? Any attempt to reduce inflation will likely lead to higher unemployment in the short run. A policymaker thus faces a trade-off between the benefits of lower inflation compared to the cost of higher unemployment.

16. Raising taxes will lead to reduced spending in the economy. This will cause a short-run increase in unemployment and a drop in prices. However, printing more money will cause a long-run rise in inflation because the value of money will be lowered.

2 THINKING LIKE AN ECONOMIST

WHAT'S NEW IN THE SIXTH EDITION:

There are some updates to the *FYI* on Who Studies Economics? There is a new *In the News* on "The Economics of President Obama." Table 1 has been updated and expanded.

LEARNING OBJECTIVES:

By the end of this chapter, students should understand:

➤ how economists apply the methods of science.

➤ how assumptions and models can shed light on the world.

➤ two simple models—the circular flow and the production possibilities frontier.

➤ the difference between microeconomics and macroeconomics.

➤ the difference between positive and normative statements.

➤ the role of economists in making policy.

➤ why economists sometimes disagree with one another.

CONTEXT AND PURPOSE:

Chapter 2 is the second chapter in a three chapter section that serves as the introduction of the text. Chapter 1 introduced ten principles of economics that will be revisited throughout the text. Chapter 2 develops how economists approach problems while Chapter 3 will explain how individuals and countries gain from trade.

 The purpose of Chapter 2 is to familiarize students with how economists approach economic problems. With practice, they will learn how to approach similar problems in this dispassionate systematic way. They will see how economists employ the scientific method, the role of assumptions in model building, and the application of two specific economic models. Students will also learn the important distinction between two roles economists can play: as scientists when we try to explain the economic world and as policymakers when we try to improve it.

15

KEY POINTS:

- Economists try to address their subject with a scientist's objectivity. Like all scientists, they make appropriate assumptions and build simplified models in order to understand the world around them. Two simple economic models are the circular-flow diagram and the production possibilities frontier.

- The field of economics is divided into two subfields: microeconomics and macroeconomics. Microeconomists study decisionmaking by households and firms and the interaction among households and firms in the marketplace. Macroeconomists study the forces and trends that affect the economy as a whole.

- A positive statement is an assertion about how the world *is*. A normative statement is an assertion about how the world *ought to be*. When economists make normative statements, they are acting more as policy advisers than scientists.

- Economists who advise policymakers offer conflicting advice either because of differences in scientific judgments or because of differences in values. At other times, economists are united in the advice they offer, but policymakers may choose to ignore it.

CHAPTER OUTLINE:

I.   The Economist as Scientist

    A.   Economists Follow the Scientific Method.

        1.   Observations help us to develop theory.

        2.   Data can be collected and analyzed to evaluate theories.

        3.   Using data to evaluate theories is more difficult in economics than in physical science because economists are unable to generate their own data and must make do with whatever data are available.

        4.   Thus, economists pay close attention to the natural experiments offered by history.

    B.   Assumptions Make the World Easier to Understand.

        1.   Example: to understand international trade, it may be helpful to start out assuming that there are only two countries in the world producing only two goods. Once we understand how trade would work between these two countries, we can extend our analysis to a greater number of countries and goods.

        2.   One important role of a scientist is to understand which assumptions one should make.

        3.   Economists often use assumptions that are somewhat unrealistic but will have small effects on the actual outcome of the answer.

    C.   Economists Use Economic Models to Explain the World Around Us.

To illustrate to the class how simple but unrealistic models can be useful, bring a road map to class. Point out how unrealistic it is. For example, it does not show where all of the stop signs, gas stations, or restaurants are located. It assumes that the earth is flat and two-dimensional. But, despite these simplifications, a map usually helps travelers get from one place to another. Thus, it is a good model.

1. Most economic models are composed of diagrams and equations.

2. The goal of a model is to simplify reality in order to increase our understanding. This is where the use of assumptions is helpful.

D. Our First Model: The Circular Flow Diagram

Figure 1

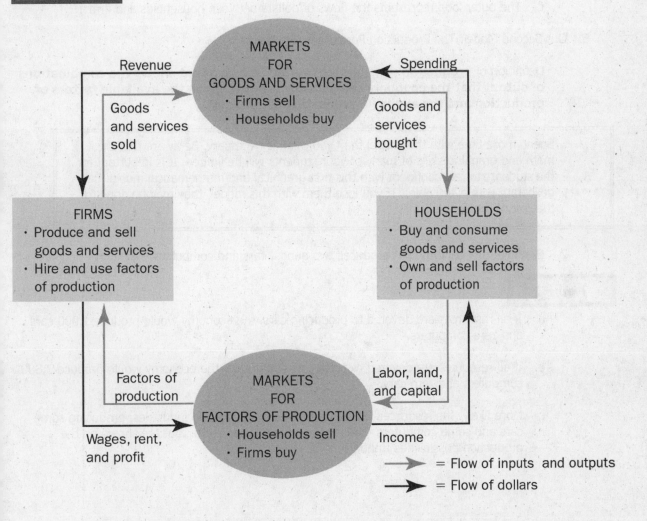

1. Definition of **circular-flow diagram: a visual model of the economy that shows how dollars flow through markets among households and firms.**

2. This diagram is a very simple model of the economy. Note that it ignores the roles of government and international trade.

   a. There are two decision makers in the model: households and firms.

   b. There are two markets: the market for goods and services and the market for factors of production.

   c. Firms are sellers in the market for goods and services and buyers in the market for factors of production.

   d. Households are buyers in the market for goods and services and sellers in the market for factors of production.

   e. The inner loop represents the flows of inputs and outputs between households and firms.

   f. The outer loop represents the flows of dollars between households and firms.

E. Our Second Model: The Production Possibilities Frontier

1. Definition of **production possibilities frontier: a graph that shows the combinations of output that the economy can possibly produce given the available factors of production and the available production technology.**

Spend more time with this model than you think is necessary. Be aware that the math and graphing skills of many of your students will be limited. It is important for the students to feel confident with this first graphical and mathematical model. Be deliberate with every point. If you lose them with this model, they may be gone for the rest of the course.

2. Example: an economy that produces two goods, cars and computers.

Figure 2

   a. If all resources are devoted to producing cars, the economy would produce 1,000 cars and zero computers.

   b. If all resources are devoted to producing computers, the economy would produce 3,000 computers and zero cars.

   c. More likely, the resources will be divided between the two industries, producing some cars and some computers. The feasible combinations of output are shown on the production possibilities frontier.

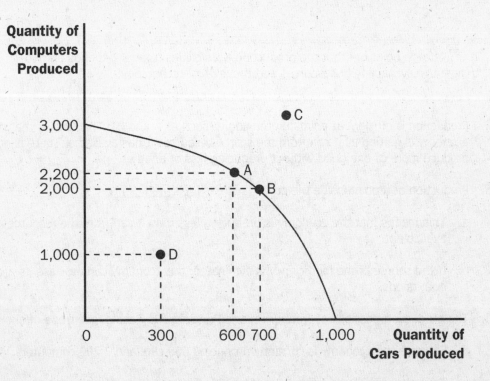

You may want to include time dimensions for variables. This will help students to realize that a new production possibilities frontier occurs for each period. Thus, the axes show the levels of output per period.

ALTERNATIVE CLASSROOM EXAMPLE:
A small country produces two goods: mp3 players and music downloads. Points on a production possibilities frontier can be shown in a table or a graph:

	A	B	C	D	E
mp3 Players	0	100	200	300	400
Music Downloads	70,000	60,000	45,000	25,000	0

The production possibilities frontier should be drawn from the numbers above.

Students should be asked to calculate the opportunity cost of increasing the number of mp3 players produced by 100:
- between 0 and 100
- between 100 and 200
- between 200 and 300
- between 300 and 400

3. Because resources are scarce, not every combination of computers and cars is possible. Production at a point outside of the curve (such as C) is not possible given the economy's current level of resources and technology.

It is useful to point out that the production possibilities frontier depends on two things: the availability of resources and the level of technology.

4. Production is <u>efficient</u> at points on the curve (such as A and B). This implies that the economy is getting all it can from the scarce resources it has available. There is no way to produce more of one good without producing less of another.

5. Production at a point inside the curve (such as D) is <u>inefficient</u>.

   a. This means that the economy is producing less than it can from the resources it has available.

   b. If the source of the inefficiency is eliminated, the economy can increase its production of both goods.

6. The production possibilities frontier reveals Principle #1: People face trade-offs.

   a. Suppose the economy is currently producing 600 cars and 2,200 computers.

   b. To increase the production of cars to 700, the production of computers must fall to 2,000.

7. Principle #2 is also shown on the production possibilities frontier: The cost of something is what you give up to get it (opportunity cost).

   a. The opportunity cost of increasing the production of cars from 600 to 700 is 200 computers.

   b. Thus, the opportunity cost of each car is two computers.

8. The opportunity cost of a car depends on the number of cars and computers currently produced by the economy.

   a. The opportunity cost of a car is high when the economy is producing many cars and few computers.

   b. The opportunity cost of a car is low when the economy is producing few cars and many computers.

9. Economists generally believe that production possibilities frontiers often have this bowed-out shape because some resources are better suited to the production of cars than computers (and vice versa).

Be aware that students often have trouble understanding why opportunity costs rise as the production of a good increases. You may want to use several specific examples of resources that are more suited to producing cars than computers (e.g., an experienced mechanic) as well as examples of resources that are more suited to producing computers than cars (e.g., an experienced computer programmer).

10. The production possibilities frontier can shift if resource availability or technology changes. Economic growth can be illustrated by an outward shift of the production possibilities frontier.

Figure 3

A Knight's Tale, Chapter 2. William (played by Heath Ledger) and two friends have won some coins in a jousting tournament. He convinces his friends to forgo current consumption and use the coins to invest in training and equipment so that they can win more in the future. This is a nice clip that allows you to explore the trade-off between current and future consumption and the effect of investment on the production possibilities curve over time.

You may also want to teach students about budget constraints at this time (call them "consumption possibilities frontiers"). This reinforces the idea of opportunity cost, and allows them to see how opportunity cost can be measured by the slope. Also, it will introduce students to the use of straight-line production possibilities frontiers (which appear in Chapter 3). However, be careful if you choose to do this as students often find the difference between straight-line and concave production possibilities frontiers challenging.

ALTERNATIVE CLASSROOM EXAMPLE:
Ivan receives an allowance from his parents of $20 each week. He spends his entire allowance on two goods: ice cream cones (which cost $2 each) and tickets to the movies (which cost $10 each).

Students should be asked to calculate the opportunity cost of one movie and the opportunity cost of one ice cream cone.

Ivan's consumption possibilities frontier (budget constraint) can be drawn. It should be noted that the slope is equal to the opportunity cost and is constant because the opportunity cost is constant.

Ask students what would happen to the consumption possibilities frontier if Ivan's allowance changes or if the price of ice cream cones or movies changes.

F. Microeconomics and Macroeconomics

1. Economics is studied on various levels.

   a. Definition of **microeconomics: the study of how households and firms make decisions and how they interact in markets.**

   b. Definition of **macroeconomics: the study of economy-wide phenomena, including inflation, unemployment, and economic growth.**

2. Microeconomics and macroeconomics are closely intertwined because changes in the overall economy arise from the decisions of individual households and firms.

3. Because microeconomics and macroeconomics address different questions, each field has its own set of models which are often taught in separate courses.

G. *FYI: Who Studies Economics?*

1. Economics can seem abstract at first, but it is fundamentally very practical and the study of economics is useful in many different career paths.

2. This box provides a sample of well-known individuals who majored in economics in college.

II. The Economist as Policy Adviser

A. Positive versus Normative Analysis

1. Example of a discussion of minimum-wage laws: Polly says, "Minimum-wage laws cause unemployment." Norma says, "The government should raise the minimum wage."

2. Definition of **positive statements: claims that attempt to describe the world as it is.**

3. Definition of **normative statements: claims that attempt to prescribe how the world should be.**

4. Positive statements can be evaluated by examining data, while normative statements involve personal viewpoints.

5. Positive views about how the world works affect normative views about which policies are desirable.

Use several examples to illustrate the differences between positive and normative statements and stimulate classroom discussion. Possible examples include the minimum wage, budget deficits, tobacco taxes, legalization of marijuana, and seat-belt laws.

Have students bring in newspaper articles and in groups, identify each statement in an editorial paragraph as being a positive or normative statement. Discuss the differences among news stories, editorials, and blogs and the analogy to economists as scientists and as policy advisers.

6. Much of economics is positive; it tries to explain how the economy works. But those who use economics often have goals that are normative. They want to understand how to improve the economy.

B. Economists in Washington

1. Economists are aware that trade-offs are involved in most policy decisions.

2. The president receives advice from the Council of Economic Advisers (created in 1946).

3. Economists are also employed by administrative departments within the various federal agencies such as the Office of Management and Budget, the Department of Treasury, the Department of Labor, the Congressional Budget Office, and the Federal Reserve.

4. The research and writings of economists can also indirectly affect public policy.

5. *In the News: The Economics of President Obama*

   a. Economist Lawrence Summers is a chief adviser to President Obama.

   b. This is a post from *The White House Blog* written by Summers describing the president's economic policies.

C. Why Economists' Advice Is Not Always Followed

   1. The process by which economic policy is made differs from the idealized policy process assumed in textbooks.

   2. Economists offer crucial input into the policy process, but their advice is only part of the advice received by policymakers.

III. Why Economists Disagree

   A. Differences in Scientific Judgments

      1. Economists may disagree about the validity of alternative positive theories or about the size of the effects of changes in the economy on the behavior of households and firms.

      2. Example: some economists feel that a change in the tax code that would eliminate a tax on income and create a tax on consumption would increase saving in this country. However, other economists feel that the change in the tax system would have little effect on saving behavior and therefore do not support the change.

   B. Differences in Values

   C. Perception versus Reality

      1. While it seems as if economists do not agree on much, this is in fact not true. Table 1 contains 20 propositions that are endorsed by a majority of economists.

Table 1

Emphasize that there is more agreement among economists than most people think. The reason for this is probably that the things that are generally agreed upon are boring to most noneconomists.

      2. Almost all economists believe that rent control adversely affects the availability and quality of housing.

      3. Most economists also oppose barriers to trade.

IV. *In the News: Environmental Economics*

    A. Some economists are working on ways to help save the planet.

    B. This is an article from the *Wall Street Journal* describing the field of environmental economics.

V. Appendix—Graphing: A Brief Review

> Many instructors may be unaware of how much trouble beginning students have grasping the most basic graphs. It is important for instructors to make sure that students are comfortable with these techniques.

> When reviewing graphing with the students, it is best to bring students to the board to be "recorders" of what the other students say as you give a series of instructions like "Draw a pie chart" or ask questions like "How tall should the bar be if the value is 120 million?" Do not make the student at the board responsible for the answer. Instead he should be simply recording what the other students say. Students are often uneasy about graphing at first and need to gain confidence.

    A. Graphs of a Single Variable

Figure A-1

        1. Pie Chart

        2. Bar Graph

        3. Time-Series Graph

    B. Graphs of Two Variables: The Coordinate System

Figure A-2

        1. Economists are often concerned with relationships between two or more variables.

        2. Ordered pairs of numbers can be graphed on a two-dimensional grid.

            a. The first number in the ordered pair is the *x*-coordinate and tells us the horizontal location of the point.

            b. The second number in the ordered pair is the *y*-coordinate and tells us the vertical location of the point.

        3. The point with both an *x*-coordinate and *y*-coordinate of zero is called the origin.

        4. Two variables that increase or decrease together have a positive correlation.

5. Two variables that move in opposite directions (one increases when the other decreases) have a negative correlation.

C. Curves in the Coordinate System

1. Often, economists want to show how one variable affects another, holding all other variables constant.

Table A-1

Figure A-3

   a. An example of this is a demand curve.

   b. The demand curve shows how the quantity of a good a consumer wants to purchase varies as its price varies, holding everything else (such as income) constant.

   c. If income does change, this will alter the amount of a good that the consumer wants to purchase at any given price. Thus, the relationship between price and quantity desired has changed and must be represented as a new demand curve.

Figure A-4

   d. A simple way to tell if it is necessary to shift the curve is to look at the axes. When a variable that is not named on either axis changes, the curve shifts.

D. Slope

Figure A-5

1. We may want to ask how strongly a consumer reacts if the price of a product changes.

   a. If the demand curve is very steep, the quantity desired does not change much in response to a change in price.

   b. If the demand curve is very flat, the quantity desired changes a great deal when the price changes.

2. The slope of a line is the ratio of the vertical distance covered to the horizontal distance covered as we move along the line ("rise over run").

$$\text{slope} = \frac{\Delta y}{\Delta x}$$

3. A small slope (in absolute value) means that the demand curve is relatively flat; a large slope (in absolute value) means that the demand curve is relatively steep.

E. Cause and Effect

1. Economists often make statements suggesting that a change in Variable A causes a change in Variable B.

2. Ideally, we would like to see how changes in Variable A affect Variable B, holding all other variables constant.

3. This is not always possible and could lead to a problem caused by omitted variables.

Figure A-6

a. If Variables A and B both change at the same time, we may conclude that the change in Variable A caused the change in Variable B.

b. But, if Variable C has also changed, it is entirely possible that Variable C is responsible for the change in Variable B.

4. Another problem is reverse causality.

Figure A-7

a. If Variable A and Variable B both change at the same time, we may believe that the change in Variable A led to the change in Variable B.

b. However, it is entirely possible that the change in Variable B led to the change in Variable A.

c. It is not always as simple as determining which variable changed first because individuals often change their behavior in response to a change in their expectations about the future. This means that Variable A may change before Variable B but only because of the expected change in Variable B.

There are two very good examples in the text that you should use in class. To discuss the omitted variable problem, point out to students that a rise in the sales of cigarette lighters is positively related to the number of individuals diagnosed with lung cancer. To discuss reverse causality, show that an increase in minivan sales is followed by an increase in birth rates.

SOLUTIONS TO TEXT PROBLEMS:

Quick Quizzes

1. Economics is like a science because economists devise theories, collect data, and analyze the data in an attempt to verify or refute their theories. In other words, economics is based on the scientific method.

Figure 1 shows the production possibilities frontier for a society that produces food and clothing. Point A is an efficient point (on the frontier), point B is an inefficient point (inside the frontier), and point C is an infeasible point (outside the frontier).

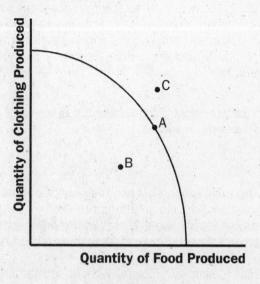

Figure 1

The effects of a drought are shown in Figure 2. The drought reduces the amount of food that can be produced, shifting the production possibilities frontier inward. (If a drought also reduced the amount of cotton available for the production of clothing, the intercept on the vertical axis would also decrease.)

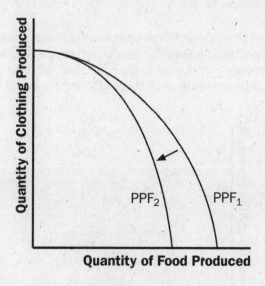

Figure 2

Microeconomics is the study of how households and firms make decisions and how they interact in markets. Macroeconomics is the study of economy-wide phenomena, including inflation, unemployment, and economic growth.

2. An example of a positive statement is "a higher price of coffee causes me to buy more tea." It is a positive statement because it is a claim that describes the world as it is. An example of a normative

statement is "the government should restrain coffee prices." It is a normative statement because it is a claim that prescribes how the world should be. Many other examples are possible.

Parts of the government that regularly rely on advice from economists are the Department of the Treasury in designing tax policy, the Department of Labor in analyzing data on the employment situation, the Department of Justice in enforcing the nation's antitrust laws, the Congressional Budget Office in evaluating policy proposals, and the Federal Reserve in analyzing economic developments. Many other answers are possible.

3. Economic advisers to the president might disagree about a question of policy because of differences in scientific judgments or differences in values.

Questions for Review

1. Economics is like a science because economists use the scientific method. They devise theories, collect data, and then analyze these data in an attempt to verify or refute their theories about how the world works. Economists use theory and observation like other scientists, but they are limited in their ability to run controlled experiments. Instead, they must rely on natural experiments.

2. Economists make assumptions to simplify problems without substantially affecting the answer. Assumptions can make the world easier to understand.

3. An economic model cannot describe reality exactly because it would be too complicated to understand. A model is a simplification that allows the economist to see what is truly important.

4. There are many possible answers.

5. There are many possible answers.

6. Figure 3 shows a production possibilities frontier between milk and cookies (PPF_1). If a disease kills half of the economy's cow population, less milk production is possible, so the PPF shifts inward (PPF_2). Note that if the economy produces all cookies, it does not need any cows and production is unaffected. But if the economy produces any milk at all, then there will be less production possible after the disease hits.

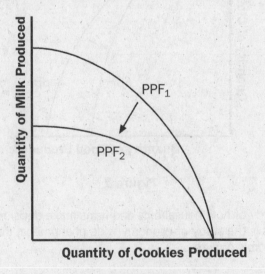

Figure 3

7. An outcome is efficient if the economy is getting all it can from the scarce resources it has available. In terms of the production possibilities frontier, an efficient point is a point on the frontier, such as point A in Figure 4. When the economy is using its resources efficiently, it cannot increase the production of one good without reducing the production of the other. A point inside the frontier, such as point B, is inefficient since more of one good could be produced without reducing the production of another good.

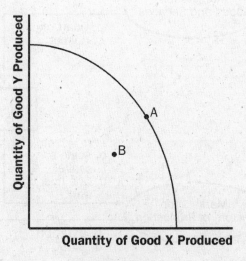

Figure 4

8. The two subfields in economics are microeconomics and macroeconomics. Microeconomics is the study of how households and firms make decisions and how they interact in specific markets. Macroeconomics is the study of economy-wide phenomena, including inflation, unemployment, and economic growth.

9. Positive statements are descriptive and make a claim about how the world is, while normative statements are prescriptive and make a claim about how the world ought to be. Here is an example. Positive: A rapid growth rate of money is the cause of inflation. Normative: The government should keep the growth rate of money low.

10. Economists sometimes offer conflicting advice to policymakers for two reasons: (1) economists may disagree about the validity of alternative positive theories about how the world works; and (2) economists may have different values and, therefore, different normative views about what public policy should try to accomplish.

Problems and Applications

1. See Figure 5; the four transactions are shown.

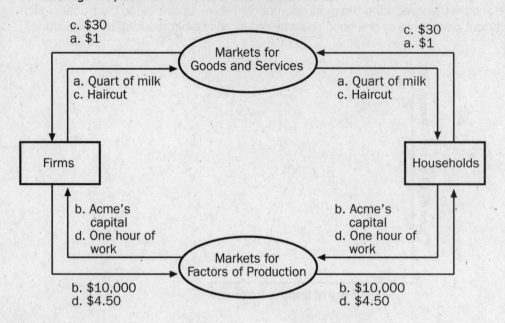

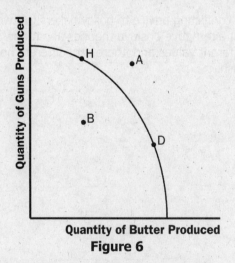

Figure 5

2. a. Figure 6 shows a production possibilities frontier between guns and butter. It is bowed out because the opportunity cost of butter depends on how much butter and how many guns the economy is producing. When the economy is producing a lot of butter, workers and machines best suited to making guns are being used to make butter, so each unit of guns given up yields a small increase in the production of butter. Thus, the frontier is steep and the opportunity cost of producing butter is high. When the economy is producing a lot of guns, workers and machines best suited to making butter are being used to make guns, so each unit of guns given up yields a large increase in the production of butter. Thus, the frontier is very flat and the opportunity cost of producing butter is low.

Quantity of Butter Produced
Figure 6

b. Point A is impossible for the economy to achieve; it is outside the production possibilities frontier. Point B is feasible but inefficient because it is inside the production possibilities frontier.

c. The Hawks might choose a point like H, with many guns and not much butter. The Doves might choose a point like D, with a lot of butter and few guns.

d. If both Hawks and Doves reduced their desired quantity of guns by the same amount, the Hawks would get a bigger peace dividend because the production possibilities frontier is much flatter at point H than at point D. As a result, the reduction of a given number of guns, starting at point H, leads to a much larger increase in the quantity of butter produced than when starting at point D.

3. See Figure 7. The shape and position of the frontier depend on how costly it is to maintain a clean environment—the productivity of the environmental industry. Gains in environmental productivity, such as the development of new way to produce electricity that emits fewer pollutants, lead to shifts of the production-possibilities frontier, like the shift from PPF$_1$ to PPF$_2$ shown in the figure.

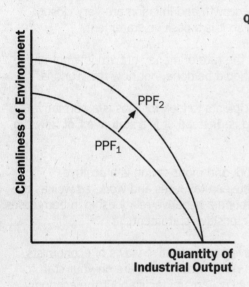

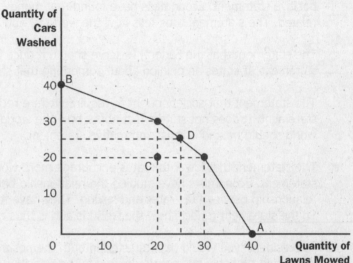

Figure 7   Figure 8

4. a. A: 40 lawns mowed; 0 washed cars
        B: 0 lawns mowed, 40 washed cars
        C: 20 lawns mowed; 20 washed cars
        D: 25 lawns mowed; 25 washed cars

    b. The production possibilities frontier is shown in Figure 8. Points A, B, and D are on the frontier, while point C is inside the frontier.

    c. Larry is equally productive at both tasks. Moe is more productive at washing cars, while Curly is more productive at mowing lawns.

    d. Allocation C is inefficient. More washed cars and mowed lawns can be produced by simply reallocating the time of the three individuals.

5. a. A family's decision about how much income to save is related to microeconomics.

    b. The effect of government regulations on auto emissions is related to microeconomics.

    c.   The impact of higher saving on economic growth is related to macroeconomics.

    d.   A firm's decision about how many workers to hire is related to microeconomics.

    e.   The relationship between the inflation rate and changes in the quantity of money is related to macroeconomics.

6. a.   The statement that society faces a short-run trade-off between inflation and unemployment is a positive statement. It deals with how the economy *is*, not how it should be. Since economists have examined data and found that there is a short-run negative relationship between inflation and unemployment, the statement is a fact, thus it is a positive statement.

    b.   The statement that a reduction in the rate of money growth will reduce the rate of inflation is a positive statement. Economists have found that money growth and inflation are very closely related. The statement thus tells how the world is, and so it is a positive statement.

    c.   The statement that the Federal Reserve should reduce the rate of money growth is a normative statement. It states an opinion about something that should be done, not how the world is.

    d.   The statement that society ought to require welfare recipients to look for jobs is a normative statement. It does not state a fact about how the world is. Instead, it is a statement of how the world should be and is thus a normative statement.

    e.   The statement that lower tax rates encourage more work and more saving is a positive statement. Economists have studied the relationship between tax rates and work, as well as the relationship between tax rates and saving. They have found a negative relationship in both cases. So the statement reflects how the world is and is thus a positive statement.

7. As the president, you would be interested in both the positive and normative views of economists, but you would probably be *most* interested in their positive views. Economists are on your staff to provide their expertise about how the economy works. They know many facts about the economy and the interaction of different sectors. So you would be most likely to call on them about questions of fact—positive analysis. Since you are the president, you are the one who has to make the normative statements as to what should be done, with an eye to the political consequences. The normative statements made by economists represent their own views, not necessarily your views or the electorate's views.

3 INTERDEPENDENCE AND THE GAINS FROM TRADE

WHAT'S NEW IN THE SIXTH EDITION:

There are no major changes to this chapter.

LEARNING OBJECTIVES:

By the end of this chapter, students should understand:

➢ how everyone can benefit when people trade with one another.

➢ the meaning of absolute advantage and comparative advantage.

➢ how comparative advantage explains the gains from trade.

➢ how to apply the theory of comparative advantage to everyday life and national policy.

CONTEXT AND PURPOSE:

Chapter 3 is the third chapter in the three-chapter section that serves as the introduction of the text. Chapter 1 introduced ten fundamental principles of economics. Chapter 2 developed how economists approach problems. This chapter shows how people and countries gain from trade (which is one of the ten principles discussed in Chapter 1).

The purpose of Chapter 3 is to demonstrate how everyone can gain from trade. Trade allows people to specialize in the production of goods for which they have a comparative advantage and then trade for goods that other people produce. Because of specialization, total output rises, and through trade we are all able to share in the bounty. This is as true for countries as it is for individuals. Because everyone can gain from trade, restrictions on trade tend to reduce welfare.

KEY POINTS:

• Each person consumes goods and services produced by many other people both in our country and around the world. Interdependence and trade are desirable because they allow everyone to enjoy a greater quantity and variety of goods and services.

- There are two ways to compare the ability of two people in producing a good. The person who can produce the good with a smaller quantity of inputs is said to have an *absolute advantage* in producing the good. The person who has the smaller opportunity cost of producing the good is said to have a *comparative advantage*. The gains from trade are based on comparative advantage, not absolute advantage.

- Trade makes everyone better off because it allows people to specialize in those activities in which they have a comparative advantage.

- The principle of comparative advantage applies to countries as well as people. Economists use the principle of comparative advantage to advocate free trade among countries.

CHAPTER OUTLINE:

Begin by explaining that there are two basic ways that individuals can satisfy their wants. The first is to be economically self-sufficient. The second is to specialize in the production of one thing and then trade with others. With rare exceptions, individuals and nations tend to rely on specialization and trade. One way to demonstrate this is to survey the students on their future plans (doctors, lawyers, teachers, etc.). Point out that they plan to specialize and trade. Ask them why this is optimal.

I.   A Parable for the Modern Economy

A.   Example: two goods—meat and potatoes; and two people—a cattle rancher and a potato farmer (each of whom likes to consume both potatoes and meat).

1.   The gains from trade are obvious if the farmer can only grow potatoes and the rancher can only raise cattle.

2.   The gains from trade are also obvious if, instead, the farmer can raise cattle as well as grow potatoes, but he is not as good at it and the rancher can grow potatoes in addition to raising cattle, but her land is not well suited for it.

3.   The gains from trade are not as clear if either the farmer or the rancher is better at producing both potatoes and meat.

Make sure that you write out all of the algebra involved in this example. If you leave out steps, students will not understand how these calculations are made.

B.   Production Possibilities

1.   The farmer and rancher both work eight hours per day and can use this time to grow potatoes, raise cattle, or both.

2.   Table 1 shows the amount of time each takes to produce one ounce of either good:

Figure 1

	Minutes Needed to Make One Ounce of:		Amount Produced in Eight Hours	
	Meat	**Potatoes**	**Meat**	**Potatoes**
Farmer	60 min./oz.	15 min./oz.	8/1=8 oz.	8/0.25=32 oz.
Rancher	20 min./oz.	10 min./oz.	8/0.33=24 oz.	8/0.16=48 oz.

ALTERNATIVE CLASSROOM EXAMPLE:
Martha and Stewart each spend eight hours a day wallpapering and painting:

	Hours Needed to Do One Room		Rooms Finished in 40 Hours	
	Paint	**Wallpaper**	**Paint**	**Wallpaper**
Martha	2 hours/room	8 hours/room	8/2=4 rooms	8/8=1 room
Stewart	4 hours/room	10 hours/room	8/4=2 rooms	8/10=0.8 room

3. The production possibilities frontiers can also be drawn.

   a. These production possibilities frontiers are drawn linearly instead of being bowed out. This assumes that the farmer's and the rancher's technology for producing meat and potatoes allows them to switch between producing one good and the other at a constant rate.

   b. As we saw in Chapter 2, these production possibilities frontiers represent the principles of trade-offs and opportunity costs.

 It is important to take the time to explain how to calculate the *x*- and *y*-intercepts. Point out that the farmer could produce 8 ounces of meat if all time is spent on meat or 32 ounces of potatoes if all time is spent on potatoes.

4. We will assume that the farmer and rancher divide their time equally between raising cattle and growing potatoes.

   a. The farmer produces (and consumes) at point A—16 ounces of potatoes and 4 ounces of meat.

   b. The rancher produces (and consumes) at point B—24 ounces of potatoes and 12 ounces of meat.

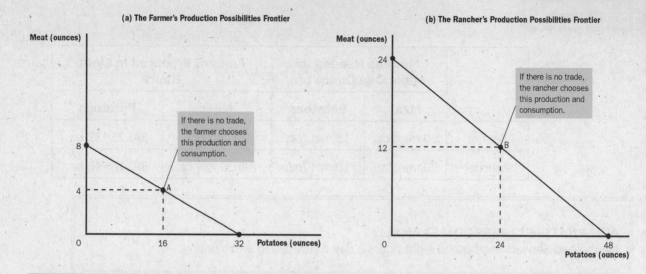

(a) The Farmer's Production Possibilities Frontier

If there is no trade, the farmer chooses this production and consumption.

(b) The Rancher's Production Possibilities Frontier

If there is no trade, the rancher chooses this production and consumption.

You should emphasize that these production possibilities frontiers represent the farmer's and the rancher's *consumption* possibilities because we are assuming that there is no trade.

C. Specialization and Trade

1. Suppose the rancher suggests that the farmer specialize in the production of potatoes and then trade with the rancher for meat.

   a. The rancher will spend six hours a day producing meat (18 ounces) and two hours a week growing potatoes (12 ounces).

   b. The farmer will spend eight hours a day growing potatoes (32 ounces).

   c. The rancher will trade 5 ounces of meat for 15 ounces of potatoes.

Students will ask how this "price" is determined. Explain the range of prices that each participant would be willing to accept.

Figure 2

2. End results:

   a. The rancher produces 18 ounces of meat and trades 5 ounces, leaving him with 13 ounces of meat. He also grows 12 ounces of potatoes and receives 15 ounces in the trade, leaving him with 27 ounces of potatoes.

   b. The farmer produces 32 ounces of potatoes and trades 15 ounces, leaving him with 17 ounces. He also receives 5 ounces of meat in the trade with the rancher.

3. In both cases, they are able to consume quantities of potatoes and meat after the trade that they could not reach before the trade.

Prove to your students that it would take each of them more than eight hours to produce these quantities on their own.

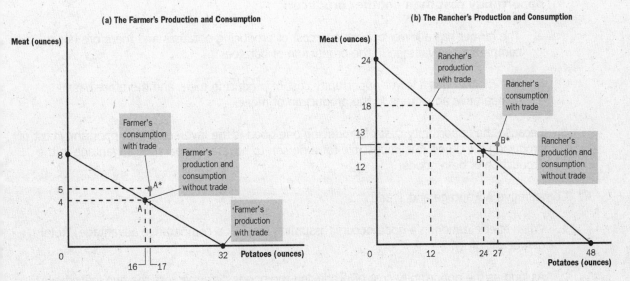

II. Comparative Advantage: The Driving Force of Specialization

A. Absolute Advantage

1. Definition of **absolute advantage: the ability to produce a good using fewer inputs than another producer does.**

2. The rancher has an absolute advantage in the production of both potatoes and meat.

B. Opportunity Cost and Comparative Advantage

1. Definition of **opportunity cost: whatever must be given up to obtain some item.**

> **Table 1**

    a. For the rancher, it takes ten minutes to produce one ounce of potatoes. Those same ten minutes could be used to produce one-half ounce of meat. Thus, the opportunity cost of producing an ounce of potatoes is one-half ounce of meat.

    b. For the farmer, it takes 15 minutes to produce one ounce of potatoes. Those same 15 minutes could be used to produce one-fourth ounce of meat. Therefore, the opportunity cost of producing one ounce of potatoes is one-fourth ounce of meat.

    c. The opportunity cost of producing one ounce of meat is the inverse of the opportunity cost of producing one ounce of potatoes.

Your students may have a hard time comprehending this. Make sure that you go through these calculations several times and write out every step on the board.

2. Definition of **comparative advantage: the ability to produce a good at a lower opportunity cost than another producer.**

   a. The farmer has a lower opportunity cost of producing potatoes and therefore has a comparative advantage in the production of potatoes.

   b. The rancher has a lower opportunity cost of producing meat and therefore has a comparative advantage in the production of meat.

3. Because the opportunity cost of producing one good is the inverse of the opportunity cost of producing the other, it is impossible for a person to have a comparative advantage in the production of both goods.

C. Comparative Advantage and Trade

1. When specialization in a good occurs (assuming there is a comparative advantage), total output will grow.

2. As long as the opportunity cost of producing the goods differs across the two individuals, both can gain from specialization and trade.

   a. The farmer buys 5 ounces of meat with 15 ounces of potatoes. This implies that the price of each ounce of meat is three ounces of potatoes, which is lower than the farmer's opportunity cost of four ounces of potatoes. Trade is beneficial to the farmer.

   b. The rancher buys 15 ounces of potatoes for 5 ounces of meat. The price of each ounce of potatoes is one-third ounce of meat. This is lower than the rancher's opportunity cost of one-half ounce of meat. Trade also benefits the rancher.

***Hannah Montana, "Mascot Love."* (Season 4, 4:05-5:04.)** While unclogging the sink, Robby (the father) realizes he is late for a meeting. When he decides to hire a plumber, his son Jackson volunteers to fix the sink for $50. The father agrees, and he admits he would have paid more. This is a nice short clip for showing comparative advantage. After the clip, discuss both Robby's and Jackson's opportunity costs.

D. The Price of the Trade

1. For both parties to gain from trade, the price at which they trade must lie between the opportunity costs.

2. In our example, the farmer and the rancher must trade at the rate of between 2 and 4 ounces of potatoes for each of meat.

Activity 1—Creating Comparative Advantage Examples

Type :	In-Class Assignment
Topics:	Specialization, interdependence, self-interest, comparative advantage
Materials needed:	3-5 candy bars (or similar items to use as prizes)
Time:	15 minutes (first day), depends on number of groups (second day)
Class limitations:	works in any size class

Purpose

This assignment allows students to further explore comparative advantage.

Instructions

Divide the class into groups of three or four to write a comparative advantage problem of their own. Tell them to make creative, humorous, yet plausible examples.

Give the students fifteen minutes to work on creating their examples at the end of class.

Instruct them to bring a neatly written copy of their examples for the next class when each group will present its example to the rest of the class. Students should include tables and figures similar to those used in class.

Let the students vote on which group has the best example and award a small prize to the group's members.

Make the examples available to all of the students in the class to use as practice problems for the exam.

E. FYI: The Legacy of Adam Smith and David Ricardo

   1. In Adam Smith's 1776 book *An Inquiry into the Nature and Causes of the Wealth of Nations,* he writes of the ability of producers to benefit through specialization and trade.

   2. In David Ricardo's 1817 book *Principles of Political Economy and Taxation,* Ricardo develops the theory of comparative advantage and argues against restrictions on free trade.

   C. The benefits of free trade are an issue that is generally agreed upon by most economists, and the theories and arguments developed by these two individuals 200 years ago are still used today.

IV. Applications of Comparative Advantage

   A. Should Tom Brady Mow His Own Lawn?

   1. Imagine that Brady can mow his lawn faster than anyone else can.

   2. This implies that he has an absolute advantage.

   3. Suppose that it takes him two hours to mow his lawn. In that same two hours, he could film a commercial for which he would earn $20,000. This means that the opportunity cost of mowing his lawn is $20,000.

4. It is likely that someone else would have a lower opportunity cost of mowing Brady's lawn; this individual would have a comparative advantage.

5. Both he and the person hired will be better off as long as he pays the individual more than the individual's opportunity cost and less than $20,000.

B. Should the United States Trade with Other Countries?

1. Just as individuals can benefit from specialization and trade, so can the populations of different countries.

2. Definition of **imports: goods produced abroad and sold domestically**.

3. Definition of **exports: goods produced domestically and sold abroad**.

4. The principle of comparative advantage suggests that each good should be produced by the country with a comparative advantage in producing that good (smaller opportunity cost).

5. Through specialization and trade, countries can have more of all goods to consume.

6. Trade issues among nations are more complex. Some individuals can be made worse off even when the country as a whole is made better off.

C. *In the News: The Changing Face of International Trade*

1. Technology is rapidly changing the goods and services that are traded across international borders.

2. This is an article from the *New York Times* that describes the work done by professional Chinese online gamers who trade online game characters and artificial currency to players of World of Warcraft and Magic Land.

 To help convince students that importing goods is not harmful to a country, ask the students to devise a way to produce coffee domestically. Point out that it is possible to grow coffee beans in the United States in enclosed nurseries, but the opportunity cost of the resources used would be significant.

 Discuss how differences in resource endowments can be significant factors in determining opportunity cost and comparative advantage. Such differences include climate, soil composition, education and training of the labor force, capital stock, and infrastructure.

SOLUTIONS TO TEXT PROBLEMS:

Quick Quizzes

1. Figure 1 shows Robinson Crusoe's production possibilities frontier for gathering coconuts and catching fish. If Crusoe lives by himself, this frontier limits his consumption of coconuts and

fish, but if he can trade with natives on the island, he will possibly be able to consume at a point outside his production possibilities frontier.

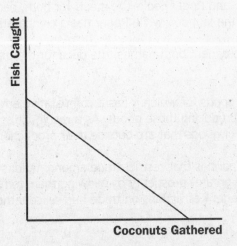

Figure 1

2. Crusoe's opportunity cost of catching one fish is 10 coconuts, since he can gather 10 coconuts in the same amount of time it takes to catch one fish. Friday's opportunity cost of catching one fish is 15 coconuts, since he can gather 30 coconuts in the same amount of time it takes to catch two fish. Friday has an absolute advantage in catching fish, since he can catch two per hour, while Crusoe can catch only one per hour. But Crusoe has a comparative advantage in catching fish, since his opportunity cost of catching a fish is less than Friday's.

3. If the world's fastest typist happens to be trained in brain surgery, she should hire a secretary because the secretary will give up less for each hour spent typing. Although the brain surgeon has an absolute advantage in typing, the secretary has a comparative advantage in typing because the secretary would have a lower opportunity cost of typing.

Questions for Review

1. The production possibilities frontier will be linear if the opportunity cost of producing a good is constant no matter how much of that good is produced. This will be most likely if the good is not produced using specialized inputs.

2. Absolute advantage reflects a comparison of the productivity of one person, firm, or nation to that of another, while comparative advantage is based on the relative opportunity costs of the persons, firms, or nations. While a person, firm, or nation may have an absolute advantage in producing every good, they cannot have a comparative advantage in the production of every good.

3. Many examples are possible. Suppose, for example, that Roger can prepare a meal of hot dogs and macaroni in just 10 minutes, while it takes Anita 20 minutes. Also suppose that Roger can do all the laundry in 3 hours, while it takes Anita 4 hours. Roger has an absolute advantage in both cooking and doing the laundry, but Anita has a comparative advantage in doing the laundry. For Anita, the opportunity cost of doing the laundry is 12 meals; for Roger, it is 18 meals.

4. Comparative advantage is more important for trade than absolute advantage. In the example in Problem 3, Anita and Roger will complete their chores more quickly if Anita does at least some of the laundry and Roger cooks the meals for both, because Anita has a comparative advantage in doing the laundry, while Roger has a comparative advantage in cooking.

5. In order for trade to benefit both parties, the price for the trade must lie between the parties' opportunity costs.

6. A nation will export goods for which it has a comparative advantage because it has a smaller opportunity cost of producing those goods. As a result, citizens of all nations are able to consume quantities of goods that are outside their production possibilities frontiers.

7. Economists oppose policies that restrict trade among nations because trade allows all countries to achieve greater prosperity by allowing them to receive the gains from comparative advantage. Restrictions on trade hurt all countries.

Problems and Applications

1. a. See Figure 2. If Maria spends all 5 hours studying economics, she can read 100 pages, so that is the vertical intercept of the production possibilities frontier. If she spends all 5 hours studying sociology, she can read 250 pages, so that is the horizontal intercept. The opportunity costs are constant, so the production possibilities frontier is a straight line.

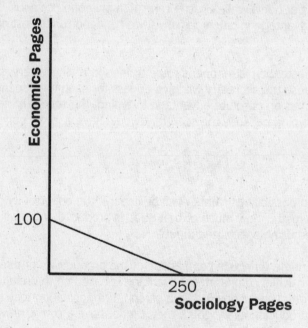

Figure 2

b. It takes Maria 2 hours to read 100 pages of sociology. In that time, she could read 40 pages of economics. So the opportunity cost of 100 pages of sociology is 40 pages of economics.

2. a.

	Workers needed to make:	
	One Car	**One Ton of Grain**
U.S.	1/4	1/10
Japan	1/4	1/5

    b. See Figure 3. With 100 million workers and 4 cars per worker, if either economy were devoted completely to cars, it could make 400 million cars. Because a U.S. worker can produce 10 tons of grain, if the United States produced only grain it would produce 1,000 million tons. Because a Japanese worker can produce 5 tons of grain, if Japan produced only grain it would produce 500 million tons. These are the intercepts of the production possibilities frontiers shown in the figure. Note that because the trade-off between cars and grain is constant for both countries, the production possibilities frontiers are straight lines.

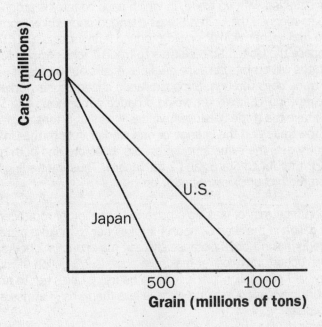

Figure 3

    c. Because a U.S. worker produces either 4 cars or 10 tons of grain, the opportunity cost of one car is 2 1/2 tons of grain, which is 10/4. Because a Japanese worker produces either 4 cars or 5 tons of grain, the opportunity cost of one car is 1 1/4 tons of grain, which is 5/4. Similarly, the U.S. opportunity cost of a ton of grain is 2/5 car (4 divided by 10) and the Japanese opportunity cost of a ton of grain is 4/5 car. This results in the following table:

	Opportunity Cost of:	
	One Car (in terms of tons of grain given up)	**One Ton of Grain (in terms of cars given up)**
U.S.	2 1/2	2/5
Japan	1 1/4	4/5

d. Neither country has an absolute advantage in producing cars, because they are equally productive (the same output per worker); the United States has an absolute advantage in producing grain, because it is more productive (greater output per worker).

e. Japan has a comparative advantage in producing cars, because it has a lower opportunity cost in terms of grain given up. The United States has a comparative advantage in producing grain, because it has a lower opportunity cost in terms of cars given up.

f. With half the workers in each country producing each of the goods, the United States would produce 200 million cars (50 million workers times 4 cars each) and 500 million tons of grain (50 million workers times 10 tons each). Japan would produce 200 million cars (50 million workers times 4 cars each) and 250 million tons of grain (50 million workers times 5 tons each).

g. From any situation with no trade, in which each country is producing some cars and some grain, suppose the United States changed one worker from producing cars to producing grain. That worker would produce 4 fewer cars and 10 additional tons of grain. Then suppose the United States offers to trade 7 tons of grain to Japan for 4 cars. The United States will do this because it values 4 cars at 10 tons of grain, so it will be better off if the trade goes through. Suppose Japan changes one worker from producing grain to producing cars. That worker would produce 4 more cars and 5 fewer tons of grain. Japan will take the trade because it values 4 cars at 5 tons of grain, so it will be better off. With the trade and the change of one worker in both the United States and Japan, each country gets the same amount of cars as before and both get additional tons of grain (3 for the United States and 2 for Japan). Thus, by trading and changing their production, both countries are better off.

3. a. Pat's opportunity cost of making a pizza is 1/2 gallon of root beer, because she could brew 1/2 gallon in the time (2 hours) it takes her to make a pizza. Pat has an absolute advantage in making pizza because she can make one in 2 hours, while it takes Kris 4 hours. Kris' opportunity cost of making a pizza is 2/3 gallon of root beer, because she could brew 2/3 of a gallon in the time (4 hours) it takes her to make a pizza. Because Pat's opportunity cost of making pizza is less than Kris', Pat has a comparative advantage in making pizza.

b. Because Pat has a comparative advantage in making pizza, she will make pizza and exchange it for root beer that Kris makes.

c. The highest price of pizza in terms of root beer that will make both roommates better off is 2/3 of a gallon of root beer. If the price were higher than that, then Kris would prefer making her own pizza (at an opportunity cost of 2/3 of a gallon of root beer) rather than trading for pizza that Pat makes. The lowest price of pizza in terms of root beer that will make both roommates better off is 1/2 gallon of root beer. If the price were lower than that, then Pat would prefer making her own root beer (she can make 1/2 gallon of root beer instead of making a pizza) rather than trading for root beer that Kris makes.

4. a. Because a Canadian worker can make either 2 cars a year or 30 bushels of wheat, the opportunity cost of a car is 15 bushels of wheat. Similarly, the opportunity cost of a bushel of wheat is 1/15 of a car. The opportunity costs are the reciprocals of each other.

b. See Figure 4. If all 10 million workers produce 2 cars each, they produce a total of 20 million cars, which is the vertical intercept of the production possibilities frontier. If all 10 million workers produce 30 bushels of wheat each, they produce a total of 300 million bushels, which is the horizontal intercept of the production possibilities frontier. Because the trade-off between cars and wheat is always the same, the production possibilities frontier is a straight line.

If Canada chooses to consume 10 million cars, it will need 5 million workers devoted to car production. That leaves 5 million workers to produce wheat, who will produce a total of 150 million bushels (5 million workers times 30 bushels per worker). This is shown as point A on Figure 4.

c. If the United States buys 10 million cars from Canada and Canada continues to consume 10 million cars, then Canada will need to produce a total of 20 million cars. So Canada will be producing at the vertical intercept of the production possibilities frontier. However, if Canada gets 20 bushels of wheat per car, it will be able to consume 200 million bushels of wheat, along with the 10 million cars. This is shown as point B in the figure. Canada should accept the deal because it gets the same number of cars and 50 million more bushes of wheat.

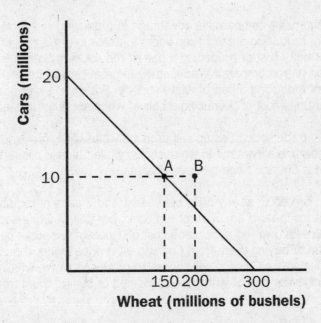

Figure 4

5. a. English workers have an absolute advantage over Scottish workers in producing scones, because English workers produce more scones per hour (50 vs. 40). Scottish workers have an absolute advantage over English workers in producing sweaters, because Scottish workers produce more sweaters per hour (2 vs. 1). Comparative advantage runs the same way. English workers, who have an opportunity cost of 1/50 sweater per scone (1 sweater per hour divided by 50 scones per hour), have a comparative advantage in scone production over Scottish workers, who have an opportunity cost of 1/20 sweater per scone (2 sweaters per hour divided by 40 scones per hour). Scottish workers, who have an opportunity cost of 20 scones per sweater (40 scones per hour divided by 2 sweaters per hour), have a comparative advantage in sweater production over English workers, who have an opportunity cost of 50 scones per sweater (50 scones per hour divided by 1 sweater per hour).

b. If England and Scotland decide to trade, Scotland will produce sweaters and trade them for scones produced in England. A trade with a price between 20 and 50 scones per sweater will benefit both countries, as they will be getting the traded good at a lower price than their opportunity cost of producing the good in their own countries.

c. Even if a Scottish worker produced just one sweater per hour, the countries would still gain from trade, because Scotland would still have a comparative advantage in producing sweaters. Its opportunity cost for sweaters would be higher than before (40 scones per sweater, instead of 20 scones per sweater before). But there are still gains from trade because England has a higher opportunity cost (50 scones per sweater).

6. a. With no trade, 1 pair of white socks trades for 1 pair of red socks in Boston, because productivity is the same for the two types of socks. The price in Chicago is 2 pairs of red socks per 1 pair of white socks.

b. Boston has an absolute advantage in the production of both types of socks, because a worker in Boston produces more (3 pairs of socks per hour) than a worker in Chicago (2 pairs of red socks per hour or 1 pair of white socks per hour).

Chicago has a comparative advantage in producing red socks, because the opportunity cost of producing a pair of red socks in Chicago is 1/2 pair of white socks, while the opportunity cost of producing a pair of red socks in Boston is 1 pair of white socks. Boston has a comparative advantage in producing white socks, because the opportunity cost of producing a pair of white socks in Boston is 1 pair of red socks, while the opportunity cost of producing a pair of white socks in Chicago is 2 pairs of red socks.

c. If they trade socks, Boston will produce white socks for export, because it has the comparative advantage in white socks, while Chicago produces red socks for export, which is Chicago's comparative advantage.

d. Trade can occur at any price between 1 and 2 pairs of red socks per pair of white socks. At a price lower than 1 pair of red socks per pair of white socks, Boston will choose to produce its own red socks (at a cost of 1 pair of red socks per pair of white socks) instead of buying them from Chicago. At a price higher than 2 pairs of red socks per pair of white socks, Chicago will choose to produce its own white socks (at a cost of 2 pairs of red socks per pair of white socks) instead of buying them from Boston.

7. a. The production possibilities frontiers for the two countries are shown in Figure 5. If, without trade, a U.S. worker spends half of his time producing each good, the United States will have 50 shirts and 10 computers. If, without trade, a worker in China spends half of his time producing each good, China will have 50 shirts and 5 computers.

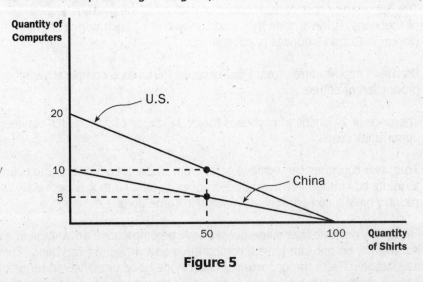

Figure 5

b. For the United States, the opportunity cost of 1 computer is 5 shirts, while the opportunity cost of a shirt is 1/5 computer. For China, the opportunity cost of 1 computer is 10 shirts, while the opportunity cost of 1 shirt is 1/10 computer. Therefore, the United States has a comparative advantage in the production of computers and China has a comparative advantage in the production of shirts.

China would export shirts. The price of a shirt will fall between 1/5 and 1/10 of a computer. An example would be a price of 1/8 computer. In other words, China could export 8 shirts and receive 1 computer in return. Both countries would benefit from trade. China would specialize in shirts (producing 100) and export 8. This would leave them with 92 shirts. In return, they would get 1 computer. The combination of 92 shirts and 1 computer was not available to China before trade. The United States could specialize in computers (producing 20) and export 1 computer to China in exchange for 8 shirts. The United States would end up with 19 computers and 8 shirts, a combination that was impossible without trade.

c. The price of a computer would fall between 5 and 10 shirts. If the price was below 5, the United States would not be willing to export computers because the opportunity cost of a shirt for the United States is 1/5 computer. If the price was greater than 10 shirts, China would not be willing to import computers because (for China) the opportunity cost of a computer is 10 shirts.

d. Once the productivity is the same in the two countries, the benefits of trade disappear. Trade is beneficial because it allows countries to exploit their comparative advantage. If China and the United States have exactly the same opportunity cost of producing shirts and computers, there will be no more gains from trade available.

8. a. An average worker in Brazil has an absolute advantage in the production of coffee because he requires less time than an average worker in Peru.

    b. An average worker in Peru has a comparative advantage in the production of coffee. The opportunity cost of each ounce of coffee for the average worker in Peru (1.5 ounces of soybeans) is lower than the opportunity cost of each ounce of coffee for the average worker in Brazil (3 ounces of soybeans).

    c. Brazil will import coffee from Peru because Peru has a comparative advantage in the production of coffee.

    d. The price of 2 ounces of soybeans for every ounce of coffee falls between the two opportunity costs.

9. a. True; two countries can achieve gains from trade even if one of the countries has an absolute advantage in the production of all goods. All that is necessary is that each country have a comparative advantage in some good.

    b. False; it is not true that some people have a comparative advantage in everything they do. In fact, no one can have a comparative advantage in everything. Comparative advantage reflects the opportunity cost of one good or activity in terms of another. If you have a comparative advantage in one thing, you must have a comparative disadvantage in the other thing.

    c. False; it is not true that if a trade is good for one person, it cannot be good for the other one. Trades can and do benefit both sides—especially trades based on comparative advantage. If both sides did not benefit, trades would never occur.

    d. False; to be good for both parties, the trade price must lie between the two opportunity costs.

    e. False; trade that makes the country better off can harm certain individuals in the country. For example, suppose a country has a comparative advantage in producing wheat and a comparative disadvantage in producing cars. Exporting wheat and importing cars will benefit the nation as a whole, as it will be able to consume more of both goods. However, the introduction of trade will likely be harmful to domestic auto workers and manufacturers.

10. This pattern of trade is consistent with the principle of comparative advantage. If the United States exports corn and aircraft, it must have a comparative advantage in the production of these goods. Because it imports oil and clothing, the United States must have a comparative disadvantage in the production of these items.

11. a. Hillary has an absolute advantage in the production of both goods because she is able to produce more in the same amount of time.

b. Bill has a comparative advantage in the production of food because he has a lower opportunity cost (1 unit of clothing per unit of food) than Hillary (1.5 units of clothing per unit of food).

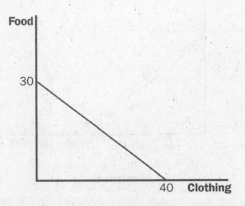

Figure 6

c. See Figure 6. If Bill and Hillary spend all of their time producing food, they can produce 30 units [(10 × 1) + (10 × 2)] per day. If they spend all of their time producing clothing, they can produce 40 units per day [(10 × 1) + (10 × 3)].

d. If no clothing is produced, Bill and Hillary can still produce only 30 units of food. If Hillary switches to clothing production, the household gives up 2/3 unit of food for every unit of clothing produced. When Hillary's 10 hours are devoted to producing clothing, she would be producing 30 units of clothing while Bill is producing 10 units of food. Of course, if Bill then begins to produce clothing, the household gives up 1 unit of food for each unit of clothing produced. Bill and Hillary could devote all their time to producing clothes. If they choose to do so, they can produce 40 units. Their production possibilities frontier is shown in Figure 7.

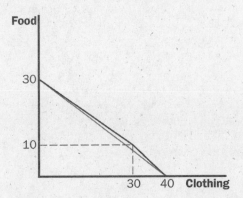

Figure 7

e. Again, Hillary and Bill can chose to produce no clothing and produce all food (30 units). To gain some clothing, Bill would produce clothing, sacrificing 1 unit of food for each unit of clothing produced. If Bill spends all of his time producing food, he would produce 10 units, while Hillary produced 20 units of food. To gain additional clothing, the household would need Hillary to reallocate her time away from food production toward clothing production (at a cost of 1/2 unit of food for each unit of clothing produced). If they choose to produce only clothing, they can produce 40 units of clothing. See Figure 8.

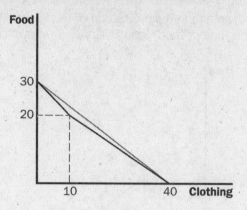

Figure 8

f. It is clear that the production possibilities expand when Hillary specializes in the production of clothing. This makes sense because she has a comparative advantage in the production of clothing.

4 THE MARKET FORCES OF SUPPLY AND DEMAND

WHAT'S NEW IN THE SIXTH EDITION:

The *In the News* feature "Price Increases after Natural Disasters" has been updated with a new article.

LEARNING OBJECTIVES:

By the end of this chapter, students should understand:

➤ what a competitive market is.

➤ what determines the demand for a good in a competitive market.

➤ what determines the supply of a good in a competitive market.

➤ how supply and demand together set the price of a good and the quantity sold.

➤ the key role of prices in allocating scarce resources in market economies.

CONTEXT AND PURPOSE:

Chapter 4 is the first chapter in a three-chapter sequence that deals with supply and demand and how markets work. Chapter 4 shows how supply and demand for a good determines both the quantity produced and the price at which the good sells. Chapter 5 will add precision to the discussion of supply and demand by addressing the concept of elasticity—the sensitivity of the quantity supplied and quantity demanded to changes in economic variables. Chapter 6 will address the impact of government policies on prices and quantities in markets.

The purpose of Chapter 4 is to establish the model of supply and demand. The model of supply and demand is the foundation for the discussion for the remainder of this text. For this reason, time spent studying the concepts in this chapter will return benefits to your students throughout their study of economics. Many instructors would argue that this chapter is the most important chapter in the text.

KEY POINTS:

- Economists use the model of supply and demand to analyze competitive markets. In a competitive market, there are many buyers and sellers, each of whom has little or no influence on the market price.

- The demand curve shows how the quantity of a good demanded depends on the price. According to the law of demand, as the price of a good falls, the quantity demanded rises. Therefore, the demand curve slopes downward.

- In addition to price, other determinants of how much consumers want to buy include income, the prices of substitutes and complements, tastes, expectations, and the number of buyers. If one of these factors changes, the demand curve shifts.

- The supply curve shows how the quantity of a good supplied depends on the price. According to the law of supply, as the price of a good rises, the quantity supplied rises. Therefore, the supply curve slopes upward.

- In addition to price, other determinants of how much producers want to sell include input prices, technology, expectations, and the number of sellers. If one of these factors changes, the supply curve shifts.

- The intersection of the supply and demand curves determines the market equilibrium. At the equilibrium price, the quantity demanded equals the quantity supplied.

- The behavior of buyers and sellers naturally drives markets toward their equilibrium. When the market price is above the equilibrium price, there is a surplus of the good, which causes the market price to fall. When the market price is below the equilibrium price, there is a shortage, which causes the market price to rise.

- To analyze how any event influences a market, we use the supply-and-demand diagram to examine how the event affects equilibrium price and quantity. To do this we follow three steps. First, we decide whether the event shifts the supply curve or the demand curve (or both). Second, we decide which direction the curve shifts. Third, we compare the new equilibrium with the initial equilibrium.

- In market economies, prices are the signals that guide economic decisions and thereby allocate scarce resources. For every good in the economy, the price ensures that supply and demand are in balance. The equilibrium price then determines how much of the good buyers choose to consume and how much sellers choose to produce.

CHAPTER OUTLINE:

I. Markets and Competition

> You may want to provide students with examples of markets other than the traditional retail store or the stock market. These include the online advertising sites such as eBay and Craigslist, the college "career services" department through which they can look for employment upon graduation, or the market for illegal drugs on a college campus. Be sure to list the good or service being sold, the buyers, and the sellers in each example.

A. What Is a Market?

1. Definition of **market: a group of buyers and sellers of a particular good or service.**

2. Markets can take many forms and may be organized (agricultural commodities) or less organized (ice cream).

B. What Is Competition?

1. Definition of **competitive market: a market in which there are so many buyers and so many sellers that each has a negligible impact on the market price.**

2. Each buyer knows that there are several sellers from which to choose. Sellers know that each buyer purchases only a small amount of the total amount sold.

> Students may find the name for this type of market misleading. You will have to point out that firms in a competitive market do not face head-to-head rivalry as in sports competitions.

C. In this chapter, we will assume that markets are perfectly competitive.

1. Characteristics of a perfectly competitive market:

    a. The goods being offered for sale are exactly the same.

    b. The buyers and sellers are so numerous that no single buyer or seller has any influence over the market price.

2. Because buyers and sellers must accept the market price as given, they are often called "price takers."

3. Not all goods are sold in a perfectly competitive market.

    a. A market with only one seller is called a monopoly market.

    b. Other markets fall between perfect competition and monopoly.

D. We will start by studying perfect competition.

1. Perfectly competitive markets are the easiest to analyze because buyers and sellers take the price as a given.

2. Because some degree of competition is present in most markets, many of the lessons that we learn by studying supply and demand under perfect competition apply in more complicated markets.

II. Demand

A. The Demand Curve: The Relationship between Price and Quantity Demanded

1. Definition of **quantity demanded: the amount of a good that buyers are willing and able to purchase.**

2. One important determinant of quantity demanded is the price of the product.

a. Quantity demanded is negatively related to price. This implies that the demand curve is downward sloping.

Make sure that you explain that, when we discuss the relationship between quantity demanded and price, we hold all other variables constant. You will need to emphasize this more than once to ensure that students understand why a change in price leads to a movement *along* the demand curve.

b. Definition of **law of demand: the claim that, other things being equal, the quantity demanded of a good falls when the price of the good rises.**

3. Definition of **demand schedule: a table that shows the relationship between the price of a good and the quantity demanded.**

Price of Ice Cream Cone	Quantity of Cones Demanded
$0.00	12
$0.50	10
$1.00	8
$1.50	6
$2.00	4
$2.50	2
$3.00	0

When you draw the demand curve for the first time, take the time to plot each of the points from the demand schedule. This way, students who have difficulty with graphs can see the relationship between the demand schedule and the demand curve. This is a good opportunity to see if students understand the (*x, y*) coordinate system.

4. Definition of **demand curve**: **a graph of the relationship between the price of a good and the quantity demanded.**

   a. Price is generally drawn on the vertical axis.

   b. Quantity demanded is represented on the horizontal axis.

ALTERNATIVE CLASSROOM EXAMPLE:
Here is a demand schedule for ink pens:

Price ($)	Quantity Demanded
.05	1000
.10	800
.15	600
.20	400
.25	200

Figure 1

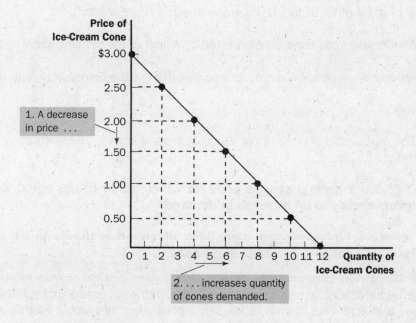

B. Market Demand versus Individual Demand

   1. The market demand is the sum of all of the individual demands for a particular good or service.

   2. The demand curves are summed horizontally—meaning that the quantities demanded are added up for each level of price.

Figure 2

3. The market demand curve shows how the total quantity demanded of a good varies with the price of the good, holding constant all other factors that affect how much consumers want to buy.

C. Shifts in the Demand Curve

Students have a difficult time understanding the difference between a change in price (which causes a movement along the demand curve) and a change in another determinant (which shifts the demand curve). You will have to emphasize what is meant by "change in quantity demanded" and "change in demand" several times using different examples. The *Case Study* on smoking will help to explain this difference as well.

Figure 3

1. Because the market demand curve holds other things constant, it need not be stable over time.

2. If any of these other factors change, the demand curve will shift.

   a. An increase in demand is represented by a shift of the demand curve to the right.

   b. A decrease in demand is represented by a shift of the demand curve to the left.

3. Income

   a. The relationship between income and quantity demanded depends on what type of good the product is.

   b. Definition of **normal good**: **a good for which, other things equal, an increase in income leads to an increase in demand.**

   c. Definition of **inferior good**: **a good for which, other things equal, an increase in income leads to a decrease in demand.**

Be careful! Students often confuse inferior goods with what economists call "bads." One way to differentiate them is to ask students whether they would ever be willing to pay for such things as pollution or garbage.

4. Prices of Related Goods

   a. Definition of **substitutes**: **two goods for which an increase in the price of one good leads to an increase in the demand for the other.**

   b. Definition of **complements**: **two goods for which an increase in the price of one good leads to a decrease in the demand for the other.**

5. Tastes

6. Expectations

   a. Future income

   b. Future prices

7. Number of Buyers

Table 1

It would be a good idea to work through an example changing each of these variables individually. Students will benefit from the discussion and the practice drawing graphs.

D. *Case Study: Two Ways to Reduce the Quantity of Smoking Demanded*

Figure 4

1. Public service announcements, mandatory health warnings on cigarette packages, and the prohibition of cigarette advertising on television are policies designed to reduce the demand for cigarettes (and shift the demand curve to the left).

2. Raising the price of cigarettes (through tobacco taxes) lowers the quantity of cigarettes demanded.

   a. The demand curve does not shift in this case, however.

   b. An increase in the price of cigarettes can be shown by a movement along the original demand curve.

3. Studies have shown that a 10% increase in the price of cigarettes causes a 4% reduction in the quantity of cigarettes demanded. For teens, a 10% increase in price leads to a 12% drop in quantity demanded.

4. Studies have also shown that a decrease in the price of cigarettes is associated with greater use of marijuana. Thus, it appears that tobacco and marijuana are complements.

The Hudsucker Proxy, Chapter 25. This clip is very useful to demonstrate the difference in a change in demand and a change in quantity demanded. A store is trying to sell Hula-Hoops with no luck. The seller tries to lower the price to raise quantity demanded. Eventually, a change in taste leads to a large rise in the demand.

III. Supply

If you have taken enough time teaching demand, students will catch on to supply more quickly. However, remember that as consumers, students can understand demand decisions more easily than supply decisions. You may want to point out to them that they are suppliers (of their time and effort) in the labor market.

A.   The Supply Curve: The Relationship between Price and Quantity Supplied

1.   Definition of **quantity supplied: the amount of a good that sellers are willing and able to sell.**

a.   Quantity supplied is positively related to price. This implies that the supply curve will be upward sloping.

b.   Definition of **law of supply: the claim that, other things equal, the quantity supplied of a good rises when the price of the good rises.**

Again you will want to point out that everything else is held constant when we discuss the relationship between price and quantity supplied. Students should understand that a change in price causes a movement along the supply curve.

2.   Definition of **supply schedule: a table that shows the relationship between the price of a good and the quantity supplied.**

3.   Definition of **supply curve: a graph of the relationship between the price of a good and the quantity supplied.**

Price of Ice Cream Cone	Quantity of Cones Supplied
$0.00	0
$0.50	0
$1.00	1
$1.50	2
$2.00	3
$2.50	4
$3.00	5

Figure 5

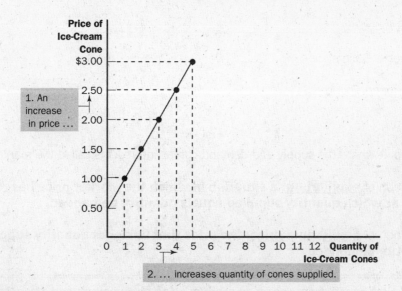

B. Market Supply versus Individual Supply

Figure 6

1. The market supply curve can be found by summing individual supply curves.

2. Individual supply curves are summed horizontally at every price.

3. The market supply curve shows how the total quantity supplied varies as the price of the good varies.

C. Shifts in the Supply Curve

Table 2

Figure 7

1. Because the market supply curve holds other things constant, the supply curve will shift if any of these factors changes.

   a. An increase in supply is represented by a shift of the supply curve to the right.

   b. A decrease in supply is represented by a shift of the supply curve to the left.

 You will want to take time to emphasize the difference between a "change in supply" and a "change in quantity supplied."

2. Input Prices

3. Technology

4. Expectations

5. Number of Sellers

IV. Supply and Demand Together

A. Equilibrium

1. The point where the supply and demand curves intersect is called the market's equilibrium.

2. Definition of **equilibrium: a situation in which the market price has reached the level at which quantity supplied equals quantity demanded.**

3. Definition of **equilibrium price: the price that balances quantity supplied and quantity demanded.**

 Students will benefit from seeing equilibrium using both a graph and a supply-and-demand schedule. The schedule will also make it easier for students to understand concepts such as shortages and surpluses.

4. The equilibrium price is often called the "market-clearing" price because both buyers and sellers are satisfied at this price.

Figure 8

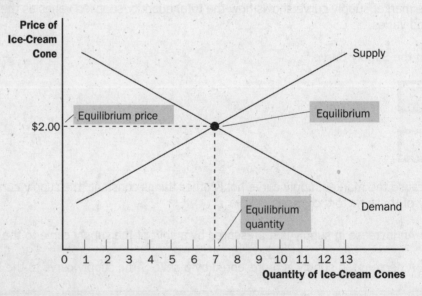

5. Definition of **equilibrium quantity: the quantity supplied and the quantity demanded at the equilibrium price.**

Activity 1—A Market Example

Type:	In-class demonstration
Topics:	Individual demand, market demand, equilibrium price, allocation
Materials needed:	A bag of Pepperidge Farm cookies (15 cookies), 5 volunteers
Time:	35 minutes
Class limitations:	Works in large lectures or small classes with over 15 students

Purpose

This is an example of a real-world market, where real goods are exchanged for real money. It is a free market, so there will be no coercion, but participants should think carefully about their answers because actual trades will take place.

Instructions

Ask five volunteers to participate in a market for Pepperidge Farm cookies. Read some of the package copy describing these "distinctively delicious" cookies. Write each volunteer's name on the board.

Ask the volunteers how many cookies they would be willing to buy at various prices. Record these prices and quantities. Give the volunteers the opportunity to revise their numbers if the figures do not accurately reflect their willingness to pay. Remind them this isn't a hypothetical exercise and they will have to pay real money.

At this point, there will be five individual demand curves, which can be graphed if desired.

Add the individual quantities at each price to find the market demand at that price. This overall demand is used to find the market equilibrium. Sketch a graph of the market demand.

Supply, in this case, is fixed at the number of cookies in the bag. There are 15 cookies. No more can be produced, and any leftovers will spoil. This gives a vertical supply curve in the very short run at $Q = 15$. (Sketch the supply curve.)

Try various prices until the individual quantities sum to 15. This will give the equilibrium price and quantity.

Distribute the cookies and collect money from each participant.

Points for Discussion

The demand curves display the typical inverse relation between price and quantity. (Remark on any unusual patterns.) These tell us about each individual's willingness to pay and reveal information about the marginal benefits of additional cookies to each consumer.

Market demand is aggregated from individual demand curves.

Notice the consumers do not get an equal number of cookies. This is typical of markets, because tastes and incomes vary across individuals.

6. If the actual market price is higher than the equilibrium price, there will be a surplus of the good.

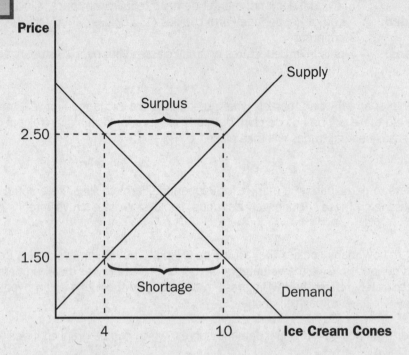

a. Definition of **surplus**: **a situation in which quantity supplied is greater than quantity demanded.**

b. To eliminate the surplus, producers will lower the price until the market reaches equilibrium.

7. If the actual price is lower than the equilibrium price, there will be a shortage of the good.

a. Definition of **shortage**: **a situation in which quantity demanded is greater than quantity supplied.**

b. Sellers will respond to the shortage by raising the price of the good until the market reaches equilibrium.

8. Definition of the **law of supply and demand**: **the claim that the price of any good adjusts to bring the supply and demand for that good into balance**.

Activity 2—Campus Parking

Type:	In-class assignment
Topics:	Demand, supply, disequilibrium, shortage, rationing
Materials needed:	A shortage of student parking on campus
Time:	35 minutes
Class limitations:	Works in large lectures or small classes, if there is a campus parking problem.

Purpose

Nothing seems to generate more heated discussion than campus parking. If your school has a parking shortage this assignment brings the ideas of price rationing and resource allocation to an issue close to the students' hearts.

A. K. Sen's parable of the bamboo flute is a good introduction to this assignment: An artist makes a beautiful instrument that becomes famous throughout the country. A number of claimants arise, each of whom argues that they deserve the flute: the artist who created it, the most talented musician, the poorest musician, the neediest citizen, the hardest working musician, etc. Who deserves the flute? Students will have different opinions on who is most deserving but many will accept a market solution—the person who is willing to pay the most (who has the highest marginal benefit, given the existing distribution of wealth and income). The allocation of campus parking spots makes a nice parallel.

Instruction

Ask the class to answer the following questions. Give them time to write an answer to a question, then discuss their answers before moving to the next question.

Common Answers and Points for Discussion

1. Write down three things that are true about the parking situation on campus.
2. What two problems do you think are most important?

The parking problem has two components in the eyes of most students. Parking permits are too expensive and there are too few spaces.

3. What policies could the administration make to resolve these problems?

Students have many policies to alleviate the situation. The most common suggestion is to ban parking for freshmen. Freshmen respond with lists of other groups who should be banned. Another popular policy would be to open faculty lots to student parking. Parking fees should be lowered or better yet eliminated. Parking violations should have lower fines. More lots should be built. Shuttles, moving sidewalks, and monorails should be installed.

Students never suggest raising prices to reach a market solution.

4. Who needs parking the most?
5. Who would pay the most for parking?

Asking about need and willingness to pay moves the discussion away from group prohibitions; freshmen may be just as needy and equally able to pay.

6. Use a supply-and-demand graph to analyze this problem.

Many students initially have difficulty graphing this problem. They want to illustrate that permit prices are too high, but then their graph will not show the shortage. Eventually they can be convinced that parking, while expensive, is actually priced too low.

7. How would your policy proposals affect the market for parking?

Analysis of the various proposals in a supply-and-demand framework shows some popular policies, like free permits, would aggravate the parking shortage. Policies to restrict demand can reduce the shortage, although there will be inefficiencies in the resulting allocation. Make sure that students realize that building more parking lots is not a shift in the supply curve, but a movement along the existing supply curve. The additional costs of new parking need to be covered by some means: higher parking fees, tuition increases, or taxpayer subsidies.

B. Three Steps to Analyzing Changes in Equilibrium

Table 3

1. Decide whether the event shifts the supply or demand curve (or perhaps both).

2. Determine the direction in which the curve shifts.

3. Use the supply-and-demand diagram to see how the shift changes the equilibrium price and quantity.

This three-step process is very important. Students often want to jump to the end without thinking the change through. They should be provided with numerous examples so that they can see the benefit of analyzing a change in equilibrium one step at a time.

C. Example: A change in market equilibrium due to a shift in demand—the effect of hot weather on the market for ice cream.

Figure 10

Go through changes in supply and demand carefully. Show students why the equilibrium price must change after one of the curves shifts. For example, point out that if demand rises, a shortage will occur at the original equilibrium price. This leads to an increase in price, which causes quantity supplied to rise and quantity demanded to fall until equilibrium is achieved. The end result is an increase in both the equilibrium price and equilibrium quantity. Also point out that an increase in demand leads to an increase in *quantity supplied,* not *supply.*

ALTERNATIVE CLASSROOM EXAMPLE:
Go through these examples of events that would shift either the demand or supply of #2 lead pencils:
- an increase in the income of consumers
- an increase in the use of standardized exams (using opscan forms)
- a decrease in the price of graphite (used in the production of pencils)
- a decrease in the price of ink pens
- the start of a school year
- new technology that lowers the cost of producing pencils.

D. Shifts in Curves versus Movements along Curves

1. A shift in the demand curve is called a "change in demand." A shift in the supply curve is called a "change in supply."

Emphasize that students should not think about the curves shifting "up" and "down" but rather think about the curves shifting "right" and "left" (or "out" and "in"). Point out that an increase in demand (or supply) is an increase in the quantity demanded (supplied) at every price. Thus, it is quantity that is getting larger. Review the same principle with a decrease in demand (or supply).

2. A movement along a fixed demand curve is called a "change in quantity demanded." A movement along a fixed supply curve is called a "change in quantity supplied."

It would helpful to students if you draw all four graphs (increase in demand, decrease in demand, increase in supply, and decrease in supply) on the board at the same time. Students will be able to see that the end result of each of these four shifts is unique. Point out to students that they can use these graphs to explain events going on in markets around them. For example, point out changes in gasoline prices seen during the past several years. Then ask students what could have led to these changes in price. Make sure that they realize that they would need to know the effect on equilibrium quantity to determine the ultimate cause.

F. Example: A change in market equilibrium due to a shift in supply—the effect of a hurricane that destroys part of the sugar-cane crop and drives up the price of sugar.

Figure 11

G. Example: Shifts in both supply and demand—the effect of hot weather and a hurricane that destroys part of the sugar cane crop.

H. *In the News: Price Increases after Natural Disasters*

1. In 2010, many towns around Boston had no access to drinkable tap water.

2. This is an article from *The Boston Globe* defending the price increase in bottled water as a natural result of market interactions.

Figure 12

Make sure that you explain to students that two possible outcomes might result, depending on the relative sizes of the shifts in the demand and supply curves. Thus, if they do not know the relative sizes of these shifts, the end effect on either equilibrium price or equilibrium quantity will be ambiguous. Teach students to shift each curve using the three-step method and to draw them on separate graphs.

I. Summary

A. When an event shifts the supply or demand curve, we can examine the effects on the equilibrium price and quantity.

B. Table 4 reports the end results of these shifts in supply and demand.

Table 4

V. Conclusion: How Prices Allocate Resources

A. The model of supply and demand is a powerful tool for analyzing markets.

B. Supply and demand together determine the prices of the economy's goods and services.

1. These prices serve as signals that guide the allocation of scarce resources in the economy.

2. Prices determine who produces each good and how much of each good is produced.

Make a big deal about how well prices serve to allocate resources to their highest valued uses. For example, suppose that consumers develop an increased taste for corn and corn products. This leads to an increase in the demand for corn, pushing the price up. This increased price provides incentives to producers to produce more corn. Thus, price signals our wants and desires. This is one reason why markets generally serve as the best way to organize economic activity.

Activity 3—Supply and Demand Article

Type: Take-home assignment
Topics: Shifts in supply or demand, changing equilibrium
Class limitations: Works in any class

Purpose

This assignment is an excellent way to determine which students need extra help in understanding supply and demand. Students who have difficulty with it often need remedial help. Allowing students to correct errors and then resubmit the assignment can be worthwhile because it is fundamental to their understanding of how markets work.

Instructions

Give the students the following assignment:

Find an article in a recent newspaper or magazine illustrating a change in price or quantity in some market. Analyze the situation using economic reasoning.

1. Has there been an increase or decrease in demand? Factors that could shift the demand curve include changes in preferences, changes in income, changes in the price of substitutes or complements, or changes in the number of consumers in the market.
2. Has there been an increase or decrease in supply? Factors that could shift the supply curve include changes in costs of materials, wages, or other inputs; changes in technology; or changes in the number of firms in the market.
3. Draw a supply-and-demand graph to explain this change. Be sure to label your graph and clearly indicate which curve shifts.

Ask students to turn in a copy of the article along with their explanation. Warn students to avoid advertisements because they contain little information. They should be wary of commodity and financial markets unless they have a good understanding of the particular market. Markets for ordinary goods and services are most easily analyzed.

Points for Discussion

Most changes will only shift one curve—either supply or demand—not both. Remind students that price changes will not cause either curve to shift. (But shifting either curve will change price.)

Equilibrium points are not fixed. They change when supply or demand changes. Prices will not necessarily return to previous levels nor will quantities.

Remind the students of the four graphs showing the shifts in supply and demand.

SOLUTIONS TO TEXT PROBLEMS:

Quick Quizzes

1. A market is a group of buyers (who determine demand) and a group of sellers (who determine supply) of a particular good or service. A perfectly competitive market is one in which there are many buyers and many sellers of an identical product so that each has a negligible impact on the market price.

2. Here is an example of a monthly demand schedule for pizza:

Price of Pizza Slice	Number of Pizza Slices Demanded
$ 0.00	10
0.25	9
0.50	8
0.75	7
1.00	6
1.25	5
1.50	4
1.75	3
2.00	2
2.25	1
2.50	0

The demand curve is graphed in Figure 1.

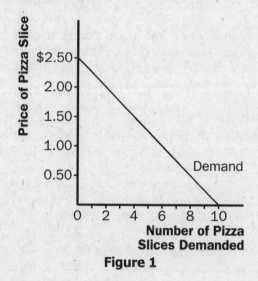

Figure 1

Examples of things that would shift the demand curve include changes in income, prices of related goods like soda or hot dogs, tastes, expectations about future income or prices, and the number of buyers.

A change in the price of pizza would not shift this demand curve; it would only lead to a movement from one point to another along the same demand curve.

3. Here is an example of a monthly supply schedule for pizza:

Price of Pizza Slice	Number of Pizza Slices Supplied
$ 0.00	0
0.25	100
0.50	200
0.75	300
1.00	400
1.25	500
1.50	600
1.75	700
2.00	800
2.25	900
2.50	1000

The supply curve is graphed in Figure 2.

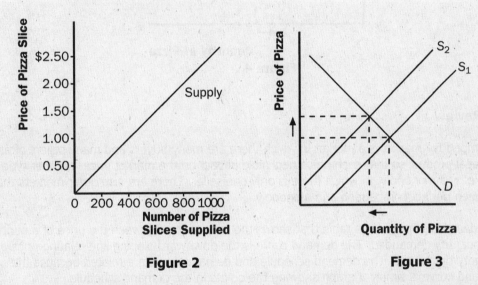

Figure 2   **Figure 3**

Examples of things that would shift the supply curve include changes in prices of inputs like tomato sauce and cheese, changes in technology like more efficient pizza ovens or automatic dough makers, changes in expectations about the future price of pizza, or a change in the number of sellers.

A change in the price of pizza would not shift this supply curve; it would only lead to a movement from one point to another along the same supply curve.

4. If the price of tomatoes rises, the supply curve for pizza shifts to the left because there has been an increase in the price of an input into pizza production, but there is no shift in demand. The shift to the left of the supply curve causes the equilibrium price to rise and the equilibrium quantity to decline, as Figure 3 shows.

If the price of hamburgers falls, the demand curve for pizza shifts to the left because the lower price of hamburgers will lead consumers to buy more hamburgers and fewer pizzas, but there is no shift in supply. The shift to the left of the demand curve causes the equilibrium price to fall and the equilibrium quantity to decline, as Figure 4 shows.

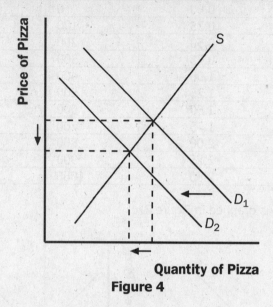

Figure 4

Questions for Review

1. A competitive market is a market in which there are many buyers and many sellers of an identical product so that each has a negligible impact on the market price. Another type of market is a monopoly, in which there is only one seller. There are also other markets that fall between perfect competition and monopoly.

2. The demand schedule is a table that shows the relationship between the price of a good and the quantity demanded. The demand curve is the downward-sloping line relating price and quantity demanded. The demand schedule and demand curve are related because the demand curve is simply a graph showing the points in the demand schedule.

   The demand curve slopes downward because of the law of demand—other things being equal, when the price of a good rises, the quantity demanded of the good falls. People buy less of a good when its price rises, both because they cannot afford to buy as much and because they switch to purchasing other goods.

3. A change in consumers' tastes leads to a shift of the demand curve. A change in price leads to a movement along the demand curve.

4. Because Popeye buys more spinach when his income falls, spinach is an inferior good for him. His demand curve for spinach shifts out as a result of the decrease in his income.

5. A supply schedule is a table showing the relationship between the price of a good and the quantity a producer is willing and able to supply. The supply curve is the upward-sloping line relating price and quantity supplied. The supply schedule and the supply curve are related because the supply curve is simply a graph showing the points in the supply schedule.

The supply curve slopes upward because when the price is high, suppliers' profits increase, so they supply more output to the market. The result is the law of supply—other things being equal, when the price of a good rises, the quantity supplied of the good also rises.

6. A change in producers' technology leads to a shift in the supply curve. A change in price leads to a movement along the supply curve.

7. The equilibrium of a market is the point at which the quantity demanded is equal to quantity supplied. If the price is above the equilibrium price, sellers want to sell more than buyers want to buy, so there is a surplus. Sellers try to increase their sales by cutting prices. That continues until they reach the equilibrium price. If the price is below the equilibrium price, buyers want to buy more than sellers want to sell, so there is a shortage. Sellers can raise their price without losing customers. That continues until they reach the equilibrium price.

8. When the price of beer rises, the demand for pizza declines, because beer and pizza are complements and people want to buy less beer. When we say the demand for pizza declines, we mean that the demand curve for pizza shifts to the left as in Figure 5. The supply curve for pizza is not affected. With a shift to the left in the demand curve, the equilibrium price and quantity both decline, as the figure shows. Thus, the quantity of pizza supplied and demanded both fall. In sum, supply is unchanged, demand is decreased, quantity supplied declines, quantity demanded declines, and the price falls.

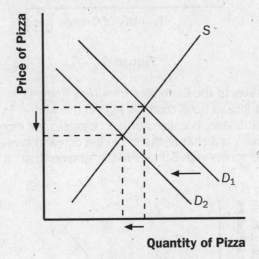

Figure 5

9. Prices play a vital role in market economies because they bring markets into equilibrium. If the price is different from its equilibrium level, quantity supplied and quantity demanded are not equal. The resulting surplus or shortage leads suppliers to adjust the price until equilibrium is restored. Prices thus serve as signals that guide economic decisions and allocate scarce resources.

Problems and Applications

1. a. Cold weather damages the orange crop, reducing the supply of oranges and raising the price of oranges. This leads to a decline in the supply of orange juice because oranges are an important input in the production of orange juice. This can be seen in Figure 6 as a shift to the left in the supply curve for orange juice. The new equilibrium price is higher than the old equilibrium price.

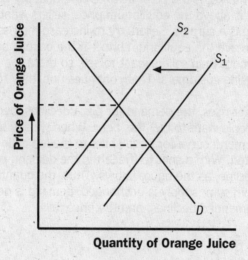

Figure 6

   b. People often travel to the Caribbean from New England to escape cold weather, so the demand for Caribbean hotel rooms is high in the winter. In the summer, fewer people travel to the Caribbean, because northern climates are more pleasant. The result, as shown in Figure 7, is a shift to the left in the demand curve. The equilibrium price of Caribbean hotel rooms is thus lower in the summer than in the winter, as the figure shows.

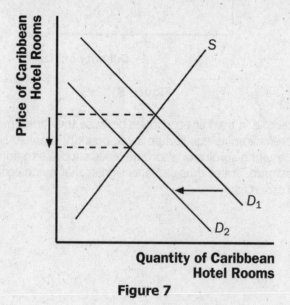

Figure 7

c. When a war breaks out in the Middle East, many markets are affected. Because a large proportion of oil production takes place there, the war disrupts oil supplies, shifting the supply curve for gasoline to the left, as shown in Figure 8. The result is a rise in the equilibrium price of gasoline. With a higher price for gasoline, the cost of operating a gas-guzzling automobile like a Cadillac will increase. As a result, the demand for used Cadillacs will decline, as people in the market for cars will not find Cadillacs as attractive. In addition, some people who already own Cadillacs will try to sell them. The result is that the demand curve for used Cadillacs shifts to the left, while the supply curve shifts to the right, as shown in Figure 9. The result is a decline in the equilibrium price of used Cadillacs.

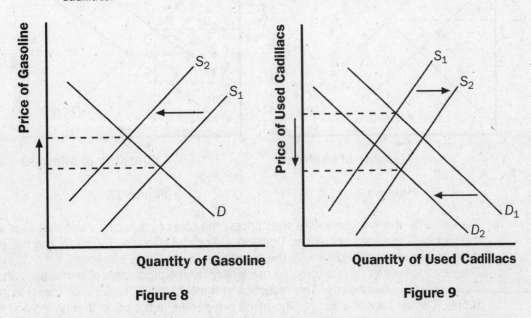

Figure 8

Figure 9

2. The statement, in general, is false. As Figure 10 shows, the increase in demand for notebooks results in an increased quantity supplied. The only way the statement would be true is if the supply curve was a vertical line, as shown in Figure 11.

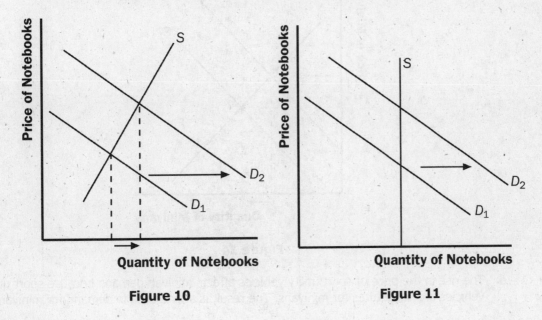

Figure 10

Figure 11

3. a. If people decide to have more children, they will want larger vehicles for hauling their kids around, so the demand for minivans will increase. Supply will not be affected. The result is a rise in both the price and the quantity sold, as Figure 12 shows.

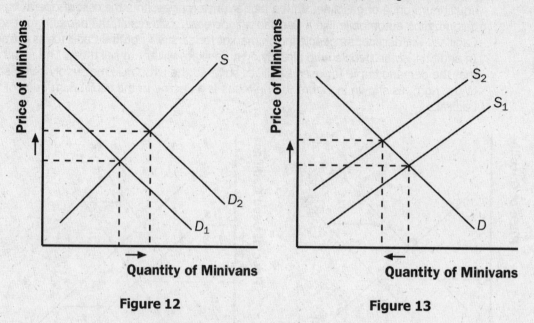

Figure 12   **Figure 13**

b. If a strike by steelworkers raises steel prices, the cost of producing a minivan rises and the supply of minivans decreases. Demand will not be affected. The result is a rise in the price of minivans and a decline in the quantity sold, as Figure 13 shows.

c. The development of new automated machinery for the production of minivans is an improvement in technology. This reduction in firms' costs will result in an increase in supply. Demand is not affected. The result is a decline in the price of minivans and an increase in the quantity sold, as Figure 14 shows.

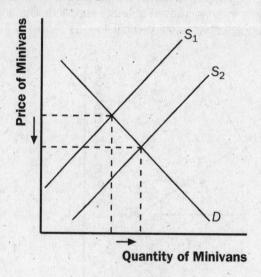

Figure 14

d. The rise in the price of sport utility vehicles affects minivan demand because sport utility vehicles are substitutes for minivans. The result is an increase in demand for minivans.

Supply is not affected. The equilibrium price and quantity of minivans both rise, as Figure 12 shows.

e. The reduction in peoples' wealth caused by a stock-market crash reduces their income, leading to a reduction in the demand for minivans, because minivans are likely a normal good. Supply is not affected. As a result, both the equilibrium price and the equilibrium quantity decline, as Figure 15 shows.

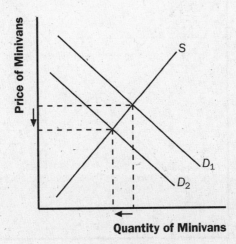

Figure 15

4. a. DVDs and TV screens are likely to be complements because you cannot watch a DVD without a television. DVDs and movie tickets are likely to be substitutes because a movie can be watched at a theater or at home. TV screens and movie tickets are likely to be substitutes for the same reason.

    b. The technological improvement would reduce the cost of producing a TV screen, shifting the supply curve to the right. The demand curve would not be affected. The result is that the equilibrium price will fall, while the equilibrium quantity will rise. This is shown in Figure 16.

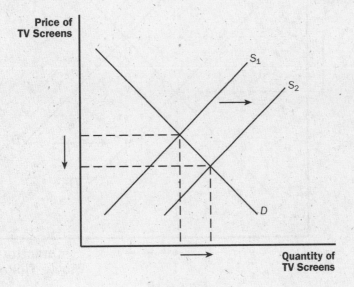

Figure 16

c. The reduction in the price of TV screens would lead to an increase in the demand for DVDs because TV screens and DVDs are complements. The effect of this increase in the demand for DVDs is an increase in both the equilibrium price and quantity, as shown in Figure 17.

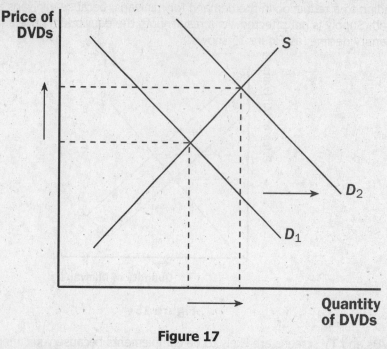

Figure 17

d. The reduction in the price of TV screens would cause a decline in the demand for movie tickets because TV screens and movie tickets are substitute goods. The decline in the demand for movie tickets would lead to a decline in the equilibrium price and quantity sold. This is shown in Figure 18.

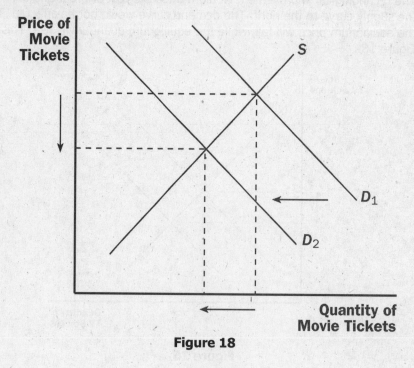

Figure 18

5. Technological advances that reduce the cost of producing computer chips represent a decline in an input price for producing a computer. The result is a shift to the right in the supply of computers, as shown in Figure 19. The equilibrium price falls and the equilibrium quantity rises, as the figure shows.

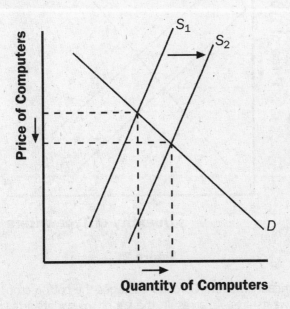

Figure 19

Because computer software is a complement to computers, the lower equilibrium price of computers increases the demand for software. As Figure 20 shows, the result is a rise in both the equilibrium price and quantity of software.

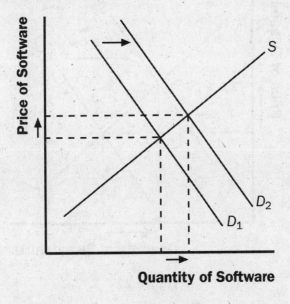

Figure 20

Because typewriters are substitutes for computers, the lower equilibrium price of computers reduces the demand for typewriters. As Figure 21 shows, the result is a decline in both the equilibrium price and quantity of typewriters.

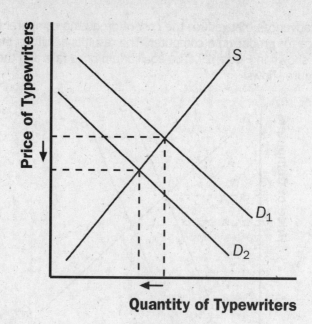

Figure 21

6. a. When a hurricane in South Carolina damages the cotton crop, it raises input prices for producing sweatshirts. As a result, the supply of sweatshirts shifts to the left, as shown in Figure 22. The new equilibrium price is higher and the new equilibrium quantity of sweatshirts is lower.

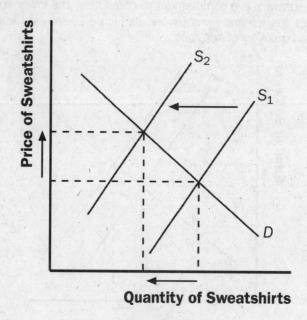

Figure 22

b. A decline in the price of leather jackets leads more people to buy leather jackets, reducing the demand for sweatshirts. The result, shown in Figure 23, is a decline in both the equilibrium price and quantity of sweatshirts.

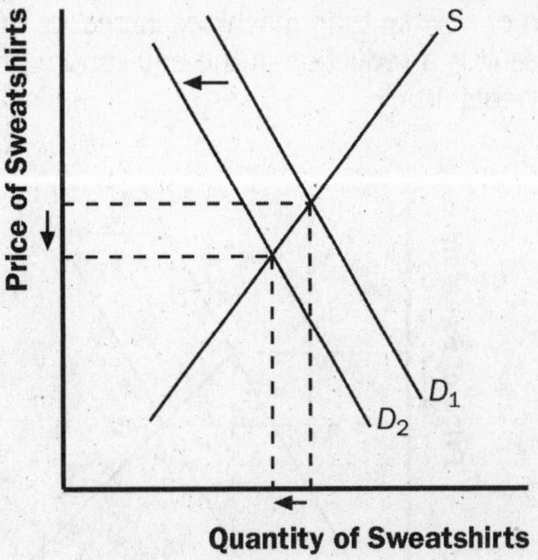

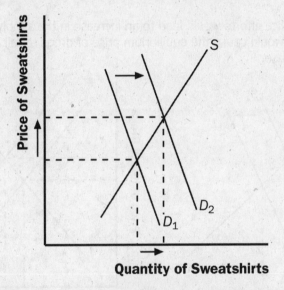

Figure 23

c. The effects of colleges requiring students to engage in morning exercise in appropriate attire raises the demand for sweatshirts, as shown in Figure 24. The result is an increase in both the equilibrium price and quantity of sweatshirts.

Figure 24

d. The invention of new knitting machines increases the supply of sweatshirts. As Figure 25 shows, the result is a reduction in the equilibrium price and an increase in the equilibrium quantity of sweatshirts.

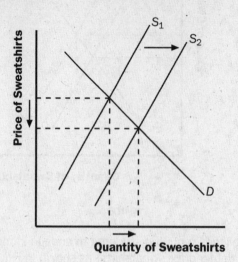

Figure 25

7. a. Reduced police efforts would lead to an increase in the supply of drugs. As Figure 26 shows, this would cause the equilibrium price of drugs to fall and the equilibrium quantity of drugs to rise.

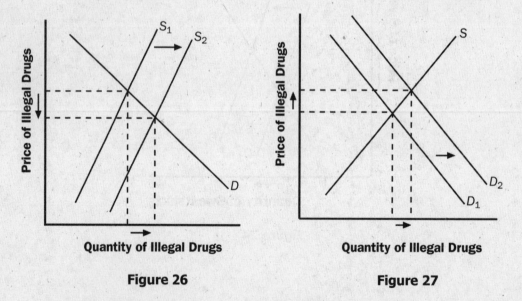

Figure 26   **Figure 27**

On the other hand, cutbacks in education efforts would lead to a rise in the demand for drugs. This would push the equilibrium price and quantity up, as shown in Figure 27.

b. A fall in the equilibrium price would lead us to believe the first hypothesis. If the equilibrium price rose, we would believe the second hypothesis.

8. A temporarily high birthrate in the year 2015 leads to opposite effects on the price of baby-sitting services in the years 2020 and 2030. In the year 2020, there are more five-year-olds who need sitters, so the demand for baby-sitting services rises, as shown in Figure 28. The result is a higher price for baby-sitting services in 2020. However, in the year 2030, the increased number of 15-year-olds shifts the supply of baby-sitting services to the right, as shown in Figure 29. The result is a decline in the price of baby-sitting services.

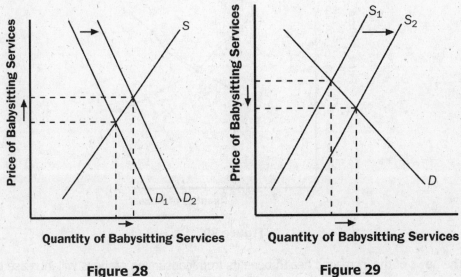

Figure 28   **Figure 29**

9. Ketchup is a complement for hot dogs. Therefore, when the price of hot dogs rises, the quantity demanded of hot dogs falls and this lowers the demand for ketchup. The end result is that both the equilibrium price and quantity of ketchup fall. Because the quantity of ketchup falls, the demand for tomatoes by ketchup producers falls, so the equilibrium price and quantity of tomatoes fall. When the price of tomatoes falls, producers of tomato juice face lower input prices, so the supply curve for tomato juice shifts out, causing the price of tomato juice to fall and the quantity of tomato juice to rise. The fall in the price of tomato juice causes people to substitute tomato juice for orange juice, so the demand for orange juice declines, causing the price and quantity of orange juice to fall. Now you can see clearly why a rise in the price of hot dogs leads to a fall in the price of orange juice!

10. Quantity supplied equals quantity demanded at a price of $6 and quantity of 81 pizzas (Figure 30). If the price were greater than $6, quantity supplied would exceed quantity demanded, so suppliers would reduce the price to gain sales. If the price were less than $6, quantity demanded would exceed quantity supplied, so suppliers could raise the price without losing sales. In both cases, the price would continue to adjust until it reached $6, the only price at which there is neither a surplus nor a shortage.

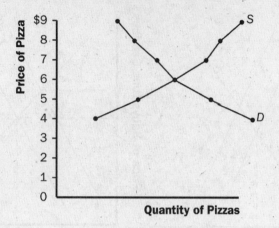

Figure 30

11. The news of the increased health benefits from consuming oranges will increase the demand for oranges, increasing both the equilibrium price and quantity. If farmers use a new fertilizer that makes orange trees more productive, the supply of oranges will increase, leading to a fall in the equilibrium price but a rise in the equilibrium quantity. If both occur at the same time, the equilibrium quantity will definitely rise, but the effect on equilibrium price will be ambiguous.

12. a. Because flour is an ingredient in bagels, a decline in the price of flour would shift the supply curve for bagels to the right. The result, shown in Figure 31, would be a fall in the price of bagels and a rise in the equilibrium quantity of bagels.

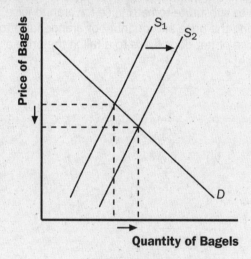

Figure 31

Because cream cheese is a complement to bagels, the fall in the equilibrium price of bagels increases the demand for cream cheese, as shown in Figure 32. The result is a rise in both the equilibrium price and quantity of cream cheese. So, a fall in the price of flour indeed raises both the equilibrium price of cream cheese and the equilibrium quantity of bagels.

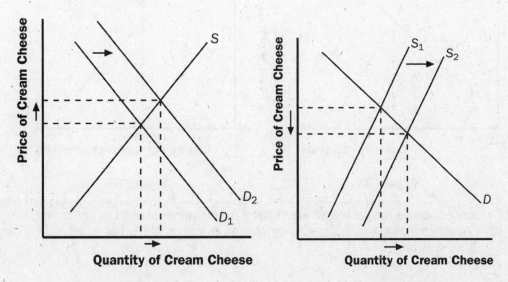

Figure 32   **Figure 33**

What happens if the price of milk falls? Because milk is an ingredient in cream cheese, the fall in the price of milk leads to an increase in the supply of cream cheese. This leads to a decrease in the price of cream cheese (Figure 33), rather than a rise in the price of cream cheese. So a fall in the price of milk could not have been responsible for the pattern observed.

b. In part (a), we found that a fall in the price of flour led to a rise in the price of cream cheese and a rise in the equilibrium quantity of bagels. If the price of flour rose, the opposite would be true; it would lead to a fall in the price of cream cheese and a fall in the equilibrium quantity of bagels. Because the question says the equilibrium price of cream cheese has risen, it could not have been caused by a rise in the price of flour.

What happens if the price of milk rises? From part (a), we found that a fall in the price of milk caused a decline in the price of cream cheese, so a rise in the price of milk would cause a rise in the price of cream cheese. Because bagels and cream cheese are complements, the rise in the price of cream cheese would reduce the demand for bagels, as Figure 34 shows. The result is a decline in the equilibrium quantity of bagels. So a rise in the price of milk does cause both a rise in the price of cream cheese and a decline in the equilibrium quantity of bagels.

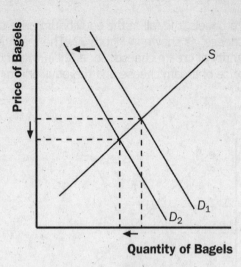

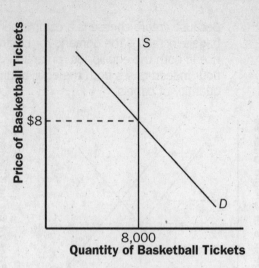

Figure 34   **Figure 35**

13. a. As Figure 35 shows, the supply curve is vertical. The constant quantity supplied makes sense because the basketball arena has a fixed number of seats at any price.

  b. Quantity supplied equals quantity demanded at a price of $8. The equilibrium quantity is 8,000 tickets.

  c.

Price	Quantity Demanded	Quantity Supplied
$4	14,000	8,000
$8	11,000	8,000
$12	8,000	8,000
$16	5,000	8,000
$20	2,000	8,000

The new equilibrium price will be $12, which equates quantity demanded to quantity supplied. The equilibrium quantity remains 8,000 tickets.

14. Equilibrium occurs where quantity demanded is equal to quantity supplied. Thus:

$$Q^d = Q^s$$
$$1,600 - 300P = 1,400 + 700P$$
$$200 = 1,000P$$
$$P = \$0.20$$

$$Q^d = 1,600 - 300(0.20) = 1,600 - 60 = 1,540$$
$$Q^s = 1,400 + 700(0.20) = 1,400 + 140 = 1,540.$$

The equilibrium price of a chocolate bar is $0.20 and the equilibrium quantity is 1,540 bars.

ELASTICITY AND ITS APPLICATION

WHAT'S NEW IN THE SIXTH EDITION:

There is a new *FYI* box reporting "A Few Elasticities from the Real World."

LEARNING OBJECTIVES:

By the end of this chapter, students should understand:

➢ the meaning of the elasticity of demand.

➢ what determines the elasticity of demand.

➢ the meaning of the elasticity of supply.

➢ what determines the elasticity of supply.

➢ the concept of elasticity in three very different markets (the market for wheat, the market for oil, and the market for illegal drugs).

CONTEXT AND PURPOSE:

Chapter 5 is the second chapter of a three-chapter sequence that deals with supply and demand and how markets work. Chapter 4 introduced supply and demand. Chapter 5 shows how much buyers and sellers respond to changes in market conditions. Chapter 6 will address the impact of government polices on competitive markets.

The purpose of Chapter 5 is to add precision to the supply-and-demand model. We introduce the concept of elasticity, which measures the responsiveness of buyers and sellers to changes in economic variables such as prices and income. The concept of elasticity allows us to make quantitative observations about the impact of changes in supply and demand on equilibrium prices and quantities.

KEY POINTS:

• The price elasticity of demand measures how much the quantity demanded responds to changes in the price. Demand tends to be more elastic if close substitutes are available, if the good is a luxury rather than a necessity, if the market is narrowly defined, or if buyers have substantial time to react to a price change.

- The price elasticity of demand is calculated as the percentage change in quantity demanded divided by the percentage change in price. If quantity demanded moves proportionately less than the price, then the elasticity is less than one, and demand is said to be inelastic. If quantity demanded moves proportionately more than the price, then the elasticity is greater than one, and demand is said to be elastic.

- Total revenue, the total amount paid for a good, equals the price of the good times the quantity sold. For inelastic demand curves, total revenue moves in the same direction as the price. For elastic demand curves, total revenue moves in the opposite direction as the price.

- The income elasticity of demand measures how much the quantity demanded responds to changes in consumers' income. The cross-price elasticity of demand measures how much the quantity demanded of one good responds to the price of another good.

- The price elasticity of supply measures how much the quantity supplied responds to changes in the price. This elasticity often depends on the time horizon under consideration. In most markets, supply is more elastic in the long run than in the short run.

- The price elasticity of supply is calculated as the percentage change in quantity supplied divided by the percentage change in price. If quantity supplied moves proportionately less than the price, then the elasticity is less than one, and supply is said to be inelastic. If quantity supplied moves proportionately more than the price, then the elasticity is greater than one, and supply is said to be elastic.

- The tools of supply and demand can be applied in many different kinds of markets. This chapter uses them to analyze the market for wheat, the market for oil, and the market for illegal drugs.

CHAPTER OUTLINE:

I.   The Elasticity of Demand

A.   Definition of **elasticity: a measure of the responsiveness of quantity demanded or quantity supplied to one of its determinants.**

B.   The Price Elasticity of Demand and Its Determinants

1.   Definition of **price elasticity of demand: a measure of how much the quantity demanded of a good responds to a change in the price of that good, computed as the percentage change in quantity demanded divided by the percentage change in price.**

2.   Determinants of the Price Elasticity of Demand

a.   Availability of Close Substitutes: the more substitutes a good has, the more elastic its demand.

b.   Necessities versus Luxuries: necessities are more price inelastic.

c. Definition of the market: narrowly defined markets (ice cream) have more elastic demand than broadly defined markets (food).

d. Time Horizon: goods tend to have more elastic demand over longer time horizons.

C. Computing the Price Elasticity of Demand

1. Formula

$$\text{Price elasticity of demand} = \frac{\text{\% change in quantity demanded}}{\text{\% change in price}}$$

 Work through a few elasticity calculations, starting with the example in the book. For principles of economics courses where there is no mathematical prerequisite, this may be difficult for some students. Working through a few simple examples will help to alleviate some of the students' anxiety. Show every step of the algebra involved.

2. Example: the price of ice cream rises by 10% and quantity demanded falls by 20%.

Price elasticity of demand = (20%)/(10%) = 2

3. Because there is an inverse relationship between price and quantity demanded (the price of ice cream rose by 10% and the quantity demanded fell by 20%), the price elasticity of demand is sometimes reported as a negative number. We will ignore the minus sign and concentrate on the absolute value of the elasticity.

 Students hate this! Explain that it really makes things easier and makes more sense because larger elasticities (in absolute value) imply greater sensitivity and responsiveness.

D. The Midpoint Method: A Better Way to Calculate Percentage Changes and Elasticities

1. Because we use percentage changes in calculating the price elasticity of demand, the elasticity calculated by going from one point to another on a demand curve will be different from an elasticity calculated by going from the second point to the first. This difference arises because the percentage changes are calculated using a different base.

a. A way around this problem is to use the midpoint method.

b. Using the midpoint method involves calculating the percentage change in either price or quantity demanded by dividing the change in the variable by the midpoint between the initial and final levels rather than by the initial level itself.

c. Example: the price rises from $4 to $6 and quantity demanded falls from 120 to 80.

% change in price = (6 − 4)/5 × 100% = 40%

% change in quantity demanded = (120 − 80)/100 = 40%

$$\text{price elasticity of demand} = 40/40 = 1$$

$$\text{Price elasticity of demand} = \frac{(Q_2 - Q_1) / [(Q_1 + Q_2) / 2]}{(P_2 - P_1) / [(P_1 + P_2) / 2]}$$

E. The Variety of Demand Curves

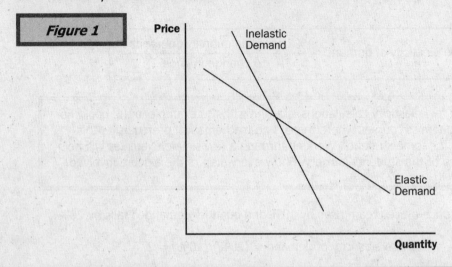

Figure 1

To clearly show the differences between relatively elastic and relatively inelastic demand curves, draw a graph on the board showing a relatively flat demand curve and one showing a relatively steep demand curve. Show that any given change in price will result in a larger change in quantity demanded if the demand curve is relatively flat. Use the same method when discussing the shape of the supply curve later in the chapter.

1. Classification of Elasticity

    a. When the price elasticity of demand is greater than one, demand is defined to be elastic.

    b. When the price elasticity of demand is less than one, the demand is defined to be inelastic.

    c. When the price elasticity of demand is equal to one, the demand is said to have unit elasticity.

Activity 1—How the Ball Bounces

Type:	In-class demonstration
Topics:	Elastic, inelastic
Materials needed:	One rubber ball and one "dead" ball. The "dead" ball is made of shock-absorbing material and doesn't bounce. Museum stores and magic shops carry them.
Time:	1 minute
Class limitations:	Works in any size class

Purpose

This quick, but memorable, demonstration can be used to introduce the concepts of elastic and inelastic.

Instructions

Bring two students to the front of the class. Give each of them a ball and ask them to bounce it off the floor and catch it. The student with the rubber ball can do this easily. The student with the "dead" ball will not be able to bounce it high enough to catch, no matter how hard he or she throws it.

Explain that one ball is elastic; it is responsive to change. The other ball is inelastic; it responds very little to change. These physical properties of elastic and inelastic are analogous to the economic concepts of elastic and inelastic.

---

2. In general, the flatter the demand curve that passes through a given point, the more elastic the demand.

3. Extreme Cases

   a. When the price elasticity of demand is equal to zero, the demand is perfectly inelastic and is a vertical line.

   b. When the price elasticity of demand is infinite, the demand is perfectly elastic and is a horizontal line.

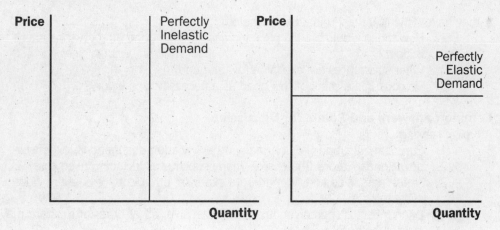

Make sure that you provide several examples of goods with these types of demand curves. You may want to point out that students will see the perfectly elastic demand curve again when competitive firms are discussed.

***The Simpsons, "I Love Lisa."* Season 4 (2:26-4:02).** Homer forgets to buy Marge a gift for Valentine's Day. At the last minute, he ends up paying almost $100 for a box of chocolates. Discuss how last-minute buying can make a consumer less sensitive to price.

4. *FYI: A Few Elasticities from the Real World*

Activity 2—Ranking Elasticities

Type:	In-class assignment
Topics:	The determinants of price elasticity of demand
Materials needed:	None
Time:	20 minutes
Class limitations:	Works in any size class

Purpose

The intent of this exercise is to get students to think about varying degrees of elasticity and the factors that determine demand elasticity.

Instructions

Give the students the following list of goods. Ask them to rank them from most to least elastic.

1. beef
2. salt
3. European vacation
4. steak
5. new Honda Accord
6. Dijon mustard

If they have difficulty, these hints can be helpful:

1. How much would a 10% price increase for the good affect a consumer's total budget?
2. What substitutes are available for the good?
3. Do consumers think of this good as a necessity or a luxury?

Common Answers and Points for Discussion

A typical ranking:

1. European vacation (luxury, many other vacation destinations, expensive)
2. new Honda Accord (expensive, many substitutes including used cars)
3. steak (perceived luxury, moderate expense, other cuts of beef are close substitutes)
4. Dijon mustard (perceived luxury, inexpensive, other types of mustard may be close substitutes)
5. beef (moderate expense, pork and chicken are substitutes)
6. salt (inexpensive, necessity, no close substitutes)

F.   Total Revenue and the Price Elasticity of Demand

Figure 2

1.   Definition of **total revenue: the amount paid by buyers and received by sellers of a good, computed as the price of the good times the quantity sold**.

Another term for price times quantity is "total expenditure." This term is sometimes used in questions found in the study guide and test bank. It is also important to point this out when discussing the market for illegal drugs at the end of the chapter.

Students find the relationship between changes in total revenue and elasticity difficult to understand. It may take several thorough discussions of this material before students will be able to master it.

2.   If demand is inelastic, the percentage change in price will be greater than the percentage change in quantity demanded.

Figure 3

a.   If price rises, quantity demanded falls, and total revenue will rise (because the increase in price will be larger than the decrease in quantity demanded).

b.   If price falls, quantity demanded rises, and total revenue will fall (because the fall in price will be larger than the increase in quantity demanded).

3.   If demand is elastic, the percentage change in quantity demanded will be greater than the percentage change in price.

a.   If price rises, quantity demanded falls, and total revenue will fall (because the increase in price will be smaller than the decrease in quantity demanded).

b.   If price falls, quantity demanded rises, and total revenue will rise (because the fall in price will be smaller than the increase in quantity demanded).

4.   If demand is unit elastic, the percentage change in price will be equal to the percentage change in quantity demanded.

a.   If price rises, quantity demanded falls, and total revenue will remain the same (because the increase in price will be equal to the decrease in quantity demanded).

b.   If price falls, quantity demanded rises, and total revenue will remain the same (because the fall in price will be equal to the increase in quantity demanded).

Point out the usefulness of elasticity from a business owner's point of view. Students should be able to see why a firm's manager would want to know the elasticity of demand for the firm's products.

G. Elasticity and Total Revenue along a Linear Demand Curve

Figure 4

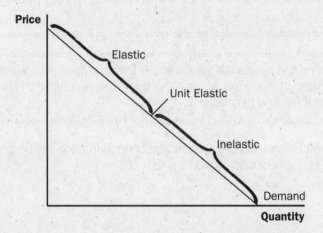

1. The slope of a linear demand curve is constant, but the elasticity is not.

   a. At points with a low price and a high quantity demanded, demand is inelastic.

   b. At points with a high price and a low quantity demanded, demand is elastic.

2. Total revenue also varies at each point along the demand curve.

 Note that when demand is elastic and price falls, total revenue rises. Also point out that once demand is inelastic, any further decrease in price results in a decrease in total revenue.

H. Other Demand Elasticities

1. Definition of **income elasticity of demand: a measure of how much the quantity demanded of a good responds to a change in consumers' income, computed as the percentage change in quantity demanded divided by the percentage change in income.**

   a. Formula

$$\text{Income elasticity of demand} = \frac{\% \text{ change in quantity demanded}}{\% \text{ change in income}}$$

b. Normal goods have positive income elasticities, while inferior goods have negative income elasticities.

ALTERNATIVE CLASSROOM EXAMPLE:

John's income rises from $20,000 to $22,000 and the quantity of hamburger he buys each week falls from 2 pounds to 1 pound.

% change in quantity demanded = (1−2)/1.5 = -0.6667 = -66.67%
% change in income = (22,000 −20,000)/21,000 = 0.0952 = 9.52%
income elasticity = 66.67%/9.52% = -7.00

Point out that hamburger is an inferior good for John.

---

c. Necessities tend to have small income elasticities, while luxuries tend to have large income elasticities.

2. Definition of **cross-price elasticity of demand**: **a measure of how much the quantity demanded of one good responds to a change in the price of another good, computed as the percentage change in the quantity demanded of the first good divided by the percentage change in the price of the second good.**

a. Formula

$$\text{Cross-price elasticity of demand} = \frac{\text{\% change in quantity demanded of good 1}}{\text{\% change in price of good 2}}$$

b. Substitutes have positive cross-price elasticities, while complements have negative cross-price elasticities.

ALTERNATIVE CLASSROOM EXAMPLE:

The price of apples rises from $1.00 per pound to $1.50 per pound. As a result, the quantity of oranges demanded rises from 8,000 per week to 9,500.

% change in quantity of oranges demanded = (9,500 − 8,000)/8,750 = 0.1714 = 17.14%
% change in price of apples = (1.50 − 1.00)/1.25 = 0.40 = 40%
cross-price elasticity = 17.14%/40% = 0.43

Because the cross-price elasticity is positive, the two goods are substitutes.

 Make sure that you explain to students why the signs of the income elasticity and the cross-price elasticity matter. This will undoubtedly lead to some confusion because we ignore the sign of the own-price elasticity of demand. You may want to put together a table to present this distinction to students.

II. The Elasticity of Supply

  A. The Price Elasticity of Supply and Its Determinants

    1. Definition of **price elasticity of supply: a measure of how much the quantity supplied of a good responds to a change in the price of that good, computed as the percentage change in quantity supplied divided by the percentage change in price.**

    2. Determinants of the Price Elasticity of Supply

       a. Flexibility of sellers: goods that are somewhat fixed in supply (beachfront property) have inelastic supplies.

       b. Time horizon: supply is usually more inelastic in the short run than in the long run.

  B. Computing the Price Elasticity of Supply

    1. Formula

$$\text{Price elasticity of supply} = \frac{\%\ \text{change in quantity supplied}}{\%\ \text{change in price}}$$

    2. Example: the price of milk increases from $2.85 per gallon to $3.15 per gallon and the quantity supplied rises from 9,000 to 11,000 gallons per month.

       % change in price = (3.15 − 2.85)/3.00 × 100% = 10%
       % change in quantity supplied = (11,000 − 9,000)/10,000 × 100% = 20%
       Price elasticity of supply = (20%)/(10%) = 2

  C. The Variety of Supply Curves

Figure 5

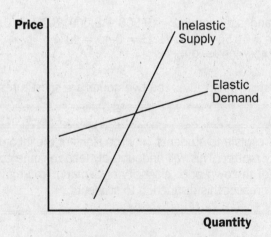

    1. In general, the flatter the supply curve that passes through a given point, the more elastic the supply.

2. Extreme Cases

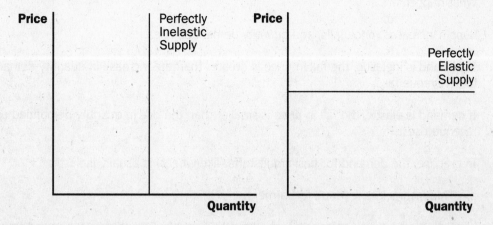

a. When the elasticity is equal to zero, the supply is said to be perfectly inelastic and is a vertical line.

b. When the elasticity is infinite, the supply is said to be perfectly elastic and is a horizontal line.

Figure 6

3. Because firms often have a maximum capacity for production, the elasticity of supply may be very high at low levels of quantity supplied and very low at high levels of quantity supplied.

 Again, you may want to present several examples of goods that may have supply curves like these.

III. Three Applications of Supply, Demand, and Elasticity

A. Can Good News for Farming Be Bad News for Farmers?

Figure 7

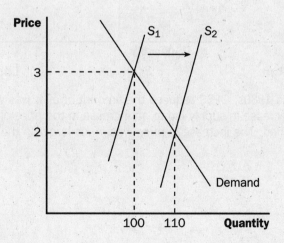

1. A new hybrid of wheat is developed that is more productive than those used in the past. What happens?

2. Supply increases, price falls, and quantity demanded rises.

3. If demand is inelastic, the fall in price is greater than the increase in quantity demanded and total revenue falls.

4. If demand is elastic, the fall in price is smaller than the rise in quantity demanded and total revenue rises.

5. In practice, the demand for basic foodstuffs (like wheat) is usually inelastic.

   a. This means less revenue for farmers.

   b. Because farmers are price takers, they still have the incentive to adopt the new hybrid so that they can produce and sell more wheat.

   c. This may help explain why the number of farms has declined so dramatically over the past two centuries.

   d. This may also explain why some government policies encourage farmers to decrease the amount of crops planted.

B. Why Did OPEC Fail to Keep the Price of Oil High?

Figure 8

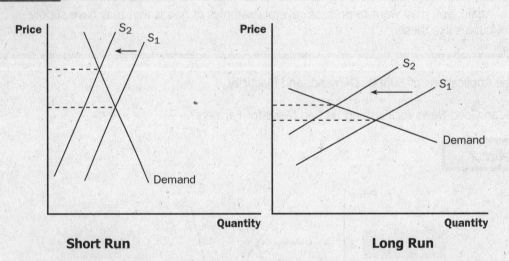

Short Run   **Long Run**

1. In the 1970s and 1980s, OPEC reduced the amount of oil it was willing to supply to world markets. The decrease in supply led to an increase in the price of oil and a decrease in quantity demanded. The increase in price was much larger in the short run than the long run. Why?

2. The demand and supply of oil are much more inelastic in the short run than the long run. The demand is more elastic in the long run because consumers can adjust to the higher price of oil by carpooling or buying a vehicle that gets better mileage. The supply is more elastic in the long run because non-OPEC producers will respond to the higher price of oil by producing more.

C. Does Drug Interdiction Increase or Decrease Drug-Related Crime?

Figure 9

1. The federal government increases the number of federal agents devoted to the war on drugs. What happens?

   a. The supply of drugs decreases, which raises the price and leads to a reduction in quantity demanded. If demand is inelastic, total expenditure on drugs (equal to total revenue) will increase. If demand is elastic, total expenditure will fall.

   b. Thus, because the demand for drugs is likely to be inelastic, drug-related crime may rise.

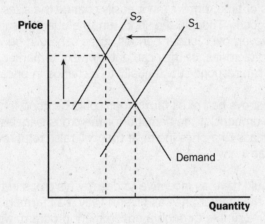

2. What happens if the government instead pursued a policy of drug education?

   a. The demand for drugs decreases, which lowers price and quantity supplied. Total expenditure must fall (because both price and quantity fall).

   b. Thus, drug education should not increase drug-related crime.

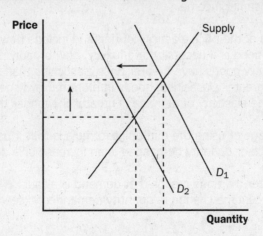

SOLUTIONS TO TEXT PROBLEMS:

Quick Quizzes

1. The price elasticity of demand is a measure of how much the quantity demanded of a good responds to a change in the price of that good, computed as the percentage change in quantity demanded divided by the percentage change in price.

    When demand is inelastic (a price elasticity less than 1), a price increase raises total revenue, and a price decrease reduces total revenue. When demand is elastic (a price elasticity greater than 1), a price increase reduces total revenue, and a price decrease increases total revenue. When demand is unit elastic (a price elasticity equal to 1), a change in price does not affect total revenue.

2. The price elasticity of supply is a measure of how much the quantity supplied of a good responds to a change in the price of that good, computed as the percentage change in quantity supplied divided by the percentage change in price.

    The price elasticity of supply might be different in the long run than in the short run because over short periods of time, firms cannot easily change the sizes of their factories to make more or less of a good. Thus, in the short run, the quantity supplied is not very responsive to the price. However, over longer periods, firms can build new factories, expand existing factories, close old factories, or they can enter or exit a market. So, in the long run, the quantity supplied can respond substantially to a change in price.

3. A drought that destroys half of all farm crops could be good for farmers (at least those unaffected by the drought) if the demand for the crops is inelastic. The shift to the left of the supply curve leads to a price increase that will raise total revenue if the price elasticity of demand is less than 1.

    No one farmer would have an incentive to destroy his crops in the absence of a drought because he takes the market price as given. Only if all farmers destroyed a portion of their crops together, for example through a government program, would this plan work to make farmers better off.

Questions for Review

1. The price elasticity of demand measures how much quantity demanded responds to a change in price. The income elasticity of demand measures how much quantity demanded responds to changes in consumer income.

2. The determinants of the price elasticity of demand include how available close substitutes are, whether the good is a necessity or a luxury, how broadly defined the market is, and the time horizon. Luxury goods have greater price elasticities than necessities, goods with close substitutes have greater elasticities, goods in more narrowly defined markets have greater elasticities, and the elasticity of demand is greater the longer the time horizon.

3. The main advantage of using the mid-point formula is that it uses a constant base whether the change in price or quantity demanded is an increase or a decrease.

4. An elasticity greater than one means that demand is elastic. When the elasticity is greater than one, the percentage change in quantity demanded exceeds the percentage change in

price. When the elasticity equals zero, demand is perfectly inelastic. There is no change in quantity demanded when there is a change in price.

5. Figure 1 presents a supply-and-demand diagram, showing the equilibrium price, the equilibrium quantity, and the total revenue received by producers. Total revenue equals the equilibrium price times the equilibrium quantity, which is the area of the rectangle shown in the figure.

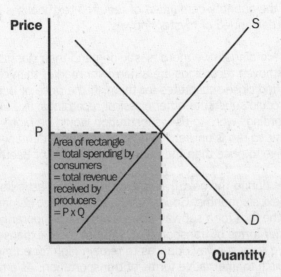

Figure 1

6. If demand is elastic, an increase in price reduces total revenue. With elastic demand, the quantity demanded falls by a greater percentage than the price rises. As a result, total revenue moves in the opposite direction as the price. Thus, if price rises, total revenue falls.

7. A good with income elasticity less than zero is called an inferior good because as income rises, the quantity demanded declines.

8. The price elasticity of supply is calculated as the percentage change in quantity supplied divided by the percentage change in price. It measures how much quantity supplied responds to changes in price.

9. The price elasticity of supply of Picasso paintings is zero, because no matter how high price rises, no more can ever be produced.

10. The price elasticity of supply is usually larger in the long run than it is in the short run. Over short periods of time, firms cannot easily change the sizes of their factories to make more or less of a good, so the quantity supplied is not very responsive to price. Over longer periods, firms can build new factories or close old ones, so the quantity supplied is more responsive to price.

11. Because the demand for drugs is likely to be inelastic, an increase in price will lead to a rise in total expenditure. Therefore, drug users may resort to theft or burglary to support their habits.

Problems and Applications

1. a. Mystery novels have more elastic demand than required textbooks, because mystery novels have close substitutes and are a luxury good, while required textbooks are a necessity with no close substitutes. If the price of mystery novels were to rise, readers could substitute other types of novels, or buy fewer novels altogether. But if the price of required textbooks were to rise, students would have little choice but to pay the higher price. Thus, the quantity demanded of required textbooks is less responsive to price than the quantity demanded of mystery novels.

    b. Beethoven recordings have more elastic demand than classical music recordings in general. Beethoven recordings are a narrower market than classical music recordings, so it is easy to find close substitutes for them. If the price of Beethoven recordings were to rise, people could substitute other classical recordings, like Mozart. But if the price of all classical recordings were to rise, substitution would be more difficult. (A transition from classical music to rap is unlikely!) Thus, the quantity demanded of classical recordings is less responsive to price than the quantity demanded of Beethoven recordings.

    c. Subway rides during the next five years have more elastic demand than subway rides during the next six months. Goods have a more elastic demand over longer time horizons. If the fare for a subway ride was to rise temporarily, consumers could not switch to other forms of transportation without great expense or great inconvenience. But if the fare for a subway ride was to remain high for a long time, people would gradually switch to alternative forms of transportation. As a result, the quantity demanded of subway rides during the next six months will be less responsive to changes in the price than the quantity demanded of subway rides during the next five years.

    d. Root beer has more elastic demand than water. Root beer is a luxury with close substitutes, while water is a necessity with no close substitutes. If the price of water were to rise, consumers have little choice but to pay the higher price. But if the price of root beer were to rise, consumers could easily switch to other sodas or beverages. So the quantity demanded of root beer is more responsive to changes in price than the quantity demanded of water.

2. a. For business travelers, the price elasticity of demand when the price of tickets rises from $200 to $250 is $[(2,000 - 1,900)/1,950]/[(250 - 200)/225] = 0.05/0.22 = 0.23$. For vacationers, the price elasticity of demand when the price of tickets rises from $200 to $250 is $[(800 - 600)/700] / [(250 - 200)/225] = 0.29/0.22 = 1.32$.

    b. The price elasticity of demand for vacationers is higher than the elasticity for business travelers because vacationers can choose more easily a different mode of transportation (like driving or taking the train). They may also choose to not travel at all. Business travelers are less likely to do so because time is more important to them and their schedules are less adaptable.

3. a. The percentage change in price is equal to $(2.20 - 1.80)/2.00 = 0.2 = 20\%$. If the price elasticity of demand is 0.2, quantity demanded will fall by 4% in the short run $[0.20 \times 0.20]$. If the price elasticity of demand is 0.7, quantity demanded will fall by 14% in the long run $[0.7 \times 0.2]$.

    b. Over time, consumers can make adjustments to their homes by purchasing alternative heat sources such as natural gas or electric furnaces. Thus, they can respond more easily to the change in the price of heating oil in the long run than in the short run.

4. If quantity demanded fell, price must have risen. If total revenue rose, then the percentage increase in the price must be greater than the percentage decline in quantity demanded. Therefore, demand is inelastic.

5. Both Billy and Valerie may be correct. If demand increases, but supply is "totally" inelastic, equilibrium price will rise but the equilibrium quantity will remain the same. This would also occur if supply decreases and demand is "totally" inelastic. Marian is incorrect. If supply and demand both rise, equilibrium quantity will increase, but the impact on equilibrium price is indeterminate.

6. a. If your income is $10,000, your price elasticity of demand as the price of DVDs rises from $8 to $10 is [(40 − 32)/36]/[(10 − 8)/9] =0.22/0.22 = 1. If your income is $12,000, the elasticity is [(50 − 45)/47.5]/[(10 − 8)/9] = 0.11/0.22 = 0.5.

   b. If the price is $12, your income elasticity of demand as your income increases from $10,000 to $12,000 is [(30 − 24)/27]/[(12,000 − 10,000)/11,000] = 0.22/0.18 = 1.22. If the price is $16, your income elasticity of demand as your income increases from $10,000 to $12,000 is [(12 − 8)/10]/[(12,000 − 10,000)/11,000] = 0.40/0.18 = 2.2.

7. Yes, an increase in income would decrease the demand for good X because the income elasticity is less than zero, indicating that good X is an inferior good. A decrease in the price of good Y will decrease the demand for good X because the two goods are substitutes (as indicated by a cross-price elasticity that is greater than zero).

8. a. If Maria always spends one-third of her income on clothing, then her income elasticity of demand is one, because maintaining her clothing expenditures as a constant fraction of her income means the percentage change in her quantity of clothing must equal her percentage change in income.

   b. Maria's price elasticity of clothing demand is also one, because every percentage point increase in the price of clothing would lead her to reduce her quantity purchased by the same percentage.

   c. Because Maria spends a smaller proportion of her income on clothing, then for any given price, her quantity demanded will be lower. Thus, her demand curve has shifted to the left. Because she will again spend a constant fraction of her income on clothing, her income and price elasticities of demand remain one.

9. a. The percentage change in price (using the midpoint formula) is (1.50 − 0.25)/(0.875) × 100% = 1.42.86%. Therefore, the price elasticity of demand is 4.3/142.86 = 0.03, which is very inelastic.

   b. Because the demand is inelastic, the Transit Authority's revenue rises when the fare rises.

   c. The elasticity estimate might be unreliable because it is only the first month after the fare increase. As time goes by, people may switch to other means of transportation in response to the price increase. So the elasticity may be larger in the long run than it is in the short run.

10. Tom's price elasticity of demand is zero, because he wants the same quantity regardless of the price. Jerry's price elasticity of demand is one, because he spends the same amount on

gas, no matter what the price, which means his percentage change in quantity is equal to the percentage change in price.

11. a.   With a price elasticity of demand of 0.4, reducing the quantity demanded of cigarettes by 20% requires a 50% increase in price, because 20/50 = 0.4. With the price of cigarettes currently $2, this would require an increase in the price to $3.33 a pack using the midpoint method (note that ($3.33 − $2)/$2.67 = .50).

   b.   The policy will have a larger effect five years from now than it does one year from now. The elasticity is larger in the long run, because it may take some time for people to reduce their cigarette usage. The habit of smoking is hard to break in the short run.

   c.   Because teenagers do not have as much income as adults, they are likely to have a higher price elasticity of demand. Also, adults are more likely to be addicted to cigarettes, making it more difficult to reduce their quantity demanded in response to a higher price.

12. In order to determine whether you should raise or lower the price of admissions, you need to know if the demand is elastic or inelastic. If demand is elastic, a decline in the price of admissions will increase total revenue. If demand is inelastic, an increase in the price of admissions will cause total revenue to rise.

13. a.   As Figure 2 shows, the increase in supply reduces the equilibrium price and increases the equilibrium quantity in both markets.

   b.   In the market for pharmaceutical drugs (with inelastic demand), the increase in supply leads to a relatively large decline in the equilibrium price and a small increase in the equilibrium quantity.

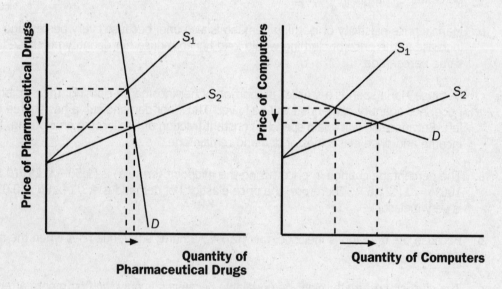

Figure 2

   c.   In the market for computers (with elastic demand), the increase in supply leads to a relatively large increase in the equilibrium quantity and a small decline in the equilibrium price.

    d.   Because demand is inelastic in the market for pharmaceutical drugs, the percentage increase in quantity will be lower than the percentage decrease in price; thus, total consumer spending will decline. Because demand is elastic in the market for computers, the percentage increase in quantity will be greater than the percentage decrease in price, so total consumer spending will increase.

14. a.   Farmers whose crops were not destroyed benefited because the destruction of some of the crops reduced the supply, causing the equilibrium price to rise.

    b.   To tell whether farmers as a group were hurt or helped by the floods, you would need to know the price elasticity of demand. It could be that the total revenue received by all farmers as a group actually rose.

15. A worldwide drought could increase the total revenue of farmers if the price elasticity of demand for grain is inelastic. The drought reduces the supply of grain, but if demand is inelastic, the reduction of supply causes a large increase in price. Total farm revenue would rise as a result. If there is only a drought in Kansas, Kansas' production is not a large enough proportion of the total farm product to have much impact on the price. As a result, price does not change (or changes by only a slight amount), while the output by Kansas farmers declines, thus reducing their income.

6 SUPPLY, DEMAND, AND GOVERNMENT POLICIES

==

WHAT'S NEW IN THE SIXTH EDITION:

There is a new *In the News* feature on "Should Unpaid Internships Be Allowed?"

LEARNING OBJECTIVES:

By the end of this chapter, students should understand:

➤ the effects of government policies that place a ceiling on prices.

➤ the effects of government policies that put a floor under prices.

➤ how a tax on a good affects the price of the good and the quantity sold.

➤ that taxes levied on sellers and taxes levied on buyers are equivalent.

➤ how the burden of a tax is split between buyers and sellers.

CONTEXT AND PURPOSE:

Chapter 6 is the third chapter in a three-chapter sequence that deals with supply and demand and how markets work. Chapter 4 developed the model of supply and demand. Chapter 5 added precision to the model of supply and demand by developing the concept of elasticity—the sensitivity of the quantity supplied and quantity demanded to changes in economic conditions. Chapter 6 addresses the impact of government policies on competitive markets using the tools of supply and demand that you learned in Chapters 4 and 5.

The purpose of Chapter 6 is to consider two types of government policies—price controls and taxes. Price controls set the maximum or minimum price at which a good can be sold while a tax creates a wedge between what the buyer pays and what the seller receives. These policies can be analyzed within the model of supply and demand. We will find that government policies sometimes produce unintended consequences.

KEY POINTS:

• A price ceiling is a legal maximum on the price of a good or service. An example is rent control. If the price ceiling is below the equilibrium price, so the price ceiling is binding, the quantity demanded

104

exceeds the quantity supplied. Because of the resulting shortage, sellers must in some way ration the good or service among buyers.

- A price floor is a legal minimum on the price of a good or service. An example is the minimum wage. If the price floor is above the equilibrium price, so the price floor is binding, the quantity supplied exceeds the quantity demanded. Because of the resulting surplus, buyers' demands for the good or service must be rationed in some way among sellers.

- When the government levies a tax on a good, the equilibrium quantity of the good falls; that is, a tax on a market shrinks the size of the market.

- A tax on a good places a wedge between the price paid by buyers and the price received by sellers. When the market moves to the new equilibrium, buyers pay more for the good and sellers receive less for it. In this sense, buyers and sellers share the tax burden. The incidence of a tax (that is, the division of the tax burden) does not depend on whether the tax is levied on buyers or sellers.

- The incidence of a tax depends on the price elasticities of supply and demand. Most of the burden falls on the side of the market that is less elastic because that side of the market can respond less easily to the tax by changing the quantity bought or sold.

CHAPTER OUTLINE:

I. Controls on Prices

 A. Definition of **price ceiling**: **a legal maximum on the price at which a good can be sold.**

 B. Definition of **price floor**: **a legal minimum on the price at which a good can be sold.**

 C. How Price Ceilings Affect Market Outcomes

> **Figure 1**

 1. There are two possible outcomes if a price ceiling is put into place in a market.

   a. If the price ceiling is higher than or equal to the equilibrium price, it is not binding and has no effect on the price or quantity sold.

   b. If the price ceiling is lower than the equilibrium price, the ceiling is a binding constraint and a shortage is created.

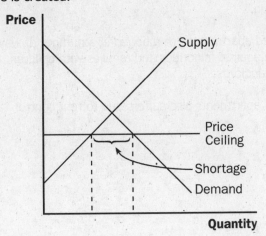

2. If a shortage for a product occurs (and price cannot adjust to eliminate it), a method for rationing the good must develop.

3. Not all buyers benefit from a price ceiling because some will be unable to purchase the product.

4. *Case Study: Lines at the Gas Pump*

Figure 2

a. In 1973, OPEC raised the price of crude oil, which led to a reduction in the supply of gasoline.

b. The federal government put a price ceiling into place and this created large shortages.

c. Motorists were forced to spend large amounts of time in line at the gas pump (which is how the gas was rationed).

d. Eventually, the government realized its mistake and repealed the price ceiling.

ALTERNATIVE CLASSROOM EXAMPLE:
Ask students about the rental market in their town. Draw a supply-and-demand graph for two-bedroom apartments asking students what they believe the equilibrium rental rate is. Then suggest that the city council is accusing landlords of taking advantage of students and thus places a price ceiling below the equilibrium price. Make sure that students can see that a shortage of apartments would result. Ask students to identify the winners and losers of this government policy.

---

5. *Case Study: Rent Control in the Short Run and the Long Run*

Figure 3

a. The goal of rent control is to make housing more affordable for the poor.

b. Because the supply of apartments is fixed (perfectly inelastic) in the short run and upward sloping (elastic) in the long run, the shortage is much larger in the long run than in the short run.

c. Rent-controlled apartments are rationed in a number of ways including long waiting lists, discrimination against minorities and families with children, and even under-the-table payments to landlords.

d. The quality of apartments also suffers due to rent control.

Seinfeld, "The Apartment." Season 2 (1:55-5:20, 9:02-9:49). Jerry lives in a rent-controlled building. The only time an apartment opens up is when Mrs. Hudwalker dies because rent controls create immobility. Elaine and Jerry find out about the opening, and because Elaine happens to be first in line, she gets it for $400 per month. Subsequently, Jerry gets worried about having Elaine living so close, and tells Elaine that she can't have the apartment—the super was offered a $5,000 bribe. This is a good clip to introduce the concept of black market transactions.

D.   How Price Floors Affect Market Outcomes

   1.   There are two possible outcomes if a price floor is put into place in a market.

Figure 4

   a.   If the price floor is lower than or equal to the equilibrium price, it is not binding and has no effect on the price or quantity sold.

   b.   If the price floor is higher than the equilibrium price, the floor is a binding constraint and a surplus is created.

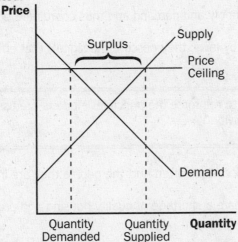

ALTERNATIVE CLASSROOM EXAMPLE:
Go through an example with an agricultural price support. Show students that, even though a price support is not a legal minimum price, its result is exactly the same as a price floor. Make sure that students can see that a surplus will result. Ask students to identify the winners and losers of this government policy. Make sure that you also point out the costs of the program (purchasing the surplus and storing it).

   2.   *Case Study: The Minimum Wage*

Figure 5

   a.   The market for labor looks like any other market: downward-sloping demand, upward-sloping supply, an equilibrium price (called a wage), and an equilibrium quantity of labor hired.

      b.   If the minimum wage is above the equilibrium wage in the labor market, a surplus of labor will develop (unemployment).

      c.   The minimum wage will be a binding constraint only in markets where equilibrium wages are low.

      d.   Thus, the minimum wage will have its greatest impact on the market for teenagers and other unskilled workers.

E.   *In the News: Should Unpaid Internships Be Allowed?*

    1.   Regulators are concerned that employers may be using unpaid internships as a way to get free labor.

    2.   This is an article from *The New York Times* discussing this concern.

F.   Evaluating Price Controls

    1.   Because most economists feel that markets are usually a good way to organize economic activity, most oppose the use of price ceilings and floors.

      a.   Prices balance supply and demand and thus coordinate economic activity.

      b.   If prices are set by laws, they obscure the signals that efficiently allocate scarce resources.

This is a good chance to reinforce the principle "Markets are usually a good way to organize economic activity."

---

    2.   Price ceilings and price floors often hurt the people they are intended to help.

      a.   Rent controls create a shortage of quality housing and provide disincentives for building maintenance.

      b.   Minimum wage laws create higher rates of unemployment for teenage and low skilled workers.

Be prepared to answer the question, "If price controls have such adverse consequences, why are they imposed?" You may want to point out that, sometimes, economic ignorance leads to unintended outcomes. You may also want to point out that economic analysis serves as only a guide to policymakers. They may choose to ignore it when forming policy. In addition, it is often interesting to encourage the students to think about the distributional effects of these government programs.

Activity 1—Ducks in a Row

Type: In-class demonstration
Topics: Price ceilings, subsidies, and unintended consequences
Materials needed: 2 toy ducks, some play money, 3 volunteers
Time: 10 minutes
Class limitations: Works in any size class

Purpose
This demonstration illustrates some common problems of government intervention in markets.

Instructions
One volunteer plays the role of the government in a poor country. Give the play money to the "government," except for $1. The government uses this money to buy ducks from the farmer and provides the ducks to the shopkeeper. The second volunteer is an urban shopkeeper. The shopkeeper asks the government for more ducks whenever he or she is sold out. Give the shopkeeper one duck. The third volunteer is a consumer. The consumer buys ducks. Give the consumer $1 in play money. The instructor is a duck farmer. The farmer keeps the second duck.

Explain this background: "Ducks are a staple food in this country but they are expensive at $3 each. The government wants to make food cheap for the urban poor to alleviate hunger. They calculate people could afford ducks if they were priced at $1. The government decides to impose a price ceiling of $1; $1 is now the maximum retail price for ducks."

Start the game. The consumer buys one duck from the shopkeeper. The shopkeeper requests more ducks from the government. The government comes to the farmer.

Points for Discussion
The instructor, as the duck farmer, controls the game. There are three points to make in this demonstration:
1.	Shortage. The farmer refuses to sell ducks at $1 each. The shopkeeper has no ducks.
2.	Subsidy. The farmer offers to sell the ducks for $3. The ducks can then be sold in the marketplace for $1. The government pays a $2 subsidy to keep food prices low.
3.	Black markets. After the farmer sells the duck to the government for $3, the duck goes to the shopkeeper for $1. The farmer buys back the original duck for $1 and resells it to the government for $3. This can continue until the government runs out of money.

Examples of unit taxes include most government excise taxes on products such as gasoline, alcohol, and tobacco.

Use this chance to reinforce the three steps learned in Chapter 4. Students should decide whether this tax law affects the demand curve or the supply curve, decide which way it shifts, and then examine how the shift affects equilibrium price and quantity.

II. Taxes

A. Definition of **tax incidence: the manner in which the burden of a tax is shared among participants in a market.**

B. How Taxes on Sellers Affect Market Outcomes

1. If the government requires the seller to pay a certain dollar amount for each unit of a good sold, this will cause a decrease in supply.

2. The supply curve will shift up by the exact amount of the tax.

Figure 6

 You will want to be very careful when discussing the "upward" shift of the supply curve given that we encourage students to think of supply and demand curves shifting "right" and "left." Make sure to emphasize the effects of the tax on sellers' willingness to sell.

3. The quantity of the good sold will decline.

4. Buyers and sellers will share the burden of the tax; buyers pay more for the good (including the tax) and sellers receive less.

5. Two lessons can be learned here.

a. Taxes discourage market activity.

b. Buyers and sellers share the burden of a tax.

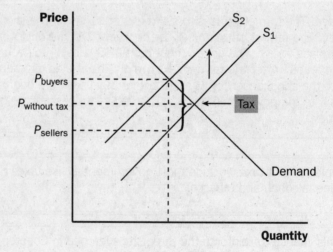

B. How Taxes on Buyers Affect Market Outcomes

Figure 7

1. If the government requires the buyer to pay a certain dollar amount for each unit of a good purchased, this will cause a decrease in demand.

2. The demand curve will shift down by the exact amount of the tax.

> Again, be very careful when discussing the "downward" shift of the demand curve. Describe the effects of the tax on buyers' willingness to buy.

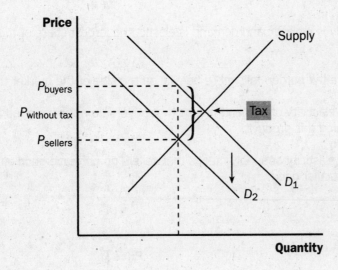

3. The quantity of the good sold will decline.

4. Buyers and sellers will share the burden of the tax; buyers pay more for the good and sellers receive less (because of the tax).

> Stress that the outcome of a tax levied on sellers is exactly the same as the outcome of a tax levied on buyers. When drawing this in class, make sure that the price that buyers end up paying and the price that sellers end up receiving is the same in both examples.

D. *Case Study: Can Congress Distribute the Burden of a Payroll Tax?*

Figure 8

1. FICA (Social Security) taxes were designed so that firms and workers would equally share the burden of the tax.

2. This type of payroll tax will simply put a wedge between the wage the firm pays and the wage the workers will receive.

3. It is true that firms and workers share the burden of this tax, but it is not necessarily 50-50.

 Go through this material slowly. Make sure that students can see how to find the burden of the tax paid by consumers and the burden of the tax paid by producers before discussing the effects of elasticity on tax incidence. If you rush through this material, you will lose them.

E. Elasticity and Tax Incidence

1. When supply is elastic and demand is inelastic, the largest share of the tax burden falls on consumers.

2. When supply is inelastic and demand is elastic, the largest share of the tax burden falls on producers.

3. In general, a tax burden falls more heavily on the side of the market that is less elastic.

    a. A small elasticity of demand means that buyers do not have good alternatives to consuming this product.

    b. A small elasticity of supply means that sellers do not have good alternatives to producing this particular good.

Figure 9

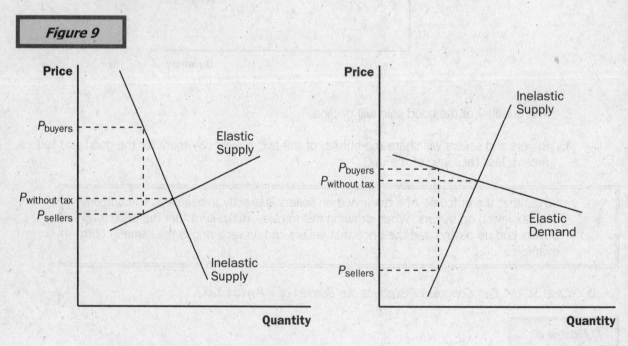

4. *Case Study: Who Pays the Luxury Tax?*

    a. In 1990, Congress adopted a new luxury tax.

b. The goal of the tax was to raise revenue from those who could most easily afford to pay.

c. Because the demand for luxuries is often relatively more elastic than supply, the burden of the tax fell on producers and their workers.

SOLUTIONS TO TEXT PROBLEMS:

Quick Quizzes

1. A price ceiling is a legal maximum on the price at which a good can be sold. Examples of price ceilings include rent controls, price controls on gasoline in the 1970s, and price ceilings on water during a drought. A price floor is a legal minimum on the price at which a good can be sold. Examples of price floors include the minimum wage and farm price supports. A price ceiling leads to a shortage, if the ceiling is binding, because suppliers will not produce enough goods to meet demand. A price floor leads to a surplus, if the floor is binding, because suppliers produce more goods than are demanded.

2. With no tax, as shown in Figure 1, the demand curve is D_1 and the supply curve is S. The equilibrium price is P_1 and the equilibrium quantity is Q_1. If the tax is imposed on car buyers, the demand curve shifts downward by the amount of the tax ($1,000) to D_2. The downward shift in the demand curve leads to a decline in the price received by sellers to P_2 and a decline in the equilibrium quantity to Q_2. The price received by sellers declines by $P_1 - P_2$, shown in the figure as ΔP_S. Buyers pay a total of $P_2 + \$1,000$, an increase in what they pay of $(P_2 + \$1,000) - P_1$, shown in the figure as ΔP_B.

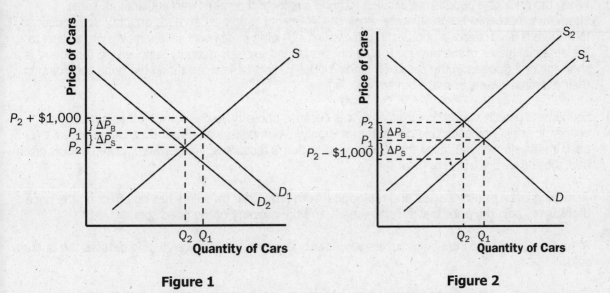

Figure 1   **Figure 2**

If the tax is imposed on car sellers, as shown in Figure 2, the supply curve shifts upward by the amount of the tax ($1,000) to S_2. The upward shift in the supply curve leads to a rise in the price paid by buyers to P_2 and a decline in the equilibrium quantity to Q_2. The price paid by buyers increases by $P_2 - P_1$, shown in the figure as ΔP_B. Sellers receive $P_2 - 1,000$, a decrease in what they receive by $P_1 - (P_2 - \$1,000)$, shown in the figure as ΔP_S.

Questions for Review

1. An example of a price ceiling is the rent control system in New York City. An example of a price floor is the minimum wage. Many other examples are possible.

2. A shortage of a good arises when there is a binding price ceiling. A binding price ceiling is one that is placed below the market equilibrium price. This leads to a shortage because quantity demanded exceeds quantity supplied. See Figure 3.

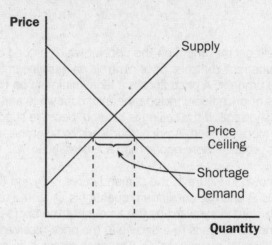

Figure 3

3. When the price of a good is not allowed to bring supply and demand into equilibrium, some alternative mechanism must allocate resources. If quantity supplied exceeds quantity demanded, so that there is a surplus of a good as in the case of a binding price floor, sellers may try to appeal to the personal biases of the buyers. If quantity demanded exceeds quantity supplied, so that there is a shortage of a good as in the case of a binding price ceiling, sellers can ration the good according to their personal biases, or make buyers wait in line.

4. Economists usually oppose controls on prices because prices have the crucial job of coordinating economic activity by balancing demand and supply. When policymakers set controls on prices, they obscure the signals that guide the allocation of society's resources. Furthermore, price controls often hurt those they are trying to help.

5. Removing a tax paid by buyers and replacing it with a tax paid by sellers has no effect on the price that buyers pay, the price that sellers receive, and the quantity of the good sold.

6. A tax on a good raises the price buyers pay, lowers the price sellers receive, and reduces the quantity sold.

7. The burden of a tax is divided between buyers and sellers depending on the elasticity of demand and supply. Elasticity represents the willingness of buyers or sellers to leave the market, which in turns depends on their alternatives. When a good is taxed, the side of the market with fewer good alternatives cannot easily leave the market and thus bears more of the burden of the tax.

Problems and Applications

1. If the price ceiling of $40 per ticket is below the equilibrium price, then quantity demanded exceeds quantity supplied, so there will be a shortage of tickets. The policy decreases the number of people

who attend classical music concerts, because the quantity supplied is lower because of the lower price.

2. a. The imposition of a binding price floor in the cheese market is shown in Figure 4. In the absence of the price floor, the price would be P_1 and the quantity would be Q_1. With the floor set at P_f, which is greater than P_1, the quantity demanded is Q_2, while quantity supplied is Q_3, so there is a surplus of cheese in the amount $Q_3 - Q_2$.

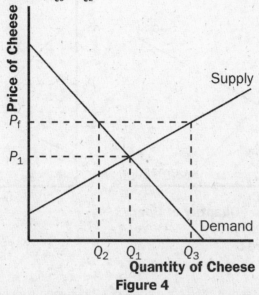

Figure 4

b. The farmers' complaint that their total revenue has declined is correct if demand is elastic. With elastic demand, the percentage decline in quantity would exceed the percentage rise in price, so total revenue would decline.

c. If the government purchases all the surplus cheese at the price floor, producers benefit and taxpayers lose. Producers would produce quantity Q_3 of cheese, and their total revenue would increase substantially. However, consumers would buy only quantity Q_2 of cheese, so they are in the same position as before. Taxpayers lose because they would be financing the purchase of the surplus cheese through higher taxes.

3. a. The equilibrium price of Frisbees is $8 and the equilibrium quantity is six million Frisbees.

b. With a price floor of $10, the new market price is $10 because the price floor is binding. At that price, only two million Frisbees are sold, because that is the quantity demanded.

c. If there's a price ceiling of $9, it has no effect, because the market equilibrium price is $8, which is below the ceiling. So the market price is $8 and the quantity sold is six million Frisbees.

4. a. Figure 5 shows the market for beer without the tax. The equilibrium price is P_1 and the equilibrium quantity is Q_1. The price paid by consumers is the same as the price received by producers.

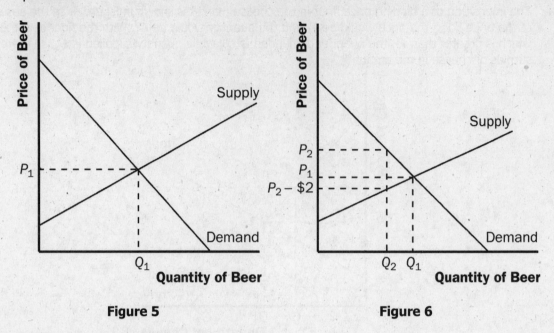

Figure 5 **Figure 6**

b. When the tax is imposed, it drives a wedge of $2 between supply and demand, as shown in Figure 6. The price paid by consumers is P_2, while the price received by producers is $P_2 - \$2$. The quantity of beer sold declines to Q_2.

5. Reducing the payroll tax paid by firms and using part of the extra revenue to reduce the payroll tax paid by workers would not make workers better off, because the division of the burden of a tax depends on the elasticity of supply and demand and not on who must pay the tax. Because the tax wedge would be larger, it is likely that both firms and workers, who share the burden of any tax, would be worse off.

6. Because a luxury car likely has an elastic demand, the price will rise by less than $500. The burden of any tax is shared by both producers and consumers—the price paid by consumers rises and the price received by producers falls, with the difference between the two equal to the amount of the tax. The only exceptions would be if the supply curve were perfectly elastic or the demand curve were perfectly inelastic, in which case consumers would bear the full burden of the tax and the price paid by consumers would rise by exactly $500.

7. a. It does not matter whether the tax is imposed on producers or consumers—the effect will be the same. With no tax, as shown in Figure 7, the demand curve is D_1 and the supply curve is S_1. If the tax is imposed on producers, the supply curve shifts up by the amount of the tax (50 cents) to S_2. Then the equilibrium quantity is Q_2, the price paid by consumers is P_2, and the price received (after taxes are paid) by producers is $P_2 - 50$ cents. If the tax is instead imposed on consumers, the demand curve shifts down by the amount of the tax (50 cents) to D_2. The downward shift in the demand curve (when the tax is imposed on consumers) is exactly the same magnitude as the upward shift in the supply curve when the tax is imposed on producers. So again, the equilibrium quantity is Q_2, the price paid by consumers is P_2 (including the tax paid to the government), and the price received by producers is $P_2 - 50$ cents.

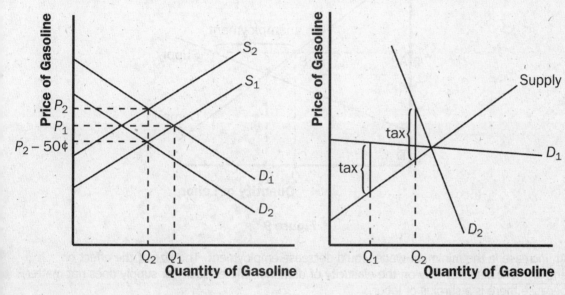

Figure 7   **Figure 8**

   b. The more elastic the demand curve is, the more effective this tax will be in reducing the quantity of gasoline consumed. Greater elasticity of demand means that quantity falls more in response to the rise in the price of gasoline. Figure 8 illustrates this result. Demand curve D_1 represents an elastic demand curve, while demand curve D_2 is more inelastic. The tax will cause a greater decline in the quantity sold when demand is elastic.

   c. The consumers of gasoline are hurt by the tax because they get less gasoline at a higher price.

   d. Workers in the oil industry are hurt by the tax as well. With a lower quantity of gasoline being produced, some workers may lose their jobs. With a lower price received by producers, wages of workers might decline.

8. a. Figure 9 shows the effects of the minimum wage. In the absence of the minimum wage, the market wage would be w_1 and Q_1 workers would be employed. With the minimum wage (w_m) imposed above w_1, the market wage is w_m, the number of employed workers is Q_2, and the number of workers who are unemployed is $Q_3 - Q_2$. Total wage payments to workers are shown as the area of rectangle ABCD, which equals w_m times Q_2.

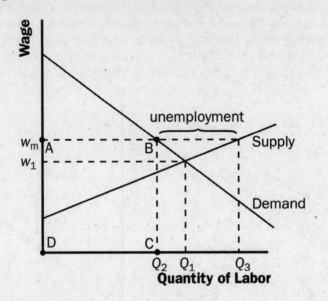

Figure 9

   b. An increase in the minimum wage would decrease employment. The size of the effect on employment depends only on the elasticity of demand. The elasticity of supply does not matter, because there is a surplus of labor.

   c. The increase in the minimum wage would increase unemployment. The size of the rise in unemployment depends on both the elasticities of supply and demand. The elasticity of demand determines the change in the quantity of labor demanded, the elasticity of supply determines the change in the quantity of labor supplied, and the difference between the quantities supplied and demanded of labor is the amount of unemployment.

   d. If the demand for unskilled labor were inelastic, the rise in the minimum wage would increase total wage payments to unskilled labor. With inelastic demand, the percentage decline in employment would be lower than the percentage increase in the wage, so total wage payments increase. However, if the demand for unskilled labor were elastic, total wage payments would decline, because then the percentage decline in employment would exceed the percentage increase in the wage.

9. a. Programs aimed at making the public aware of the dangers of smoking reduce the demand for cigarettes, shown in Figure 10 as a shift from demand curve D_1 to D_2. The price support program increases the price of tobacco, which is the main ingredient in cigarettes. As a result, the supply of cigarettes shifts to the left, from S_1 to S_2. The effect of both programs is to reduce the quantity of cigarette consumption from Q_1 to Q_2.

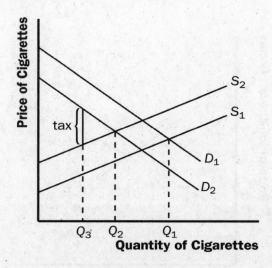

Figure 10

   b. The combined effect of the two programs on the price of cigarettes is ambiguous. The education campaign reduces demand for cigarettes, which tends to reduce the price. The tobacco price supports raising the cost of production of cigarettes, which tends to increase the price. The end result on price depends on the relative sizes of these two effects.

   c. The taxation of cigarettes further reduces cigarette consumption, because it increases the price to consumers. As shown in the figure, the quantity falls to Q_3.

10. Since the supply of seats is perfectly inelastic, the entire burden of the tax will fall on the team's owners. Figure 11 shows that the price the buyers pay for the tickets will fall by the exact amount of the tax.

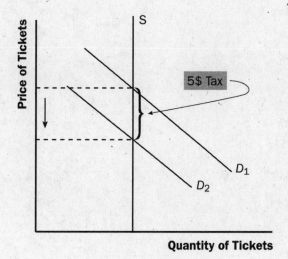

Figure 11

11. a. The effect of a $0.50 per cone subsidy is to shift the demand curve up by $0.50 at each quantity, because at each quantity a consumer's willingness to pay is $0.50 higher. The effects of such a subsidy are shown in Figure 12. Before the subsidy, the price is P_1. After the subsidy, the price received by sellers is P_S and the effective price paid by consumers is P_D, which equals P_S minus $0.50. Before the subsidy, the quantity of cones sold is Q_1; after the subsidy the quantity increases to Q_2.

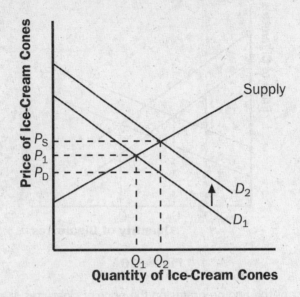

Figure 12

   b. Because of the subsidy, consumers are better off, because they consume more at a lower price. Producers are also better off, because they sell more at a higher price. The government loses, because it has to pay for the subsidy.

13. a. If gasoline refineries are operating at near full capacity, supply is likely to be highly inelastic.

   b. The burden of a tax falls on the side of the market that is relatively more inelastic. Thus, it will be suppliers who will benefit from the temporary suspension of the federal gasoline tax.

7 CONSUMERS, PRODUCERS, AND THE EFFICIENCY OF MARKETS

WHAT'S NEW IN THE SIXTH EDITION:

There are no major changes to this chapter.

LEARNING OBJECTIVES:

By the end of this chapter, students should understand:

➤ the link between buyers' willingness to pay for a good and the demand curve.

➤ how to define and measure consumer surplus.

➤ the link between sellers' costs of producing a good and the supply curve.

➤ how to define and measure producer surplus.

➤ that the equilibrium of supply and demand maximizes total surplus in a market.

CONTEXT AND PURPOSE:

Chapter 7 is the first chapter in a three-chapter sequence on welfare economics and market efficiency. Chapter 7 employs the supply and demand model to develop consumer surplus and producer surplus as a measure of welfare and market efficiency. These concepts are then utilized in Chapters 8 and 9 to determine the winners and losers from taxation and restrictions on international trade.

The purpose of Chapter 7 is to develop *welfare economics*—the study of how the allocation of resources affects economic well-being. Chapters 4 through 6 employed supply and demand in a positive framework, which focused on the question, "What is the equilibrium price and quantity in a market?" This chapter now addresses the normative question, "Is the equilibrium price and quantity in a market the best possible solution to the resource allocation problem, or is it simply the price and quantity that balance supply and demand?" Students will discover that under most circumstances the equilibrium price and quantity is also the one that maximizes welfare.

KEY POINTS:

- Consumer surplus equals buyers' willingness to pay for a good minus the amount they actually pay for it, and it measures the benefit buyers get from participating in a market. Consumer surplus can be computed by finding the area below the demand curve and above the price.

- Producer surplus equals the amount sellers receive for their goods minus their costs of production, and it measures the benefit sellers get from participating in a market. Producer surplus can be computed by finding the area below the price and above the supply curve.

- An allocation of resources that maximizes the sum of consumer and producer surplus is said to be efficient. Policymakers are often concerned with the efficiency, as well as the equality, of economic outcomes.

- The equilibrium of supply and demand maximizes the sum of consumer and producer surplus. That is, the invisible hand of the marketplace leads buyers and sellers to allocate resources efficiently.

- Markets do not allocate resources efficiently in the presence of market failures such as market power or externalities.

CHAPTER OUTLINE:

I. Definition of **welfare economics: the study of how the allocation of resources affects economic well-being.**

 Students often are confused by the use of the word "welfare." Remind them that we are talking about social well-being and not public assistance.

II. Consumer Surplus

   A. Willingness to Pay

      1. Definition of **willingness to pay: the maximum amount that a buyer will pay for a good.**

      2. Example: You are auctioning a mint-condition recording of Elvis Presley's first album. Four buyers show up. Their willingness to pay is as follows:

 Students will understand consumer surplus if you take the time to work through the Elvis Presley example. If you start with this simple example, students will have no trouble understanding how to find consumer surplus on a graph.

> Table 1

Buyer	Willingness to Pay
John	$100
Paul	$80
George	$70
Ringo	$50

If the bidding goes to slightly higher than $80, all buyers drop out except for John. Because John is willing to pay more than he has to for the album, he derives some benefit from participating in the market.

3. Definition of **consumer surplus: the amount a buyer is willing to pay for a good minus the amount the buyer actually pays for it.**

4. Note that if you had more than one copy of the album, the price in the auction would end up being lower (a little over $70 in the case of two albums) and both John and Paul would gain consumer surplus.

Activity 1—Value of a Time Machine

Type:	In-class demonstration
Topics:	Consumer surplus
Materials needed:	None
Time:	10 minutes
Class limitations:	Works in any size class

Purpose
Consumer surplus can be a hard concept for students because it is based on avoided expense rather than on money that is actually exchanged. This example puts a specific dollar value on consumer surplus.

Instructions
Tell the class, "A new technology has been developed that allows individuals to travel backward or forward in time. We want to identify the value this time machine provides to consumers. Let's assume the four consumers who most desire this product are in this class."

Choose four student names and use them in the following example:

   "Scott is the consumer who most values this product. He wants to go back to the time of the dinosaurs. He is willing to pay $3,000."
   "Carol is the consumer with the next highest willingness to pay. She would like to see 200 years in the future. She'd pay $2,500."
   "Steve is the next highest bidder. He'd like to relive this entire semester. He'll pay up to $800."
   "Jeanne is our fourth consumer. She'd pay $200 to move the clock forward to the end of this class period."

On the board write:
Scott	$3,000
Carol	$2,500
Steve	$800
Jeanne	$200

"This represents the demand curve for the time machine. Consumer surplus is the difference between what consumers are willing to pay and the amount they actually have to pay. The market price will determine who uses the time machine and how much surplus they keep."

"If the price of a time machine ride was $500, three rides would be sold—one to Scott, one to Carol, and one to Steve. Jeanne is not willing to pay $500, so she wouldn't time travel."

"We can calculate the consumer surplus of three time trips. Scott would pay $3,000 but only pays $500, leaving $2,500 of net benefits." (Put these numbers on the board.) "Carol has net benefits of $2,000. Steve has $300 in net benefits. Adding up these net savings gives $4,800 in consumer surplus."

Points for Discussion
The consumer surplus depends on a good's selling price and the number of consumers who are willing to purchase the good at that price. The lower the price, the greater the consumer surplus.

B. Using the Demand Curve to Measure Consumer Surplus

1. We can use the information on willingness to pay to derive a demand curve for the rare Elvis Presley album.

Price	Buyers	Quantity Demanded
More than $100	None	0
$80 to $100	John	1
$70 to $80	John, Paul	2
$50 to $70	John, Paul, George	3
$50 or less	John, Paul, George, Ringo	4

Figure 1

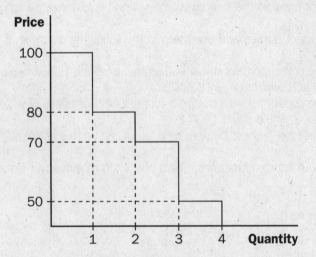

2. At any given quantity, the price given by the demand curve reflects the willingness to pay of the *marginal buyer*. Because the demand curve shows the buyers' willingness to pay, we can use the demand curve to measure consumer surplus.

Figure 2

3. Consumer surplus can be measured as the area below the demand curve and above the price.

C. How a Lower Price Raises Consumer Surplus

Figure 3

1. As price falls, consumer surplus increases for two reasons.

   a. Those already buying the product will receive additional consumer surplus because they are paying less for the product than before (area A on the graph).

   b. Because the price is now lower, some new buyers will enter the market and receive consumer surplus on these additional units of output purchased (area B on the graph).

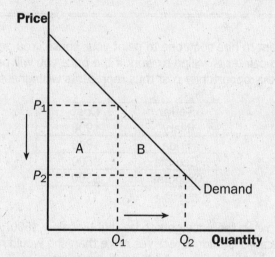

D. What Does Consumer Surplus Measure?

 It is important to stress that consumer surplus is measured in monetary terms. Consumer surplus gives us a way to place a monetary cost on inefficient market outcomes (due to government involvement or market failure).

1. Remember that consumer surplus is the difference between the amount that buyers are willing to pay for a good and the price that they actually pay.

2. Thus, it measures the benefit that consumers receive from the good as the buyers themselves perceive it.

ALTERNATIVE CLASSROOM EXAMPLE:

Review the material on price ceilings from Chapter 6. Redraw the market for two-bedroom apartments in your town. Draw in a price ceiling below the equilibrium price.

Then go through:
- consumer surplus before the price ceiling is put into place.
- consumer surplus after the price ceiling is put into place.

III. Producer Surplus

    A. Cost and the Willingness to Sell

        1. Definition of <u>**cost**</u>: **the value of everything a seller must give up to produce a good**.

 You will need to take some time to explain the relationship between the producers' willingness to sell and the cost of producing the good. The relationship between cost and the supply curve is not as apparent as the relationship between the demand curve and willingness to pay.

        2. Example: You want to hire someone to paint your house. You accept bids for the work from four sellers. Each painter is willing to work if the price you will pay exceeds her opportunity cost. (Note that this opportunity cost thus represents willingness to sell.) The costs are:

Seller	Cost
Mary	$900
Frida	$800
Georgia	$600
Grandma	$500

Table 2

        3. Bidding will stop when the price gets to be slightly below $600. All sellers will drop out except for Grandma. Because Grandma receives more than she would require to paint the house, she derives some benefit from producing in the market.

        4. Definition of <u>**producer surplus**</u>: **the amount a seller is paid for a good minus the seller's cost of providing it.**

        5. Note that if you had more than one house to paint, the price in the auction would end up being higher (a little under $800 in the case of two houses) and both Grandma and Georgia would gain producer surplus.

B. Using the Supply Curve to Measure Producer Surplus

1. We can use the information on cost (willingness to sell) to derive a supply curve for house painting services.

Price	Sellers	Quantity Supplied
$900 or more	Mary, Frida, Georgia, Grandma	4
$800 to $900	Frida, Georgia, Grandma	3
$600 to $800	Georgia, Grandma	2
$500 to $600	Grandma	1
less than $500	None	0

2. At any given quantity, the price given by the supply curve represents the cost of the *marginal seller*. Because the supply curve shows the sellers' cost (willingness to sell), we can use the supply curve to measure producer surplus.

Figure 4

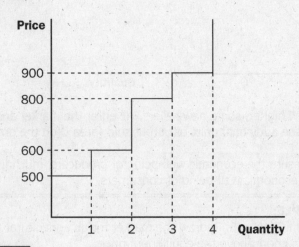

Figure 5

3. Producer surplus can be measured as the area above the supply curve and below the price.

C. How a Higher Price Raises Producer Surplus

Figure 6

1. As price rises, producer surplus increases for two reasons.

   a. Those already selling the product will receive additional producer surplus because they are receiving more for the product than before (area C on the graph).

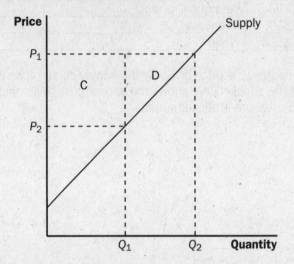

   b. Because the price is now higher, some new sellers will enter the market and receive producer surplus on these additional units of output sold (area D on the graph).

D. Producer surplus is used to measure the economic well-being of producers, much like consumer surplus is used to measure the economic well-being of consumers.

ALTERNATIVE CLASSROOM EXAMPLE:
Review the material on price floors from Chapter 6. Redraw the market for an agricultural product such as corn. Draw in a price support above the equilibrium price.

Then go through:
- producer surplus before the price support is put in place.
- producer surplus after the price support is put in place.

Make sure that you discuss the cost of the price support to taxpayers.

Pretty Woman, Chapter 6. Vivien (Julia Roberts) and Edward (Richard Gere) negotiate a price. Afterward, Vivien reveals she would have accepted a lower price, while Edward admits he would have paid more. If you have done a good job of introducing consumer and producer surplus, you will see the light bulbs go off above your students' heads as they watch this clip.

IV. Market Efficiency

A. The Benevolent Social Planner

1. The economic well-being of everyone in society can be measured by total surplus, which is the sum of consumer surplus and producer surplus:

    Total Surplus = Consumer Surplus + Producer Surplus

    Total Surplus = (Value to Buyers − Amount Paid by Buyers) +
    (Amount Received by Sellers − Cost to Sellers)

    Because the Amount Paid by Buyers = Amount Received by Sellers:

    > Total Surplus = Value to Buyers − Cost to Sellers

2. Definition of **efficiency: the property of a resource allocation of maximizing the total surplus received by all members of society**.

3. Definition of **equality: the property of distributing economic prosperity uniformly the members of society**.

Now might be a good time to point out that many government policies involve a trade-off between efficiency and equity. When you evaluate government policies, like price ceilings or floors, you can explain them in terms of equity and efficiency.

B. Evaluating the Market Equilibrium

> **Figure 7**

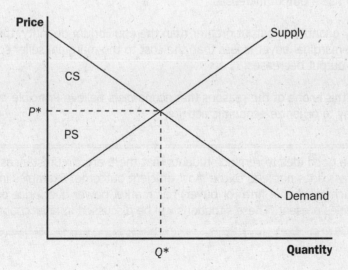

1. At the market equilibrium price:

   a. Buyers who value the product more than the equilibrium price will purchase the product; those who do not, will not purchase the product. In other words, the free market allocates the supply of a good to the buyers who value it most highly, as measured by their willingness to pay.

   b. Sellers whose costs are lower than the equilibrium price will produce the product; those whose costs are higher, will not produce the product. In other words, the free market allocates the demand for goods to the sellers who can produce it at the lowest cost.

2. Total surplus is maximized at the market equilibrium.

Figure 8

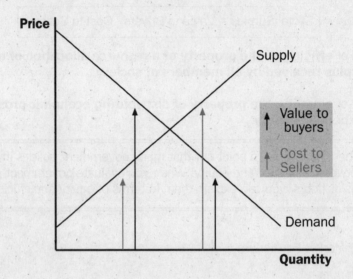

   a. At any quantity of output smaller than the equilibrium quantity, the value of the product to the marginal buyer is greater than the cost to the marginal seller so total surplus would rise if output increases.

   b. At any quantity of output greater than the equilibrium quantity, the value of the product to the marginal buyer is less than the cost to the marginal seller so total surplus would rise if output decreases.

3. Note that this is one of the reasons that economists believe Principle #6: Markets are usually a good way to organize economic activity.

 It would be a good idea to remind students that there are circumstances when the market process does not lead to the most efficient outcome. Examples include situations such as when a firm (or buyer) has market power over price or when there are externalities present. These situations will be discussed in later chapters.

   C. *In the News: Ticket Scalping*

      1. Ticket scalping is an example of how markets work to achieve an efficient outcome.

      2. This article from *The Boston Globe* describes economist Chip Case's experience with ticket scalping.

   D. *Case Study: Should There Be a Market in Organs?*

      1. As a matter of public policy, people are not allowed to sell their organs.

         a. In essence, this means that there is a price ceiling on organs of $0.

         b. This has led to a shortage of organs.

      2. The creation of a market for organs would lead to a more efficient allocation of resources, but critics worry about the equity of a market system for organs.

V. Market Efficiency and Market Failure

   A. To conclude that markets are efficient, we made several assumptions about how markets worked.

      1. Perfectly competitive markets.

      2. No externalities.

   B. When these assumptions do not hold, the market equilibrium may not be efficient.

   C. When markets fail, public policy can potentially remedy the situation.

SOLUTIONS TO TEXT PROBLEMS:

Quick Quizzes

1. Figure 1 shows the demand curve for turkey. The price of turkey is P_1 and the consumer surplus that results from that price is denoted CS. Consumer surplus is the amount a buyer is willing to pay for a good minus the amount the buyer actually pays for it. It measures the benefit to buyers of participating in a market.

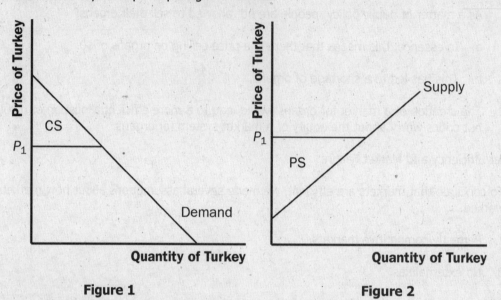

Figure 1   **Figure 2**

2. Figure 2 shows the supply curve for turkey. The price of turkey is P_1 and the producer surplus that results from that price is denoted PS. Producer surplus is the amount sellers are paid for a good minus the sellers' cost of providing it (measured by the supply curve). It measures the benefit to sellers of participating in a market.

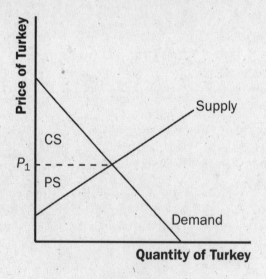

Figure 3

3. Figure 3 shows the supply and demand for turkey. The price of turkey is P_1, consumer surplus is CS, and producer surplus is PS. Producing more turkeys than the equilibrium

quantity would lower total surplus because the value to the marginal buyer would be lower than the cost to the marginal seller on those additional units.

Questions for Review

1. The price a buyer is willing to pay, consumer surplus, and the demand curve are all closely related. The height of the demand curve represents the willingness to pay of the buyers. Consumer surplus is the area below the demand curve and above the price, which equals the price that each buyer is willing to pay minus the price actually paid.

2. Sellers' costs, producer surplus, and the supply curve are all closely related. The height of the supply curve represents the costs of the sellers. Producer surplus is the area below the price and above the supply curve, which equals the price received minus each seller's costs of producing the good.

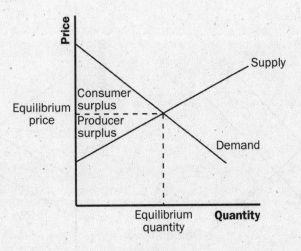

Figure 4

3. Figure 4 shows producer and consumer surplus in a supply-and-demand diagram.

4. An allocation of resources is efficient if it maximizes total surplus, the sum of consumer surplus and producer surplus. But efficiency may not be the only goal of economic policymakers; they may also be concerned about equity—the fairness of the distribution of well-being.

5. The invisible hand of the marketplace guides the self-interest of buyers and sellers into promoting general economic well-being. Despite decentralized decision making and self-interested decision makers, free markets often lead to an efficient outcome.

6. Two types of market failure are market power and externalities. Market power may cause market outcomes to be inefficient because firms may cause price and quantity to differ from the levels they would be under perfect competition, which keeps total surplus from being maximized. Externalities are side effects that are not taken into account by buyers and sellers. As a result, the free market does not maximize total surplus.

Problems and Applications

1. a. Consumer surplus is equal to willingness to pay minus the price paid. Therefore, Melissa's willingness to pay must be $200 ($120 + $80).

    b. Her consumer surplus at a price of $90 would be $200 − $90 = $110.

    c. If the price of an iPod was $250, Melissa would not have purchased one because the price is greater than her willingness to pay. Therefore, she would receive no consumer surplus.

2. If an early freeze in California sours the lemon crop, the supply curve for lemons shifts to the left, as shown in Figure 5. The result is a rise in the price of lemons and a decline in consumer surplus from A + B + C to just A. So consumer surplus declines by the amount B + C.

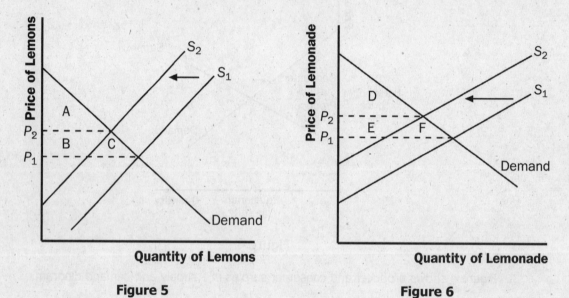

Figure 5   **Figure 6**

In the market for lemonade, the higher cost of lemons reduces the supply of lemonade, as shown in Figure 6. The result is a rise in the price of lemonade and a decline in consumer surplus from D + E + F to just D, a loss of E + F. Note that an event that affects consumer surplus in one market often has effects on consumer surplus in other markets.

3. A rise in the demand for French bread leads to an increase in producer surplus in the market for French bread, as shown in Figure 7. The shift of the demand curve leads to an increased price, which increases producer surplus from area A to area A + B + C.

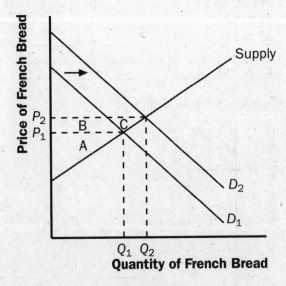

Figure 7

The increased quantity of French bread being sold increases the demand for flour, as shown in Figure 8. As a result, the price of flour rises, increasing producer surplus from area D to D + E + F. Note that an event that affects producer surplus in one market leads to effects on producer surplus in related markets.

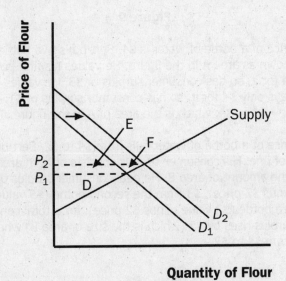

Figure 8

4. a. Bert's demand schedule is:

Price	Quantity Demanded
More than $7	0
$5 to $7	1
$3 to $5	2
$1 to $3	3
$1 or less	4

Bert's demand curve is shown in Figure 9.

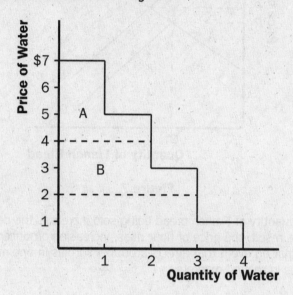

Figure 9

b. When the price of a bottle of water is $4, Bert buys two bottles of water. His consumer surplus is shown as area A in the figure. He values his first bottle of water at $7, but pays only $4 for it, so has consumer surplus of $3. He values his second bottle of water at $5, but pays only $4 for it, so has consumer surplus of $1. Thus Bert's total consumer surplus is $3 + $1 = $4, which is the area of A in the figure.

c. When the price of a bottle of water falls from $4 to $2, Bert buys three bottles of water, an increase of one. His consumer surplus consists of both areas A and B in the figure, an increase in the amount of area B. He gets consumer surplus of $5 from the first bottle ($7 value minus $2 price), $3 from the second bottle ($5 value minus $2 price), and $1 from the third bottle ($3 value minus $2 price), for a total consumer surplus of $9. Thus consumer surplus rises by $5 (which is the size of area B) when the price of a bottle of water falls from $4 to $2.

5. a. Ernie's supply schedule for water is:

Price	Quantity Supplied
More than $7	4
$5 to $7	3
$3 to $5	2
$1 to $3	1
Less than $1	0

Ernie's supply curve is shown in Figure 10.

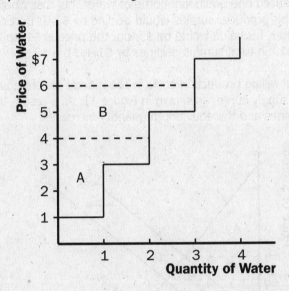

Figure 10

b. When the price of a bottle of water is $4, Ernie sells two bottles of water. His producer surplus is shown as area A in the figure. He receives $4 for his first bottle of water, but it costs only $1 to produce, so Ernie has producer surplus of $3. He also receives $4 for his second bottle of water, which costs $3 to produce, so he has producer surplus of $1. Thus Ernie's total producer surplus is $3 + $1 = $4, which is the area of A in the figure.

c. When the price of a bottle of water rises from $4 to $6, Ernie sells three bottles of water, an increase of one. His producer surplus consists of both areas A and B in the figure, an increase by the amount of area B. He gets producer surplus of $5 from the first bottle ($6 price minus $1 cost), $3 from the second bottle ($6 price minus $3 cost), and $1 from the third bottle ($6 price minus $5 price), for a total producer surplus of $9. Thus producer surplus rises by $5 (which is the size of area B) when the price of a bottle of water rises from $4 to $6.

6. a. From Ernie's supply schedule and Bert's demand schedule, the quantity demanded and supplied are:

Price	Quantity Supplied	Quantity Demanded
$2	1	3
$4	2	2
$6	3	1

Only a price of $4 brings supply and demand into equilibrium, with an equilibrium quantity of two.

b. At a price of $4, consumer surplus is $4 and producer surplus is $4, as shown in Problems 3 and 4 above. Total surplus is $4 + $4 = $8.

c. If Ernie produced one less bottle, his producer surplus would decline to $3, as shown in Problem 4 above. If Bert consumed one less bottle, his consumer surplus would decline to $3, as shown in Problem 3 above. So total surplus would decline to $3 + $3 = $6.

d. If Ernie produced one additional bottle of water, his cost would be $5, but the price is only $4, so his producer surplus would decline by $1. If Bert consumed one additional bottle of water, his value would be $3, but the price is $4, so his consumer surplus would decline by $1. So total surplus declines by $1 + $1 = $2.

7. a. The effect of falling production costs in the market for stereos results in a shift to the right in the supply curve, as shown in Figure 11. As a result, the equilibrium price of stereos declines and the equilibrium quantity increases.

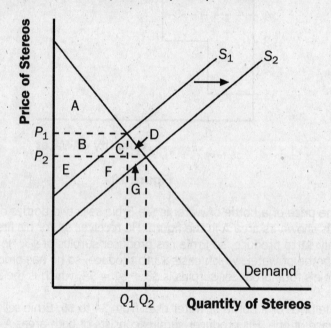

Figure 11

b. The decline in the price of stereos increases consumer surplus from area A to A + B + C + D, an increase in the amount B + C + D. Prior to the shift in supply, producer surplus was areas B + E (the area above the supply curve and below the price). After the shift in supply, producer surplus is areas E + F + G. So producer surplus changes by the amount F + G − B, which may be positive or negative. The increase in quantity increases producer surplus, while the decline in the price reduces producer surplus. Because consumer surplus rises by B + C + D and producer surplus rises by F + G − B, total surplus rises by C + D + F + G.

c. If the supply of stereos is very elastic, then the shift of the supply curve benefits consumers most. To take the most dramatic case, suppose the supply curve were horizontal, as shown in Figure 12. Then there is no producer surplus at all. Consumers capture all the benefits of falling production costs, with consumer surplus rising from area A to area A + B.

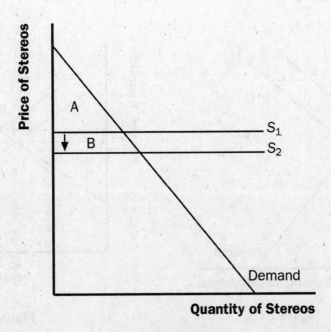

Figure 12

8. Figure 13 shows supply and demand curves for haircuts. Supply equals demand at a quantity of three haircuts and a price between $4 and $5. Firms A, C, and D should cut the hair of Ellen, Jerry, and Phil. Oprah's willingness to pay is too low and firm B's costs are too high, so they do not participate. The maximum total surplus is the area between the demand and supply curves, which totals $11 ($8 value minus $2 cost for the first haircut, plus $7 value minus $3 cost for the second, plus $5 value minus $4 cost for the third).

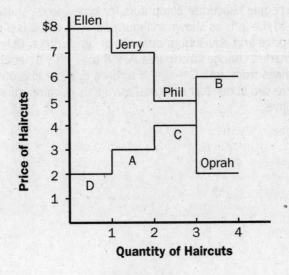

Figure 13

9. a. The effect of falling production costs in the market for computers results in a shift to the right in the supply curve, as shown in Figure 14. As a result, the equilibrium price of computers declines and the equilibrium quantity increases. The decline in the price of computers increases consumer surplus from area A to A + B + C + D, an increase in the amount B + C + D.

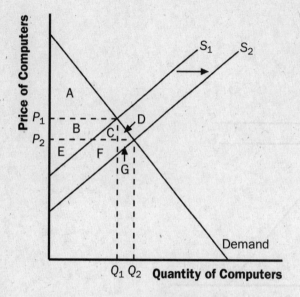

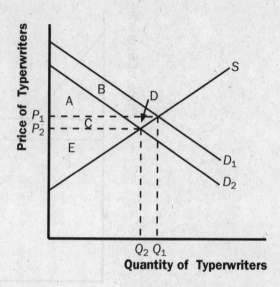

Figure 14   **Figure 15**

Prior to the shift in supply, producer surplus was areas B + E (the area above the supply curve and below the price). After the shift in supply, producer surplus is areas E + F + G. So producer surplus changes by the amount F + G − B, which may be positive or negative. The increase in quantity increases producer surplus, while the decline in the price reduces producer surplus. Because consumer surplus rises by B + C + D and producer surplus rises by F + G − B, total surplus rises by C + D + F + G.

b. Because typewriters are substitutes for computers, the decline in the price of computers means that people substitute computers for typewriters, shifting the demand for typewriters to the left, as shown in Figure 15. The result is a decline in both the equilibrium price and equilibrium quantity of typewriters. Consumer surplus in the typewriter market changes from area A + B to A + C, a net change of C − B. Producer surplus changes from area C + D + E to area E, a net loss of C + D. Typewriter producers are sad about technological advances in computers because their producer surplus declines.

c. Because software and computers are complements, the decline in the price and increase in the quantity of computers means that the demand for software increases, shifting the demand for software to the right, as shown in Figure 16. The result is an increase in both the price and quantity of software. Consumer surplus in the software market changes from B + C to A + B, a net change of A − C. Producer surplus changes from E to C + D + E, an increase of C + D, so software producers should be happy about the technological progress in computers.

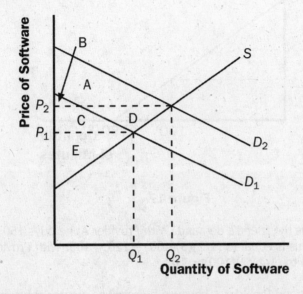

Figure 16

d. Yes, this analysis helps explain why Bill Gates is one the world's richest people, because his company produces a lot of software that is a complement with computers and there has been tremendous technological advance in computers.

10. a. With Provider A, the cost of an extra minute is $0. With Provider B, the cost of an extra minute is $1.

b. With Provider A, my friend will purchase 150 minutes [= 150 − (50)(0)]. With Provider B, my friend would purchase 100 minutes [= 150 − (50)(1)].

c. With Provider A, he would pay $120. The cost would be $100 with Provider B.

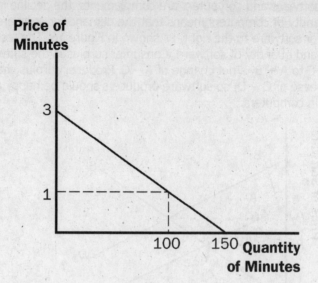

Figure 17

d. Figure 17 shows the friend's demand. With Provider A, he buys 150 minutes and his consumer surplus is equal to $(1/2)(3)(150) - 120 = 105$. With Provider B, his consumer surplus is equal to $(1/2)(2)(100) = 100$.

e. I would recommend Provider A because he receives greater consumer surplus.

11. a. Figure 18 illustrates the demand for medical care. If each procedure has a price of $100, quantity demanded will be Q_1 procedures.

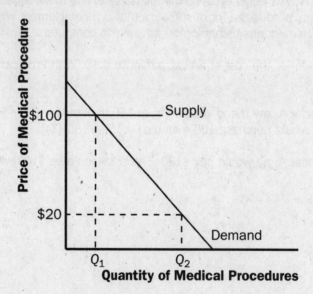

Figure 18

b. If consumers pay only $20 per procedure, the quantity demanded will be Q_2 procedures. Because the cost to society is $100, the number of procedures performed is too large to maximize total surplus. The quantity that maximizes total surplus is Q_1 procedures, which is less than Q_2.

c. The use of medical care is excessive in the sense that consumers get procedures whose value is less than the cost of producing them. As a result, the economy's total surplus is reduced.

d. To prevent this excessive use, the consumer must bear the marginal cost of the procedure. But this would require eliminating insurance. Another possibility would be that the insurance company, which pays most of the marginal cost of the procedure ($80, in this case) could decide whether the procedure should be performed. But the insurance company does not get the benefits of the procedure, so its decisions may not reflect the value to the consumer.

# 8 APPLICATION: THE COSTS OF TAXATION

WHAT'S NEW IN THE SIXTH EDITION:

A new *In the News* box on "New Research on Taxation" has been added.

LEARNING OBJECTIVES:

By the end of this chapter, students should understand:

➤ how taxes reduce consumer and producer surplus.

➤ the meaning and causes of the deadweight loss from a tax.

➤ why some taxes have larger deadweight losses than others.

➤ how tax revenue and deadweight loss vary with the size of a tax.

CONTEXT AND PURPOSE:

Chapter 8 is the second chapter in a three-chapter sequence dealing with welfare economics. In the previous section on supply and demand, Chapter 6 introduced taxes and demonstrated how a tax affects the price and quantity sold in a market. Chapter 6 also described the factors that determine how the burden of the tax is divided between the buyers and sellers in a market. Chapter 7 developed welfare economics—the study of how the allocation of resources affects economic well-being. Chapter 8 combines the lessons learned in Chapters 6 and 7 and addresses the effects of taxation on welfare. Chapter 9 will address the effects of trade restrictions on welfare.

The purpose of Chapter 8 is to apply the lessons learned about welfare economics in Chapter 7 to the issue of taxation that was addressed in Chapter 6. Students will learn that the cost of a tax to buyers and sellers in a market exceeds the revenue collected by the government. Students will also learn about the factors that determine the degree by which the cost of a tax exceeds the revenue collected by the government.

144

KEY POINTS:

- A tax on a good reduces the welfare of buyers and sellers of the good, and the reduction in consumer and producer surplus usually exceeds the revenue raised by the government. The fall in total surplus—the sum of consumer surplus, producer surplus, and tax revenue—is called the deadweight loss of the tax.

- Taxes have deadweight losses because they cause buyers to consume less and sellers to produce less, and these changes in behavior shrink the size of the market below the level that maximizes total surplus. Because the elasticities of supply and demand measure how much market participants respond to market conditions, larger elasticities imply larger deadweight losses.

- As a tax grows larger, it distorts incentives more, and its deadweight loss grows larger. Because a tax reduces the size of a market, however, tax revenue does not continually increase. It first rises with the size of a tax, but if a tax gets large enough, tax revenue starts to fall.

CHAPTER OUTLINE:

I.   The Deadweight Loss of Taxation

   A.   Remember that it does not matter who a tax is levied on; buyers and sellers will likely share in the burden of the tax.

   B.   If there is a tax on a product, the price that a buyer pays will be greater than the price the seller receives. Thus, there is a tax wedge between the two prices and the quantity sold will be smaller if there was no tax.

Figure 1

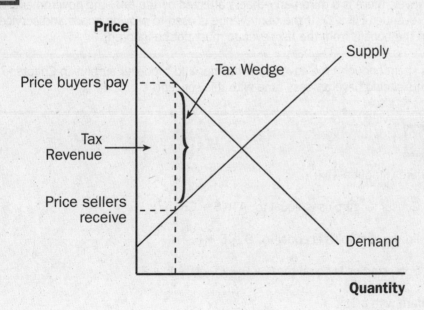

C. How a Tax Affects Market Participants

Figure 2

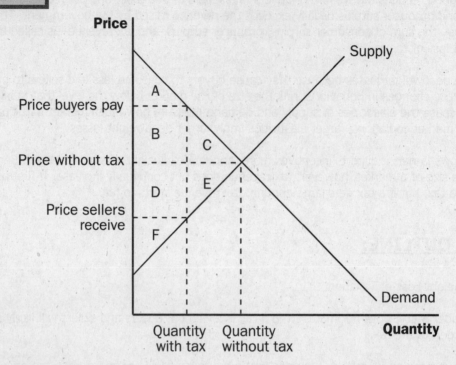

1. We can measure the effects of a tax on consumers by examining the change in consumer surplus. Similarly, we can measure the effects of the tax on producers by looking at the change in producer surplus.

2. However, there is a third party that is affected by the tax—the government, which gets total tax revenue of T × Q. If the tax revenue is used to provide goods and services to the public, then the benefit from the tax revenue must not be ignored.

 If you spent enough time covering consumer and producer surplus in Chapter 7, students should have an easy time with this concept.

Figure 3

3. Welfare without a Tax

    a. Consumer surplus is equal to: A + B + C.

    b. Producer surplus is equal to: D + E + F.

    c. Total surplus is equal to: A + B + C + D + E + F.

4. Welfare with a Tax

    a. Consumer surplus is equal to: A.

b. Producer surplus is equal to: F.

c. Tax revenue is equal to: B + D.

d. Total surplus is equal to: A + B + D + F.

5. Changes in Welfare

a. Consumer surplus changes by: −(B + C).

b. Producer surplus changes by: −(D + E).

c. Tax revenue changes by: +(B + D).

d. Total surplus changes by: −(C + E).

6. Definition of **deadweight loss: the fall in total surplus that results from a market distortion, such as a tax.**

D. Deadweight Losses and the Gains from Trade

Figure 4

1. Taxes cause deadweight losses because they prevent buyers and sellers from benefiting from trade.

2. This occurs because the quantity of output declines; trades that would be beneficial to both the buyer and seller will not take place because of the tax.

Show the students that the nature of this deadweight loss stems from the reduction in the quantity of the output exchanged. Stress the idea that goods that are not produced, consumed, or taxed do not generate benefits for anyone.

3. The deadweight loss is equal to areas C and E (the drop in total surplus).

4. Note that output levels between the equilibrium quantity without the tax and the quantity with the tax will not be produced, yet the value of these units to consumers (represented by the demand curve) is larger than the cost of these units to producers (represented by the supply curve).

II. The Determinants of the Deadweight Loss

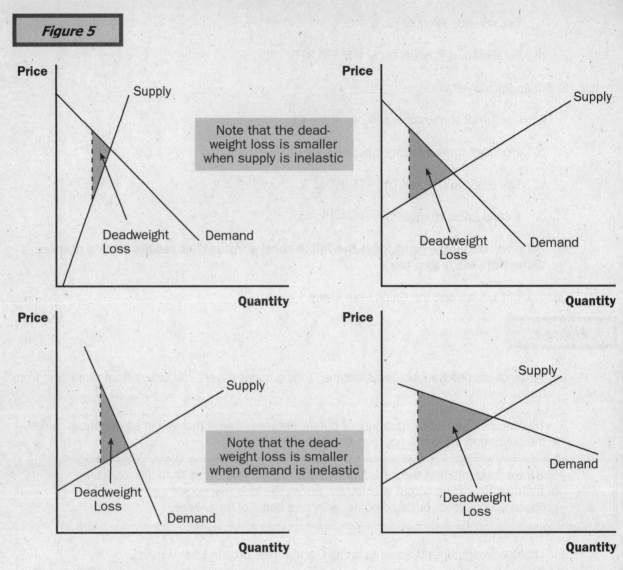

Figure 5

A. The price elasticities of supply and demand will determine the size of the deadweight loss that occurs from a tax.

1. Given a stable demand curve, the deadweight loss is larger when supply is relatively elastic.

2. Given a stable supply curve, the deadweight loss is larger when demand is relatively elastic.

B. *Case Study: The Deadweight Loss Debate*

1. Social Security tax and federal income tax are taxes on labor earnings. A labor tax places a tax wedge between the wage the firm pays and the wage that workers receive.

2. There is considerable debate among economists concerning the size of the deadweight loss from this wage tax.

3. The size of the deadweight loss depends on the elasticity of labor supply and demand, and there is disagreement about the magnitude of the elasticity of supply.

a. Economists who argue that labor taxes do not greatly distort market outcomes believe that labor supply is fairly inelastic.

b. Economists who argue that labor taxes lead to large deadweight losses believe that labor supply is more elastic.

Activity 1—Labor Taxes

Type:	In-class discussion
Topics:	Deadweight loss, taxation
Materials needed:	None
Time:	10 minutes
Class limitations:	Works in any size class

Purpose

Most students have not spent a great deal of time considering the effects of taxation on labor supply. This in-class exercise gives them the opportunity to consider the effects of proposed tax rates on their own willingness to supply labor.

Instructions

Ask students to assume that they are full-time workers earning $10 per hour, $80 per day, $400 per week, $20,000 per year.

Ask them if they would quit their jobs or keep working if the tax rate was 10%, 20%, 30%, ... (up to 100%).

Keep a tally as they show hands indicating that they are leaving the labor force.

Ask students what they think the "best" tax rate is.

Points for Discussion

Many students have no idea that current marginal tax rates are greater than 30% for many taxpayers.

Students will likely say that a tax rate of zero would be best, but remind them that there would be no roads, libraries, parks, or national defense without at least some revenue raised by the government.

III. Deadweight Loss and Tax Revenue as Taxes Vary

> **Figure 6**

A. As taxes increase, the deadweight loss from the tax increases.

B. In fact, as taxes increase, the deadweight loss rises more quickly than the size of the tax.

1. The deadweight loss is the area of a triangle and the area of a triangle depends on the square of its size.

2. If we double the size of a tax, the base and height of the triangle both double so the area of the triangle (the deadweight loss) rises by a factor of four.

C. As the tax increases, the level of tax revenue will eventually fall.

D. *Case Study: The Laffer Curve and Supply-Side Economics*

1. The relationship between the size of a tax and the level of tax revenues is called a Laffer curve.

2. Supply-side economists in the 1980s used the Laffer curve to support their belief that a drop in tax rates could lead to an increase in tax revenue for the government.

3. Economists continue to debate Laffer's argument.

    a. Many believe that the 1980s refuted Laffer's theory.

    b. Others believe that the events of the 1980s tell a more favorable supply-side story.

    c. Some economists believe that, while an overall cut in taxes normally decreases revenue, some taxpayers may find themselves on the wrong side of the Laffer curve.

ALTERNATIVE CLASSROOM EXAMPLE:
Draw a graph showing the demand and supply of paper clips. (Draw each curve as a 45-degree line so that buyers and sellers will share any tax equally.) Mark the equilibrium price as $0.50 (per box) and the equilibrium quantity as 1,000 boxes. Show students the areas of producer and consumer surplus.

Impose a $0.20 tax on each box. Assume that sellers are required to "pay" the tax to the government. Show students that:

- the price buyers pay will rise to $0.60.
- the price sellers receive will fall to $0.40.
- the quantity of toilet paper purchased will fall (assume to 800 units).
- tax revenue would be equal to $160 ($0.20 × 800).

Have students calculate the area of deadweight loss. (You may have to remind students how to calculate the area of a triangle.)

Show students that as the tax increases (to $0.40, $0.60, and $0.80), tax revenue rises and then falls, and the deadweight loss increases.

E. *In the News: New Research on Taxation*

1. The latest economic research indicates that some European countries may be on the declining side of the Laffer curve.

2. This is an article from the *Wall Street Journal* that describes research by economists comparing the positions of the U.S. and several European countries with respect to the Laffer curve.

Activity 2—Tax Alternatives

Type: In-class assignment
Topics: Taxes and deadweight loss
Materials needed: None
Time: 20 minutes
Class limitations: Works in any size class

Purpose
The market impact of taxes can be a new concept to many students. This exercise helps them think about the effects of taxes on different goods. Taxes that may be appealing for equity reasons can be distortionary from a market perspective.

Instructions
Tell the class, "The state has decided to increase funding for public education. They are considering four alternative taxes to finance these expenditures. All four taxes would raise the same amount of revenue." List these options on the board:
1.   A sales tax on food.
2.   A tax on families with school-age children.
3.   A property tax on vacation homes.
4.   A sales tax on jewelry.

Ask the students to answer the following questions. Give them time to write an answer, and then discuss their answers before moving to the next question:
A.   Taxes change incentives. How might individuals change their behavior because of each of these taxes?
B.   Rank these taxes from smallest deadweight loss to largest deadweight loss. Explain.
C.   Is deadweight loss the only thing to consider when designing a tax system?

Common Answers and Points for Discussion
A.   Taxes change incentives. How might individuals change their behavior because of each of these taxes?
   1. A sales tax on food: At the margin, some consumers will purchase less food. Overall food purchases will not decrease substantially because the tax will be spread over a large number of consumers and demand is relatively inelastic.
   2. A tax on families with school-age children: No families would put their children up for adoption to avoid taxes. A large tax could have implications for family planning; couples may choose not to have children, or to have fewer children, over time. A more realistic concern would be relocation to other states by mobile families.
   3. A property tax on vacation homes: This tax would be concentrated on fewer households. A large tax would discourage people from buying vacation homes. Developers would build fewer vacation homes in the long run. In many areas, people could choose an out-of-state vacation home.
   4. A sales tax on jewelry: This tax would also be relatively concentrated. People would buy less jewelry, or they would buy jewelry in other states with lower taxes.

B.   Rank these taxes from smallest deadweight loss to largest deadweight loss.
      Lowest deadweight loss—tax on children, very inelastic.
      Then—tax on food. Demand is inelastic; supply is elastic.
      Third—tax on vacation homes. Demand is elastic; short-run supply is inelastic.
      Most deadweight loss—tax on jewelry. Demand is elastic; supply is elastic.

C.   Is deadweight loss the only thing to consider when designing a tax system?
      No. This can generate a lively discussion. There are a variety of equity or fairness
      concerns. The taxes on children and on food would be regressive. Each of the taxes
      would tax certain households at much higher rates than other households with similar
      incomes.

SOLUTIONS TO TEXT PROBLEMS:

Quick Quizzes

1. Figure 1 shows the supply and demand curves for cookies, with equilibrium quantity Q_1 and
    equilibrium price P_1. When the government imposes a tax on cookies, the price to buyers
    rises to P_B, the price received by sellers declines to P_S, and the equilibrium quantity falls to
    Q_2. The deadweight loss is the triangular area below the demand curve and above the supply
    curve between quantities Q_1 and Q_2. The deadweight loss shows the fall in total surplus that
    results from the tax.

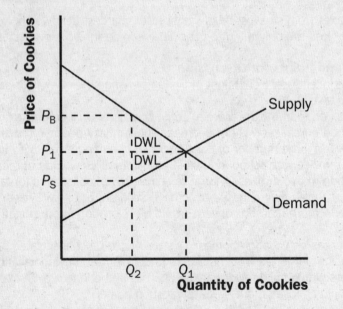

Figure 1

2. The deadweight loss of a tax is greater the greater is the elasticity of demand. Therefore, a
    tax on beer would have a larger deadweight loss than a tax on milk because the demand for
    beer is more elastic than the demand for milk.

3. If the government doubles the tax on gasoline, the revenue from the gasoline tax could rise or fall depending on whether the size of the tax is on the upward or downward sloping portion of the Laffer curve. However, if the government doubles the tax on gasoline, you can be sure that the deadweight loss of the tax rises because deadweight loss always rises as the tax rate rises.

Questions for Review

1. When the sale of a good is taxed, both consumer surplus and producer surplus decline. The decline in consumer surplus and producer surplus exceeds the amount of government revenue that is raised, so society's total surplus declines. The tax distorts the incentives of both buyers and sellers, so resources are allocated inefficiently.

2. Figure 2 illustrates the deadweight loss and tax revenue from a tax on the sale of a good. Without a tax, the equilibrium quantity would be Q_1, the equilibrium price would be P_1, consumer surplus would be A + B + C, and producer surplus would be D + E + F. The imposition of a tax places a wedge between the price buyers pay, P_B, and the price sellers receive, P_S, where $P_B = P_S + $ tax. The quantity sold declines to Q_2. Now consumer surplus is A, producer surplus is F, and government revenue is B + D. The deadweight loss of the tax is C+E, because that area is lost due to the decline in quantity from Q_1 to Q_2.

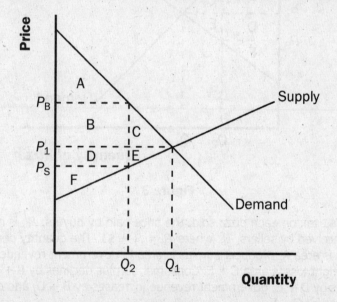

Figure 2

3. The greater the elasticities of demand and supply, the greater the deadweight loss of a tax. Because elasticity measures the response of quantity to a change in price, higher elasticity means the tax induces a greater reduction in quantity, and therefore, a greater distortion to the market.

4. Experts disagree about whether labor taxes have small or large deadweight losses because they have different views about the elasticity of labor supply. Some believe that labor supply is inelastic, so a tax on labor has a small deadweight loss. But others think that workers can adjust their hours worked in various ways, so labor supply is elastic, and thus a tax on labor has a large deadweight loss.

5. The deadweight loss of a tax rises more than proportionally as the tax rises. Tax revenue, however, may increase initially as a tax rises, but as the tax rises further, revenue eventually declines.

Problems and Applications

1. a. Figure 3 illustrates the market for pizza. The equilibrium price is P_1, the equilibrium quantity is Q_1, consumer surplus is area A + B + C, and producer surplus is area D + E + F. There is no deadweight loss, as all the potential gains from trade are realized; total surplus is the entire area between the demand and supply curves: A + B + C + D + E + F.

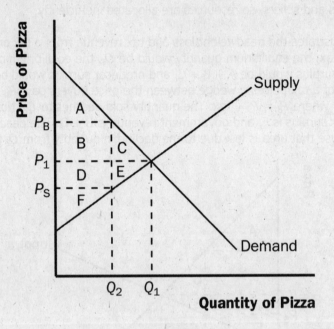

Figure 3

b. With a $1 tax on each pizza sold, the price paid by buyers, P_B, is now higher than the price received by sellers, P_S, where $P_B = P_S + \$1$. The quantity declines to Q_2, consumer surplus is area A, producer surplus is area F, government revenue is area B + D, and deadweight loss is area C + E. Consumer surplus declines by B + C, producer surplus declines by D + E, government revenue increases by B + D, and deadweight loss increases by C + E.

c. If the tax were removed and consumers and producers voluntarily transferred B + D to the government to make up for the lost tax revenue, then everyone would be better off than without the tax. The equilibrium quantity would be Q_1, as in the case without the tax, and the equilibrium price would be P_1. Consumer surplus would be A + C, because consumers get surplus of A + B + C, then voluntarily transfer B to the government. Producer surplus would be E + F, because producers get surplus of D + E + F, then voluntarily transfer D to the government. Both consumers and producers are better off than the case when the tax was imposed. If consumers and producers gave a little bit more than B + D to the government, then all three parties, including the government, would be better off. This illustrates the inefficiency of taxation.

2. a. The statement, "A tax that has no deadweight loss cannot raise any revenue for the government," is incorrect. An example is the case of a tax when either supply or demand is perfectly inelastic. The tax has neither an effect on quantity nor any deadweight loss, but it does raise revenue.

    b. The statement, "A tax that raises no revenue for the government cannot have any deadweight loss," is incorrect. An example is the case of a 100% tax imposed on sellers. With a 100% tax on their sales of the good, sellers will not supply any of the good, so the tax will raise no revenue. Yet the tax has a large deadweight loss, because it reduces the quantity sold to zero.

3. a. With very elastic supply and very inelastic demand, the burden of the tax on rubber bands will be borne largely by buyers. As Figure 4 shows, consumer surplus declines considerably, by area A + B, but producer surplus does not fall much at all, just by area C + D.

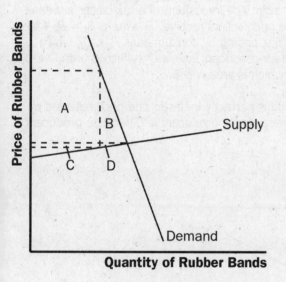

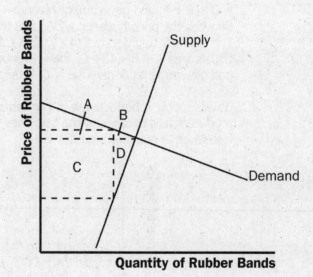

Figure 4   **Figure 5**

    b. With very inelastic supply and very elastic demand, the burden of the tax on rubber bands will be borne largely by sellers. As Figure 5 shows, consumer surplus does not decline much, just by area A + B, while producer surplus falls substantially, by area C + D. Compared to part (a), producers bear much more of the burden of the tax, and consumers bear much less.

4. a. The deadweight loss from a tax on heating oil is likely to be greater in the fifth year after it is imposed rather than the first year. In the first year, the elasticity of demand is fairly low, as people who own oil heaters are not likely to get rid of them right away. But over time they may switch to other energy sources and people buying new heaters for their homes will more likely choose gas or electric, so the tax will have a greater impact on quantity. Thus, the deadweight loss of the tax will get larger over time.

    b. The tax revenue is likely to be higher in the first year after it is imposed than in the fifth year. In the first year, demand is more inelastic, so the quantity does not decline as much and tax revenue is relatively high. As time passes and more people substitute away from oil, the quantity sold declines, as does tax revenue.

5. Because the demand for food is inelastic, a tax on food is a good way to raise revenue because it does not lead to much of a deadweight loss; thus taxing food is less inefficient than taxing other things. But it is not a good way to raise revenue from an equity point of view, because poorer people spend a higher proportion of their income on food. The tax would hit them harder than it would hit wealthier people.

6. a. This tax has such a high rate that it is not likely to raise much revenue. Because of the high tax rate, the equilibrium quantity in the market is likely to be at or near zero.

   b. Senator Moynihan's goal was probably to ban the use of hollow-tipped bullets. In this case, the tax could be as effective as an outright ban.

7. a. Figure 6 illustrates the market for socks and the effects of the tax. Without a tax, the equilibrium quantity would be Q_1, the equilibrium price would be P_1, total spending by consumers equals total revenue for producers, which is $P_1 \times Q_1$, which equals area B + C + D + E + F, and government revenue is zero. The imposition of a tax places a wedge between the price buyers pay, P_B, and the price sellers receive, P_S, where $P_B = P_S + tax$. The quantity sold declines to Q_2. Now total spending by consumers is $P_B \times Q_2$, which equals area A + B + C + D, total revenue for producers is $P_S \times Q_2$, which is area C + D, and government tax revenue is $Q_2 \times tax$, which is area A + B.

   b. Unless supply is perfectly elastic or demand is perfectly inelastic, the price received by producers falls because of the tax. Total receipts for producers fall, because producers lose revenue equal to area B + E + F.

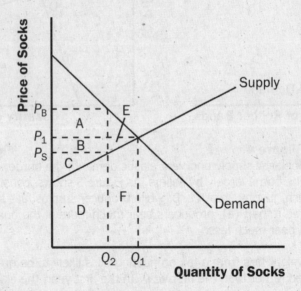

Figure 6

   c. The price paid by consumers rises, unless demand is perfectly elastic or supply is perfectly inelastic. Whether total spending by consumers rises or falls depends on the price elasticity of demand. If demand is elastic, the percentage decline in quantity exceeds the percentage increase in price, so total spending declines. If demand is inelastic, the percentage decline in quantity is less than the percentage increase in price, so total spending rises. Whether total consumer spending falls or rises, consumer surplus declines because of the increase in price and reduction in quantity.

8. Because the tax on gadgets was eliminated, all tax revenue must come from the tax on widgets. The tax revenue from the tax on widgets equals the tax per unit times the quantity produced. Assuming that neither the supply nor the demand curves for widgets are perfectly elastic or inelastic and because the increased tax causes a smaller quantity of widgets to be produced, then it is impossible for tax revenue to double—multiplying the tax per unit (which doubles) times the quantity (which declines) gives a number that is less than double the original tax revenue from widgets. So the government's tax change will yield less money than before.

9. Figure 7 illustrates the effects of the $2 subsidy on a good. Without the subsidy, the equilibrium price is P_1 and the equilibrium quantity is Q_1. With the subsidy, buyers pay price P_B, producers receive price P_S (where $P_S = P_B + \$2$), and the quantity sold is Q_2. The following table illustrates the effect of the subsidy on consumer surplus, producer surplus, government revenue, and total surplus. Because total surplus declines by area D + H, the subsidy leads to a deadweight loss in that amount.

	OLD	NEW	CHANGE
Consumer Surplus	A + B	A + B + E + F + G	+(E + F + G)
Producer Surplus	E + I	B + C + E + I	+(B + C)
Government Revenue	0	−(B + C + D + E + F + G + H)	−(B + C + D + E + F + G + H)
Total Surplus	A + B + E + I	A + B − D + E − H + I	−(D + H)

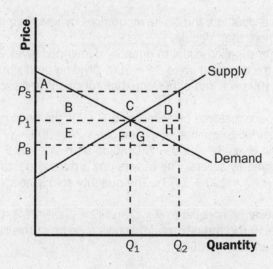

Figure 7

10. a. Figure 8 shows the effect of a $10 tax on hotel rooms. The tax revenue is represented by areas A + B, which are equal to ($10)(900) = $9,000. The deadweight loss from the tax is represented by areas C + D, which are equal to (0.5)($10)(100) = $500.

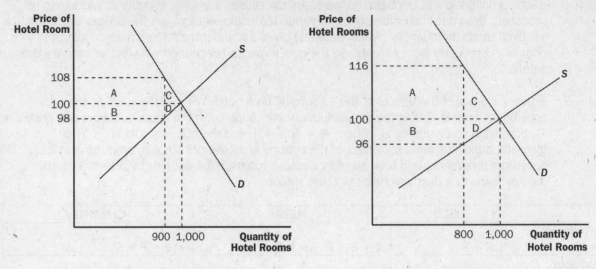

Figure 8   **Figure 9**

b. Figure 9 shows the effect of a $20 tax on hotel rooms. The tax revenue is represented by areas A + B, which are equal to ($20)(800) = $16,000. The deadweight loss from the tax is represented by areas C + D, which are equal to (0.5)($20)(200) = $2,000.

When the tax is doubled, the tax revenue rises by less than double, while the deadweight loss rises by more than double.

11. a. Setting quantity supplied equal to quantity demanded gives $2P = 300 - P$. Adding P to both sides of the equation gives $3P = 300$. Dividing both sides by 3 gives $P = 100$. Plugging $P = 100$ back into either equation for quantity demanded or supplied gives $Q = 200$.

b. Now P is the price received by sellers and $P + T$ is the price paid by buyers. Equating quantity demanded to quantity supplied gives $2P = 300 - (P+T)$. Adding P to both sides of the equation gives $3P = 300 - T$. Dividing both sides by 3 gives $P = 100 - T/3$. This is the price received by sellers. The buyers pay a price equal to the price received by sellers plus the tax ($P + T = 100 + 2T/3$). The quantity sold is now $Q = 2P = 200 - 2T/3$.

c. Because tax revenue is equal to $T \times Q$ and $Q = 200 - 2T/3$, tax revenue equals $200T - 2T^2/3$. Figure 10 (on the next page) shows a graph of this relationship. Tax revenue is zero at $T = 0$ and at $T = 300$.

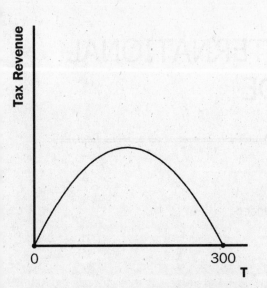

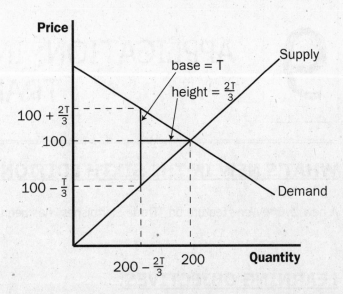

Figure 10   **Figure 11**

d. As Figure 11 shows, the area of the triangle (laid on its side) that represents the deadweight loss is 1/2 × base × height, where the base is the change in the price, which is the size of the tax (T) and the height is the amount of the decline in quantity ($2T/3$). So the deadweight loss equals $1/2 \times T \times 2T/3 = T^2/3$. This rises exponentially from 0 (when $T = 0$) to 30,000 when $T = 300$, as shown in Figure 12.

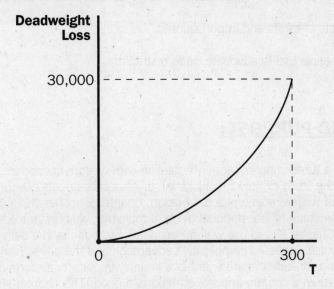

Figure 12

e. A tax of $200 per unit is a bad idea, because it is in a region in which tax revenue is declining. The government could reduce the tax to $150 per unit, get more tax revenue ($15,000 when the tax is $150 versus $13,333 when the tax is $200), and reduce the deadweight loss (7,500 when the tax is $150 compared to 13,333 when the tax is $200).

9 APPLICATION: INTERNATIONAL TRADE

WHAT'S NEW IN THE SIXTH EDITION:

A new *In the News* feature on "Trade Skirmishes" has been added.

LEARNING OBJECTIVES:

By the end of this chapter, students should understand:

➤ what determines whether a country imports or exports a good.

➤ who wins and who loses from international trade.

➤ that the gains to winners from international trade exceed the losses to losers.

➤ the welfare effects of tariffs and import quotas.

➤ the arguments people use to advocate trade restrictions.

CONTEXT AND PURPOSE:

Chapter 9 is third in a three-chapter sequence dealing with welfare economics. Chapter 7 introduced welfare economics: the study of how the allocation of resources affects economic well-being. Chapter 8 applied the lessons of welfare economics to taxation. Chapter 9 applies the tools of welfare economics from Chapter 7 to the study of international trade, a topic that was first introduced in Chapter 3.

The purpose of Chapter 9 is to use welfare economics to address the gains from trade more precisely than in Chapter 3, which discussed comparative advantage and the gains from trade. This chapter develops the conditions that determine whether a country imports or exports a good and discusses who wins and who loses when a country imports or exports a good. This chapter will show that when free trade is allowed, the gains of the winners exceed the losses of the losers. Because there are gains from trade, restrictions on free trade reduce the gains from trade and cause deadweight losses similar to those generated by a tax.

KEY POINTS:

- The effects of free trade can be determined by comparing the domestic price without trade to the world price. A low domestic price indicates that the country has a comparative advantage in producing the good and that the country will become an exporter. A high domestic price indicates that the rest of the world has a comparative advantage in producing the good and that the country will become an importer.

- When a country allows trade and becomes an exporter of a good, producers of the good are better off, and consumers of the good are worse off. When a country allows trade and becomes an importer of a good, consumers are better off, and producers are worse off. In both cases, the gains from trade exceed the losses.

- A tariff—a tax on imports—moves a market closer to the equilibrium that would exist without trade and, therefore, reduces the gains from trade. Although domestic producers are better off and the government raises revenue, the losses to consumers exceed these gains.

- There are various arguments for restricting trade: protecting jobs, defending national security, helping infant industries, preventing unfair competition, and responding to foreign trade restrictions. Although some of these arguments have some merit in some cases, economists believe that free trade is usually the better policy.

CHAPTER OUTLINE:

This chapter may be difficult to teach and very difficult for students to understand and accept. Be prepared for a skeptical reaction from students who have been told that free international trade is detrimental to a country. For various historical, cultural, and political reasons, free trade has few defenders outside of the economics profession.

Point out that international trade issues are no different from trading as it applies to individuals within a community or between states and regions within a country. The gains from trade between countries occur for the same reasons that we observe gains from trade between individuals.

Pick a state adjacent to yours. Ask students why we do not seem to worry about "importing" goods from other states the same way in which we worry about importing goods from other countries.

I. The Determinants of Trade

A. Example used throughout the chapter: The market for textiles in a country called Isoland.

B. The Equilibrium without Trade

1. If there is no trade, the domestic price in the textile market will balance supply and demand.

2. A new leader is elected who is interested in pursuing trade. A committee of economists is organized to determine the following:

    a. If the government allows trade, what will happen to the price of textiles and the quantity of textiles sold in the domestic market?

    b. Who will gain from trade, who will lose, and will the gains exceed the losses?

    c. Should a tariff (a tax on imported textiles) be part of the new trade policy?

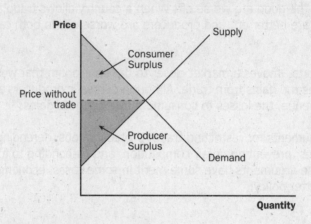

C. The World Price and Comparative Advantage

1. The first issue is to decide whether Isoland should import or export textiles.

    a. The answer depends on the relative price of textiles in Isoland compared with the price of textiles in other countries.

    b. Definition of **world price: the price of a good that prevails in the world market for that good.**

2. If the world price is greater than the domestic price, Isoland should export textiles; if the world price is lower than the domestic price, Isoland should import textiles.

    a. Note that the domestic price represents the opportunity cost of producing textiles in Isoland, while the world price represents the opportunity cost of producing textiles abroad.

    b. Thus, if the domestic price is low, this implies that the opportunity cost of producing textiles in Isoland is low, suggesting that Isoland has a comparative advantage in the production of textiles. If the domestic price is high, the opposite is true.

II. The Winners and Losers from Trade

A. We can use welfare analysis to determine who will gain and who will lose if free trade begins in Isoland.

B. We will assume that, because Isoland would be such a small part of the market for textiles, they will be price takers in the world economy. This implies that they take the world price as given and must sell (or buy) at that price.

C. The Gains and Losses of an Exporting Country

1. If the world price is higher than the domestic price, Isoland will export textiles. Once free trade begins, the domestic price will rise to the world price.

2. As the price of textiles rises, the domestic quantity of textiles demanded will fall and the domestic quantity of textiles supplied will rise. Thus, with trade, the domestic quantity demanded will not be equal to the domestic quantity supplied.

> Have students come to the board and label the areas of consumer and producer surplus after you have drawn each of the figures. This should not be a problem as they are likely familiar enough with consumer and producer surplus after completing Chapters 7 and 8.

Figure 2

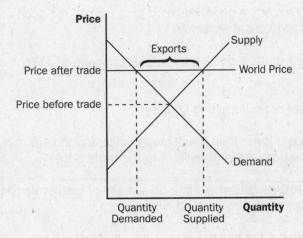

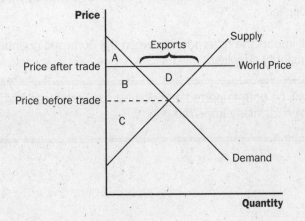

3. Welfare without Trade

   a. Consumer surplus is equal to: A + B.

   b. Producer surplus is equal to: C.

   c. Total surplus is equal to: A + B + C.

4. Welfare with Trade

   a. Consumer surplus is equal to: A.

   b. Producer Surplus is equal to: B + C + D.

   c. Total surplus is equal to: A + B + C + D.

5. Changes in Welfare

   a. Consumer surplus changes by: −B.

   b. Producer surplus changes by: +(B + D).

   c. Total surplus changes by: +D.

6. When a country exports a good, domestic producers of the good are better off and domestic consumers of the good are worse off.

7. When a country exports a good, total surplus is increased and the economic well-being of the country rises.

D. The Gains and Losses of an Importing Country

   1. If the world price is lower than the domestic price, Isoland will import textiles. Once free trade begins, the domestic price will fall to the world price.

   2. As the price of textiles falls, the domestic quantity of textiles demanded will rise and the domestic quantity of textiles supplied will fall.

      a. Thus, with trade, the domestic quantity demanded will not be equal to the domestic quantity supplied.

      b. Isoland will import the difference between the domestic quantity demanded and the domestic quantity supplied.

Note that there will be both imported and domestically produced textiles sold in this country. This is true for many imported goods.

Figure 3

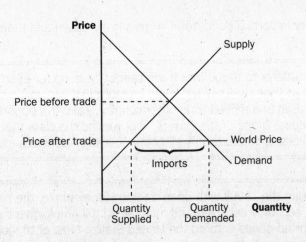

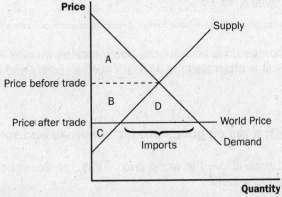

3. Welfare without Trade

   a. Consumer surplus is equal to: A.

   b. Producer surplus is equal to: B + C.

   c. Total surplus is equal to: A + B + C.

4. Welfare with Trade

   a. Consumer surplus is equal to: A + B + D.

   b. Producer surplus is equal to: C.

   c. Total surplus is equal to: A + B + C + D.

5. Changes in Welfare

   a. Consumer surplus changes by: +(B + D).

   b. Producer surplus changes by: −B.

   c. Total surplus changes by: +D.

6. When a country imports a good, domestic consumers of the good are better off and domestic producers of the good are worse off.

7. When a country imports a good, total surplus is increased and the economic well-being of the country rises.

Be prepared for students to argue that trade cannot be good for everyone. More than likely at least one of your students will know an individual who lost his or her job when a factory closed and moved to another country. Take this opportunity to point out that this individual is one of the "losers," but remind the class that the gains from trade exceed the losses, so the total well-being of society is increased.

Point out that during the 1990s with open trading (for example, the passage of NAFTA), the U.S. economy achieved and maintained full employment even as large quantities of imported goods entered the United States. Most of the jobs that "left the country" were low-skill, low-wage jobs.

E. Trade policy is often contentious because the policy creates winners and losers. If the losers have political clout, the result is often trade restrictions such as tariffs and quotas.

F. The Effects of a Tariff

1. Definition of **tariff: a tax on goods produced abroad and sold domestically.**

2. A tariff raises the price above the world price. Thus, the domestic price of textiles will rise to the world price plus the tariff.

3. As the price rises, the domestic quantity of textiles demanded will fall and the domestic quantity of textiles supplied will rise. The quantity of imports will fall and the market will move closer to the domestic market equilibrium that occurred before trade.

4. Welfare before the Tariff (with trade)

   a. Consumer surplus is equal to: A + B + C + D + E + F.

   b. Producer surplus is equal to: G.

   c. Government revenue is equal to: zero.

   d. Total surplus is equal to: A + B + C + D + E + F + G.

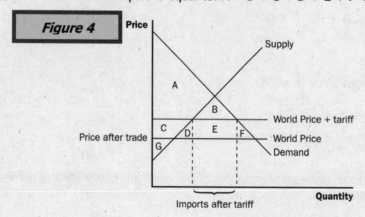

Figure 4

5. Welfare after the Tariff

   a. Consumer surplus is equal to: A + B.

   b. Producer surplus is equal to: C + G.

   c. Government revenue is equal to: E.

   d. Total surplus is equal to: A + B + C + E + G.

6. Changes in Welfare

   a. Consumer surplus changes by: −(C + D + E + F).

   b. Producer surplus changes by: +C.

   c. Government revenue changes by: +E.

   d. Total surplus changes by: −(D + F).

G. *FYI: Import Quotas: Another Way to Restrict Trade*

   1. An import quota is a limit on the quantity of a good that can be produced abroad and sold domestically.

   2. Import quotas are much like tariffs.

      a. Both tariffs and quotas raise the domestic price of the good, reduce the welfare of domestic consumers, increase the welfare of domestic producers, and cause deadweight losses.

      b. However, a tariff raises revenue for the government, whereas a quota creates surplus for license holders.

      c. A quota can potentially cause a larger deadweight loss than a tariff, depending on the mechanism used to allocate the import licenses.

H. The Lessons for Trade Policy

 This section provides a good opportunity to review what the students have learned thus far about trade. You should reinforce the idea that total surplus rises when trade is introduced, but falls once trade restrictions are imposed.

   1. If trade is allowed, the price of textiles will be driven to the world price. If the domestic price is higher than the world price, the country will become an importer and the domestic price will fall. If the domestic price is lower than the world price, the country will become an exporter and the domestic price will rise.

   2. If a country imports a product, domestic producers are made worse off, domestic consumers are made better off, and the gains of consumers outweigh the losses of producers. If a country exports a product, domestic producers are made better off, domestic consumers are made worse off, and the gains of producers outweigh the losses of consumers.

3. A tariff would create a deadweight loss because total surplus would fall.

I. *In the News: Trade Skirmishes*

1. In recent years, trade between the U.S. and China has not been completely free.

2. This is an article from *The New York Times* describing how trade policy often results in strategic moves between countries.

J. Other Benefits of International Trade

1. In addition to increasing total surplus, there are several other benefits of free trade.

2. These include an increased variety of goods, lower costs through economies of scale, increased competition, and an enhanced flow of ideas.

III. The Arguments for Restricting Trade

A. The Jobs Argument

1. If a country imports a product, domestic producers of the product will have to lay off workers because they will decrease domestic output when the price declines to the world price.

2. Free trade, however, will create job opportunities in other industries where the country enjoys a comparative advantage.

 Outsourced, Chapter 1. A call center in Seattle is outsourced to India. Todd is asked by his boss to travel to India to train his replacement, who earns only $11,000 per year. This is a nice clip to begin a class discussion on the factors that affect the success of outsourcing jobs.

B. The National-Security Argument

1. Certain industries may produce key resources needed to produce products necessary for national security.

2. In many of the cases for which this argument is used, the role of the particular market in providing national security is exaggerated.

C. The Infant-Industry Argument

1. New industries need time to establish themselves to be able to compete in world markets.

2. Sometimes older industries argue that they need temporary protection to help them adjust to new conditions.

3. Even if this argument is legitimate, it is nearly impossible for the government to choose which industries will be profitable in the future and it is even more difficult to remove trade restrictions in an industry once they are in place.

D. The Unfair-Competition Argument

1. It is unfair if firms in one country are forced to comply with more regulations than firms in another country, or if another government subsidizes the production of a good.

2. Even if another country is subsidizing the production of a product so that it can be exported to a country at a lower price, the domestic consumers who import the product gain more than the domestic producers lose.

E. The Protection-as-a-Bargaining-Chip Argument

1. Threats of protectionism can make other countries more willing to reduce the amounts of protectionism they use.

2. If the threat does not work, the country has to decide if it would rather reduce the economic well-being of its citizens (by carrying out the threat) or lose credibility in negotiations (by reneging on its threat).

F. *In the News: Second Thoughts about Free Trade*

1. Some economists worry about the impact of international trade on the distribution of income.

2. This is a column by economist Paul Krugman expressing such concerns.

G. *Case Study: Trade Agreements and the World Trade Organization*

1. Countries wanting to achieve freer trade can take two approaches to cutting trade restrictions: a unilateral approach or a multilateral approach.

2. A unilateral approach occurs when a country lowers its trade restrictions on its own. A multilateral approach occurs when a country reduces its trade restrictions while other countries do the same.

3. The North America Free Trade Agreement (NAFTA) and the General Agreement on Tariffs and Trade (GATT) are multilateral approaches to reducing trade barriers.

4. The rules established under GATT are now enforced by the World Trade Organization (WTO).

5. The functions of the WTO are to administer trade agreements, provide a forum for negotiation, and handle disputes that arise among member countries.

 Make sure that you point out the conclusion in this chapter. The chapter ends with a very effective parable about the discovery of comparative advantage, its adoption, its beneficial consequences, and finally, its abandonment for political reasons.

SOLUTIONS TO TEXT PROBLEMS:

Quick Quizzes

1. Since wool suits are cheaper in neighboring countries, Autarka would import suits if it were to allow free trade.

2. Figure 1 shows the supply and demand for wool suits in Autarka. With no trade, the price of suits is 3 ounces of gold, consumer surplus is area A, producer surplus is area B + C, and total surplus is area A + B + C. When trade is allowed, the price falls to 2 ounces of gold, consumer surplus rises to A + B + D (an increase of B + D), producer surplus falls to C (a decline of B), so total surplus rises to A + B + C + D (an increase of D). A tariff on suit imports would reduce the increase in consumer surplus, reduce the decline in producer surplus, and reduce the gain in total surplus.

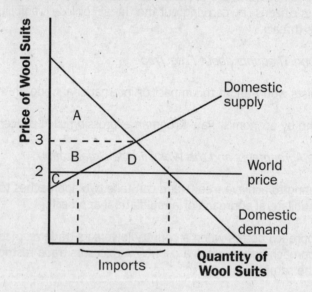

Figure 1

3. Lobbyists for the textile industry might make five arguments in favor of a ban on the import of wool suits: (1) imports of wool suits destroy domestic jobs; (2) the wool-suit industry is vital for national security; (3) the wool-suit industry is just starting up and needs protection from foreign competition until it gets stronger; (4) other countries are unfairly subsidizing their wool-suit industries; and (5) the ban on the importation of wool suits can be used as a bargaining chip in international negotiations.

In defending free trade in wool suits, you could argue that: (1) free trade creates jobs in some industries even as it destroys jobs in the wool-suit industry and allows Autarka to enjoy a higher standard of living; (2) the role of wool suits for the military may be exaggerated; (3) government protection is not needed for an industry to grow on its own; (4) it would be good for the citizens of Autarka to be able to buy wool suits at a subsidized price; and (5) threats against free trade may backfire, leading to lower levels of trade and lower economic welfare for everyone.

Questions for Review

1. If the domestic price that prevails without international trade is above the world price, the country does not have a comparative advantage in producing the good. If the domestic price is below the world price, the country has a comparative advantage in producing the good.

2. A country will export a good for which its domestic price is lower than the prevailing world price. Thus, if a country has a comparative advantage in producing a good, it will become an exporter when trade is allowed. A country will import a product for which its domestic price is greater than the prevailing world price. Thus, if a country does not have a comparative advantage in producing a good, it will become an importer when trade is allowed.

3. Figure 2 illustrates supply and demand for an importing country. Before trade is allowed, consumer surplus is area A and producer surplus is area B + C. After trade is allowed, consumer surplus is area A + B + D and producer surplus is area C. The change in total surplus is an increase of area D.

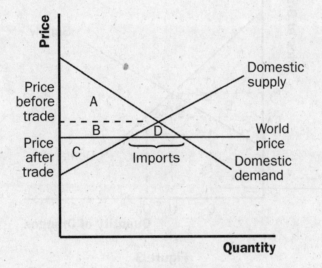

Figure 2

4. A tariff is a tax on goods produced abroad and sold domestically. If a country is an importer of a good, a tariff reduces the quantity of imports and moves the domestic market closer to its equilibrium without trade, increasing the price of the good, reducing consumer surplus and total surplus, while raising producer surplus and government revenue.

5. The arguments given to support trade restrictions are: (1) trade destroys jobs; (2) industries threatened with competition may be vital for national security; (3) new industries need trade restrictions to help them get started; (4) some countries unfairly subsidize their firms, so competition is not fair; and (5) trade restrictions can be useful bargaining chips. Economists disagree with these arguments: (1) trade may destroy some jobs, but it creates other jobs; (2) arguments about national security tend to be exaggerated; (3) the government cannot easily identify new industries that are worth protecting; (4) if countries subsidize their exports, doing so simply benefits consumers in importing countries; and (5) bargaining over trade is a risky business, because it may backfire, making the country worse off without trade.

6. A unilateral approach to achieving free trade occurs when a country removes trade restrictions on its own. Under a multilateral approach, a country reduces its trade restrictions while other countries do the same, based on an agreement reached through bargaining. The unilateral approach was taken by Great Britain in the 1800s and by Chile and South Korea in recent years. Examples of the multilateral approach include NAFTA in 1993 and the GATT negotiations since World War II.

Problems and Applications

1. a. In Figure 3, with no international trade the equilibrium price is P_1 and the equilibrium quantity is Q_1. Consumer surplus is area A and producer surplus is area B + C, so total surplus is A + B + C.

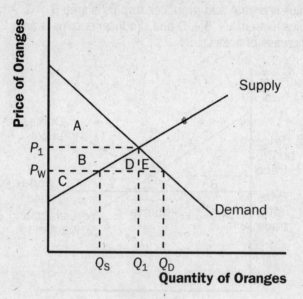

Figure 3

b. When the Mexican orange market is opened to trade, the new equilibrium price is P_W, the quantity consumed is Q_D, the quantity produced domestically is Q_S, and the quantity imported is $Q_D - Q_S$. Consumer surplus increases from A to A + B + D + E. Producer surplus decreases from B + C to C. Total surplus changes from A + B + C to A + B + C + D + E, an increase of D + E.

2. a. Figure 4 illustrates the Canadian market for wine, where the world price of wine is P_1. The following table illustrates the results under the heading "P_1."

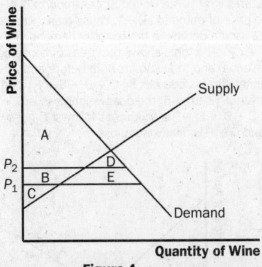

Figure 4

b. The shift in the Gulf Stream destroys some of the grape harvest in Europe and raises the world price of wine to P_2. The table shows the new areas of consumer, producer, and total surplus, as well as the changes in these surplus measures. Consumers lose, producers win, and Canada as a whole is worse off.

	P_1	P_2	CHANGE
Consumer Surplus	A + B + D + E	A + D	−(B + E)
Producer Surplus	C	B + C	+B
Total Surplus	A + B + C + D + E	A + B + C + D	−E

3. The impact of a tariff on imported autos is shown in Figure 6. Without the tariff, the price of an auto is P_W, the quantity produced in the United States is Q_1^S, and the quantity purchased in the United States is Q_1^D. The United States imports $Q_1^D - Q_1^S$ autos. The imposition of the tariff raises the price of autos to $P_W + t$, causing an increase in quantity supplied by U.S. producers to Q_2^S and a decline in the quantity demanded to Q_2^D. This reduces the number of imports to $Q_2^D - Q_2^S$. The table shows the areas of consumer surplus, producer surplus, government revenue, and total surplus both before and after the imposition of the tariff. Because consumer surplus declines by C + D + E + F while producer surplus rises by C and government revenue rises by E, the deadweight loss is D + F. The loss of consumer surplus in the amount C + D + E + F is split up as follows: C goes to producers, E goes to the government, and D + F is deadweight loss.

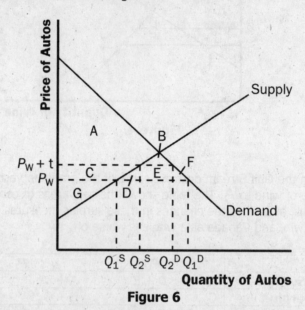

Figure 6

	Before Tariff	After Tariff	CHANGE
Consumer Surplus	A + B + C + D + E + F	A + B	−(C + D + E + F)
Producer Surplus	G	C + G	+C
Government Revenue	0	E	+E
Total Surplus	A + B + C + D + E + F + G	A + B + C + E + G	−(D + F)

4. a. For a country that imports clothing, the effects of a decline in the world price are shown in Figure 7. The initial price is P_{w1} and the initial level of imports is $Q^d_1 - Q^s_1$. The new world price is P_{w2} and the new level of imports is $Q^d_2 - Q^s_2$. The table below shows the changes in consumer surplus, producer surplus, and total surplus. Domestic consumers are made better off, while domestic producers are made worse off. Total surplus rises by areas D + E + F.

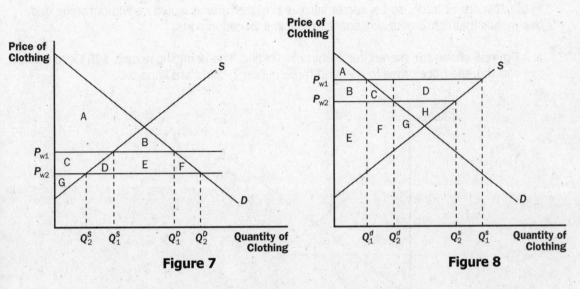

Figure 7   **Figure 8**

	P_{w1}	P_{w2}	CHANGE
Consumer Surplus	A+B	A+B+C+D+E+F	C+D+E+F
Producer Surplus	C+G	G	–C
Total Surplus	A+C+G	A+B+C+D+E+F+G	D+E+F

b. For a country that exports clothing, the effects of a decline in the world price are shown in Figure 8. The initial price is P_{w1} and the initial level of exports is $Q^s_1 - Q^d_1$. The new world price is P_{w2} and the new level of exports is $Q^s_2 - Q^d_2$. The table below shows the changes in consumer surplus, producer surplus, and total surplus. Domestic consumers are made better off, while domestic producers are made worse off. Total surplus falls by area D.

	P_{w1}	P_{w2}	CHANGE
Consumer Surplus	A	A + B + C	B + C
Producer Surplus	B + C + D + E + F + G + H	E + F + G + H	–B – C – D
Total Surplus	A + C + G	A + B + C + E + F + G + H	–D

c. Overall, importing countries benefit from the fall in the world price of clothing, while exporting countries are harmed.

5. The tax on wine from California is just like a tariff imposed by one country on imports from another. As a result, Washington producers would be better off and Washington consumers would be worse off. The higher price of wine in Washington means producers would produce more wine, so they would hire more workers. Tax revenue would go to the government of Washington. So both claims are true, but it is a bad policy because the losses to Washington consumers exceed the gains to producers and the state government.

6. a. There are many possible answers.

   b. There are many possible answers.

7. Senator Hollings is correct that the price of clothing is the world price. When trade is allowed, the domestic price of clothing is driven to the world price. The price is lower than it would be in the absence of trade, so consumer surplus is higher than it would be without trade and this means that consumers *do* benefit from lower-priced imports.

8. a. Figure 9 shows the market for T-shirts in Textilia. The domestic price is $20 Once trade is allowed, the price drops to $16 and three million T-shirts are imported.

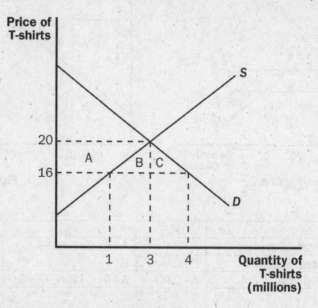

Figure 9

   b. Consumer surplus increases by areas A + B + C. Area A is equal to ($4)(1 million) +(0.5)($4)(2 million) = $8 million. Area B is equal to (0.5)($4)(2 million) = $4 million. Area C is equal to (0.5)($4)(1 million) = $2 million. Thus, consumer surplus increases by $14 million.

   Producer surplus declines by area A. Thus, producer surplus falls by $8 million.

   Total surplus rises by areas B + C. Thus, total surplus rises by $6 million.

9. a. Figure 10 shows the market for grain in an exporting country. The world price is P_W.

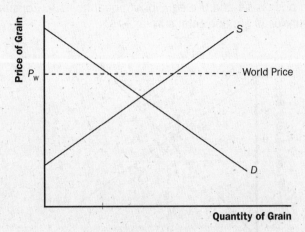

Figure 10

b. An export tax will reduce the effective world price received by the exporting nation.

c. An export tax will increase domestic consumer surplus, decrease domestic producer surplus, and increase government revenue.

d. Total surplus will fall because the decline in producer surplus is less than the sum of the changes in consumer surplus and government revenue. Thus, there is a deadweight loss as a result of the tax.

10. a. This statement is true. For a given world price that is lower than the domestic price, quantity demanded will rise more when demand is elastic. Therefore, the rise in consumer surplus will be greater when demand is elastic.

b. This statement is false. Quantity demanded would remain unchanged, but buyers would pay a lower price. This would increase consumer surplus. Domestic producer surplus will fall, but by less than the rise in consumer surplus. Gains from trade will increase.

c. This statement is false. Even though quantity demanded does not rise when trade is allowed, consumer surplus rises, because consumers are paying a lower price.

11. a. Figure 11 shows the market for jelly beans in Kawmin if trade is not allowed. The market equilibrium price is $4 and the equilibrium quantity is 4. Consumer surplus is $8, producer surplus is $8, and total surplus is $16.

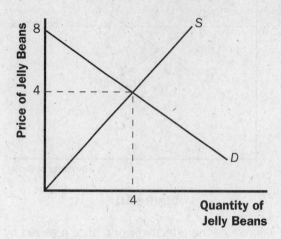

Figure 11

b. Since the world price is $1, kawmin will become an importer of jelly beans. Figure 12 shows that the domestic quantity supplied will be 1, quantity demanded will be 7, and 6 bags will be imported. Consumer surplus is $24.50, producer surplus is $0.50, so total surplus is $25.

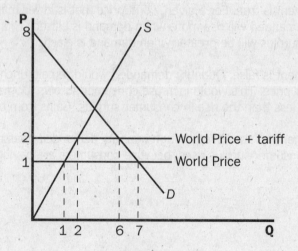

Figure 12

c. The tariff raises the world price to $2. This reduces domestic consumption to 6 bags and raises domestic production to 2 bags. Imports fall to 4 bags (see Figure 12). Consumer surplus is now $18, producer surplus is $2, government revenue is $4, and total surplus is $24.

d. When trade was opened, total surplus increases from $16 to $25. The deadweight loss of the tariff is $1 ($25 − $24).

12. a. Using Figure 4 from the text, the quantity demanded will fall to Q_2^D, the same quantity demanded under the tariff. However, quantity supplied will not change because the price sellers receive will be the world price. Thus, quantity supplied will remain at Q_1^S.

   b. The effects of the consumption tax can be seen in the table below:

	World price	World price + tax	CHANGE
Consumer Surplus	A + B + C + D + E + F	A + B	-C - D - E - F
Producer Surplus	G	G	None
Government Revenue	None	C + D + E	C + D + E
Total Surplus	A + B + C + D + E + F + G	A + B + C + D + E + G	-F

   c. The consumption tax raises more government revenue because the tax is on all units (not just the imported units). Thus, the deadweight loss is smaller than that associated with a tariff.

13. a. When a technological advance lowers the world price of televisions, the effect on the United States, an importer of televisions, is shown in Figure 13. Initially the world price of televisions is P_1, consumer surplus is A + B, producer surplus is C + G, total surplus is A + B + C + G, and the amount of imports is shown as "Imports₁". After the improvement in technology, the world price of televisions declines to P_2 (which is P_1 − 100), consumer surplus increases by D + E + F, producer surplus declines by C, total surplus rises by D + E + F, and the amount of imports rises to "Imports₂".

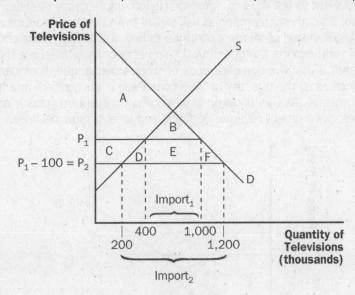

Figure 13

	P_1	P_2	CHANGE
Consumer Surplus	A + B	A + B + C + D + E + F	C + D + E + F
Producer Surplus	C + G	G	−C
Total Surplus	A + B + C + G	A + B + C + D + E + F + G	D + E + F

   b. The areas are calculated as follows: Area C = 200,000($100) + (0.5)(200,000)($100) = $30 million. Area D = (0.5)(200,000)($100) = $10 million. Area E = (600,000)($100) = $60 million. Area F = (0.5)(200,000)($100) = $10 million.

Therefore, the change in consumer surplus is $110 million. The change in producer surplus is -$30 million. Total surplus rises by $80 million.

c. If the government places a $100 tariff on imported televisions, consumer and producer surplus would return to their initial values. That is, consumer surplus would fall by areas C + D + E + F (a decline of $110 million). Producer surplus would rise by $30 million. The government would gain tariff revenue equal to ($100)(600,000) = $60 million. The deadweight loss from the tariff would be areas D and F (a value of $20 million). This is not a good policy from the standpoint of U.S. welfare because total surplus is reduced after the tariff is introduced. However, domestic producers will be happier as they benefit from the tariff.

d. It makes no difference why the world price dropped in terms of our analysis. The drop in the world price benefits domestic consumers more than it harms domestic producers and total welfare improves.

14. An export subsidy increases the price of steel exports received by producers by the amount of the subsidy, s, as shown in Figure 14. The figure shows the world price, P_W, before the subsidy is put in place. At that price, domestic consumers buy quantity Q_1^D of steel, producers supply Q_1^S units, and the country exports the quantity $Q_1^S - Q_1^D$. With the subsidy put in place, suppliers get a total price per unit of $P_W + s$, because they receive the world price for their exports P_W, and the government pays them the subsidy of s. However, note that domestic consumers can still buy steel at the world price, P_W, by importing it. Domestic firms do not want to sell steel to domestic customers, because they do not get the subsidy for doing so. So domestic companies will sell all the steel they produce abroad, in total quantity Q_2^S. Domestic consumers continue to buy quantity Q_1^D. The country imports steel in quantity Q_1^D and exports the quantity Q_2^S, so net exports of steel are the quantity $Q_2^S - Q_1^D$. The end result is that the domestic price of steel is unchanged, the quantity of steel produced increases, the quantity of steel consumed is unchanged, and the quantity of steel exported increases. As the following table shows, consumer surplus is unaffected, producer surplus rises, government revenue declines, and total surplus declines.

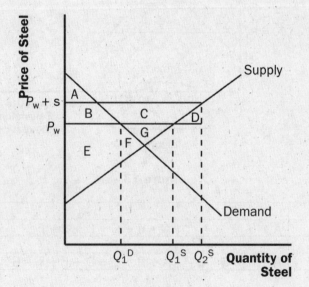

Figure 14

Thus, it is not a good policy from an economic standpoint because there is a decline in total surplus.

	Without Subsidy	With Subsidy	CHANGE
Consumer Surplus	A + B	A + B	0
Producer Surplus	E + F + G	B + C + E + F + G	+(B + C)
Government Revenue	0	−(B + C + D)	−(B + C + D)
Total Surplus	A + B + E + F + G	A + B − D + E + F + G	−D

10 MEASURING A NATION'S INCOME

WHAT'S NEW IN THE SIXTH EDITION:

There is a new *In the News* box on "Beyond Gross Domestic Product."

LEARNING OBJECTIVES:

By the end of this chapter, students should understand:

➢ why an economy's total income equals its total expenditure.

➢ how gross domestic product (GDP) is defined and calculated.

➢ the breakdown of GDP into its four major components.

➢ the distinction between real GDP and nominal GDP.

➢ whether GDP is a good measure of economic well-being.

CONTEXT AND PURPOSE:

Chapter 10 is the first chapter in the macroeconomic section of the text. It is the first of a two-chapter sequence that introduces students to two vital statistics that economists use to monitor the macroeconomy—GDP and the consumer price index. Chapter 10 develops how economists measure production and income in the macroeconomy. The following chapter, Chapter 11, develops how economists measure the level of prices in the macroeconomy. Taken together, Chapter 10 concentrates on the *quantity* of output in the macroeconomy while Chapter 11 concentrates on the *price* of output in the macroeconomy.

The purpose of this chapter is to provide students with an understanding of the measurement and the use of gross domestic product (GDP). GDP is the single most important measure of the health of the macroeconomy. Indeed, it is the most widely reported statistic in every developed economy.

KEY POINTS:

- Because every transaction has a buyer and a seller, the total expenditure in the economy must equal the total income in the economy.

- Gross domestic product (GDP) measures an economy's total expenditure on newly produced goods and services and the total income earned from the production of these goods and services. More precisely, GDP is the market value of all final goods and services produced within a country in a given period of time.

- GDP is divided among four components of expenditure: consumption, investment, government purchases, and net exports. Consumption includes spending on goods and services by households, with the exception of purchases of new housing. Investment includes spending on new equipment and structures, including households' purchases of new housing. Government purchases include spending on goods and services by local, state, and federal governments. Net exports equal the value of goods and services produced domestically and sold abroad (exports) minus the value of goods and services produced abroad and sold domestically (imports).

- Nominal GDP uses current prices to value the economy's production of goods and services. Real GDP uses constant base-year prices to value the economy's production of goods and services. The GDP deflator—calculated from the ratio of nominal to real GDP—measures the level of prices in the economy.

- GDP is a good measure of economic well-being because people prefer higher incomes to lower incomes. But it is not a perfect measure of well-being. For example, GDP excludes the value of leisure and the value of a clean environment.

CHAPTER OUTLINE:

Regardless of whether microeconomics is taught before macroeconomics or vice versa, students need to be reminded of the differences between the two areas of study. Begin by defining the two terms and contrasting and comparing their focus.

I. Review of the Definitions of Microeconomics and Macroeconomics

   A. Definition of **microeconomics: the study of how households and firms make decisions and how they interact in markets**.

   B. Definition of **macroeconomics: the study of economy-wide phenomena including inflation, unemployment, and economic growth**.

II. The Economy's Income and Expenditure

   A. To judge whether or not an economy is doing well, it is useful to look at Gross Domestic Product (GDP).

Students have heard of GDP and they are often interested in learning more about what it is. The basic point that you must get across is that GDP is a measure of *both* aggregate production and aggregate income in a nation over a period of one year. You can demonstrate this by using the circular-flow diagram and explaining that production generates income, which provides the purchasing power that generates the demand for the products.

1. GDP measures the total income of everyone in the economy.

2. GDP measures total expenditure on an economy's output of goods and services.

B. For an economy as a whole, total income must equal total expenditure.

1. If someone pays someone else $100 to mow a lawn, the expenditure on the lawn service ($100) is exactly equal to the income earned from the production of the lawn service ($100).

2. We can also use the circular-flow diagram from Chapter 2 to show why total income and total expenditure must be equal.

Figure 1

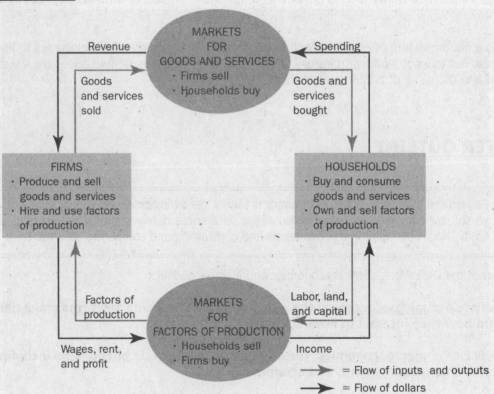

a. Households buy goods and services from firms; firms use this money to pay for resources purchased from households.

b. In the simple economy described by this circular-flow diagram, calculating GDP could be done by adding up the total purchases of households or summing total income earned by households.

    c.   Note that this simple diagram is somewhat unrealistic as it omits saving, taxes, government purchases, and investment purchases by firms. However, because a transaction always has a buyer and a seller, total expenditure in the economy must be equal to total income.

III. The Measurement of Gross Domestic Product

  A. Definition of **gross domestic product (GDP)**: **the market value of all final goods and services produced within a country in a given period of time**.

> To put GDP in terms that students may understand better, explain to them that GDP represents the amount of money one would need to purchase one year's worth of the economy's production of all final goods and services.

> Have a contest and see which student can come closest in guessing the level of GDP for the United States last year.

  B. "GDP Is the Market Value . . ."

    1. To add together different items, market values are used.

    2. Market values are calculated by using market prices.

  C. ". . . Of All . . ."

    1. GDP includes all items produced and sold legally in the economy.

    2. The value of housing services is somewhat difficult to measure.

      a. If housing is rented, the value of the rent is used to measure the value of the housing services.

      b. For housing that is owned (or mortgaged), the government estimates the rental value and uses this figure to value the housing services.

    3. GDP does not include illegal goods or services or items that are not sold in markets.

      a. When you hire someone to mow your lawn, that production is included in GDP.

      b. If you mow your own lawn, that production is not included in GDP.

  D. ". . . Final . . ."

    1. Intermediate goods are not included in GDP.

> Make sure that students realize that investment goods (such as structures and vehicles used in production) are not intermediate goods. Investment goods represent products purchased for final use by business firms.

    2. The value of intermediate goods is already included as part of the value of the final good.

3. Goods that are placed into inventory are considered to be "final" and included in GDP as a firm's inventory investment.

    a. Goods that are sold out of inventory are counted as a decrease in inventory investment.

    b. The goal is to count the production when the good is finished, which is not necessarily the same time that the product is sold.

E. ". . . Goods and Services . . ."

    1. GDP includes both tangible goods and intangible services.

F. ". . . Produced . . ."

    1. Only current production is counted.

    2. Used goods that are sold do not count as part of GDP.

G. ". . . Within a Country . . ."

    1. GDP measures the production that takes place within the geographical boundaries of a particular country.

    2. If a Canadian citizen works temporarily in the United States, the value of his output is included in GDP for the United States. If an American owns a factory in Haiti, the value of the production of that factory is not included in U.S. GDP.

Students sometimes have trouble understanding that the production of a foreign firm operating in the United States is part of U.S. GDP. Help them make the connection by using the circular-flow diagram. Show them that, even if it is a foreign firm, the firm's workers are living in the United States and buying clothes, groceries, and other goods in the United States. Thus, the workers in the foreign firm operating in the United States are fueling the domestic economy.

H. ". . . in a Given Period of Time."

    1. The usual interval of time used to measure GDP is a quarter (three months).

    2. When the government reports GDP, the data are generally reported on an annual basis.

    3. In addition, data are generally adjusted for regular seasonal changes (such as Christmas).

I. In addition to summing expenditure, the government also calculates GDP by adding up total income in the economy.

    1. The two ways of calculating GDP almost exactly give the same answer.

    2. The difference between the two calculations of GDP is called the *statistical discrepancy*.

J.   *FYI: Other Measures of Income*

 It can be a challenge to teach all of these definitions without putting your students to sleep. Concentrate on the measures that will mean the most to students as the semester progresses.

A. Gross National Product (GNP) is the total income earned by a nation's permanent residents.

1.   GNP includes income that American citizens earn abroad.

2.   GNP excludes income that foreigners earn in the United States.

B. Net National Product (NNP) is the total income of a nation's residents (GNP) minus losses from depreciation (wear and tear on an economy's stock of equipment and structures).

C. National income is the total income earned by a nation's residents in the production of goods and services.

1.   National income differs from NNP by excluding indirect business taxes and including business subsidies.

2.   NNP and national income also differ due to "statistical discrepancy."

D. Personal income is the income that households and noncorporate businesses receive.

E. Disposable personal income is the income that households and noncorporate businesses have left after taxes and other obligations to the government.

IV. The Components of GDP

A. GDP (*Y*) can be divided into four components: consumption (*C*), investment (*I*), government purchases (*G*), and net exports (*NX*).

$$Y = C + I + G + NX$$

 Students will ask why GDP is called "*Y*." Remind them that in equilibrium GDP expenditures must be equal to income. The "*Y*" stands for income because the letter "*I*" is used for investment.

B. Definition of **consumption: spending by households on goods and services, with the exception of purchases of new housing**.

C. Definition of **investment: spending on capital equipment, inventories, and structures, including household purchases of new housing**.

1.   GDP accounting uses the word "investment" differently from how we use the term in everyday conversation.

2.   When a student hears the word "investment," he or she thinks of financial instruments such as stocks and bonds.

3. In GDP accounting, investment means purchases of investment goods such as capital equipment, inventories, or structures.

D. Definition of **government purchases**: **spending on goods and services by local, state, and federal governments**.

1. Salaries of government workers are counted as part of the government purchases component of GDP.

2. Transfer payments are not included as part of the government purchases component of GDP.

Spend some time in class distinguishing between government purchases and transfer payments. Point out that transfer payments are actually negative taxes representing payments from the government to individuals (with no good or service provided in return) rather than payments from individuals to the government. Define net taxes as the difference between taxes and transfers.

E. Definition of **net exports**: **spending on domestically produced goods by foreigners (exports) minus spending on foreign goods by domestic residents (imports)**.

Table 1

F. *Case Study: The Components of U.S. GDP*

1. Table 1 shows these four components of GDP for 2009.

2. The data for GDP come from the Bureau of Economic Analysis, which is part of the Department of Commerce.

Make sure that you point out Table 1. Call attention to the importance of consumption and the negative number in the net exports column.

V. Real Versus Nominal GDP

A. There are two possible reasons for total spending to rise from one year to the next.

1. The economy may be producing a larger output of goods and services.

2. Goods and services could be selling at higher prices.

B. When studying GDP over time, economists would like to know if output has changed (not prices).

C. Thus, economists measure real GDP by valuing output using a fixed set of prices.

D. A Numerical Example

Make sure that you do this example or a similar numerical example in class. If you feel comfortable improvising, let the students pick two goods and then make up an example with them.

Table 2

1. Two goods are being produced: hot dogs and hamburgers.

Year	Price of Hot Dogs	Quantity of Hot Dogs	Price of Hamburgers	Quantity of Hamburgers
2010	$1	100	$2	50
2011	$2	150	$3	100
2012	$3	200	$4	150

2. Definition of **nominal GDP: the production of goods and services valued at current prices**.

> Nominal GDP for 2010 = ($1 × 100) + ($2 × 50) = $200.
> Nominal GDP for 2011 = ($2 × 150) + ($3 × 100) = $600.
> Nominal GDP for 2012 = ($3 × 200) + ($4 × 150) = $1,200.

3. Definition of **real GDP: the production of goods and services valued at constant prices**.

> Let's assume that the base year is 2008.

> Real GDP for 2010 = ($1 × 100) + ($2 × 50) = $200.
> Real GDP for 2011 = ($1 × 150) + ($2 × 100) = $350.
> Real GDP for 2012 = ($1 × 200) + ($2 × 150) = $500.

Make sure that it is clear to students how to calculate these numbers so that they can compute nominal GDP and real GDP on their own.

E. Because real GDP is unaffected by changes in prices over time, changes in real GDP reflect changes in the amount of goods and services produced.

Emphasize that when there is inflation, nominal GDP can increase while real GDP actually declines. Make sure that students understand that real GDP will be used as a proxy for aggregate production throughout the course.

ALTERNATIVE CLASSROOM EXAMPLE:

The country of _____ (insert name based on school mascot such as "Pantherville" or "Owlstown") produces two goods: footballs and basketballs. Below is a table showing prices and quantities of output for three years:

Year	Price of Footballs	Quantity of Footballs	Price of Basketballs	Quantity of Basketballs
Year 1	$10	120	$12	200
Year 2	12	200	15	300
Year 3	14	180	18	275

Nominal GDP in Year 1 = ($10 × 120) + ($12 × 200) = $3,600
Nominal GDP in Year 2 = ($12 × 200) + ($15 × 300) = $6,900
Nominal GDP in Year 3 = ($14 × 180) + ($18 × 275) = $7,470

Using Year 1 as the Base Year:
Real GDP in Year 1 = ($10 × 120) + ($12 × 200) = $3,600
Real GDP in Year 2 = ($10 × 200) + ($12 × 300) = $5,600
Real GDP in Year 3 = ($10 × 180) + ($12 × 275) = $5,100
(Note that nominal GDP rises from Year 2 to Year 3, but real GDP falls.)

GDP deflator for Year 1 = ($3,600/$3,600) × 100 = 1 × 100 = 100
GDP deflator for Year 2 = ($6,900/$5,600) × 100 = 1.2321 × 100 = 123.21
GDP deflator for Year 3 = ($7,470/$5,100) × 100 = 1.4647 × 100 = 146.47

F. The GDP Deflator

1. Definition of **GDP deflator: a measure of the price level calculated as the ratio of nominal GDP to real GDP times 100**.

$$\text{GDP deflator} = \frac{\text{Nominal GDP}}{\text{Real GDP}} \times 100$$

2. Example Calculations

GDP Deflator for 2010 = ($200 / $200) × 100 = 100.
GDP Deflator for 2011 = ($600 / $350) × 100 = 171.
GDP Deflator for 2012 = ($1200 / $500) × 100 = 240.

Make sure that you point out that nominal GDP and real GDP will be equal in the base year. This implies that the GDP deflator for the base year will always be equal to 100.

G. *Case Study: Real GDP over Recent History*

Figure 2

1. Figure 2 shows quarterly data on real GDP for the United States since 1965.

2. We can see that real GDP has increased over time.

3. We can also see that there are times when real GDP declines. These periods are called recessions.

VI. Is GDP a Good Measure of Economic Well-Being?

> Get students involved in a discussion of the merits and problems involved with using GDP as a measure of well-being. Students are often as interested in what is not included in GDP as they are in what is included. Have the students break into small groups and list the things that might be missing if we use GDP as a measure of well-being. Then, have each group report their results and summarize them on the board.

A. GDP measures both an economy's total income and its total expenditure on goods and services.

B. GDP per person tells us the income and expenditure level of the average person in the economy.

C. GDP, however, may not be a very good measure of the economic well-being of an individual.

1. GDP omits important factors in the quality of life including leisure, the quality of the environment, and the value of goods produced but not sold in formal markets.

2. GDP also says nothing about the distribution of income.

3. However, a higher GDP does help us achieve a good life. Nations with larger GDP generally have better education and better health care.

D. *In the News: The Underground Economy*

1. The measurement of GDP misses many transactions that take place in the underground economy.

2. This article compares the underground economies of the United States and several other countries.

E. *Case Study: International Differences in GDP and the Quality of Life*

Table 3

1. Table 3 shows real GDP per person, life expectancy, adult literacy rates, and Internet usage for 12 countries.

2. In rich countries, life expectancy is higher and adult literacy and Internet usage rates are also high.

3. In poor countries, people typically live only into their 50s, only about half of the adult population is literate, and Internet usage is very rare.

Activity 1—GDP and Well-Being

Type: In-class demonstration
Topics: Per capita GDP
Materials needed: None
Time: 15 minutes
Class limitations: Works in any size class

Purpose

This activity examines the usefulness and limits of measures of GDP. Students often have difficulty accepting the use of GDP as a proxy for well-being. Per capita GDP does not directly measure well-being but it is highly correlated with direct measures. Making this correlation explicit helps students understand the emphasis on GDP in macroeconomics.

Instructions

Ask students the following questions. Discuss each before moving to the next question.

1. If GDP is a good measure of well-being, why is Switzerland's GDP so much lower than India's GDP or China's GDP?
2. What measures would be better to compare the well-being of different countries?
3. How do you expect these direct measures to correlate with per capita GDP?

Common Answers and Points for Discussion

1. GDP itself tells very little; Switzerland's GDP is much lower than that of India or China, yet Swiss citizens have one of the highest standards of living in the world. The difference, of course, is population. Switzerland is a small country, so its GDP is relatively small, despite its wealth. The appropriate comparison is per capita GDP. A more interesting question is "Is per capita GDP a good measure of well-being?" Or worded another way: "What constitutes well-being?"
2. Well-being can be measured directly in a variety of ways. Students often suggest these:
    Health care
    Food
    Education
    These are certainly better measures than money income, but they can be difficult to collect and interpret.
3. Although per capita GDP is not a direct measure of well-being, it can be used as a proxy for direct measures. The wealthiest countries have per capita incomes over 10 times higher than the poorest.

F. *In the News: Beyond Gross Domestic Product*

1. Some economists wonder if we need a better measure of economic well-being.

2. This is an article from *The New York Times* describing some criticisms of using GDP solely to measure economic well-being.

SOLUTIONS TO TEXT PROBLEMS:

Quick Quizzes:

1. Gross domestic product measures two things at once: (1) the total income of everyone in the economy and (2) the total expenditure on the economy's output of final goods and services. It can measure both of these things at once because all expenditure in the economy ends up as someone's income.

2. The production of a pound of caviar contributes more to GDP than the production of a pound of hamburger because the contribution to GDP is measured by market value and the price of a pound of caviar is much higher than the price of a pound of hamburger.

3. The four components of expenditure are: (1) consumption; (2) investment; (3) government purchases; and (4) net exports. The largest component is consumption, which accounts for more than 70 percent of total expenditure.

4. Real GDP is the production of goods and services valued at constant prices. Nominal GDP is the production of goods and services valued at current prices. Real GDP is a better measure of economic well-being because changes in real GDP reflect changes in the amount of output being produced. Thus, a rise in real GDP means people have produced more goods and services, but a rise in nominal GDP could occur either because of increased production or because of higher prices.

5. Although GDP is not a perfect measure of well-being, policymakers should care about it because a larger GDP means that a nation can afford better healthcare, better educational systems, and more of the material necessities of life.

Questions for Review:

1. An economy's income must equal its expenditure, because every transaction has a buyer and a seller. Thus, expenditure by buyers must equal income by sellers.

2. The production of a luxury car contributes more to GDP than the production of an economy car because the luxury car has a higher market value.

3. The contribution to GDP is $3, the market value of the bread, which is the final good that is sold.

4. The sale of used records does not affect GDP at all because it involves no current production.

5. The four components of GDP are consumption, such as the purchase of a DVD; investment, such as the purchase of a computer by a business; government purchases, such as an order for military aircraft; and net exports, such as the sale of American wheat to Russia. (Many other examples are possible.)

6. Economists use real GDP rather than nominal GDP to gauge economic well-being because real GDP is not affected by changes in prices, so it reflects only changes in the amounts being produced. You cannot determine if a rise in nominal GDP has been caused by increased production or higher prices.

7.

Year	Nominal GDP	Real GDP	GDP Deflator
2010	100 X $2 = $200	100 X $2 = $200	($200/$200) X 100 = 100
2011	200 X $3 = $600	200 X $2 = $400	($600/$400) X 100 = 150

The percentage change in nominal GDP is (600 − 200)/200 x 100% = 200%. The percentage change in real GDP is (400 − 200)/200 x 100% = 100%. The percentage change in the deflator is (150 − 100)/100 x 100% = 50%.

8. It is desirable for a country to have a large GDP because people could enjoy more goods and services. But GDP is not the only important measure of well-being. For example, laws that restrict pollution cause GDP to be lower. If laws against pollution were eliminated, GDP would be higher but the pollution might make us worse off. Or, for example, an earthquake would raise GDP, as expenditures on cleanup, repair, and rebuilding increase. But an earthquake is an undesirable event that lowers our welfare.

Problems and Applications

1. a. Consumption increases because a refrigerator is a good purchased by a household.
   b. Investment increases because a house is an investment good.
   c. Consumption increases because a car is a good purchased by a household, but investment decreases because the car in Ford's inventory had been counted as an investment good until it was sold.
   d. Consumption increases because pizza is a good purchased by a household.
   e. Government purchases increase because the government spent money to provide a good to the public.
   f. Consumption increases because the bottle is a good purchased by a household, but net exports decrease because the bottle was imported.
   g. Investment increases because new structures and equipment were built.

2. With transfer payments, nothing is produced, so there is no contribution to GDP.

3. If GDP included goods that are resold, it would be counting output of that particular year, plus sales of goods produced in a previous year. It would double-count goods that were sold more than once and would count goods in GDP for several years if they were produced in one year and resold in another.

4. a. Calculating nominal GDP:
   2010: ($1 per qt. of milk × 100 qts. milk) + ($2 per qt. of honey × 50 qts. honey) = $200
   2011: ($1 per qt. of milk × 200 qts. milk) + ($2 per qt. of honey × 100 qts. honey) = $400
   2012: ($2 per qt. of milk × 200 qts. milk) + ($4 per qt. of honey × 100 qts. honey) = $800

   Calculating real GDP (base year 2010):
   2010: ($1 per qt. of milk × 100 qts. milk) + ($2 per qt. of honey × 50 qts. honey) = $200
   2011: ($1 per qt. of milk × 200 qts. milk) + ($2 per qt. of honey × 100 qts. honey) = $400
   2012: ($1 per qt. of milk × 200 qts. milk) + ($2 per qt. of honey × 100 qts. honey) = $400

      Calculating the GDP deflator:
      2010: ($200/$200) × 100 = 100
      2011: ($400/$400) × 100 = 100
      2012: ($800/$400) × 100 = 200

b. Calculating the percentage change in nominal GDP:
     Percentage change in nominal GDP in 2011 = [($400 − $200)/$200] × 100% = 100%.
     Percentage change in nominal GDP in 2012 = [($800 − $400)/$400] × 100% = 100%.

     Calculating the percentage change in real GDP:
     Percentage change in real GDP in 2011 = [($400 − $200)/$200] × 100% = 100%.
     Percentage change in real GDP in 2012 = [($400 − $400)/$400] × 100% = 0%.

     Calculating the percentage change in GDP deflator:
     Percentage change in the GDP deflator in 2011 = [(100 − 100)/100] × 100% = 0%.
     Percentage change in the GDP deflator in 2012 = [(200 − 100)/100] × 100% = 100%.

     Prices did not change from 2010 to 2011. Thus, the percentage change in the GDP deflator is zero. Likewise, output levels did not change from 2011 to 2012. This means that the percentage change in real GDP is zero.

c. Economic well-being rose more in 2010 than in 2011, since real GDP rose in 2011 but not in 2012. In 2011, real GDP rose but prices did not. In 2012, real GDP did not rise but prices did.

5. a. Calculating Nominal GDP:

     Year 1: (3 bars × $4) = $12
     Year 2: (4 bars × $5) = $20
     Year 3: (5 bars × $6) = $30

  b. Calculating Real GDP:

     Year 1: (3 bars × $4) = $12
     Year 2: (4 bars × $4) = $16
     Year 3: (5 bars × $4) = $20

  c. Calculating the GDP delator:

     Year 1: $12/$12 × 100 = 100
     Year 2: $20/$16 × 100 = 125
     Year 3: $30/$20 × 100 = 150

  d. The growth rate from Year 2 to Year 3 = (16 − 12)/12 × 100% = 4/12 × 100% = 33.3%

  e. The inflation rate from Year 2 to Year 3 = (150 − 125)/125 × 100% = 25/125 × 100% = 20%.

  f. To calculate the growth rate of real GDP, we could simply calculate the percentage change in the quantity of bars. To calculate the inflation rate, we could measure the percentage change in the price of bars.

6.

Year	Nominal GDP (billions)	GDP Deflator (base year: 2005)
2009	$14,256	109.8
1999	$9,353	86.8

a. The growth rate of nominal GDP = $100\% \times [(\$14,256/\$9,353)^{0.10} - 1] = 4.3\%$

b. The growth rate of the deflator = $100\% \times [(109.886.8)^{0.10} - 1] = 2.4\%$

c. Real GDP in 1999 (in 2005 dollars) is $9,353/(86.8/100) = $10,775.35.

d. Real GDP in 2009 (in 2005 dollars) is $14,256/(109.8/100) = $12,983.61.

e. The growth rate of real GDP = $100\% \times [(\$12,983.61/\$10,775.35)^{0.10} - 1] = 1.9\%$

f. The growth rate of nominal GDP is higher than the growth rate of real GDP because of inflation.

7. Many answers are possible.

8. a. GDP is the market value of the final good sold, $180.

b. Value added for the farmer: $100.
Value added for the miller: $150 − $100 = $50.
Value added for the baker: $180 − $150 = $30.

c. Together, the value added for the three producers is $100 + $50 + $30 = $180. This is the value of GDP.

9. In countries like India, people produce and consume a fair amount of food at home that is not included in GDP. So GDP per person in India and the United States will differ by more than their comparative economic well-being.

10. a. The increased labor-force participation of women has increased GDP in the United States, because it means more people are working and production has increased.

b. If our measure of well-being included time spent working in the home and taking leisure, it would not rise as much as GDP, because the rise in women's labor-force participation has reduced time spent working in the home and taking leisure.

c. Other aspects of well-being that are associated with the rise in women's increased labor-force participation include increased self-esteem and prestige for women in the workforce, especially at managerial levels, but decreased quality time spent with children, whose parents have less time to spend with them. Such aspects would be quite difficult to measure.

11. a. GDP equals the dollar amount Barry collects, which is $400.
b. NNP = GDP − depreciation = $400 − $50 = $350.
c. National income = NNP = $350.
d. Personal income = national income − retained earnings − indirect business taxes = $350 − $100 − $30 = $220.
e. Disposable personal income = personal income − personal income tax = $220 − $70 = $150.

11 MEASURING THE COST OF LIVING

WHAT'S NEW IN THE SIXTH EDITION:

A new *In the News* feature on "Shopping for the CPI" has been added.

s

LEARNING OBJECTIVES:

By the end of this chapter, students should understand:

➢ how the consumer price index (CPI) is constructed.

➢ why the CPI is an imperfect measure of the cost of living.

➢ how to compare the CPI and the GDP deflator as measures of the overall price level.

➢ how to use a price index to compare dollar figures from different times.

➢ the distinction between real and nominal interest rates.

CONTEXT AND PURPOSE:

Chapter 11 is the second chapter of a two-chapter sequence that deals with how economists measure output and prices in the macroeconomy. Chapter 10 addressed how economists measure output. Chapter 11 develops how economists measure the overall price level in the macroeconomy.

The purpose of Chapter 11 is twofold: first, to show students how to generate a price index and, second, to teach them how to employ a price index to compare dollar figures from different points in time and to adjust interest rates for inflation. In addition, students will learn some of the shortcomings of using the consumer price index as a measure of the cost of living.

KEY POINTS:

- The consumer price index (CPI) shows the cost of a basket of goods and services relative to the cost of the same basket in the base year. The index is used to measure the overall level of prices in the economy. The percentage change in the consumer price index measures the inflation rate.

- The consumer price index is an imperfect measure of the cost of living for three reasons. First, it does not take into account consumers' ability to substitute toward goods that become relatively cheaper over time. Second, it does not take into account increases in the purchasing power of the dollar due to the introduction of new goods. Third, it is distorted by unmeasured changes in the quality of goods and services. Because of these measurement problems, the CPI overstates annual inflation by about one percentage point.

- Like the consumer price index, the GDP deflator also measures the overall level of prices in the economy. Although the two price indexes usually move together, there are important differences. The GDP deflator differs from the CPI because it includes goods and services produced rather than goods and services consumed. As a result, imported goods affect the consumer price index but not the GDP deflator. In addition, while the consumer price index uses a fixed basket of goods, the GDP deflator automatically changes the group of goods and services over time as the composition of GDP changes.

- Dollar figures from different times do not represent a valid comparison of purchasing power. To compare a dollar figure from the past to a dollar figure today, the older figure should be inflated using a price index.

- Various laws and private contracts use price indexes to correct for the effects of inflation. The tax laws, however, are only partially indexed for inflation.

- A correction for inflation is especially important when looking at data on interest rates. The nominal interest rate is the interest rate usually reported; it is the rate at which the number of dollars in a savings account increases over time. By contrast, the real interest rate takes into account changes in the value of the dollar over time. The real interest rate equals the nominal interest rate minus the rate of inflation.

CHAPTER OUTLINE:

I. The Consumer Price Index

    A. Definition of **consumer price index (CPI): a measure of the overall cost of the goods and services bought by a typical consumer**.

    B. How the Consumer Price Index Is Calculated

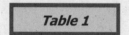

       1. Fix the basket.

          a. The Bureau of Labor Statistics uses surveys to determine a representative bundle of goods and services purchased by a typical consumer.

          b. Example: 4 hot dogs and 2 hamburgers.

2. Find the prices.

    a. Prices for each of the goods and services in the basket must be determined for each time period.

    b. Example:

Year	Price of Hot Dogs	Price of Hamburgers
2010	$1	$2
2011	$2	$3
2012	$3	$4

3. Compute the basket's cost.

    a. By keeping the basket the same, only prices are being allowed to change. This allows us to isolate the effects of price changes over time.

    b. Example:

    Cost in 2010 = ($1 × 4) + ($2 × 2) = $8.
    Cost in 2011 = ($2 × 4) + ($3 × 2) = $14.
    Cost in 2012 = ($3 × 4) + ($4 × 2) = $20.

It is very important that students understand how to make these calculations. Students often have a difficult time recreating the steps taken in class without the instructor's help.

ALTERNATIVE CLASSROOM EXAMPLE:
Using the example from Chapter 10:

1. Fix the basket: 3 footballs and 4 basketballs.

2. Find the prices:

Year	Price of Footballs	Price of Basketballs
Year 1	$10	$12
Year 2	12	15
Year 3	14	18

3. Compute the Cost of the Basket:
    Cost in Year 1 = (3 × $10) + (4 × $12) = $78
    Cost in Year 2 = (3 × $12) + (4 × $15) = $96
    Cost in Year 3 = (3 × $14) + (4 × $18) = $114

4. Using Year 1 as the base year, compute the index:
    CPI in Year 1 = ($78/$78) × 100 = 1 × 100 = 100
    CPI in Year 2 = ($96/$78) × 100 = 1.2308 × 100 = 123.08
    CPI in Year 3 = ($114/$78) × 100 = 1.4615 × 100 = 146.15

5. Compute the inflation rate:
    Inflation rate for Year 2 = [(123.08 − 100)/100] × 100% = 23.08%
    Inflation rate for Year 3 = [(146.15 − 123.08)/123.08] × 100% = 18.74%

Activity 1—Create a Student Price Index

Type: Take-home assignment
Topics: Consumer price index
Class limitations: Works in any size class

Purpose

This assignment gives students a practical look at how price indices are measured. It also establishes base prices for calculating inflation rates later in the term.

Instructions

The students should pick real transaction prices for goods they actually purchase. If the indices will be used to calculate inflation rate, they should save a copy of this assignment in a safe place. They should not use prices from catalogs because such prices will not be subject to much change over the semester.

Points for Discussion

This assignment makes a good introduction to a discussion of market basket selection for price indices. The goods that students usually pick for their market basket account for a relatively small portion of consumer spending compared to housing, medical care, transportation, etc. Ask the students which goods are likely to change price frequently.

This can be used to introduce problems with the measurement of the consumer price index.

Assignment

The consumer price index includes the prices of hundreds of goods purchased by consumers. It is possible to construct many other price indexes.

Your mission: Create a personalized student price index.

1. Choose five (or more) different products.
   — be specific e.g., unleaded gasoline, Budweiser beer
2. Pick a quantity for each product. This will be your market basket.
   — e.g., 15 gallons gasoline, 12 pack of Budweiser
3. Find the actual price for each product.
4. Calculate the total cost of buying these products.

At the end of the semester, have students find the prices for these same five products and recalculate the cost of their market basket. Then, have them calculate their SPI (Student Price Index) and the rate of inflation.

4. Choose a base year and compute the index.

   a. The base year is the benchmark against which other years are compared.

   b. The formula for calculating the price index is:

$$CPI = \left(\frac{\text{cost of basket in current year}}{\text{cost of basket in base year}} \right) \times 100$$

   c. Example (using 2010 as the base year):

$$\text{CPI for 2010} = (\$8)/(\$8) \times 100 = 100.$$
$$\text{CPI for 2011} = (\$14)/(\$8) \times 100 = 175.$$
$$\text{CPI for 2012} = (\$20)/(\$8) \times 100 = 250.$$

 Point out that the CPI must be equal to 100 in the base year.

5. Compute the inflation rate.

   a. Definition of **inflation rate: the percentage change in the price index from the preceding period**.

 Make sure that you explain that inflation does not mean that the prices of all goods in the economy are rising. Inflation means that prices *on average* are rising. In fact, the prices of many electronic goods (such as computers and DVD players) have fallen over time.

   b. The formula used to calculate the inflation rate is:

$$\text{inflation rate} = \left(\frac{\text{CPI}_{\text{Year 2}} - \text{CPI}_{\text{Year 1}}}{\text{CPI}_{\text{Year 1}}} \right) \times 100\%$$

   c. Example:

$$\text{Inflation Rate for 2011} = (175 - 100)/100 \times 100\% = 75\%.$$
$$\text{Inflation Rate for 2012} = (250 - 175)/175 \times 100\% = 43\%.$$

 Be sure to point out to students that it is possible for the CPI to fall if deflation is present. Point out to students that, even though they have not experienced deflation in their lifetimes, it has occurred during several periods of U.S. history (especially during the Great Depression).

C. The Producer Price Index

   1. Definition of **producer price index (PPI): a measure of the cost of a basket of goods and services bought by firms**.

   2. Because firms eventually pass on higher costs to consumers in the form of higher prices on products, the producer price index is believed to be useful in predicting changes in the CPI.

D. *FYI: What Is in the CPI's Basket?*

Figure 1

   1. Figure 1 shows the makeup of the market basket used to compute the CPI.

   2. The largest category is housing, which makes up 43% of a typical consumer's budget.

One way to highlight this is to draw the pie chart on the board without the category names and let the students decide what goes where. Most likely, they will be surprised by the sizes of recreation and medical care.

E. Problems in Measuring the Cost of Living

1. Substitution Bias

   a. When the price of one good changes, consumers often respond by substituting another good in its place.

   b. The CPI does not allow for this substitution; it is calculated using a fixed basket of goods and services.

   c. This implies that the CPI overstates the increase in the cost of living over time.

2. Introduction of New Goods

   a. When a new good is introduced, consumers have a wider variety of goods and services to choose from.

   b. This makes every dollar more valuable, which lowers the cost of maintaining the same level of economic well-being.

   c. Because the market basket is not revised often enough, these new goods are left out of the bundle of goods and services included in the basket.

3. Unmeasured Quality Change

   a. If the quality of a good falls from one year to the next, the value of a dollar falls; if quality rises, the value of the dollar rises.

   b. Attempts are made to correct prices for changes in quality, but it is often difficult to do so because quality is hard to measure.

4. The size of these problems is also difficult to measure.

5. Most studies indicate that the CPI overstates the rate of inflation by approximately one percentage point per year.

6. The issue is important because many government transfer programs (such as Social Security) are tied to increases in the CPI.

F. *In the News: Shopping for the CPI*

1. To collect the data for the CPI, thousands of individuals must check prices in stores.

2. This is an article that chronicles a day in the life of one of these shoppers.

G. The GDP Deflator versus the Consumer Price Index

1. The GDP deflator reflects the prices of all goods produced domestically, while the CPI reflects the prices of all goods bought by consumers.

Figure 2

2. The CPI compares the prices of a *fixed* basket of goods over time, while the GDP deflator compares the prices of the goods *currently produced* to the prices of the goods produced in the base year. This means that the group of goods and services used to compute the GDP deflator changes automatically over time as output changes.

3. Figure 2 shows the inflation rate as measured by both the CPI and the GDP deflator.

II. Correcting Economic Variables for the Effects of Inflation

A. Dollar Figures from Different Times

1. To change dollar values from one year to the next, we can use this formula:

$$\text{Value in Year 2 dollars} = \text{Value in Year 1 dollars} \times \left(\frac{\text{Price level in Year 2}}{\text{Price level in Year 1}} \right)$$

2. Example: Babe Ruth's 1931 salary in 2009 dollars:

$$\text{Salary in 2009 dollars} = \text{Salary in 1931 dollars} \times \frac{\text{Price level in 2009}}{\text{Price level in 1931}}$$

Salary in 2009 dollars = $80,000 × (214.5/15.2).
Salary in 2009 dollars = $1,128,947.

ALTERNATIVE CLASSROOM EXAMPLE:
Your father graduated from school and took his first job in 1972, which paid a salary of $7,000. What is this salary worth in 2009 dollars?

CPI in 1972 = 41.8
CPI in 2009 = 214.5

Value in 2009 dollars = 1972 salary × (CPI in 2009/CPI in 1972)
Value in 2009 dollars = $7,000 × (214.5/41.8) = $7,000 × 5.13 = $35,910

---

3. *FYI: Mr. Index Goes to Hollywood*

a. Reports of box office success are often made in terms of the dollar values of ticket sales.

b. These ticket sales are then compared with ticket sales of movies in the past.

c. However, no correction for changes in the value of a dollar are made.

Activity 2—You Paid How Much?

Type:	Take-home assignment
Topics:	Consumer price index
Class limitations:	Works in any size class

Purpose

This assignment gives students a chance to see how dollar values have changed over time. It also provides them some practice at using the formula to calculate changes in dollar values over time.

Instructions

Have students ask their parents (or grandparents) how much they paid for their first car and in what year they bought it. (If there are older students in the class, ask them to remember how much they paid for their first car.) Students can then determine how much they would have to pay in current dollars using the consumer price index.

Austin Powers: International Man of Mystery, Chapter 6. Austin Powers has been cryogenically frozen for 30 years and has no idea of the changes in prices that have occurred since the 1960s. This clip is a good way to illustrate how dollar values have changed over time.

B. Indexation

1. Definition **of** <u>indexation</u>: **the automatic correction of a dollar amount for the effects of inflation by law or contract**.

2. As mentioned above, many government transfer programs use indexation for the benefits. The government also indexes the tax brackets used for federal income tax.

3. There are uses of indexation in the private sector as well. Many labor contracts include cost-of-living allowances (COLAs).

C. Real and Nominal Interest Rates

Use an example to make the importance of real interest rates clear. Suppose a student has $100 in his savings account earning 3% interest. Ask students what will happen to the purchasing power of that money if prices rise 3% during the year. Then, change the inflation rate to 5% and then 1% and go through the example again.

---

1. Example: Sally Saver deposits $1,000 into a bank account that pays an annual interest rate of 10%. A year later, she withdraws $1,100.

2. What matters to Sally is the *purchasing power* of her money.

   a. If there is zero inflation, her purchasing power has risen by 10%.

   b. If there is 6% inflation, her purchasing power has risen by about 4%.

   c. If there is 10% inflation, her purchasing power has remained the same.

   d. If there is 12% inflation, her purchasing power has declined by about 2%.

   e. If there is 2% deflation, her purchasing power has risen by about 12%.

3. Definition of **nominal interest rate: the interest rate as usually reported without a correction for the effects of inflation**.

4. Definition of **real interest rate: the interest rate corrected for the effects of inflation**.

> real interest rate = nominal interest rate − inflation rate .

5. *Case Study: Interest Rates in the U.S. Economy*

Figure 3

   a. Figure 3 shows real and nominal interest rates from 1965 to the present.

   b. The nominal interest rate is always greater than the real interest rate in this diagram because there was always inflation during this period.

   c. Note that in the late 1970s the real interest rate was negative because the inflation rate exceeded the nominal interest rate.

SOLUTIONS TO TEXT PROBLEMS:

Quick Quizzes

1. The consumer price index measures the overall cost of the goods and services bought by a typical consumer. It is constructed by surveying consumers to determine a basket of goods and services that the typical consumer buys. Prices of these goods and services are used to compute the cost of the basket at different times, and a base year is chosen. To compute the index, we divide the cost of the market basket in the current year by the cost of the market basket in the base year and multiply by 100.

    The CPI is an imperfect measure of the cost of living because of (1) substitution bias, (2) the introduction of new goods, and (3) unmeasured quality changes.

2. Since Henry Ford paid his workers $5 a day in 1914 and the consumer price index was 10 in 1914 and 218 in 2010, then the Ford paycheck was worth $5 × 218 / 10 = $109 a day in 2010 dollars.

Questions for Review

1. A 10% increase in the price of chicken has a greater effect on the consumer price index than a 10% increase in the price of caviar because chicken is a bigger part of the average consumer's market basket.

2. The three problems in the consumer price index as a measure of the cost of living are: (1) substitution bias, which arises because people substitute toward goods that have become relatively less expensive; (2) the introduction of new goods, which are not reflected quickly in the CPI; and (3) unmeasured quality change.

3. If the price of a Navy submarine rises, there is no effect on the consumer price index, because Navy submarines are not consumer goods. But the GDP price index is affected, because Navy submarines are included in GDP as a part of government purchases.

4. Because the overall price level doubled, but the price of the candy bar rose sixfold, the real price (the price adjusted for inflation) of the candy bar tripled.

5. The nominal interest rate is the rate of interest paid on a loan in dollar terms. The real interest rate is the rate of interest corrected for inflation. The real interest rate is the nominal interest rate minus the rate of inflation.

Problems and Applications

1. Answers will vary. Students should multiply $100 by the CPI for the year in which they were born and then divide by 100.

2. a. Find the price of each good in each year:

Year	Cauliflower	Broccoli	Carrots
2010	$2	$1.50	$0.10
2011	$3	$1.50	$0.20

    b. If 2010 is the base year, the market basket used to compute the CPI is 100 heads of cauliflower, 50 bunches of broccoli, and 500 carrots. We must now calculate the cost of the market basket in each year:
    2010: $(100 \times \$2) + (50 \times \$1.50) + (500 \times \$.10) = \$325$
    2011: $(100 \times \$3) + (50 \times \$1.50) + (500 \times \$.20) = \$475$

    Then, using 2010 as the base year, we can compute the CPI in each year:
    2010: $\$325/\$325 \times 100 = 100$
    2011: $\$475/\$325 \times 100 = 146$

    c. We can use the CPI to compute the inflation rate for 2011:
    $(146 - 100)/100 \times 100\% = 46\%$

3. a. The percentage change in the price of tennis balls is $(2 - 2)/2 \times 100\% = 0\%$.
    The percentage change in the price of golf balls is $(6 - 4)/4 \times 100\% = 50\%$.
    The percentage change in the price of Gatorade is $(2 - 1)/1 \times 100\% = 100\%$.

    b. The cost of the market basket in 2011 is $(\$2 \times 100) + (\$4 \times 100) + (\$1 \times 200) = \$200 + \$400 + \$200 = \$800$.

The cost of the market basket in 2012 is ($2 × 100) + ($6 × 100) + ($2 × 200) = $200 + $600 + $400 = $1,200.

The percentage change in the cost of the market basket from 2011 to 2012 is (1,200 − 800)/800 × 100% = 50%.

c. This would lower my estimation of the inflation rate because the value of a bottle of Gatorade is now greater than before. The comparison should be made on a per-ounce basis.

d. More flavors enhance consumers' well-being. Thus, this would be considered a change in quality and would also lower my estimate of the inflation rate.

4. Answers will vary.

5. a. The cost of the market basket in 2011 is (1 × $40) + (3 × $10) = $40 + $30 = $70.

The cost of the market basket in 2012 is (1 × $60) + (3 × $12) = $60 + $36 = $96.

Using 2011 as the base year, we can compute the CPI in each year:
2011: $70/$70 × 100 = 100
2012: $96/$70 × 100 = 137.14

We can use the CPI to compute the inflation rate for 2012:
(137.14 − 100)/100 × 100% = 37.14%

b. Nominal GDP for 2011 = (10 × $40) + (30 × $10) = $400 + $300 = $700.

Nominal GDP for 2012 = (12 × $60) + (50 × $12) = $720 + $600 = $1,320.

Real GDP for 2011 = (10 × $40) + (30 × $10) = $400 + $300 = $700.

Real GDP for 2012 = (12 × $40) + (50 × $10) = $480 + $500 = $980.

The GDP deflator for 2011 = (700/700) × 100 = 100.

The GDP deflator for 2012 = (1,320/980) × 100 = 134.69.

The rate of inflation for 2012 = (134.69 − 100)/100 × 100% = 34.69%.

c. No, it is not the same. The rate of inflation calculated by the CPI holds the basket of goods and services constant, while the GDP deflator allows it to change.

6. a. introduction of new goods; b. unmeasured quality change; c. substitution bias; d. unmeasured quality change; e. substitution bias

7. a. ($2.00 − $0.15)/$0.15 × 100% = 1,233%.

b. ($20.42 − $3.23)/$3.23 × 100% = 532%.

c. In 1970: $0.15/($3.23/60) = 2.8 minutes. In 2009: $2.00/($20.42/60) = 5.9 minutes.

    d. Workers' purchasing power fell in terms of newspapers.

8. a. If the elderly consume the same market basket as other people, Social Security would provide the elderly with an improvement in their standard of living each year because the CPI overstates inflation and Social Security payments are tied to the CPI.

    b. Because the elderly consume more health care than younger people do, and because health care costs have risen faster than overall inflation, it is possible that the elderly are worse off. To investigate this, you would need to put together a market basket for the elderly, which would have a higher weight on health care. You would then compare the rise in the cost of the "elderly" basket with that of the general basket for CPI.

9. In deciding how much income to save for retirement, workers should consider the real interest rate, because they care about their purchasing power in the future, not simply the number of dollars they will have.

10. a. When inflation is higher than was expected, the real interest rate is lower than expected. For example, suppose the market equilibrium has an expected real interest rate of 3% and people expect inflation to be 4%, so the nominal interest rate is 7%. If inflation turns out to be 5%, the real interest rate is 7% minus 5% equals 2%, which is less than the 3% that was expected.

    b. Because the real interest rate is lower than was expected, the lender loses and the borrower gains. The borrower is repaying the loan with dollars that are worth less than was expected.

    c. Homeowners in the 1970s who had fixed-rate mortgages from the 1960s benefited from the unexpected inflation, while the banks that made the mortgage loans were harmed.

PRODUCTION AND GROWTH

WHAT'S NEW IN THE SIXTH EDITION:

There is a new *In the News* box on "One Economist's Answer:"

LEARNING OBJECTIVES:

By the end of this chapter, students should understand:

➢ how much economic growth differs around the world.

➢ why productivity is the key determinant of a country's standard of living.

➢ the factors that determine a country's productivity.

➢ how a country's policies influence its productivity growth.

CONTEXT AND PURPOSE:

Chapter 12 is the first chapter in a four-chapter sequence on the production of output in the long run. Chapter 12 addresses the determinants of the level and growth rate of output. We find that capital and labor are among the primary determinants of output. In Chapter 13, we address how saving and investment in capital goods affect the production of output, and in Chapter 14, we learn about some of the tools people and firms use when choosing capital projects in which to invest. In Chapter 15, we address the market for labor.

The purpose of Chapter 12 is to examine the long-run determinants of both the level and the growth rate of real GDP per person. Along the way, we will discover the factors that determine the productivity of workers and address what governments might do to improve the productivity of their citizens.

KEY POINTS:

- Economic prosperity, as measured by GDP per person, varies substantially around the world. The average income in the world's richest countries is more than ten times that in the world's poorest countries. Because growth rates of real GDP also vary substantially, the relative positions of countries can change dramatically over time.

209

- The standard of living in an economy depends on the economy's ability to produce goods and services. Productivity, in turn, depends on the amounts of physical capital, human capital, natural resources, and technological knowledge available to workers.

- Government policies can try to influence the economy's growth rate in many ways: encouraging saving and investment, encouraging investment from abroad, fostering education, promoting good health, maintaining property rights and political stability, allowing free trade, and promoting the research and development of new technologies.

- The accumulation of capital is subject to diminishing returns: The more capital an economy has, the less additional output the economy gets from an extra unit of capital. As a result, while higher saving leads to higher growth for a period of time, growth eventually slows down as the economy approaches a higher level of capital, productivity, and income. Also because of diminishing returns, the return to capital is especially high in poor countries. Other things being equal, these countries can grow faster because of the catch-up effect.

- Population growth has a variety of effects on economic growth. On the one hand, more rapid population growth may lower productivity by stretching the supply of natural resources and by reducing the amount of capital available for each worker. On the other hand, a larger population may enhance the rate of technological progress because there are more scientists and engineers.

CHAPTER OUTLINE:

I. Economic Growth Around the World

Table 1

A. Table 1 shows data on real GDP per person for 13 countries during different periods of time.

   1. The data reveal the fact that living standards vary a great deal between these countries.

   2. Growth rates are also reported in the table. Japan has had the largest growth rate over time, 2.76% per year (on average).

> Use Table 1 to make the point that a one-percentage point change in a country's growth rate can make a significant difference over several generations. The powerful effects of compounding should be used to underscore the process of economic growth.

   3. Because of different growth rates, the ranking of countries by income per person changes over time.

      a. In the late 19th century, the United Kingdom was the richest country in the world.

      b. Today, income per person is lower in the United Kingdom than in the United States (a former colony of the United Kingdom).

B. *FYI: Are You Richer Than the Richest American?*

1. According to the magazine *American Heritage*, the richest American of all time is John B. Rockefeller, whose wealth today would be the equivalent of approximately $200 billion.

2. Yet, because Rockefeller lived from 1839 to 1937, he did not get the chance to enjoy many of the conveniences we take for granted today such as television, air conditioning, and modern medicine.

3. Thus, because of technological advances, the average American today may enjoy a "richer" life than the richest American who lived a century ago.

C. *FYI: A Picture Is Worth a Thousand Statistics*

1. This box presents three photos showing a typical family in three countries – the United Kingdom, Mexico, and Mali. Each family was photographed outside their home, together with all of their material possessions.

2. These photos demonstrate the vast difference in the standards of living in these countries.

II. Productivity: Its Role and Determinants

A. Why Productivity Is So Important

1. Example: Robinson Crusoe

a. Because he is stranded alone, he must catch his own fish, grow his own vegetables, and make his own clothes.

b. His standard of living depends on his ability to produce goods and services.

2. Definition of **productivity: the amount of goods and services a worker produces in each hour of work.**

3. Review of Principle #8: A Country's Standard of Living Depends on Its Ability to Produce Goods and Services.

B. How Productivity Is Determined

1. Physical Capital per Worker

a. Definition of **physical capital: the stock of equipment and structures that are used to produce goods and services**.

b. Example: Crusoe will catch more fish if he has more fishing poles.

2. Human Capital per Worker

a. Definition of **human capital: the knowledge and skills that workers acquire through education, training, and experience**.

b. Example: Crusoe will catch more fish if he has been trained in the best fishing techniques or as he gains experience fishing.

3. Natural Resources per Worker

    a. Definition of **natural resources: the inputs into the production of goods and services that are provided by nature, such as land, rivers, and mineral deposits**.

    b. Example: Crusoe will have better luck catching fish if there is a plentiful supply around his island.

4. Technological Knowledge

    a. Definition of **technological knowledge: society's understanding of the best ways to produce goods and services**.

    b. Example: Crusoe will catch more fish if he has invented a better fishing lure.

    c. *Case Study: Are Natural Resources a Limit to Growth?* This section points out that as the population has grown over time, we have discovered ways to lower our use of natural resources. Thus, most economists are not worried about shortages of natural resources.

 Cast Away. Chuck Noland is stranded on an island alone. His ability to consume is solely dependent on his ability to produce.

C. *FYI: The Production Function*

1. A production function describes the relationship between the quantity of inputs used in production and the quantity of output from production.

2. The production function generally is written like this:

$$Y = A\,F(L,\ K,\ H,\ N)$$

where Y = output, L = quantity of labor, K = quantity of physical capital, H = quantity of human capital, N = quantity of natural resources, A reflects the available production technology, and $F()$ is a function that shows how inputs are combined to produce output.

3. Many production functions have a property called constant returns to scale.

    a. This property implies that as all inputs are doubled, output will exactly double.

    b. This implies that the following must be true:

$$xY = A\,F(xL,\ xK,\ xH,\ xN)$$

    where $x = 2$ if inputs are doubled.

    c. This also means that if we want to examine output per worker we could set $x = 1/L$ and we would get the following:

$$Y/L = A\,F(1,\ K/L,\ H/L,\ N/L)$$

This shows that output per worker depends on the amount of physical capital per worker (K/L), the amount of human capital per worker (H/L), and the amount of natural resources per worker (N/L).

III. Economic Growth and Public Policy

 Start out by asking students what factors they believe will lead to greater economic growth in the future.

A. Saving and Investment

1. Because capital is a produced factor of production, a society can change the amount of capital that it has.

2. However, there is an opportunity cost of doing so; if resources are used to produce capital goods, fewer goods and services are produced for current consumption.

B. Diminishing Returns and the Catch-Up Effect

1. Definition of **diminishing returns: the property whereby the benefit from an extra unit of an input declines as the quantity of the input increases**.

Figure 1

a. As the capital stock rises, the extra output produced from an additional unit of capital will fall.

b. This can be seen in Figure 1, which shows how the amount of capital per worker determines the amount of output per worker, holding constant all other determinants of output.

c. Thus, if workers already have a large amount of capital to work with, giving them an additional unit of capital will not increase their productivity by much.

d. In the long run, a higher saving rate leads to a higher level of productivity and income, but not to higher growth rates in these variables.

2. An important implication of diminishing returns is the catch-up effect.

a. Definition of **catch-up effect: the property whereby countries that start off poor tend to grow more rapidly than countries that start off rich**.

b. When workers have very little capital to begin with, an additional unit of capital will increase their productivity by a great deal.

C. Investment from Abroad

1. Saving by domestic residents is not the only way for a country to invest in new capital.

2. Investment in the country by foreigners can also occur.

      a. Foreign direct investment occurs when a capital investment is owned and operated by a foreign entity.

      b. Foreign portfolio investment occurs when a capital investment is financed with foreign money but operated by domestic residents.

  3. Some of the benefits of foreign investment flow back to foreign owners. But the economy still experiences an increase in the capital stock, which leads to higher productivity and higher wages.

  4. The World Bank is an organization that tries to encourage the flow of investment to poor countries.

      a. The World Bank obtains funds from developed countries such as the United States and makes loans to less-developed countries so that they can invest in roads, sewer systems, schools, and other types of capital.

      b. The World Bank also offers these countries advice on how best to use these funds.

D. Education

  1. Investment in human capital also has an opportunity cost.

      a. When students are in class, they cannot be producing goods and services for consumption.

      b. In less-developed countries, this opportunity cost is considered to be high; as a result, children often drop out of school at a young age.

  2. Because there are positive externalities in education, the effect of lower education on the economic growth rate of a country can be large.

  3. Many poor countries also face a "brain drain"—the best educated often leave to go to other countries where they can enjoy a higher standard of living.

  4. *In the News: Promoting Human Capital*

      a. Human capital is a key to economic growth.

      b. This is an article that describes how some developing countries now give parents an immediate financial incentive to keep their children in school.

E. Health and Nutrition

  1. Human capital can also be used to describe another type of investment in people: expenditures that lead to a healthier population.

  2. Other things being equal, healthier workers are more productive.

  3. Making the right investments in the health of the population is one way for a nation to increase productivity.

F. Property Rights and Political Stability

1. Protection of property rights and promotion of political stability are two other important ways that policymakers can improve economic growth.

2. There is little incentive to produce products if there is no guarantee that they cannot be taken. Contracts must also be enforced.

3. Countries with questionable enforcement of property rights or an unstable political climate will also have difficulty in attracting foreign (or even domestic) investment.

G. Free Trade

1. Some countries have tried to achieve faster economic growth by avoiding transacting with the rest of the world.

2. However, trade allows a country to specialize in what it does best and thus consume beyond its production possibilities.

3. When a country trades wheat for steel, it is as well off as it would be if it had developed a new technology for turning wheat into steel.

4. The amount a nation trades is determined not only by government policy but also by geography.

    a. Countries with good, natural seaports find trade easier than countries without this resource.

    b. Countries with more than 80 percent of their population living within 100 kilometers of a coast have an average GDP per person that is four times as large as countries with 20 percent of their population living near a coast.

H. Research and Development

1. The primary reason why living standards have improved over time has been due to large increases in technological knowledge.

2. Knowledge can be considered a public good.

3. The U.S. government promotes the creation of new technological information by providing research grants and providing tax incentives for firms engaged in research.

4. The patent system also encourages research by granting an inventor the exclusive right to produce the product for a specified number of years.

I. Population Growth

1. Stretching Natural Resources

    a. Thomas Malthus (an English minister and early economic thinker) argued that an ever-increasing population meant that the world was doomed to live in poverty forever.

   b. However, he failed to understand that new ideas would be developed to increase the production of food and other goods, including pesticides, fertilizers, mechanized equipment, and new crop varieties.

2. Diluting the Capital Stock

   a. High population growth reduces GDP per worker because rapid growth in the number of workers forces the capital stock to be spread more thinly.
   b. Countries with a high population growth have large numbers of school-age children, placing a burden on the education system.

3. Some countries have already instituted measures to reduce population growth rates.

4. Policies that foster equal treatment for women should raise economic opportunities for women leading to lower rates of population.

5. Promoting Technological Progress

   a. Some economists have suggested that population growth has driven technological progress and economic prosperity.

   b. In a 1993 journal article, economist Michael Kremer provided evidence that increases in population lead to technological progress.

Start a class discussion of the trade-offs that are necessary to sustain economic growth. Point out that current consumption must be forgone for higher consumption in the future. Ask students to examine the trade-offs involved with each of the public policies discussed.

   J. *In the News: One Economist's Answer*

   1. Why do some nations thrive while others do not?

   2. This is an article by economist Daron Acemoglu providing his ideas on the answers to this question.

SOLUTIONS TO TEXT PROBLEMS:

Quick Quizzes

1. The approximate growth rate of real GDP per person in the United States is 1.80 percent (based on Table 1) from 1870 to 2008. Countries that have had faster growth include Japan, Brazil, Mexico, Germany, Canada, China, and Argentina; countries that have had slower growth include United Kingdom, India, Indonesia, Pakistan, and Bangladesh.

2. The four determinants of a country's productivity are: (1) physical capital, which is the stock of equipment and structures that are used to produce goods and services; (2) human capital, which is the knowledge and skills that workers acquire through education, training, and experience; (3) natural resources, which are inputs into production that are provided by

nature, such as land, rivers, and mineral deposits; and (4) technological knowledge, which is society's understanding of the best ways to produce goods and services.

3. Ways in which a government policymaker can try to raise the growth in living standards in a society include: (1) investing more current resources in the production of capital, which has the drawback of reducing the resources used for producing current consumption; (2) encouraging investment from abroad, which has the drawback that some of the benefits of investment flow to foreigners; (3) increasing education, which has an opportunity cost in that students are not engaged in current production; (4) protecting property rights and promoting political stability, for which no drawbacks are obvious; (5) pursuing outward-oriented policies to encourage free trade, which may have the drawback of making a country more dependent on its trading partners; (6) reducing the rate of population growth, which may have the drawbacks of reducing individual freedom and lowering the rate of technological progress; and (7) encouraging research and development, which (like investment) may have the drawback of reducing current consumption.

Questions for Review

1. The level of a nation's GDP measures both the total income earned in the economy and the total expenditure on the economy's output of goods and services. The level of real GDP is a good gauge of economic prosperity, and the growth of real GDP is a good gauge of economic progress. You would rather live in a nation with a high level of GDP, even though it had a low growth rate, than in a nation with a low level of GDP and a high growth rate, because the level of GDP is a measure of prosperity.

2. The four determinants of productivity are: (1) physical capital, which is the stock of equipment and structures that are used to produce goods and services; (2) human capital, which consists of the knowledge and skills that workers acquire through education, training, and experience; (3) natural resources, which are inputs into production that are provided by nature; and (4) technological knowledge, which is society's understanding of the best ways to produce goods and services.

3. A college degree is a form of human capital. The skills learned in earning a college degree increase a worker's productivity.

4. Higher saving means fewer resources are devoted to consumption and more to producing capital goods. The rise in the capital stock leads to rising productivity and more rapid growth in GDP for a while. In the long run, the higher saving rate leads to a higher standard of living. A policymaker might be deterred from trying to raise the rate of saving because doing so requires that people reduce their consumption today and it can take a long time to get to a higher standard of living.

5. A higher rate of saving leads to a higher growth rate temporarily, not permanently. In the short run, increased saving leads to a larger capital stock and faster growth. But as growth continues, diminishing returns to capital mean growth slows down and eventually settles down to its initial rate, though this may take several decades.

6. Removing a trade restriction, such as a tariff, would lead to more rapid economic growth because the removal of the trade restriction acts like an improvement in technology. Free trade allows all countries to consume more goods and services.

7. The higher the rate of population growth, the lower is the level of GDP per person because there's less capital per person, hence lower productivity.

8. The U.S. government tries to encourage advances in technological knowledge by providing research grants through the National Science Foundation and the National Institute of Health, with tax breaks for firms engaging in research and development, and through the patent system.

Problems and Applications

1. The facts that countries import many goods and services yet must produce a large quantity of goods and services themselves to enjoy a high standard of living are reconciled by noting that there are substantial gains from trade. In order to be able to afford to purchase goods from other countries, an economy must generate income. By producing many goods and services, then trading them for goods and services produced in other countries, a nation maximizes its standard of living.

2. a. More investment would lead to faster economic growth in the short run.

   b. The change would benefit many people in society who would have higher incomes as the result of faster economic growth. However, there might be a transition period in which workers and owners in consumption-good industries would get lower incomes, and workers and owners in investment-good industries would get higher incomes. In addition, some group would have to reduce their spending for some time so that investment could rise.

3. a. Private consumption spending includes buying food and buying clothes; private investment spending includes people buying houses and firms buying computers. Many other examples are possible. Education can be considered as both consumption and investment.

   b. Government consumption spending includes paying workers to administer government programs; government investment spending includes buying military equipment and building roads. Many other examples are possible. Government spending on health programs is an investment in human capital. This is truer for spending on health programs for the young rather than those for the elderly.

4. The opportunity cost of investing in capital is the loss of consumption that results from redirecting resources toward investment. Over-investment in capital is possible because of diminishing marginal returns. A country can "over-invest" in capital if people would prefer to have higher consumption spending and less future growth. The opportunity cost of investing in human capital is also the loss of consumption that is needed to provide the resources for investment. A country could "over-invest" in human capital if people were too highly educated for the jobs they could get—for example, if the best job a Ph.D. in philosophy could find is managing a restaurant.

5. a. When a German firm opens a factory in South Carolina, it represents foreign direct investment.

   b. The investment increases U.S. GDP because it increases production in the United States. The effect on U.S. GNP would be smaller because the owners would get paid a return on their investment that would be part of German GNP rather than U.S. GNP.

6. a. The United States benefited from the Chinese and Japanese investment because it made our capital stock larger, increasing our economic growth.

   b. It would have been better for the United States to make the investments itself because then it would have received the returns on the investment itself, instead of the returns going to China and Japan.

7. Greater educational opportunities for women could lead to faster economic growth in these developing countries because increased human capital would increase productivity and there would be external effects from greater knowledge in the country. Second, increased educational opportunities for young women may lower the population growth rate because such opportunities raise the opportunity cost of having a child.

8. a. Individuals with higher incomes have better access to clean water, medical care, and good nutrition.

   b. Healthier individuals are likely to be more productive.

   c. Understanding the direction of causation will help policymakers place proper emphasis on the programs that will achieve both greater health and higher incomes.

9. a. Political stability could lead to strong economic growth by making the country attractive to investors. The increased investment would raise economic growth.

   b. Strong economic growth could lead to political stability because when people have high incomes they tend to be satisfied with the political system and are less likely to overthrow or change the government.

10. a. If output is rising and the number of workers is declining, then output per worker must be rising.

    b. Policymakers should not be concerned as long as output in the manufacturing sector is not declining. The reduction in manufacturing jobs will allow labor resources to move to other industries, increasing total output in the economy. An increase in productivity of workers (as measured by output per worker) is beneficial to the economy.

13 SAVING, INVESTMENT, AND THE FINANCIAL SYSTEM

WHAT'S NEW IN THE SIXTH EDITION:

A new *FYI* box on "Financial Crises" has been added. The *Case Study* on "The History of U.S. Government Debt" has been updated.

LEARNING OBJECTIVES:

By the end of this chapter, students should understand:

➤ some of the important financial institutions in the U.S. economy.

➤ how the financial system is related to key macroeconomic variables.

➤ the model of the supply and demand for loanable funds in financial markets.

➤ how to use the loanable-funds model to analyze various government policies.

➤ how government budget deficits affect the U.S. economy.

CONTEXT AND PURPOSE:

Chapter 13 is the second chapter in a four-chapter sequence on the production of output in the long run. In Chapter 12, we found that capital and labor are among the primary determinants of output. For this reason, Chapter 13 addresses the market for saving and investment in capital, and Chapter 14 addresses the tools people and firms use when choosing capital projects in which to invest. Chapter 15 will address the market for labor.

The purpose of Chapter 13 is to show how saving and investment are coordinated by the loanable funds market. Within the framework of the loanable funds market, we are able to see the effects of taxes and government deficits on saving, investment, the accumulation of capital, and ultimately, the growth rate of output.

KEY POINTS:

• The U.S. financial system is made up of many types of financial institutions, such as the bond market, the stock market, banks, and mutual funds. All of these institutions act to direct the resources of households that want to save some of their income into the hands of households and firms who want to borrow.

220

- National income accounting identities reveal some important relationships among macroeconomic variables. In particular, for a closed economy, national saving must equal investment. Financial institutions are the mechanism through which the economy matches one person's saving with another person's investment.

- The interest rate is determined by the supply and demand for loanable funds. The supply of loanable funds comes from households who want to save some of their income and lend it out. The demand for loanable funds comes from households and firms who want to borrow for investment. To analyze how any policy or event affects the interest rate, one must consider how it affects the supply and demand for loanable funds.

- National saving equals private saving plus public saving. A government budget deficit represents negative public saving and, therefore, reduces national saving and the supply of loanable funds available to finance investment. When a government budget deficit crowds out investment, it reduces the growth of productivity and GDP.

CHAPTER OUTLINE:

I. Definition of **financial system: the group of institutions in the economy that help to match one person's saving with another person's investment**.

II. Financial Institutions in the U.S. Economy

   A. Financial Markets

      1. Definition of **financial markets: financial institutions through which savers can directly provide funds to borrowers**.

      2. The Bond Market

         a. Definition of **bond: a certificate of indebtedness**.

         b. A bond identifies the date of maturity and the rate of interest that will be paid periodically until the loan matures.

         c. One important characteristic that determines a bond's value is its term. The term is the length of time until the bond matures. All else being equal, long-term bonds pay higher rates of interest than short-term bonds.

         d. Another important characteristic of a bond is its credit risk, which is the probability that the borrower will fail to pay some of the interest or principal. All else being equal, the more risky a bond is, the higher its interest rate.

         e. A third important characteristic of a bond is its tax treatment. For example, when state and local governments issue bonds (called municipal bonds), the interest income earned by the holders of these bonds is not taxed by the federal government. This makes the bonds more attractive, lowering the interest rate needed to entice people to buy them.

3. The Stock Market

   a. Definition of **stock: a claim to partial ownership in a firm**.

   b. The sale of stock to raise money is called *equity finance*; the sale of bonds to raise money is called *debt finance*.

   c. Stocks are sold on organized stock exchanges (such as the New York Stock Exchange or NASDAQ) and the prices of stocks are determined by supply and demand.

   d. The price of a stock generally reflects the perception of a company's future profitability.

   e. A *stock index* is computed as an average of a group of stock prices.

   f. *FYI: Key Numbers for Stock Watchers* describes three key numbers that are reported on the financial pages.

B. Financial Intermediaries

   1. Definition of **financial intermediaries: financial institutions through which savers can indirectly provide funds to borrowers**.

   2. Banks

      a. The primary role of banks is to take in deposits from people who want to save and then lend them out to others who want to borrow.

      b. Banks pay depositors interest on their deposits and charge borrowers a slightly higher rate of interest to cover the costs of running the bank and provide the bank owners with some amount of profit.

      c. Banks also play another important role in the economy by allowing individuals to use checking deposits as a medium of exchange.

   3. Mutual Funds

      a. Definition of **mutual fund: an institution that sells shares to the public and uses the proceeds to buy a portfolio of stocks and bonds**.

      b. The primary advantage of a mutual fund is that it allows individuals with small amounts of money to diversify.

      c. Mutual funds called "index funds" buy all of the stocks of a given stock index. These funds have generally performed better than funds with active fund managers. This may be true because they trade stocks less frequently and they do not have to pay the salaries of fund managers.

Activity 1—Create a Portfolio

Type: Take-home assignment
Topics: Financial markets
Class limitations: Works in any size class

Purpose
This assignment requires students to use the financial pages of the newspaper to create their own portfolio. Many students are unfamiliar with the basic elements of stock and bond tables. This assignment then asks students to analyze elements that would affect their portfolio.

Instructions
Ask the students to do the following assignment. Many possible variations exist. It can be worthwhile to have students reevaluate their portfolio at the end of the semester.

1. Assume you have $100,000 in savings. Create a portfolio of securities worth $100,000. Decide what financial instruments you would like to use, then find their current prices in the newspaper. Calculate your holdings of each security based on current prices.
2. What objectives do you have for this portfolio? Was it chosen to maximize short-term gains, long-term stability, or some other objective?
3. Explain how each of the following economic events would affect the value of your portfolio:
   a. an increase or decrease in interest rates
   b. a recession
   c. rapid inflation
   d. a depreciation of the U.S. dollar

Common Answers and Points for Discussion
Most students pick a mix of common stocks, mutual funds, and bonds. Some choose familiar, low-risk, but low-yielding bank accounts and certificates of deposit. A few may choose more sophisticated financial instruments.

This can be used to introduce the trade-off between risk and return and the concept of the risk premium.

The impact of macroeconomic events on financial markets usually interests students. Portfolios heavily invested in cyclical stocks will give low returns in the event of recession. Bonds and cash perform poorly with unanticipated inflation. Foreign-denominated assets may give high returns if the dollar depreciates. Interest rate changes can cause large swings in the value of bond-heavy portfolios.

C. Summing Up

   1. There are many financial institutions in the U.S. economy.

   2. These institutions all serve the same goal—moving funds from savers to borrowers.

D. *FYI: Financial Crises*

   1. What are the key elements of a financial crisis?

      a. A large decline in asset prices.

b. Insolvencies at some financial institutions.

c. A decline in confidence in financial institutions.

d. A credit crunch.

e. An economic downturn.

f. A vicious circle.

2. Financial crises do have serious consequences but eventually end.

III. Saving and Investment in the National Income Accounts

 Make sure that you work through all of the algebraic steps here. Students will not understand this material if you skip steps.

A. Some Important Identities

1. Remember that GDP can be divided up into four components: consumption, investment, government purchases, and net exports.

$$Y = C + I + G + NX$$

2. We will assume that we are dealing with a closed economy (an economy that does not engage in international trade or international borrowing and lending). This implies that GDP can now be divided into only three components:

$$Y = C + I + G$$

3. To isolate investment, we can subtract C and G from both sides:

$$Y - C - G = I$$

4. The left-hand side of this equation ($Y - C - G$) is the total income in the economy after paying for consumption and government purchases. This amount is called national saving.

5. Definition of **national saving (saving): the total income in the economy that remains after paying for consumption and government purchases**.

6. Substituting saving (S) into our identity gives us:

$$S = I$$

7. This equation tells us that saving equals investment.

8. Let's go back to our definition of national saving once again:

$$S = Y - C - G$$

9. We can add taxes (T) and subtract taxes (T):

$$S = (Y - C - T) + (T - G)$$

10. The first part of this equation ($Y - T - C$) is called private saving; the second part ($T - G$) is called public saving.

   a. Definition of **private saving: the income that households have left after paying for taxes and consumption**.

   b. Definition of **public saving: the tax revenue that the government has left after paying for its spending**.

   c. Definition of **budget surplus: an excess of tax revenue over government spending**.

   d. Definition of **budget deficit: a shortfall of tax revenue from government spending**.

The important point to make here is that with a government budget deficit, public saving is negative and the public sector is thus "dissaving." To make up for this shortfall, it must go to the loanable funds market and borrow the money. This will reduce the supply of loanable funds available for investment.

11. The fact that $S = I$ means that (for the economy as a whole) saving must be equal to investment.

   a. The bond market, the stock market, banks, mutual funds, and other financial markets and institutions stand between the two sides of the $S = I$ equation.

   b. These markets and institutions take in the nation's saving and direct it to the nation's investment.

B. The Meaning of Saving and Investment

1. In macroeconomics, investment refers to the purchase of new capital, such as equipment or buildings.

You will have to keep reminding students what the term "investment" means to economists. Outside of the economics profession, most people use the terms "saving" and "investing" interchangeably.

2. If an individual spends less than he earns and uses the rest to buy stocks or mutual funds, economists call this saving.

IV. The Market for Loanable Funds

   A. Definition of **market for loanable funds: the market in which those who want to save supply funds and those who want to borrow to invest demand funds.**

   B. Supply and Demand for Loanable Funds

Figure 1

   1. The supply of loanable funds comes from those who spend less than they earn. The supply can occur directly through the purchase of some stock or bonds or indirectly through a financial intermediary.

   2. The demand for loanable funds comes from households and firms who wish to borrow funds to make investments. Families generally invest in new homes while firms may borrow to purchase new equipment or to build factories.

   3. The price of a loan is the interest rate.

 Students will wonder which interest rate is the price of a loan. Explain to them that interest rates in the economy do vary because of the things discussed earlier (term, risk, and tax treatment), but that these interest rates tend to move together when changes in the loanable funds market occur. Thus, it is appropriate to talk of one interest rate.

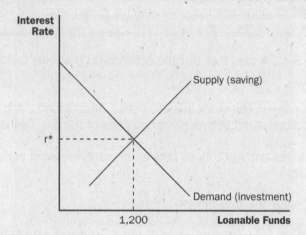

   a. All else equal, as the interest rate rises, the quantity of loanable funds supplied will increase.

   b. All else equal, as the interest rate rises, the quantity of loanable funds demanded will fall.

 Make sure that you spend time discussing why the demand for loanable funds is downward sloping and why the supply of loanable funds is upward sloping. It is important for students to understand the relationships among the interest rate, saving, and investment.

---

4. At equilibrium, the quantity of funds demanded is equal to the quantity of funds supplied.

   a. If the interest rate in the market is greater than the equilibrium rate, the quantity of funds demanded would be smaller than the quantity of funds supplied. Lenders would compete for borrowers, driving the interest rate down.

   b. If the interest rate in the market is less than the equilibrium rate, the quantity of funds demanded would be greater than the quantity of funds supplied. The shortage of loanable funds would encourage lenders to raise the interest rate they charge.

> It is a good idea to remind students that the supply of loanable funds comes from saving and the demand for loanable funds comes from investment by putting "(saving)" next to the supply curve and "(investment)" next to the demand curve as shown above.

5. The supply and demand for loanable funds depends on the real (rather than nominal) interest rate because the real rate reflects the true return to saving and the true cost of borrowing.

> When examining the next three sections on different policies, encourage students to follow the three-step process developed in Chapter 4. First, determine which curve is affected. Then, decide which way it shifts to determine the effects on the equilibrium interest rate and quantity of funds.

C. Policy 1: Saving Incentives

Figure 2

1. Savings rates in the United States are relatively low when compared with other countries such as Japan and Germany.

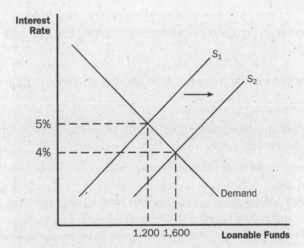

2. Suppose that the government changes the tax code to encourage greater saving.

   a. This will cause an increase in saving, shifting the supply of loanable funds to the right.

   b. The equilibrium interest rate will fall and the equilibrium quantity of funds will rise.

3. Thus, the result of the new tax laws would be a decrease in the equilibrium interest rate and greater saving and investment.

If you would like, now would be a good time to discuss the debate in Chapter 23 concerning whether the tax laws should be reformed to encourage saving.

D. Policy 2: Investment Incentives

Figure 3

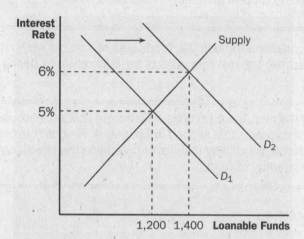

1. Suppose instead that the government passed a new law lowering taxes for any firm building a new factory or buying a new piece of equipment (through the use of an investment tax credit).

   a. This will cause an increase in investment, causing the demand for loanable funds to shift to the right.

   b. The equilibrium interest rate will rise, and the equilibrium quantity of funds will increase as well.

2. Thus, the result of the new tax laws would be an increase in the equilibrium interest rate and greater saving and investment.

Point out that both Policy 1 (a law to increase saving) and Policy 2 (a law to increase investment) each lead to an increase in both saving and investment. the difference between these two policies lies in their effects on the interest rate.

E. Policy 3: Government Budget Deficits and Surpluses

Figure 4

1. A budget deficit occurs if the government spends more than it receives in tax revenue.

2. This implies that public saving ($T - G$) falls, which will lower national saving.

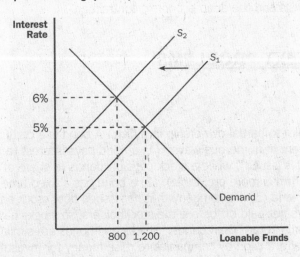

a. The supply of loanable funds will shift to the left.

b. The equilibrium interest rate will rise, and the equilibrium quantity of funds will decrease.

3. When the interest rate rises, the quantity of funds demanded for investment purposes falls.

4. Definition of **crowding out: a decrease in investment that results from government borrowing**.

5. When the government reduces national saving by running a budget deficit, the interest rate rises and investment falls.

6. Government budget surpluses work in the opposite way. The supply of loanable funds increases, the equilibrium interest rate falls, and investment rises.

Now might be a good time to move to the section in Chapter 23 concerning the debate on whether or not the government should balance its budget.

7. *Case Study: The History of U.S. Government Debt*

Figure 5

a. Figure 5 shows the debt of the U.S. government expressed as a percentage of GDP.

b. Throughout history, the primary cause of fluctuations in government debt has been wars. However, the U.S. debt also increased substantially during the 1980s when taxes were cut but government spending was not.

c. By the late 1990s, the debt-to-GDP ratio began declining due to budget surpluses.

d. The debt-to-GDP ratio began rising again during the first few years of the George W. Bush presidency. The causes have been threefold: tax cuts, a recession, and an increase in government spending for the war on terrorism.

e. A very large increase in the debt-to-GDP ratio started occurring in 2008 because of the financial crisis and the deep economic contraction.

SOLUTIONS TO TEXT PROBLEMS:

Quick Quizzes

1. A stock is a claim to partial ownership in a firm. A bond is a certificate of indebtedness. They are different in numerous ways: (1) a bond pays interest (a fixed payment determined when the bond is issued), while a stock pays dividends (a share of the firm's profits that can increase if the firm is more profitable); (2) a bond has a fixed time to maturity, while a stock never matures; and (3) if a company that has issued both stock and bonds goes bankrupt, the bondholders get paid off before the stockholders, so stocks have greater risk and potentially greater return than bonds. Stocks and bonds are similar in that both are financial instruments that are used by companies to raise money for investment, both are traded on exchanges, both entail a degree of risk, and the returns to both are taxed (usually).

2. Private saving is the amount of income that households have left after paying their taxes and paying for their consumption. Public saving is the amount of tax revenue that the government has left after paying for its spending. National saving is equal to the total income in the economy that remains after paying for consumption and government purchases. Investment is the purchase of new capital, such as equipment or buildings.

   These terms are related in two ways: (1) National saving is the sum of public saving and private saving.. (2) In a closed economy, national saving equals investment.

3. If more Americans adopted a "live for today" approach to life, they would spend more and save less. This would shift the supply curve to the left in the market for loanable funds. At the new equilibrium, there would be less saving and investment and a higher interest rate.

Questions for Review

1. The financial system's role is to help match one person's saving with another person's investment. Two markets that are part of the financial system are the bond market, through which large corporations, the federal government, or state and local governments borrow, and the stock market, through which corporations sell ownership shares. Two financial intermediaries are banks, which take in deposits and use the deposits to make loans, and mutual funds, which sell shares to the public and use the proceeds to buy a portfolio of financial assets.

2. It is important for people who own stocks and bonds to diversify their holdings because then they will have only a small stake in each asset, which reduces risk. Mutual funds make such diversification easy by allowing a small investor to purchase parts of hundreds of different stocks and bonds.

3. National saving is the amount of a nation's income that is not spent on consumption or government purchases. Private saving is the amount of income that households have left after paying their taxes and paying for their consumption. Public saving is the amount of tax revenue that the government has left after paying for its spending. The three variables are related because national saving equals private saving plus public saving.

4. Investment refers to the purchase of new capital, such as equipment or buildings. It is equal to national saving.

5. A change in the tax code that might increase private saving is the expansion of eligibility for special accounts that allow people to shelter some of their saving from taxation. This would increase the supply of loanable funds, lower interest rates, and increase investment.

6. A government budget deficit arises when the government spends more than it receives in tax revenue. Because a government budget deficit reduces national saving, it raises interest rates, reduces private investment, and thus reduces economic growth.

Problems and Applications

1. a. The bond of an eastern European government would pay a higher interest rate than the bond of the U.S. government because there would be a greater risk of default.

   b. A bond that repays the principal in 2040 would pay a higher interest rate than a bond that repays the principal in 2015 because it has a longer term to maturity, so there is more risk to the principal.

   c. A bond from a software company you run in your garage would pay a higher interest rate than a bond from Coca-Cola because your software company has more credit risk.

   d. A bond issued by the federal government would pay a higher interest rate than a bond issued by New York State because an investor does not have to pay federal income tax on the bond from New York State.

2. Companies encourage their employees to hold stock in the company because it gives the employees the incentive to care about the firm's profits, not just their own salaries. Then, if employees see waste or see areas in which the firm can improve, they will take actions that benefit the company because they know the value of their stock will rise as a result. It also gives employees an additional incentive to work hard, knowing that if the firm does well, they will profit.

   But from an employee's point of view, owning stock in the company for which she or he works can be risky. The employee's wages or salary is already tied to how well the firm performs. If the firm has trouble, the employee could be laid off or have her or his salary reduced. If the employee owns stock in the firm, then there is a double whammy—the employee is unemployed or gets a lower salary and the value of the stock falls as well. So owning stock in your own company is a very risky proposition. Most employees would be better off diversifying—owning stock or bonds in other companies—so their fortunes would not depend so much on the firm for which they work.

3. To a macroeconomist, saving occurs when a person's income exceeds his consumption, while investment occurs when a person or firm purchases new capital, such as a house or business equipment.

   a. When your family takes out a mortgage and buys a new house, that is investment because it is a purchase of new capital.

   b.   When you use your $200 paycheck to buy stock in AT&T, that is saving because your income of $200 is not being spent on consumption goods.

   c.   When your roommate earns $100 and deposits it in her account at a bank, that is saving because the money is not spent on consumption goods.

   d.   When you borrow $1,000 from a bank to buy a car to use in your pizza-delivery business, that is investment because the car is a capital good.

4. Given that $Y = 8$, $T = 1.5$, $S_{private} = 0.5 = Y - T - C$, $S_{public} = 0.2 = T - G$.
    Because $S_{private} = Y - T - C$, then rearranging gives $C = Y - T - S_{private} = 8 - 1.5 - 0.5 = 6$.
    Because $S_{public} = T - G$, then rearranging gives $G = T - S_{public} = 1.5 - 0.2 = 1.3$.
    Because $S =$ national saving $= S_{private} + S_{public} = 0.5 + 0.2 = 0.7$.
    Finally, because $I =$ investment $= S$, $I = 0.7$.

5. Private saving is equal to $(Y - C - T) = 10,000 - 6,000 - 1,500 = 2,500$.

    Public saving is equal to $(T - G) = 1,500 - 1,700 = -200$.

    National saving is equal to $(Y - C - G) = 10,000 - 6,000 - 1,700 = 2,300$.

    Investment is equal to saving $= 2,300$.

    The equilibrium interest rate is found by setting investment equal to 2,300 and solving for r:
       $3,300 - 100r = 2,300$.
       $100r = 1,000$.
       $r = 10$ percent.

6. a. If interest rates increase, the costs of borrowing money to build the factory become higher, so the returns from building the new plant may not be sufficient to cover the costs. Thus, higher interest rates make it less likely that Intel will build the new factory.

   b. Even if Intel uses its own funds to finance the factory, the rise in interest rates still matters. There is an opportunity cost on the use of the funds. Instead of investing in the factory, Intel could invest the money in the bond market to earn the higher interest rate available there. Intel will compare its potential returns from building the factory to the potential returns from the bond market. If interest rates rise, so that bond market returns rise, Intel is again less likely to invest in the factory.

7. a. Harry will have $1,000(1 + 0.05) = $1,050. Ron will have $1,000(1 + 0.08) = $1,080. Hermione will have $1,000(1 + 0.20) = $1,200.

   b. Each student would compare the expected rate of return on his or her own project with the market rate of interest (r). If the expected rate of return is greater than r, the student would borrow. If the expected rate of return is less than r, the student would lend.

   c. If $r = 7\%$, Harry would want to lend while Ron and Hermione would want to borrow. The quantity of funds demanded would be $2,000, while the quantity supplied would be $1,000.

      If $r = 10\%$, only Hermione would want to borrow. The quantity of funds demanded would be $1,000, while the quantity supplied would be $2,000.

d. The loanable funds market would be in equilibrium at an interest rate of 8%. Harry would want to lend and Hermione would want to borrow. Ron would use his own savings for his project, but would want to neither borrow nor lend. Thus quantity demanded = quantity supplied = $1,000.

e. Harry will have $1,000(1 + 0.08) = $1,080. Ron will have $1,000(1 + 0.08) = $1,080. Hermione will have $2,000(1 + 0.20) − $1,000(1 + 0.08) = $2,400 − $1,080 = $2,320. Both borrowers and lenders are better off. No one is worse off.

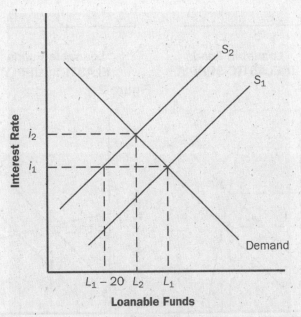

Figure 1

8. a. Figure 1 illustrates the effect of the $20 billion increase in government borrowing. Initially, the supply of loanable funds is curve S_1, the equilibrium real interest rate is i_1, and the quantity of loanable funds is L_1. The increase in government borrowing by $20 billion reduces the supply of loanable funds at each interest rate by $20 billion, so the new supply curve, S_2, is shown by a shift to the left of S_1 by exactly $20 billion. As a result of the shift, the new equilibrium real interest rate is i_2. The interest rate has increased as a result of the increase in government borrowing.

    b. Because the interest rate has increased, investment and national saving decline and private saving increases. The increase in government borrowing reduces public saving. From the figure you can see that total loanable funds (and thus both investment and national saving) decline by less than $20 billion, while public saving declines by $20 billion and private saving rises by less than $20 billion.

    c. The more elastic is the supply of loanable funds, the flatter the supply curve would be, so the interest rate would rise by less and thus national saving would fall by less, as Figure 2 shows.

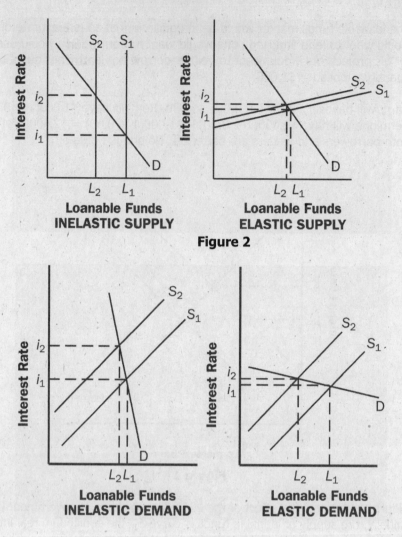

Figure 2

Figure 3

d. The more elastic the demand for loanable funds, the flatter the demand curve would be, so the interest rate would rise by less and thus national saving would fall by more, as Figure 3 shows.

e. If households believe that greater government borrowing today implies higher taxes to pay off the government debt in the future, then people will save more so they can pay the higher future taxes. Thus, private saving will increase, as will the supply of loanable funds. This will offset the reduction in public saving, thus reducing the amount by which the equilibrium quantity of investment and national saving decline, and reducing the amount that the interest rate rises.

If the rise in private saving was exactly equal to the increase in government borrowing, there would be no shift in the national saving curve, so investment, national saving, and the interest rate would all be unchanged. This is the case of Ricardian equivalence.

9. a. If new regulations increase the cost of investment, the demand for loanable funds will decline as shown in Figure 4. This will reduce the equilibrium interest rate along with the levels of saving and investment. With a reduction in investment, the economy will face a lower rate of economic growth in the long run.

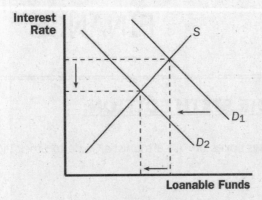

Figure 4

b. If the new regulations improve savers' confidence in the financial system, the supply of loanable funds will increase. The impact can be seen in Figure 5. The interest rate will fall, but saving and investment will rise. Greater investment will increase the rate of economic growth in the long run.

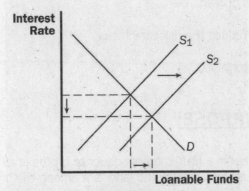

Figure 5

10. a. Investment can be increased by reducing taxes on private saving or by reducing the government budget deficit. But reducing taxes on private saving has the effect of increasing the government budget deficit, unless some other taxes are increased or government spending is reduced. So it is difficult to engage in both policies at the same time.

b. To know which of these policies would be a more effective way to raise investment, you would need to know: (1) what the elasticity of private saving is with respect to the after-tax real interest rate, because that would determine how much private saving would increase if you reduced taxes on saving; (2) how private saving responds to changes in the government budget deficit, because, for example, if Ricardian equivalence holds, the decline in the government budget deficit would be matched by an equal decline in private saving, so national saving would not increase at all; and (3) how elastic investment is with respect to the interest rate, because if investment is quite inelastic, neither policy will have much of an impact on investment.

THE BASIC TOOLS OF FINANCE

WHAT'S NEW IN THE SIXTH EDITION:

There are two new *In the News* boxes on "A Cartoonist's Guide to Stock Picking" and "Is the Efficient Markets Hypothesis Kaput?"

LEARNING OBJECTIVES:

By the end of this chapter, students should understand:

➢ the relationship between present value and future value.

➢ the effects of compound growth.

➢ how risk-averse people reduce the risk they face.

➢ how asset prices are determined.

CONTEXT AND PURPOSE:

Chapter 14 is the third chapter in a four-chapter sequence on the level and growth of output in the long run. In Chapter 12, we discuss how capital and labor are among the primary determinants of output and growth. In Chapter 13, we addressed how saving and investment in capital goods affect the production of output. In Chapter 15, we will show some of the tools people and firms use when choosing capital projects in which to invest. Because both capital and labor are among the primary determinants of output, Chapter 15 will address the market for labor.

  The purpose of Chapter 14 is to introduce the students to some tools that people use when they participate in financial markets. We will show how people compare different sums of money at different points in time, how they manage risk, and how these concepts combine to help determine the value of a financial asset, such as a share of stock.

KEY POINTS:

- Because savings can earn interest, a sum of money today is more valuable than the same sum of money in the future. A person can compare sums from different times using the concept of present value. The present value of any future sum is the amount that would be needed today, given prevailing interest rates, to produce that future sum.

236

- Because of diminishing marginal utility, most people are risk averse. Risk-averse people can reduce risk by buying insurance, diversifying their holdings, and choosing a portfolio with lower risk and lower return.

- The value of an asset equals the present value of the cash flows the owner of the share will receive. For a share of stock, cash flows include the stream of dividends and the final share price. According to the efficient markets hypothesis, financial markets process valuable information rationally, so a stock price always equals the best estimate of the value of the underlying business. Some economists question the efficient markets hypothesis, however, and believe that irrational psychological factors also influence asset prices.

CHAPTER OUTLINE:

I. Definition of **finance: the field that studies how people make decisions regarding the allocation of resources over time and the handling of risk.**

   A. Many of the basic insights of finance are central to understanding how the economy works.

   B. The tools of finance help us think through some of the decisions that we must make in our lives.

II. Present Value: Measuring the Time Value of Money

   A. Money today is more valuable than the same amount of money in the future.

   B. Definition of **present value: the amount of money today that would be needed to produce, using prevailing interest rates, a given future amount of money.**

      1. Example: you put $100 in a bank account today. How much will it be worth in N years?

      2. Definition of **future value: the amount of money in the future that an amount of money today will yield, given prevailing interest rates.**

         a. Definition of **compounding: the accumulation of a sum of money in, say, a bank account where the interest earned remains in the account to earn additional interest in the future.**

         b. If we invest $100 at an interest rate of 5% for 10 years, the future value will be $(1.05)^{10} \times \$100 = \$163$.

         c. Example: You expect to receive $200 in N years. What is the present value of $200 that will be paid in N years?

            i) To compute a present value from a future value, we divide by the factor $(1 + r)^N$.

            ii) If the interest rate is 5% and the $200 will be received 10 years from now, the present value is $\$200/(1.05)^{10} = \$123$.

> If r is the interest rate, then an amount $\$X$ to be received in N years has a present value of $\$X/(1+r)^N$.

d. The higher the interest rate, the more you can earn by depositing your money at the bank, so the more attractive having $100 today becomes.

e. The concept of present value also helps to explain why investment is inversely related to the interest rate.

***Futurama, "Fishful of Dollars."* Season 1 (5:55-6:43).** Fry discovers that his bank account interest (for more than 1 million years) has made him a billionaire.

C. *FYI: The Magic of Compounding and the Rule of 70*

1. Growth rates that seem small in percentage terms seem large after they are compounded for many years.

2. Example: Finn and Quinn both graduate from college at the age of 22 and take jobs earning $30,000 per year.

    a. Finn lives in an economy where incomes grow at 1% per year.

    b. Quinn lives in an economy where incomes grow at 3% per year.

    c. Forty years later (when both are 62), Finn will be earning $45,000 and Quinn will be earning $98,000.

3. The Rule of 70 can help us understand the effects of compounding:

> Rule of 70: If a variable grows at X% per year, then that variable will double in approximately $70/X$ years.

This is a good time to explain to students how important saving can be while they are young. Show students how the magic of compounding can turn a small amount of saving (say, $1,000 per year) into a large amount in 25 or 30 years.

III. Managing Risk

A. Risk Aversion

1. Most people are risk averse.

    a. People dislike bad things happening to them.

    b. In fact, they dislike bad things more than they like comparable good things.

Figure 1

    c. For a risk-averse person, the pain from losing the $1,000 would exceed the pleasure from winning $1,000.

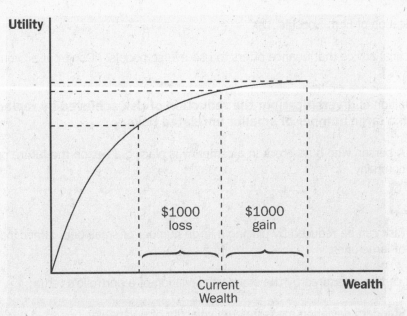

2. Economists have developed models of risk aversion using the concept of utility, which is a person's subjective measure of well-being or satisfaction.

   a. A utility function exhibits the property of diminishing marginal utility: the more wealth a person has, the less utility he gets from an additional dollar.

   b. Because of diminishing marginal utility, the utility lost from losing $1,000 is greater than the utility of winning $1,000.

B. The Markets for Insurance

1. One way to deal with risk is to purchase insurance.

2. From the standpoint of the economy as a whole, the role of insurance is not to eliminate the risks inherent in life but to spread them around more efficiently.

   a. Owning insurance does not prevent bad things from happening to you.

   b. However, the risk is shared among thousands of insurance-company stockholders rather than being borne by you alone.

3. The markets for insurance suffer from two types of problems that impede their ability to spread risk.

   a. A high-risk person is more likely to apply for insurance than a low-risk person because a high-risk person would benefit more from insurance protection. This is *adverse selection*.

   b. After people buy insurance, they have less incentive to be careful about their risky behavior because the insurance company will cover much of the resulting losses. This is *moral hazard*.

C. Diversification of Firm-Specific Risk

1. Practical advice that finance offers to risk-averse people: "Don't put all your eggs in one basket."

2. Definition of **diversification: the reduction of risk achieved by replacing a single risk with a large number of smaller unrelated risks.**

    a. A person who buys stock in a company is placing a bet on the future profitability of that company.

Figure 2

    b. Risk can be reduced by placing a large number of small bets rather than a small number of large ones.

3. Risk can be measured by the standard deviation of a portfolio's return.

    a. Standard deviation measures the volatility of a variable.

    b. The higher the standard deviation of a portfolio's return, the riskier it is.

    c. The risk of a stock portfolio falls as the number of stocks increases.

4. It is impossible to eliminate all risk by increasing the number of stocks in the portfolio.

    a. Definition of **firm-specific risk: risk that affects only a single economic actor.**

    b. Definition of **market risk: risk that affects all economic actors at once.**

    c. Diversification can eliminate firm-specific risk, but will not affect market risk.

Seinfeld, "The Marine Biologist." **Season 5 (3:40-4:18, 9:02-10:30, 13:35-14:00).** Kramer gives Elaine an electronic organizer, which through a series of unfortunate events, gets lost. Elaine goes to Kramer bemoaning the fact that she had put everything in the organizer, and had thrown away her paper organizer. If she hadn't put all her eggs in one basket, she would have lowered her exposure to risk.

D. The Trade-off between Risk and Return

1. Principle #1: People face trade-offs.

2. Risk-averse people are willing to accept the risk inherent in holding stock because they are compensated for doing so.

3. When deciding how to allocate their savings, people have to decide how much risk they are willing to undertake to earn a higher return.

Figure 3

4. The choice of a particular combination of risk and return depends on a person's risk aversion, which reflects a person's own preferences.

IV. Asset Valuation

A. The price of a share of stock is determined by supply and demand.

B. To understand stock prices, we need to understand what determines a person's willingness to pay for a share of stock.

C. Fundamental Analysis

1. Definition of **fundamental analysis: the study of a company's accounting statements and future prospects to determine its value.**

2. If the price of a share of stock is less than the value, the stock is said to be *undervalued*.

3. If the price of a share of stock is greater than its value, the stock is said to be *overvalued*.

4. If the price of a share of stock is equal to its value, the stock is said to be *fairly valued*.

5. The value of a stock to a shareholder is what he receives from owning it, which includes the present value of dividend payments and the final sale price.

   a. Both of these are highly related to the firm's ability to earn profits.

   b. The firm's profitability depends on a large number of factors that affect the demand for its product and its costs of doing business.

6. There are three ways to rely on fundamental analysis to select a stock portfolio.

   a. Do all of the necessary research yourself.

   b. Rely on the advice of Wall Street analysts.

   c. Buy a mutual fund.

7. *In the News: A Cartoonist's Guide to Stock Picking*

   a. Scott Adams, the creator of *Dilbert*, was an economics major in college.

   b. This is a *Wall Street Journal* article in which Adams provides some financial advice.

D. The Efficient Markets Hypothesis

1. Definition of the **efficient markets hypothesis: the theory according to which asset prices reflect all publicly available information about the value of an asset.**

2. Each company listed on a major stock exchange is followed closely by money managers who monitor news stories and conduct fundamental analysis to determine a stock's value.

3. At the equilibrium market price of a share of stock, the number of shares being offered for sale is exactly equal to the number of shares that people want to buy.

      a. At the market price, the number of people who think that the stock is overvalued exactly balances the number of people who think it is undervalued.

      b. As judged by the typical person in the market, all stocks are fairly valued all of the time.

4. Definition of **informationally efficient**: **reflecting all available information in a rational way.**

      a. Stock prices change when information changes.

      b. When the good (bad) news about a company's prospects becomes public, the value and the price of the stock will rise (fall).

5. Definition of **random walk: the path of a variable whose changes are hard to predict.**

      a. Changes in stock prices are impossible to predict from available information.

      b. The only thing that can move stock prices is news that changes the market's perception of the company's value.

      c. Because news is unpredictable, changes in stock prices should be unpredictable.

6. *Case Study: Random Walks and Index Funds*

      a. Some of the best evidence in favor of the efficient markets hypothesis comes from the performance of index funds.

      b. In practice, funds that are actively managed by a professional rarely beat index funds and often do worse.

E. Market Irrationality

1. The efficient markets hypothesis assumes that people buying and selling stock rationally process all of the information they have about the stock's underlying value.

2. There is a long tradition suggesting that fluctuations in stock prices are partly psychological.

      a. In the 1930s, John Maynard Keynes suggested that asset markets are driven by the "animal spirits" of investors.

      b. In the 1990s, Federal Reserve Chairman Alan Greenspan questioned whether the stock market boom was due to "irrational exuberance."

3. The value of a stock depends on the final sale price expected in the future.

      a. A person may be willing to pay more than a stock is worth today if he believes that another person will pay even more in the future.

      b. Therefore, to evaluate a stock, you have to estimate not only the value of the business but also what other people may believe the business is worth in the future.

4.   There is much debate among economists about whether departures from rational pricing are important or rare.

   a.   Believers in market irrationality point out that the stock market often moves in ways that are hard to explain on the basis of news that might alter a rational valuation.

   b.   Believers in the efficient markets hypothesis point out that it is difficult to know the correct, rational valuation of a company so it is hard to tell if any particular valuation is irrational.

F.   *In the News: Is the Efficient Markets Hypothesis Kaput?*

   1.   Some individuals suggest that the financial crisis of 2008 and 2009 indicates that the efficient markets hypothesis is wrong.

   2.   This is an article by economist Jeremy Siegel who argues the contrary.

SOLUTIONS TO TEXT PROBLEMS:

Quick Quizzes

1.   The present value of $150 to be received in 10 years if the interest rate is 7 percent is $150 / $(1.07)^{10}$ = $76.25.

2.   There are three ways in which a risk-averse person may reduce the risk he faces: (1) purchase insurance, (2) diversify his portfolio, or (3) choose safer alternatives by accepting a lower rate of return.

3.   No. According to the efficient markets hypothesis, the price of a share of stock should reflect all available information about its value. Thus, the stocks on this list should perform no better on average than other stocks listed on the stock exchange.

Questions for Review

1.   If the interest rate is 7%, the present value of $200 to be received in 10 years is $200/(1.07)^{10}$ = $101.67. If the interest rate is 7%, the present value of $300 to be received 20 years from now is $300/(1.07)^{20}$ = $77.53.

2.   Purchasing insurance allows an individual to reduce the level of risk he faces. Two problems that impede the insurance industry from working correctly are adverse selection and moral hazard. Adverse selection occurs because a high-risk person is more likely to apply for insurance than a low-risk person is. Moral hazard occurs because people have less incentive to be careful about their risky behavior after they purchase insurance.

3.   Diversification is the reduction of risk achieved by replacing a single risk with a large number of smaller unrelated risks. A stockholder will get more diversification going from 1 to 10 stocks than from 100 to 120 stocks.

4. Stocks have more risk because their value depends on the future value of the firm. Because of its higher risk, shareholders will demand a higher return. There is a positive relationship between risk and return.

5. A stock analyst will consider the future profitability of a firm when determining the value of the stock.

6. The efficient markets hypothesis suggests that stock prices reflect all available information. This means that we cannot use current information to predict future changes in stock prices. One piece of evidence that supports this theory is the fact that many index funds outperform mutual funds that are actively managed by a professional portfolio manager.

7. Economists who are skeptical of the efficient markets hypothesis believe that fluctuations in stock prices are partly psychological. People may in fact be willing to purchase a stock that is overvalued if they believe that someone will be willing to pay even more in the future. This means that the stock price may not be a rational valuation of the firm.

Problems and Applications

1. The future value of $24 invested for 400 years at an interest rate of 7% is $(1.07)^{400} \times \$24 = \$13,600,000,000,000 = \$13.6$ trillion.

2. a. The present value of $15 million to be received in four years at an interest rate of 11% is $15 million/$(1.11)^4 = \$9.88$ million. Because the present value of the payoff is less than the cost, the project should not be undertaken.

    The present value of $15 million to be received in four years at an interest rate of 10% is $15 million/$(1.10)^4 = \$10.25$ million. Because the present value of the payoff is greater than the cost, the project should be undertaken.

    The present value of $15 million to be received in four years at an interest rate of 9% is $15 million/$(1.09)^4 = \$10.63$ million. Because the present value of the payoff is greater than the cost, the project should be undertaken.

    The present value of $15 million to be received in four years at an interest rate of 8% is $15 million/$(1.08)^4 = \$11.03$ million. Because the present value of the payoff is greater than the cost, the project should be undertaken.

    b. The exact cutoff for the interest rate between profitability and nonprofitability is the interest rate that will equate the present value of receiving $15 million in four years with the current cost of the project ($10 million):

    $$\$10 = 15/(1 + x)^4$$
    $$10(1 + x)^4 = 15$$
    $$(1 + x)^4 = 1.5$$
    $$1 + x = (1.5)^{0.25}$$
    $$1 + x = 1.1067$$
    $$x = 0.1067$$

    Therefore, an interest rate of 10.67% would be the cutoff between profitability and nonprofitability.

3. a. Bond A: $8,000/(1 + 0.035)^{20}$ = $8,000/1.9898 = $4,020.50
   Bond B: $8,000/(1 + 0.035)^{40}$ = $8,000/3.9593 = $2,020.56

   b. Bond A: $8,000/(1 + 0.07)^{20}$ = $8,000/3.870 = $2,067.18
   Bond B: $8,000/(1 + 0.07)^{40}$ = $8,000/14.974 = $539.26

   Bond B has the larger percentage change in value.

   c. The value of a bond *falls* when the interest rate increases, and bonds with a longer time to maturity are *more* sensitive to changes in the interest rate.

4. The value of the stock is equal to the present value of its dividends and its final sale price. This is equal to $5/1.08 + $5/(1.08)^2 + ($5 + $120)/(1.08)^3$ = $4.63 + $4.29 + $99.23 = $108.15. Since this is lower than the initial selling price of $110, XYZ stock is not a good investment.

5. a. A sick person is more likely to apply for health insurance than a well person is. This is adverse selection. Once a person has health insurance, he may be less likely to take good care of himself. This is moral hazard.

   b. A risky driver is more likely than a safe driver to apply for car insurance. This is adverse selection. Once a driver has insurance, he may drive more recklessly. This is adverse selection.

6. A stock that is very sensitive to economic conditions will have more risk associated with it. Thus, we would expect for that stock to pay a higher return. To get stockholders to be willing to accept the risk, the expected return must be larger than average.

7. Shareholders will likely demand a higher return due to the stock's firm-specific risk. Firm-specific risk is risk that affects only that particular stock. All stocks in the economy are subject to market risk.

8. a. If a roommate is buying stocks in companies that everyone believes will experience big profits in the future, the price-earnings ratio is likely to be high. The price is high because it reflects everyone's expectations about the firm's future earnings. The largest disadvantage in buying these stocks is that they may be currently overvalued and may not pay off in the future.

   b. Firms with low price-earnings ratios will likely have lower future earnings. The reason why these stocks are cheap is that everyone has lower expectations about the future profitability of these firms. The largest disadvantage to buying this stock is that the market may be correct and the firm's stock may provide a low return.

9. a. Answers will vary, but may include things like information on new products under development or information concerning future government regulations that will affect the profitability of the firm.

   b. The fact that those who trade stocks based on inside information earn very high rates of return does not violate the efficient markets hypothesis. The efficient market hypothesis suggests that the price of a stock reflects all available information concerning the future profitability of the firm. Inside information is not readily available to the public and thus is not reflected in the stock's price.

c. Insider trading is illegal because it gives some buyers or sellers an unfair advantage in the stock market.

10. a. Yes, Jamal is risk averse. The marginal utility of an additional dollar of wealth is diminishing. Figure 1 shows Jamal's utility function.

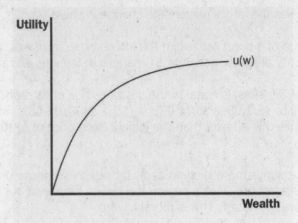

Figure 1

b. The expected value of option A = U(W = $4 million) = 2,000.

The expected value of option B = (0.6) × U(W = $1 million) + 0.4 × U(W = $9 million) = (0.6) × 1,000 + (0.4) × 3,000 = 600 + 1,200 = 1,800.

Jamal should choose option A.

15 UNEMPLOYMENT

WHAT'S NEW IN THE SIXTH EDITION:

Two new *In the News* boxes on "The Rise of Long-Term Unemployment" and "How Much Do the Unemployed Respond to Incentives?" have been added.

LEARNING OBJECTIVES:

By the end of this chapter, students should understand:

➢ the data used to measure the amount of unemployment.

➢ how unemployment can result from minimum-wage laws.

➢ how unemployment can arise from bargaining between firms and unions.

➢ how unemployment results when firms choose to pay efficiency wages.

CONTEXT AND PURPOSE:

Chapter 15 is the fourth chapter in a four-chapter sequence on the level and growth of output in the long run. In Chapter 12, we learned that capital and labor are among the primary determinants of output and growth. In Chapter 13, we addressed how saving and investment in capital goods affect the production of output. In Chapter 14, we learned about some of the tools people and firms use when choosing capital projects in which to invest. In Chapter 15, we see how full utilization of our labor resources improves the level of production and our standard of living.

The purpose of Chapter 15 is to introduce students to the labor market. We will see how economists measure the performance of the labor market using unemployment statistics. We will also address a number of sources of unemployment and some policies that the government might use to lower certain types of unemployment.

KEY POINTS:

- The unemployment rate is the percentage of those who would like to work but do not have jobs. The Bureau of Labor Statistics calculates this statistic monthly based on a survey of thousands of households.

247

- The unemployment rate is an imperfect measure of joblessness. Some people who call themselves unemployed may actually not want to work, and some people who would like to work have left the labor force after an unsuccessful search and therefore are not counted as employed.

- In the U.S. economy, most people who become unemployed find work within a short period of time. Nonetheless, most unemployment observed at any given time is attributable to the few people who are unemployed for long periods of time.

- One reason for unemployment is the time it takes for workers to search for jobs that best suit their tastes and skills. This frictional unemployment is increased as a result of unemployment insurance, a government policy designed to protect workers' incomes.

- A second reason why our economy always has some unemployment is minimum-wage laws. By raising the wage of unskilled and inexperienced workers above the equilibrium level, minimum-wage laws raise the quantity of labor supplied and reduce the quantity demanded. The resulting surplus of labor represents unemployment.

- A third reason for unemployment is the market power of unions. When unions push the wages in unionized industries above the equilibrium level, they create a surplus of labor.

- A fourth reason for unemployment is suggested by the theory of efficiency wages. According to this theory, firms find it profitable to pay wages above the equilibrium level. High wages can improve worker health, lower worker turnover, raise worker quality, and increase worker effort.

CHAPTER OUTLINE:

I. Unemployment can be divided into two categories.

    A. The economy's natural rate of unemployment refers to the amount of unemployment that the economy normally experiences.

    B. Cyclical unemployment refers to the year-to-year fluctuations in unemployment around its natural rate.

II. Identifying Unemployment

    A. How Is Unemployment Measured?

        1. The Bureau of Labor Statistics (BLS) surveys 60,000 households every month.

        2. The BLS places each adult (age 16 or older) into one of three categories: employed, unemployed, or not in the labor force.

> **Figure 1**
>
> Ask students which category they are in. Remind them that to be considered to be unemployed, they must be without a job and looking for work. Many students are not in the labor force, but may consider themselves to be unemployed simply because they do not have a job. Explain to students that the unemployment rate is a useful statistic because it answers the following question: Of those in the economy who want to work, what percentage cannot find a job?

3. Definition of **labor force: the total number of workers, including both the employed and the unemployed**.

$$\text{Labor force} = \text{Number of employed} + \text{Number of unemployed}$$

4. Definition of **unemployment rate: the percentage of the labor force that is unemployed**.

$$\text{Unemployment rate} = \left(\frac{\text{Number of unemployed}}{\text{Labor force}} \right) \times 100\%$$

5. Definition of **labor-force participation rate: the percentage of the adult population that is in the labor force**.

$$\text{Labor-force participation rate} = \left(\frac{\text{Labor force}}{\text{Adult population}} \right) \times 100\%$$

6. Example: Data from 2009. In that year, there were 139.9 million employed people and 14.3 million unemployed people.

   a. Labor Force = 139.9 + 14.3 = 154.2 million.

   b. Unemployment Rate = (14.3/154.2) × 100% = 9.3%.

   c. If the adult population was 235.8 million, the labor-force participation rate was:

   Labor-Force Participation Rate = (154.2/235.8) × 100% = 65.4%.

 Make sure that students understand how to make these calculations. Make sure that the formula is written on the board and refer to it often.

ALTERNATIVE CLASSROOM EXAMPLE:
The country of Bada has collected the following information:

Population	240,000
Employed	180,000
Unemployed	30,000

Labor Force = 180,000 + 30,000 = 210,000
Unemployment rate = (30,000/210,000) × 100% = 14.3%
Labor-force participation rate = (210,000/240,000) × 100% = 87.5%

Table 1

7. Table 1 shows unemployment and labor-force participation rates for various sub-groups of the U.S. population.

a. Women ages 20 and older have lower labor-force participation rates than men, and, once in the labor market, have lower unemployment rates than men.

b. Blacks ages 20 and older have similar labor-force participation rates to whites, but have higher rates of unemployment.

c. Teenagers have lower labor-force participation rates than adults, but have higher unemployment rates.

Figure 2

8. Figure 2 shows the unemployment rate in the United States since 1960.

B. Definition of the **natural rate of unemployment: the normal rate of unemployment around which the unemployment rate fluctuates**.

C. Definition of **cyclical unemployment: the deviation of unemployment from its natural rate**.

> Discuss how the age composition of the labor force and other demographic and social factors can cause the natural rate of unemployment to vary over time. For 2009, economists at the Congressional Budget Office have estimated a natural rate of 5.0%.

D. *Case Study: Labor-Force Participation of Men and Women in the U.S. Economy*

1. There has been a dramatic rise in the labor-force participation rates of women over the past 50 years.

Figure 3

2. Figure 3 shows this rise in the labor-force participation rate of women. The figure also shows that the labor-force participation rates for men have actually fallen by a small amount over the same time period.

E. Does the Unemployment Rate Measure What We Want It To?

1. Measuring the unemployment rate is not as straightforward as it may seem.

2. There is a tremendous amount of movement into and out of the labor force.

a. Many of the unemployed are new entrants or reentrants looking for work.

b. Many unemployment spells end with a person leaving the labor force as opposed to actually finding a job.

3. There may be individuals who are calling themselves unemployed to qualify for government assistance, yet they are not trying hard to find work. These individuals are more likely not a part of the true labor force, but they will be counted as unemployed.

4. Definition of **discouraged workers: individuals who would like to work but have given up looking for a job**.

   a. These individuals will not be counted as part of the labor force.

   b. Thus, while they are likely a part of the unemployed, they will not show up in the unemployment statistics.

***Mad Money, Chapter 1* (4:35-7:40).** Don's wife asks him why he has not applied for any jobs. He replies that he has given up after searching for a job for a year without success. Meanwhile, his wife finds it difficult to find a job because she has no computing skills.

---

5. Table 2 presents other measures of labor underutilization calculated by the Bureau of Labor Statistics.

Activity 1—Who Is Unemployed?

Type:	In-class assignment
Topics:	Unemployment categories
Materials needed:	None
Time:	5 minutes
Class limitations:	Works in any size class

Purpose
This assignment helps familiarize students with labor-force statistics.

Instructions
Ask the students to classify each of the following individuals in one of the following categories: employed, unemployed, or not in the labor force.

1. Steve worked 40 hours last week in an office supply store.
2. Last week, Elizabeth worked 10 hours as a computer programmer for the National Video Company and attended night classes at the local college. She would prefer a full-time job.
3. Roger lost his job at the R-gone Manufacturing Company. Since then he has been trying to find a job at other local factories.
4. Linda is a homemaker. Last week she was occupied with her normal household chores. She neither held a job nor looked for a job.
5. Linda's father is unable to work.
6. Scott has a Ph.D. He worked full-time but does not like his job as a dishwasher. He has applied for jobs with three companies and five universities. As soon as he gets an offer, he will quit his current job.
7. Mary-Helen has been out of work for a full year. She would take a job if it was offered, but no local companies are hiring. She is not actively searching for work.

Common Answers and Points for Discussion
Steve, Elizabeth, and Scott are employed. Roger is unemployed. Linda, Linda's father, and Mary-Helen are not in the labor force.

This assignment can also be used to discuss measurement problems such as underemployment (Elizabeth and Scott are examples) and discouraged workers (Mary-Helen provides an example).

F. How Long Are the Unemployed without Work?

1. Another important variable that policymakers may be concerned with is the duration of unemployment.

Table 2

2. Most spells of unemployment are short, and most unemployment observed at any given time is long term.

3. *In the News: The Rise of Long-Term Unemployment*

a. During the recession of 2008 and 2009, the number of individuals who were unemployed long term was very high.

b. This is an article from *The Wall Street Journal* detailing the hardships faced by those unemployed for long stretches of time.

G. Why Are There Always Some People Unemployed?

1. In an ideal labor market, wages would adjust so that the quantity of labor supplied and the quantity of labor demanded would be equal.

2. However, there is always unemployment even when the economy is doing well. The unemployment rate is never zero; it fluctuates around the natural rate.

a. Definition of **frictional unemployment: unemployment that results because it takes time for workers to search for the jobs that best suit their tastes and skills**.

b. Definition of **structural unemployment: unemployment that results because the number of jobs available in some labor markets is insufficient to provide a job for everyone who wants one**.

c. Three possible reasons for structural unemployment are minimum-wage laws, unions, and efficiency wages.

Seinfeld, "The Revenge." **Season 2 (3:00-6:18, 21:06-21:28).** George is out of work after quitting his job and considers a career change. The poor housing market has led to cyclical unemployment. George laments that unions control his desired job of movie projectionist (structural unemployment). He would also like to be a college professor, but lacks the human capital (frictional unemployment).

H. *FYI: The Jobs Number*

1. When the Bureau of Labor Statistics announces the unemployment rate each month, it also announces the number of jobs the economy gained or lost.

2. This information comes from a survey of 160,000 business establishments.

III. Job Search

A. Definition of **job search: the process by which workers find appropriate jobs given their tastes and skills**.

B. Because workers differ from one another in terms of their skills and tastes and jobs differ in their attributes, it is often difficult for workers to match with the appropriate job.

C. Why Some Frictional Unemployment Is Inevitable

1. Frictional unemployment often occurs because of a change in the demand for labor among different firms.

    a. When consumers decide to stop buying a good produced by Firm A and instead start buying a good produced by Firm B, some workers at Firm A will likely lose their jobs.

    b. New jobs will be created at Firm B, but it will take some time to move the displaced workers from Firm A to Firm B.

    c. The result of this transition is temporary unemployment.

    d. The same situation can occur across industries and regions as well.

2. This implies that, because the economy is always changing, frictional unemployment is inevitable. Workers in declining industries will find themselves looking for new jobs, and firms in growing industries will be seeking new workers.

D. Public Policy and Job Search

1. The faster information spreads about job openings and worker availability, the more rapidly the economy can match workers and firms.

2. Government programs can help to reduce the amount of frictional unemployment.

    a. Government-run employment agencies give out information on job vacancies.

    b. Public training programs can ease the transition of workers from declining to growing industries and help disadvantaged groups escape poverty.

3. Critics of these programs argue that the private labor market will do a better job of matching workers with employers and therefore the government should not be involved in the process of job search.

E. Unemployment Insurance

1. Definition of **unemployment insurance: a government program that partially protects workers' incomes when they become unemployed**.

2. Because unemployment insurance reduces the hardship of unemployment, it also increases the amount of unemployment that exists.

3. Many studies have shown that more generous unemployment insurance benefits lead to reduced job search effort and, as a result, more unemployment.

4. *In the News: How Much Do the Unemployed Respond to Incentives?*

    a. During the recession of 2008 and 2009, policymakers worried about the (dis)incentives provided by unemployment insurance.

    b. This is an article from *The Wall Street Journal* discussing these concerns in consideration of increasing the length of time the unemployed may receive unemployment benefits.

IV. Minimum-Wage Laws

A. Unemployment can also occur because of minimum-wage laws.

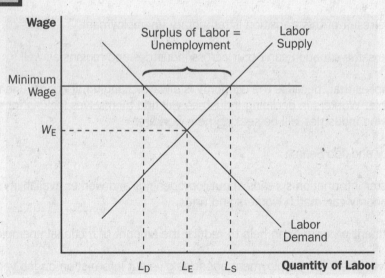

B. The minimum wage is a price floor.

1. If the minimum wage is set above the equilibrium wage in the labor market, a surplus of labor will occur.

2. However, this is a binding constraint only when the minimum wage is set above the equilibrium wage.

    a. Most workers in the economy earn a wage above the minimum wage.

      b.   Minimum-wage laws therefore have the largest affect on workers with low skill and little experience (such as teenagers).

C. *FYI: Who Earns the Minimum Wage?*

    1. In 2010, the Department of Labor released a study concerning workers who reported earnings at or below the minimum wage.

       a.   Of all workers paid an hourly rate in the United States, about 4% of men and 6% of women reported wages at or below the minimum wage.

       b.   Minimum-wage workers tend to be young, with about half under the age of 25.

       c.   Minimum-wage workers tend to be less educated. Of those workers ages 16 and over with a high school education, only 4% earned the minimum wage.

       d.   The industry with the highest proportion of workers with reported wages at or below the minimum wage was leisure and hospitality.

       e.   The proportion of workers earning the prevailing minimum wage has trended downward since 1979.

D. Anytime a wage is kept above the equilibrium level for any reason, the result is unemployment.

    1. Other causes of this situation include unions and efficiency wages.

    2. This situation is different from frictional unemployment where the search for the *right* job is the reason for unemployment.

V. Unions and Collective Bargaining

A. Definition of **<u>union</u>: a worker association that bargains with employers over wages and working conditions**.

B. Unions play a smaller role in the U.S. economy today than they did in the past. However, unions continue to be prevalent in many European countries.

C. The Economics of Unions

    1. Definition of **<u>collective bargaining</u>: the process by which unions and firms agree on the terms of employment**.

    2. Unions try to negotiate for higher wages, better benefits, and better working conditions than the firm would offer if there were no union.

    3. Definition of **<u>strike</u>: the organized withdrawal of labor from a firm by a union**.

    4. Economists have found that union workers typically earn 10% to 20% more than similar workers who do not belong to unions.

5. This implies that unions raise the wage above the equilibrium wage, resulting in unemployment.

    a. Unions are often believed to cause conflict between *insiders* (who benefit from high union wages) and *outsiders* (who do not get the union jobs).

    b. Outsiders will either remain unemployed or find jobs in firms that are not unionized.

    c. The supply of workers in nonunion firms will increase, pushing wages at those firms down.

D. Are Unions Good or Bad for the Economy?

    1. Critics of unions argue that unions are a cartel, which causes inefficiency because fewer workers end up being hired at the higher union wage.

    2. Advocates of unions argue that unions are an answer to the problems that occur when a firm has too much power in the labor market (for example, if it is the only major employer in town). In addition, by representing workers' views, unions help firms provide the right mix of job attributes.

VI. The Theory of Efficiency Wages

A. Definition of **efficiency wages: above-equilibrium wages paid by firms in order to increase worker productivity**.

B. Efficiency wages raise the wage above the market equilibrium wage, resulting in unemployment.

C. There are several reasons why a firm may pay efficiency wages.

    1. Worker Health

        a. Better-paid workers can afford to eat better and can afford good medical care.

        b. This is more applicable in developing countries where inadequate nutrition can be a significant problem.

    2. Worker Turnover

        a. A firm can reduce turnover by paying a wage greater than its workers could receive elsewhere.

        b. This is especially helpful for firms that face high hiring and training costs.

    3. Worker Quality

        a. Offering higher wages attracts a better pool of applicants.

        b. This is especially helpful for firms that are not able to perfectly gauge the quality of job applicants.

4. Worker Effort

    a. Again, if a firm pays a worker more than he or she can receive elsewhere, the worker will be more likely to try to protect his or her job by working harder.

    b. This is especially helpful for firms that have difficulty monitoring their workers.

5. *Case Study: Henry Ford and the Very Generous $5-a-Day Wage*

    a. Henry Ford used a high wage (about twice the going rate) to attract better employees.

    b. After instituting this higher wage policy, the company's production costs actually fell due to reduced turnover, absenteeism, and shirking.

When discussing the material in this chapter, you may find that students want to begin discussing possible policies to deal with unemployment. Keep the focus on institutional responses such as unemployment insurance, job training, and government-sponsored employment agencies.

SOLUTIONS TO TEXT PROBLEMS:

Quick Quizzes

1. The unemployment rate is measured through a survey of 60,000 households to determine the percentage of the labor force that is unemployed. The unemployment rate overstates the amount of joblessness because some of those who report being unemployed may not, in fact, be trying hard to find a job. But the unemployment rate may understate the amount of joblessness because discouraged workers are considered not in the labor force even though they are workers without jobs.

2. An increase in the world price of oil increases the amount of frictional unemployment as oil-producing firms increase output and employment, but other firms, such as those in the auto industry, reduce output and employment. The sectoral shift from the auto industry to oil firms causes higher frictional unemployment for a time until workers have shifted from the auto industry to the oil industry. Although no increase in unemployment is really desirable, this type of frictional unemployment is a natural outcome of the reallocation of resources between different sectors. Public policies that might affect the unemployment caused by this change in the price of oil include government-run employment agencies, which can help autoworkers move into the oil industry, job-training programs to help workers adapt to a new industry, and unemployment insurance, which keeps workers from suffering economic hardship while changing from one industry to another.

3. Figure 1 shows the supply curve (*S*) and the demand curve (*D*) for labor. The wage (*W*) is above the equilibrium wage (*W*ₑ). The result is unemployment, equal to the amount by which the quantity of labor supplied (*L*ₛ) exceeds the quantity of labor demanded (*L*ₒ).

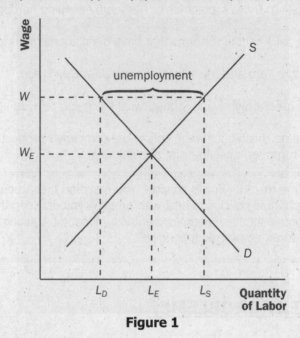

Figure 1

4. A union in the auto industry raises the wages of workers employed by General Motors and Ford by threatening to strike. To prevent the costs of a strike, the firms generally pay higher wages than they would if there were no union. However, the higher wages reduce employment at General Motors and Ford. The unemployed autoworkers seek jobs elsewhere, reducing wages and increasing employment in the nonunion sector.

5. There are four reasons that firms might find it profitable to pay wages above the level that balances the quantity of labor supplied and the quantity of labor demanded: (1) to ensure that workers are in good health so they will be more productive; (2) to reduce worker turnover because it is costly to hire new workers; (3) to make workers eager to keep their jobs, thus discouraging them from shirking; and (4) to attract a better pool of workers.

Questions for Review

1. The BLS categorizes each adult (16 years of age and older) as either employed, unemployed, or not in the labor force. The labor force consists of the sum of the employed and the unemployed. The unemployment rate is the percentage of the labor force that is unemployed. The labor-force participation rate is the percentage of the total adult population that is in the labor force.

2. Unemployment is typically short term. Most people who become unemployed are able to find new jobs fairly quickly. But some unemployment is attributable to the relatively few workers who are jobless for long periods of time.

3. Frictional unemployment is inevitable because the economy is always changing. Some firms are shrinking while others are expanding. Some regions are experiencing faster growth than other regions. Transitions of workers between firms and between regions are accompanied by temporary unemployment.

The government could help to reduce the amount of frictional unemployment through public policies that provide information about job vacancies in order to match workers and jobs more quickly, and through public training programs that help ease the transition of workers from declining to expanding industries and help disadvantaged groups escape poverty.

4. Minimum-wage laws are a better explanation for unemployment among teenagers than among college graduates. Teenagers have fewer job-related skills than college graduates do, so their wages are low enough to be affected by the minimum wage. College graduates' wages generally exceed the minimum wage.

5. Unions may affect the natural rate of unemployment via the effect on insiders and outsiders. Because unions raise the wage above the equilibrium level, the quantity of labor demanded declines while the quantity supplied of labor rises, so there is unemployment. Insiders are those who keep their jobs. Outsiders, workers who become unemployed, have two choices: either get a job in a firm that is not unionized, or remain unemployed and wait for a job to open up in the union sector. As a result, the natural rate of unemployment is higher than it would be without unions.

6. Advocates of unions claim that unions are good for the economy because they are an antidote to the market power of the firms that hire workers and they are important for helping firms respond efficiently to workers' concerns.

7. Four reasons why a firm's profits might increase when it raises wages are: (1) better paid workers are healthier and more productive; (2) worker turnover is reduced; (3) the firm can attract higher quality workers; and (4) worker effort is increased.

Problems and Applications

1. The labor force consists of the number of employed (139,445,000) plus the number of unemployed (15,260,000), which equals 154,705,000.

   To find the labor-force participation rate, we need to know the size of the adult population. Adding the labor force (154,705,000) to the number of people not in the labor force (82,614,000) gives the adult population of 237,319,000. The labor-force participation rate is the labor force (154,705,000) divided by the adult population (237,319,000) times 100%, which equals 65.2%.

   The unemployment rate is the number of unemployed (15,260,000) divided by the labor force (154,705,000) times 100%, which equals 9.9%.

2. Many answers are possible.

3. The fact that employment increased 6.8 million while unemployment declined 1.1 million is consistent with growth in the labor force of 5.7 million workers. The labor force constantly increases as the population grows and as labor-force participation increases, so the increase in the number of people employed may always exceed the reduction in the number unemployed.

4. a. If an auto company goes bankrupt and its workers immediate begin looking for work, the unemployment rate will rise and the employment-population ratio will fall.

b. If some of the unemployed auto workers give up looking for a job, the unemployment rate will fall and the employment-population ratio will remain the same.

c. If numerous students graduate from college and cannot find work, the unemployment rate will rise and the employment-population ratio will remain unchanged.

d. If numerous students graduate from college and immediately begin new jobs, the unemployment rate will fall and the employment-population ratio will rise.

e. If a stock market boom induces earlier retirement, the unemployment rate will rise and the employment-population ratio will fall.

f. Advances in health care that prolong the life of retirees will not affect the unemployment rate and will lower the employment-population ratio.

5. a. A construction worker who is laid off because of bad weather is likely to experience short-term unemployment, because the worker will be back to work as soon as the weather clears up.

b. A manufacturing worker who loses her job at a plant in an isolated area is likely to experience long-term unemployment, because there are probably few other employment opportunities in the area. She may need to move somewhere else to find a suitable job, which means she will be out of work for some time.

c. A worker in the stagecoach industry who was laid off because of the growth of railroads is likely to be unemployed for a long time. The worker will have a lot of trouble finding another job because his entire industry is shrinking. He will probably need to gain additional training or skills to get a job in a different industry.

d. A short-order cook who loses his job when a new restaurant opens is likely to find another job fairly quickly, perhaps even at the new restaurant, and thus will probably have only a short spell of unemployment.

e. An expert welder with little education who loses her job when the company installs automatic welding machinery is likely to be without a job for a long time, because she lacks the technological skills to keep up with the latest equipment. To remain in the welding industry, she may need to go back to school and learn the newest techniques.

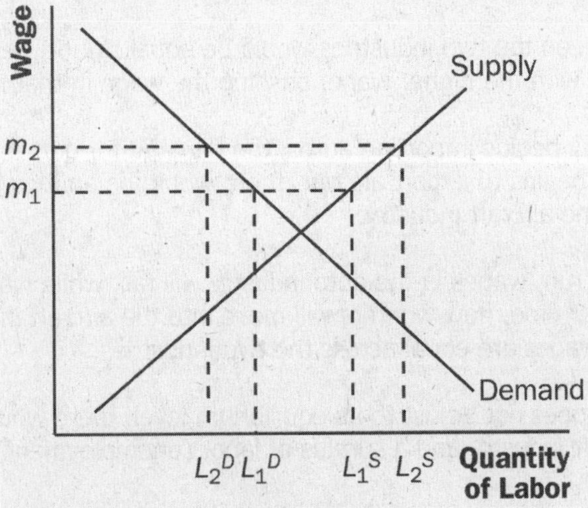

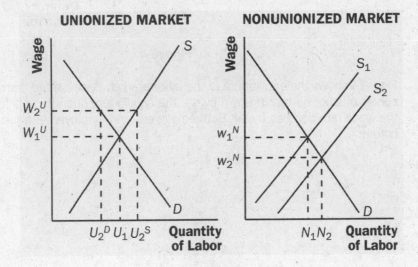

Figure 2

6. Figure 2 shows a diagram of the labor market with a binding minimum wage. At the initial minimum wage (m_1), the quantity of labor supplied L_1^S is greater than the quantity of labor demanded L_1^D, and unemployment is equal to $L_1^S - L_1^D$. An increase in the minimum wage to m_2 leads to an increase in the quantity of labor supplied to L_2^S and a decrease in the quantity of labor demanded to L_2^D. As a result, unemployment increases as the minimum wage rises.

7. a. Figure 3 illustrates the effect of a union being established in the manufacturing labor market. In the figure on the left, the wage rises from w_1^U to w_2^U and the quantity of labor demanded declines from U_1 to U_2^D. Because the wage is higher, the quantity supplied of labor increases to U_2^S, so there are $U_2^S - U_2^D$ unemployed workers in the unionized manufacturing sector.

   b. When those workers who become unemployed in the manufacturing sector seek employment in the service labor market, shown in the figure on the right, the supply of labor shifts to the right from S_1 to S_2. The result is a decline in the wage in the nonunionized service sector from w_1^N to w_2^N and an increase in employment in the nonunionized service sector from N_1 to N_2.

Figure 3

8. a. Wages between the two industries would be equal. If not, new workers would choose the industry with the higher wage, pushing the wage in that industry down.

   b. If the country begins importing autos, the demand for domestic auto workers will fall. If the country begins to export aircraft, there would be an increase in the demand for workers in the aircraft industry.

   c. In the short run, wages in the auto industry will fall, while wages in the aircraft industry will rise. Over time, new workers will move into the aircraft industry bringing its wage down until wages are equal across the two industries.

   d. If the wage does not adjust to its equilibrium level, there would be a shortage of workers in the aircraft industry and a surplus of labor (unemployment) in the auto industry.

9. a. If a firm was not providing such benefits prior to the legislation, the curve showing the demand for labor would shift down by exactly $4 at each quantity of labor, because the firm would not be willing to pay as high a wage given the increased cost of the benefits.

   b. If employees value the benefit by exactly $4 per hour, they would be willing to work the same amount for a wage that's $4 less per hour, so the supply curve of labor shifts down by exactly $4.

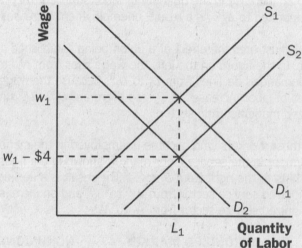

Figure 4

   c. Figure 4 shows the equilibrium in the labor market. Because the demand and supply curves of labor both shift down by $4, the equilibrium quantity of labor is unchanged and the wage rate declines by $4. Both employees and employers are just as well off as before.

d. If the minimum wage prevents the wage from falling, the result will be increased unemployment, as Figure 5 shows. Initially, the equilibrium quantity of labor is L_1 and the equilibrium wage is w_1, which is $3 lower than the minimum wage w_m. After the law is passed, demand falls to D_2 and supply rises to S_2. Because of the minimum wage, the quantity of labor demanded (L_2^D) will be smaller than the quantity supplied (L_2^S). Thus, there will be unemployment equal to $L_2^S - L_2^D$.

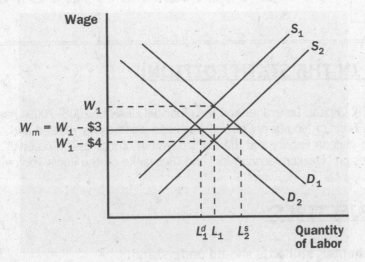

Figure 5

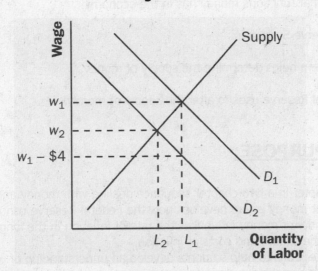

Figure 6

e. If the workers do not value the mandated benefit at all, the supply curve of labor does not shift down. As a result, the wage rate will decline by less than $4 and the equilibrium quantity of labor will decline, as shown in Figure 6. Employers are worse off, because they now pay a greater total wage plus benefits for fewer workers. Employees are worse off, because they get a lower wage and fewer are employed.

16 THE MONETARY SYSTEM

WHAT'S NEW IN THE SIXTH EDITION:

A new section on "Bank Capital, Leverage, and the Financial Crisis of 2008–2009" has been added. The section on "The Fed's Tools of Monetary Control" has been significantly revised and now includes a discussion of the term Auction Facility and the Fed's payment of interest on reserves. There are also two new *In the News* boxes on "Mackereleconomics" and "Bernanke on the Fed's Toolbox."

LEARNING OBJECTIVES:

By the end of this chapter, students should understand:

➢ what money is and what functions money has in the economy.

➢ what the Federal Reserve System is.

➢ how the banking system helps determine the supply of money.

➢ what tools the Federal Reserve uses to alter the supply of money.

CONTEXT AND PURPOSE:

Chapter 16 is the first chapter in a two-chapter sequence dealing with money and prices in the long run. Chapter 16 describes what money is and develops how the Federal Reserve controls the quantity of money. Because the quantity of money influences the rate of inflation in the long run, the following chapter concentrates on the causes and costs of inflation.

The purpose of Chapter 16 is to help students develop an understanding of what money is, what forms money takes, how the banking system helps create money, and how the Federal Reserve controls the quantity of money. An understanding of money is important because the quantity of money affects inflation and interest rates in the long run, and production and employment in the short run.

KEY POINTS:

- The term *money* refers to assets that people regularly use to buy goods and services.

- Money serves three functions. As a medium of exchange, it provides the item used to make transactions. As a unit of account, it provides the way in which prices and other economic values are recorded. As a store of value, it provides a way of transferring purchasing power from the present to the future.

- Commodity money, such as gold, is money that has intrinsic value: It would be valued even if it were not used as money. Fiat money, such as paper dollars, is money without intrinsic value: It would be worthless if it were not used as money.

- In the U.S. economy, money takes the form of currency and various types of bank deposits, such as checking accounts.

- The Federal Reserve, the central bank of the United States, is responsible for regulating the U.S. monetary system. The Fed chairman is appointed by the president and confirmed by Congress every four years. The chairman is the lead member of the Federal Open Market Committee, which meets about every six weeks to consider changes in monetary policy.

- Bank depositors provide resources to banks by depositing their funds into bank accounts. These deposits are part of a bank's liabilities. Bank owners also provide resources (called bank capital) for the bank. Because of leverage (the use of borrowed funds for investment), a small change in the value of a bank's assets can lead to a large change in the value of the bank's capital. To protect depositors, bank regulators require banks to hold a certain minimum amount of capital.

- The Fed controls the money supply primarily through open-market operations. The purchase of government bonds increases the money supply, and the sale of government bonds decreases the money supply. The Fed also uses other tools to control the money supply. It can expand the money supply by decreasing the discount rate, increasing its lending to banks, lowering reserve requirements, or decreasing the interest rate on reserves. It can contract the money supply by increasing the discount rate, decreasing its lending to banks, raising reserve requirements or increasing the interest rate on reserves.

- When individuals deposit money in banks and banks loan out some of these deposits, the quantity of money in the economy increases. Because the banking system influences the money supply in this way, the Fed's control of the money supply is imperfect.

- The Federal Reserve has in recent years set monetary policy by choosing a target for the federal funds rate, a short-term interest rate at which banks make loans to one another. As the Fed achieves its target, it adjusts the money supply.

CHAPTER OUTLINE:

> This is a good chapter to "win back" the students who were bored with national income accounting. Students are generally interested in learning more about the banking system and the Federal Reserve. The Federal Reserve offers a free, 13-minute video entitled "The Fed Today" that discusses the history and operations of the Fed.

I. The Meaning of Money

> Begin the analysis by asking students, "What is money?" Students will likely want to start right in with a discussion of the functions that money serves. Stop them. Ask them instead to describe money. Hold up a dollar bill and a piece of paper cut to the same size. Ask the students which they would prefer and why.

A. Definition of **money: the set of assets in an economy that people regularly use to buy goods and services from other people**.

B. The Functions of Money

1. Money serves three functions in our economy.

a. Definition of **medium of exchange: an item that buyers give to sellers when they want to purchase goods and services**.

b. Definition of **unit of account: the yardstick people use to post prices and record debts**.

c. Definition of **store of value: an item that people can use to transfer purchasing power from the present to the future**.

2. Definition of **liquidity: the ease with which an asset can be converted into the economy's medium of exchange**.

a. Money is the most liquid asset available.

b. Other assets (such as stocks, bonds, and real estate) vary in their liquidity.

c. When people decide in what forms to hold their wealth, they must balance the liquidity of each possible asset against the asset's usefulness as a store of value.

C. The Kinds of Money

1. Definition of **commodity money: money that takes the form of a commodity with intrinsic value**.

2. Definition of **fiat money: money without intrinsic value that is used as money because of government decree**.

3. *In the News: Mackereleconomics*

a. Even prisoners need a form of money.

b. This is an article from *The Wall Street Journal* describing how containers of mackerel are now a common currency in U.S. prisons.

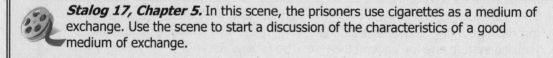

> ***Stalog 17, Chapter 5.*** In this scene, the prisoners use cigarettes as a medium of exchange. Use the scene to start a discussion of the characteristics of a good medium of exchange.

D. Money in the U.S. Economy

1. The quantity of money circulating in the United States is sometimes called the *money stock*.

2. Included in the measure of the money supply are currency, demand deposits, and other monetary assets.

a. Definition of **currency: the paper bills and coins in the hands of the public**.

Figure 1

b. Definition of **demand deposits: balances in bank accounts that depositors can access on demand by writing a check**.

3. Figure 1 shows the monetary assets included in two important measures of the money supply, M1 and M2.

Point out to students that currency only makes up about 30% of the value of M1, with the remaining 70% in the form of checking deposits. Students need to understand that the majority of the money in the economy is actually made up of account balances rather than stacks of currency in a vault.

Make sure that students realize that the assets included in M1 and M2 differ in terms of their liquidity. Also note that there are other measures of the money supply (M3 and MZM), which include less liquid assets like large time deposits.

4. *FYI: Why Credit Cards Aren't Money*

a. Credit cards are not a form of money; when a person uses a credit card, he or she is simply deferring payment for the item.

Students are quite curious about whether credit cards are considered money. You can satisfy their curiosity in part by pointing out that credit cards actually lead to a drop in the quantity of money people need to carry because they allow households to consolidate bills for payment once a month.

b. Because using a debit card is like writing a check, the account balances that lie behind debit cards are included in the measures of money.

5. *Case Study: Where Is All the Currency?*

a. If we divide the amount of outstanding currency in the United States by the adult population, we find that the average adult should have approximately $3,653 in currency.

b. Of course, most adults carry a much smaller amount.

c. One explanation is that a great deal of U.S. currency may be held in other countries.

d. Another explanation is that large amounts of currency may be held by criminals because transactions that use currency leave no paper trail.

II. The Federal Reserve System

A. Definition of **Federal Reserve (Fed): the central bank of the United States**.

B. Definition of **central bank: An institution designed to oversee the banking system and regulate the quantity of money in the economy.**

Activity 1—What Can Be Learned from a Dollar?

Type:	In-class demonstration
Topics:	Money, Federal Reserve
Materials needed:	None
Time:	5 minutes
Class limitations:	Works in any size class

Purpose
This activity introduces the role of the Federal Reserve in controlling the money supply.

Instructions
Ask the class to take a dollar bill from wallets (or a $5, $10, $20, or $100). Students without any currency can share with someone who does. Ask the class to read the bill.

After a minute, ask them what they have learned.

Common Answers and Points for Discussion
Most students focus on the statement "This note is legal tender for all debts, public and private." This statement is the only "backing" U.S. currency has—the note is not convertible into gold or silver. This can be used to introduce the difference between fiat money and commodity money.

Someone will usually point to the phrase printed at the top of the face of each bill: "Federal Reserve Note." Explain the Fed functions as the United States' central bank—controlling the money supply and supplying currency to banks.

Information about the structure of the Federal Reserve can be found in the seal to the left of Washington's portrait. The writing around the seal says "Federal Reserve Bank of _____."

If the class is big enough, all 12 Federal Reserve Banks will be represented: Boston, New York, Philadelphia, Richmond, Atlanta, Cleveland, Chicago, St. Louis, Minneapolis, Kansas City, Dallas, and San Francisco.

This is a good place to introduce the Federal Reserve Districts, and the Banks' roles in those regions. These include check clearing, holding commercial bank reserves, supplying currency, lending to commercial banks, and collecting and analyzing regional economic data.

C. The Fed's Organization

Highlight the Federal Reserve's independence from the federal government. Students are surprised to find that the Fed actually earns more than enough to finance its operations without being funded by Congress.

2. The Fed is run by a Board of Governors with 7 members who serve 14-year terms.

a. The Board of Governors has a chairman who is appointed for a four-year term.

b. The current chairman is Ben Bernanke.

3. The Federal Reserve System is made up of 12 regional Federal Reserve Banks located in major cities around the country.

Have students pull out dollar bills and read the name of the city of the district bank on the bill. However, make sure that they are actually reading off dollar bills and not just guessing the names of large cities.

4. One job performed by the Fed is the regulation of banks to ensure the health of the nation's banking system.

a. The Fed monitors each bank's financial condition and facilitates bank transactions by clearing checks.

b. The Fed also makes loans to banks when they want (or need) to borrow.

5. The second job of the Fed is to control the quantity of money available in the economy.

a. Definition of **money supply: the quantity of money available in the economy**.

b. Definition of **monetary policy: the setting of the money supply by policymakers in the central bank**.

D. The Federal Open Market Committee

1. The Federal Open Market Committee (FOMC) consists of the 7 members of the Board of Governors and 5 of the 12 regional Federal Reserve District Bank presidents.

Introduce students to the idea of open market operations here, but do not be surprised if they do not catch on quickly. You can return to this topic later in the chapter.

2. The primary way in which the Fed increases or decreases the supply of money is through open market operations (which involve the purchase or sale of U.S. government bonds).

a. If the Fed wants to increase the supply of money, it creates dollars and uses them to purchase government bonds from the public through the nation's bond markets.

b. If the Fed wants to lower the supply of money, it sells government bonds from its portfolio to the public. Money is then taken out of the hands of the public and the supply of money falls.

III. Banks and the Money Supply

 The process of money creation in the banking system is one of the more difficult things to teach at the Principles level. Nearly every aspect of the process will be new to students and nothing is obvious or intuitive. Therefore, it is extremely important that each step in the process is shown through T-accounts so that students can see how the banking system creates money as banks carry out their normal functions of accepting deposits and giving out loans.

A. The Simple Case of 100-Percent-Reserve Banking

1. Example: Suppose that currency is the only form of money and the total amount of currency is $100.

2. A bank is created as a safe place to store currency; all deposits are kept in the vault until the depositor withdraws them.

a. Definition of **reserves: deposits that banks have received but have not loaned out**.

b. Under the example described above, we have 100-percent-reserve banking.

 Make sure that you explain why bank reserves are an asset from the bank's perspective, but customer deposits are a liability.

3. The financial position of the bank can be described with a T-account:

FIRST NATIONAL BANK			
Assets		**Liabilities**	
Reserves	$100.00	Deposits	$100.00

 Students will either catch on to T-accounts immediately or be completely confused. It is a good idea to explain them and then let students work together in small groups of two or three. You can check each group to identify the students who will require individualized attention.

4. The money supply in this economy is unchanged by the creation of a bank.

a. Before the bank was created, the money supply consisted of $100 worth of currency.

b. Now, with the bank, the money supply consists of $100 worth of deposits.

5. This means that, if banks hold all deposits in reserve, banks do not influence the supply of money.

B. Money Creation with Fractional-Reserve Banking

1. Definition of **fractional-reserve banking: a banking system in which banks hold only a fraction of deposits as reserves**.

2. Definition of **reserve ratio: the fraction of deposits that banks hold as reserves**.

3. Example: Same as before, but First National decides to set its reserve ratio equal to 10% and lend the remainder of the deposits.

4. The bank's T-account would look like this:

FIRST NATIONAL BANK			
Assets		**Liabilities**	
Reserves	$10.00	Deposits	$100.00
Loans	$90.00		

5. When the bank makes these loans, the money supply changes.

   a. Before the bank made any loans, the money supply was equal to the $100 worth of deposits.

   b. Now, after the loans, deposits are still equal to $100, but borrowers now also hold $90 worth of currency from the loans.

   c. Therefore, when banks hold only a fraction of deposits in reserve, banks create money.

6. Note that, while new money has been created, so has debt. There is no new wealth created by this process.

C. The Money Multiplier

1. The creation of money does not stop at this point.

2. Borrowers usually borrow money to purchase something and then the money likely becomes redeposited at a bank.

3. Suppose a person borrowed the $90 to purchase something and the funds then get redeposited in Second National Bank. Here is this bank's T-account (assuming that it also sets its reserve ratio to 10%):

SECOND NATIONAL BANK			
Assets		**Liabilities**	
Reserves	$9.00	Deposits	$90.00
Loans	$81.00		

4. If the $81 in loans becomes redeposited in another bank, this process will go on and on.

5. Each time the money is deposited and a bank loan is created, more money is created.

6. Definition of **money multiplier: the amount of money the banking system generates with each dollar of reserves**.

> money multiplier = 1/reserve ratio

7. In our example, the money supply increased from $100 to $1,000 after the establishment of fractional-reserve banking.

ALTERNATIVE CLASSROOM EXAMPLE:
Reserve ratio = 12.5%
Money multiplier = 1/0.125 = 8

 Spend some time showing students how the multiplier changes as reserve requirements change. Make sure that you explain why the multiplier changes when the reserve ratio changes. Students will catch on to the math fairly quickly; it is the intuition that is most difficult for them.

D. Bank Capital, Leverage, and the Financial Crisis of 2008–2009

1. In reality, banks also get funds from issuing debt and equity.

2. Definition of **bank capital: the resources a bank's owners have put into the institution**.

3. A more realistic balance sheet for a bank:

MORE REALISTIC NATIONAL BANK			
Assets		**Liabilities**	
Reserves	$200.00	Deposits	$800.00
Loans	$700.00	Debt	$150.00
Securities	$100.00	Capital (owner's equity)	$50.00

4. Definition of **leverage: the use of borrowed money to supplement existing funds for purposes of investment**.

5. Definition of **leverage ratio: the ratio of assets to bank capital**.

   a. The leverage ratio is $1,000/$50 = 20.

   b. A leverage ratio of 20 means that, for every dollar of capital that has been contributed by the owners, the bank has $20 of assets.

   c. Because of leverage, a small change in assets can lead to a large change in owner's equity.

6. Definition of **capital requirement: a government regulation specifying a minimum amount of bank capital**.

7. In 2008 and 2009, many banks found themselves with too little capital because the value of their assets had fallen dramatically.

IV. The Fed's Tools of Monetary Control

   A. How the Fed Influences the Quantity of Reserves

   1. Open Market Operations

---

a. Definition of **open market operations**: **the purchase and sale of U.S. government bonds by the Fed**.

b. If the Fed wants to increase the supply of money, it creates dollars and uses them to purchase government bonds from the public in the nation's bond markets.

c. If the Fed wants to lower the supply of money, it sells government bonds from its portfolio to the public in the nation's bond markets. Money is then taken out of the hands of the public and the supply of money falls.

d. If the sale or purchase of government bonds affects the amount of deposits in the banking system, the effect will be made larger by the money multiplier.

> You may wish to use T-accounts to show the effects of an open market purchase or sale. This way, students can see that the effect of an open market operation can be quite large because of the money multiplier.

d. Open market operations are easy for the Fed to conduct and are therefore the tool of monetary policy that the Fed uses most often.

2. Fed Lending to Banks

a. The Fed can also lend reserves to banks.

b. Definition of **discount rate**: **the interest rate on the loans that the Fed makes to banks**.

c. A higher discount rate discourages banks from borrowing from the Fed and likely encourages banks to hold onto larger amounts of reserves. This in turn lowers the money supply.

d. A lower discount rate encourages banks to lend their reserves (and borrow from the Fed). This will increase the money supply.

e. In recent years, the Fed has set up new mechanisms for banks to borrow from the Fed.

B. How the Fed Influences the Reserve Ratio

1. Reserve Requirements

a. Definition of **reserve requirements**: **regulations on the minimum amount of reserves that banks must hold against deposits**.

b. This can affect the size of the money supply through changes in the money multiplier.

c. The Fed rarely uses this tool because of the disruptions in the banking industry that would be caused by frequent alterations of reserve requirements. (It is also not effective when banks hold a lot of excess reserves.)

2. Paying Interest on Reserves

a. In October of 2008, the Fed began paying banks interest on reserves.

    b. The higher the interest rate, the more reserves a bank will want to hold. This will reduce the money multiplier.

C. Problems in Controlling the Money Supply

    1. The Fed does not control the amount of money that consumers choose to deposit in banks.

        a. The more money that households deposit, the more reserves the banks have, and the more money the banking system can create.

        b. The less money that households deposit, the smaller the amount of reserves banks have, and the less money the banking system can create.

    2. The Fed does not control the amount that bankers choose to lend.

        a. The amount of money created by the banking system depends on loans being made.

        b. If banks choose to hold onto a greater level of reserves than required by the Fed (called excess reserves), the money supply will fall.

    3. Therefore, in a system of fractional-reserve banking, the amount of money in the economy depends in part on the behavior of depositors and bankers.

    4. Because the Fed cannot control or perfectly predict this behavior, it cannot perfectly control the money supply.

D. *Case Study: Bank Runs and the Money Supply*

    1. Bank runs create a large problem under fractional-reserve banking.

    2. Because the bank only holds a fraction of its deposits in reserve, it will not have the funds to satisfy all of the withdrawal requests from its depositors.

    3. Today, deposits are guaranteed through the Federal Depository Insurance Corporation (FDIC).

It's a Wonderful Life, Chapter 12. George finds a mob standing outside the Building and Loan and he allows the people to come into the lobby. His uncle tells him that he has given out most of the cash the bank has and has closed the bank to prevent a riot. George pleads with the people and tries to explain how the banking system works. The bank doesn't keep all depositors' money, but lends it out to borrowers for new homes and businesses.

Activity 2—Money Creation

Type:	In-class demonstration
Topics:	The banking system and deposit expansion
Materials needed:	two volunteers, a paper with "$1,000" written on it
Time:	25 minutes
Class limitations:	Works in any size class

Purpose

This activity demonstrates the role of the banking system in expanding the money supply.

Instructions

The two volunteers are bankers. Have each of them draw a balance sheet on the board.

BankTwo		AmerBankCorp	
Assets	Liabilities	Assets	Liabilities
0	0	0	0

The rest of the class is the public. They are all eager borrowers and depositors.

The instructor is the Federal Reserve. The Federal Reserve sets the reserve requirement at 20% of deposits.

The Federal Reserve also conducts open-market operations. Use the $1,000 paper to buy a baseball cap from a student. (Explain that the Fed actually buys government bonds from the public because the market for used baseball caps is small.)

The capless student now has $1,000 to spend with any other member of the class. This student receives $1,000 and puts it in the bank of his or her choice.

The bank now has $1,000 in deposits (a liability) and $1,000 in cash (an asset). The bank needs to keep $200 in reserve (20%) but can loan the other $800. Have the banker tear off 20% of the bill and give the rest to another student.

Revise the banks' balance sheets.

Now the borrower spends the $800 and the recipient deposits it in a bank. This bank now has $800 in deposits and $800 in cash. Of that, $160 needs to be kept in reserve and $640 can be lent. Have the banker save 20% of the paper and give the rest to another eager borrower.

Revise the banks' balance sheets.

Continue this process for a few more iterations.

At the end, ask everyone who has money in the bank to stand. The total deposits in the bank will far exceed the initial $1,000 that the Fed put into the economy.

Show the final balance sheet for each bank.

Points for Discussion

Banks are important to the process of money creation. The banking system, as a whole, literally expands the money supply.

If the process is carried on far enough, you can derive the money multiplier.

F. The Federal Funds Rate

1. Definition of **federal funds rate: the short-term interest rate that banks charge one another for loans.**

2. When the federal funds rate rises or falls, other interest rates often move in the same direction.

3. In recent years, the Fed has set a target for the federal funds rate.

G. *In the News: Bernanke on the Fed's Toolbox*

1. During the financial crisis of 2008 and 2009, the Fed expanded reserves to help struggling banks.

2. This is an article written by Fed chairman Ben Bernanke discussing the Fed's options for reversing this policy once the economy recovers from this deep recession.

SOLUTIONS TO TEXT PROBLEMS:

Quick Quizzes

1. The three functions of money are: (1) medium of exchange; (2) unit of account; and (3) store of value. Money is a medium of exchange because money is the item people use to purchase goods and services. Money is a unit of account because it is the yardstick people use to post prices and record debts. Money is a store of value because people use it to transfer purchasing power from the present to the future.

2. The primary responsibilities of the Federal Reserve are to regulate banks, to ensure the health of the banking system, and to control the quantity of money that is made available in the economy. If the Fed wants to increase the supply of money, it usually does so by creating dollars and using them to purchase government bonds from the public in the nation's bond markets.

3. Banks create money when they hold a fraction of their deposits in reserve and lend out the remainder. If the Fed wanted to use all three of its tools to decrease the money supply, it would: (1) sell government bonds from its portfolio in the open market to reduce the number of dollars in circulation; (2) increase reserve requirements to reduce the money created by banks; and (3) increase the discount rate to discourage banks from borrowing reserves from the Fed.

Questions for Review

1. Money is different from other assets in the economy because it is the most liquid asset available. Other assets vary widely in their liquidity.

2. Commodity money is money with intrinsic value, like gold, which can be used for purposes other than as a medium of exchange. Fiat money is money without intrinsic value; it has no value other than its use as a medium of exchange. Our economy today uses fiat money.

3. Demand deposits are balances in bank accounts that depositors can access on demand simply by writing a check or using a debit card. They should be included in the supply of money because they can be used as a medium of exchange.

4. The Federal Open Market Committee (FOMC) is responsible for setting monetary policy in the United States. The FOMC consists of the 7 members of the Federal Reserve Board of Governors and 5 of the 12 presidents of Federal Reserve Banks. Members of the Board of Governors are appointed by the president of the United States and confirmed by the U.S. Senate. The presidents of the Federal Reserve Banks are chosen by each bank's board of directors.

5. If the Fed wants to increase the supply of money with open-market operations, it purchases U.S. government bonds from the public on the open market. The purchase increases the number of dollars in the hands of the public, thus raising the money supply.

6. Banks do not hold 100% reserves because it is more profitable to use the reserves to make loans, which earn interest, instead of leaving the money as reserves, which earn no interest. The amount of reserves banks hold is related to the amount of money the banking system creates through the money multiplier. The smaller the fraction of reserves banks hold, the larger the money multiplier, because each dollar of reserves is used to create more money.

7. Bank B will show a larger change in bank capital. The drop in assets will render Bank B insolvent because its assets will fall below its liabilities. Bank A will suffer a large decline in bank capital (70%) but will remain solvent.

8. The discount rate is the interest rate on loans that the Federal Reserve makes to banks. If the Fed raises the discount rate, fewer banks will borrow from the Fed, so both banks' reserves and the money supply will be lower.

9. Reserve requirements are regulations on the minimum amount of reserves that banks must hold against deposits. An increase in reserve requirements raises the reserve ratio, lowers the money multiplier, and decreases the money supply.

10. The Fed cannot control the money supply perfectly because: (1) the Fed does not control the amount of money that households choose to hold as deposits in banks; and (2) the Fed does not control the amount that bankers choose to lend. The actions of households and banks affect the money supply in ways the Fed cannot perfectly control or predict.

Problems and Applications

1. a. A U.S. penny is money in the U.S. economy because it is used as a medium of exchange to buy goods or services, it serves as a unit of account because prices in stores are listed in terms of dollars and cents, and it serves as a store of value for anyone who holds it over time.

   b. A Mexican peso is not money in the U.S. economy, because it is not used as a medium of exchange, and prices are not given in terms of pesos, so it is not a unit of account. It could serve as a store of value, though.

   c. A Picasso painting is not money, because you cannot exchange it for goods or services, and prices are not given in terms of Picasso paintings. It does, however, serve as a store of value.

d. A plastic credit card is similar to money, but represents deferred payment rather than immediate payment. So credit cards do not fully represent the medium of exchange function of money, nor are they really stores of value, because they represent short-term loans rather than being an asset like currency.

2. When your uncle repays a $100 loan from Tenth National Bank (TNB) by writing a check from his TNB checking account, the result is a change in the assets and liabilities of both your uncle and TNB, as shown in these T-accounts:

Your Uncle			
Assets		**Liabilities**	
Before:			
Checking Account	$100	Loans	$100
After:			
Checking Account	$0	Loans	$0

Tenth National Bank			
Assets		**Liabilities**	
Before:			
Loans	$100	Deposits	$100
After:			
Loans	$0	Deposits	$0

By paying off the loan, your uncle simply eliminated the outstanding loan using the assets in his checking account. Your uncle's wealth has not changed; he simply has fewer assets and fewer liabilities.

3. a. Here is BSB's T-account:

Beleaguered State Bank			
Assets		**Liabilities**	
Reserves	$25 million	Deposits	$250 million
Loans	$225 million		

b. When BSB's largest depositor withdraws $10 million in cash and BSB reduces its loans outstanding to maintain the same reserve ratio, its T-account is now:

Beleaguered State Bank			
Assets		**Liabilities**	
Reserves	$24 million	Deposits	$240 million
Loans	$216 million		

c. Because BSB is cutting back on its loans, other banks will find themselves short of reserves and they may also cut back on their loans as well.

d. BSB may find it difficult to cut back on its loans immediately, because it cannot force people to pay off loans. Instead, it can stop making new loans. But for a time it might find itself with more loans than it wants. It could try to attract additional deposits to get additional reserves, or borrow from another bank or from the Fed.

4. If you take $100 that you held as currency and put it into the banking system, then the total amount of deposits in the banking system increases by $1,000, because a reserve ratio of 10% means the money multiplier is 1/0.10 = 10. Thus, the money supply increases by $900, because deposits increase by $1,000 but currency declines by $100.

5. a.

Happy Bank			
Assets		**Liabilities**	
Reserves	$100	Deposits	$800
Loans	$900	Bank Capital	$200

    b. The leverage ratio = $1,000/$200 = 5.

    c.

Happy Bank			
Assets		**Liabilities**	
Reserves	$100	Deposits	$800
Loans	$810	Bank Capital	$110

    Assets decline by 0.9%. Bank capital declines by 4.5%. Bank capital is smaller than assets.

6. With a required reserve ratio of 10%, the money multiplier could be as high as 1/0.10 = 10, if banks hold no excess reserves and people do not keep some additional currency. So the maximum increase in the money supply from a $10 million open-market purchase is $100 million. The smallest possible increase is $10 million if all of the money is held by banks as excess reserves.

7. The money supply will expand more if the Fed buys $2,000 worth of bonds. Both deposits will lead to monetary expansion, but the Fed's deposit is new money. The $2,000 from the cookie jar is already part of the money supply.

8. a. If the required reserve ratio is 5%, then ABC Bank's required reserves are $500,000 × 0.05 = $25,000. Because the bank's total reserves are $100,000, it has excess reserves of $75,000.

    b. With a required reserve ratio of 5%, the money multiplier is 1/0.05 = 20. If ABC Bank lends out its excess reserves of $75,000, the money supply will eventually increase by $75,000 × 20 = $1,500,000.

9. a. With a required reserve ratio of 10% and no excess reserves, the money multiplier is 1/0.10 = 10. If the Fed sells $1 million of bonds, reserves will decline by $1 million and the money supply will contract by 10 × $1 million = $10 million.

    b. Banks might wish to hold excess reserves if they need to hold the reserves for their day-to-day operations, such as paying other banks for customers' transactions, making change, cashing paychecks, and so on. If banks increase excess reserves such that there is no overall change in the total reserve ratio, then the money multiplier does not change and there is no effect on the money supply.

10. a. With banks holding only required reserves of 10%, the money multiplier is 1/0.10 = 10. Because reserves are $100 billion, the money supply is 10 × $100 billion = $1,000 billion.

b. If the required reserve ratio is raised to 20%, the money multiplier declines to 1/0.20 = 5. With reserves of $100 billion, the money supply would decline to $500 billion, a decline of $500 billion. Reserves would be unchanged.

11. a. To expand the money supply, the Fed should buy bonds.

b. With a reserve requirement of 20%, the money multiplier is 1/0.20 = 5. Therefore to expand the money supply by $40 million, the Fed should buy $40 million/5 = $8 million worth of bonds.

12. a. If people hold all money as currency, the quantity of money is $2,000.

b. If people hold all money as demand deposits at banks with 100% reserves, the quantity of money is $2,000.

c. If people have $1,000 in currency and $1,000 in demand deposits, the quantity of money is $2,000.

d. If banks have a reserve ratio of 10%, the money multiplier is 1/0.10 = 10. So if people hold all money as demand deposits, the quantity of money is 10 × $2,000 = $20,000.

e. If people hold equal amounts of currency (C) and demand deposits (D) and the money multiplier for reserves is 10, then two equations must be satisfied: (1) $C = D$, so that people have equal amounts of currency and demand deposits; and (2) 10 × ($2,000 − C) = D, so that the money multiplier (10) times the number of dollar bills that are not being held by people ($2,000 − C) equals the amount of demand deposits (D). Using the first equation in the second gives 10 × ($2,000 − D) = D, or $20,000 − 10$D$ = D, or $20,000 = 11 D, so D = $1,818.18. Then C = $1,818.18. The quantity of money is $C + D$ = $3,636.36.

MONEY GROWTH AND INFLATION

WHAT'S NEW IN THE SIXTH EDITION:

A new section on "Inflation is Bad, but Deflation May be Worse" has been added. There is a new *FYI* box on "Hyperinflation in Zimbabwe" and a new *In the News* feature on "Inflation Targets."

LEARNING OBJECTIVES:

By the end of this chapter, students should understand:

➢ why inflation results from rapid growth in the money supply.

➢ the meaning of the classical dichotomy and monetary neutrality.

➢ why some countries print so much money that they experience hyperinflation.

➢ how the nominal interest rate responds to the inflation rate.

➢ the various costs that inflation imposes on society.

CONTEXT AND PURPOSE:

Chapter 17 is the second chapter in a two-chapter sequence dealing with money and prices in the long run. Chapter 16 explained what money is and how the Federal Reserve controls the quantity of money. Chapter 17 establishes the relationship between the rate of growth of money and the inflation rate. The purpose of this chapter is to acquaint students with the causes and costs of inflation. Students will find that, in the long run, there is a strong relationship between the growth rate of money and inflation. Students will also find that there are numerous costs to the economy from high inflation, but that there is not a consensus on the importance of these costs when inflation is moderate.

KEY POINTS:

* The overall level of prices in an economy adjusts to bring money supply and money demand into balance. When the central bank increases the supply of money, it causes the price level to rise. Persistent growth in the quantity of money supplied leads to continuing inflation.

- The principle of monetary neutrality asserts that changes in the quantity of money influence nominal variables but not real variables. Most economists believe that monetary neutrality approximately describes the behavior of the economy in the long run.

- A government can pay for some of its spending simply by printing money. When countries rely heavily on this "inflation tax," the result is hyperinflation.

- One application of the principle of monetary neutrality is the Fisher effect. According to the Fisher effect, when the inflation rate rises, the nominal interest rate rises by the same amount, so that the real interest rate remains the same.

- Many people think that inflation makes them poorer because it raises the cost of what they buy. This view is a fallacy, however, because inflation also raises nominal incomes.

- Economists have identified six costs of inflation: shoeleather costs associated with reduced money holdings, menu costs associated with more frequent adjustment of prices, increased variability of relative prices, unintended changes in tax liabilities due to nonindexation of the tax code, confusion and inconvenience resulting from a changing unit of account, and arbitrary redistributions of wealth between debtors and creditors. Many of these costs are large during hyperinflation, but the size of these costs for moderate inflation is less clear.

CHAPTER OUTLINE:

I.   The inflation rate is measured as the percentage change in the Consumer Price Index, the GDP deflator, or some other index of the overall price level.

   A.   Over the past 70 years, prices have risen an average of about 4% per year in the United States.

      1.   There has been substantial variation in the rate of price changes over time.

      2.   During the 1990s, prices rose at an average rate of 2% per year, while prices rose by 7% per year during the 1970s.

   B.   International data shows an even broader range of inflation experiences. In 2009, inflation was 9% in Russia and 25% in Venezuela.

II. The Classical Theory of Inflation

> Start off the chapter by differentiating between a "once-and-for-all" increase in the average level of prices and a continuous increase in the price level. Also make sure that students realize that inflation means that the average level of prices in the economy is rising rather than the prices of all goods.

> It is instructive to review the inflation history of the United States. While your students are likely fully aware of inflation, they may not realize that, prior to World War II, the United States experienced several periods of deflation. Also point out to the students that the rate of inflation has varied significantly since World War II.

A. The Level of Prices and the Value of Money

    1. When the price level rises, people have to pay more for the goods and services that they purchase.

    2. A rise in the price level also means that the value of money is now lower because each dollar now buys a smaller quantity of goods and services.

    3. If P is the price level, then the quantity of goods and services that can be purchased with $1 is equal to $1/P$.

    4. Suppose you live in a country with one good (ice cream cones).

        a. When the price of an ice cream cone is $2, the value of a dollar is 1/2 cone.

        b. When the price of an ice cream cone rises to $3, the value of a dollar is 1/3 cone.

B. Money Supply, Money Demand, and Monetary Equilibrium

    1. The value of money is determined by the supply and demand for money.

    2. For the most part, the supply of money is determined by the Fed.

        a. This implies that the quantity of money supplied is fixed (until the Fed decides to change it).

        b. Thus, the supply of money will be vertical (perfectly inelastic).

    3. The demand for money reflects how much wealth people want to hold in liquid form.

        a. One variable that is very important in determining the demand for money is the price level.

        b. The higher prices are, the more money that is needed to perform transactions.

Figure 1

        c. Thus, a higher price level (and a lower value of money) leads to a higher quantity of money demanded.

    4. In the long run, the overall price level adjusts to the level at which the demand for money equals the supply of money.

        a. If the price level is above the equilibrium level, people will want to hold more money than is available and prices will have to decline.

        b. If the price level is below equilibrium, people will want to hold less money than that available and the price level will rise.

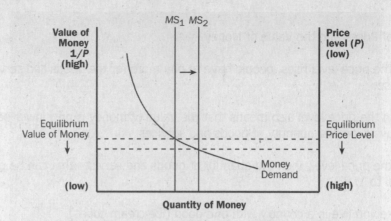

5. We can show the supply and demand for money using a graph.

  a. The left-hand vertical axis is the value of money, measured by $1/P$.

  b. The right-hand vertical axis is the price level (P). Note that it is inverted—a high value of money means a low price level and vice versa.

  c. At the equilibrium, the quantity of money demanded is equal to the quantity of money supplied.

C. The Effects of a Monetary Injection

  1. Assume that the economy is currently in equilibrium and the Fed suddenly increases the supply of money.

  2. The supply of money shifts to the right.

Figure 2

  3. The equilibrium value of money falls and the price level rises.

  4. When an increase in the money supply makes dollars more plentiful, the result is an increase in the price level that makes each dollar less valuable.

  5. Definition of **quantity theory of money: a theory asserting that the quantity of money available determines the price level and that the growth rate in the quantity of money available determines the inflation rate**.

D. A Brief Look at the Adjustment Process

  1. The immediate effect of an increase in the money supply is to create an excess supply of money.

  2. People try to get rid of this excess supply in a variety of ways.

    a. They may buy goods and services with the excess funds.

b. They may use these excess funds to make loans to others by buying bonds or depositing the money in a bank account. These loans will then be used to buy goods and services.

c. In either case, the increase in the money supply leads to an increase in the demand for goods and services.

d. Because the supply of goods and services has not changed, the result of an increase in the demand for goods and services will be higher prices.

Futurama, "Three-Hundred Big Boys." **Season 4 (0:30-1:15; 2:34-2:38).**
The government gives all citizens $300. Prices immediately rise.

E. The Classical Dichotomy and Monetary Neutrality

1. In the 18th century, David Hume and other economists wrote about the relationship between monetary changes and important macroeconomic variables such as production, employment, real wages, and real interest rates.

2. They suggested that economic variables should be divided into two groups: nominal variables and real variables.

   a. Definition of **nominal variables**: **variables measured in monetary units**.

   b. Definition of **real variables**: **variables measured in physical units**.

3. Definition of **classical dichotomy**: **the theoretical separation of nominal and real variables**.

4. Prices in the economy are nominal (because they are quoted in units of money), but relative prices are real (because they are not measured in money terms).

5. Classical analysis suggested that different forces influence real and nominal variables.

   a. Changes in the money supply affect nominal variables but not real variables.

   b. Definition of **monetary neutrality**: **the proposition that changes in the money supply do not affect real variables**.

Mankiw's analogy of changing the size of a yard from 36 inches to 18 inches is a useful way to explain the confusion that a change in a unit of measurement (or a unit of account) can cause.

F. Velocity and the Quantity Equation

1. Definition of **velocity of money**: **the rate at which money changes hands**.

2. To calculate velocity, we divide nominal GDP by the quantity of money.

$$\text{velocity} = \text{nominal GDP/money supply}$$

3. If *P* is the price level (the GDP deflator), *Y* is real GDP, and *M* is the quantity of money:

$$\text{velocity} = \frac{P \times Y}{M}$$

4. Rearranging, we get the quantity equation:

$$M \times V = P \times Y$$

ALTERNATIVE CLASSROOM EXAMPLE:

Suppose that:

Real GDP = $5,000
Velocity = 5
Money supply = $2,000
Price level = 2

We can show that:

M x V = P x Y
$2,000 x 5 = 2 x $5,000
$10,000 = $10,000

---

5. Definition of **quantity equation**: the equation **$M \times V = P \times Y$, which relates the quantity of money, the velocity of money, and the dollar value of the economy's output of goods and services**.

   a. The quantity equation shows that an increase in the quantity of money must be reflected in one of the other three variables.

   b. Specifically, the price level must rise, output must rise, or velocity must fall.

Figure 3

   c. Figure 3 shows nominal GDP, the quantity of money (as measured by M2) and the velocity of money for the United States since 1960. It appears that velocity is fairly stable, while GDP and the money supply have grown dramatically.

6. We can now explain how an increase in the quantity of money affects the price level using the quantity equation.

   a. The velocity of money is relatively stable over time.

   b. When the central bank changes the quantity of money (*M*), it will proportionately change the nominal value of output ($P \times Y$).

   c. The economy's output of goods and services (*Y*) is determined primarily by available resources and technology. Because money is neutral, changes in the money supply do not affect output.

d. This must mean that *P* increases proportionately with the change in *M*.

e. Thus, when the central bank increases the money supply rapidly, the result is a high level of inflation.

Now would be a good time to discuss the debate in Chapter 23 on whether monetary policy should be made by rule or discretion.

G. *Case Study: Money and Prices during Four Hyperinflations*

1. Hyperinflation is generally defined as inflation that exceeds 50% per month.

Figure 4

2. Figure 4 shows data from four classic periods of hyperinflation during the 1920s in Austria, Hungary, Germany, and Poland.

3. We can see that, in each graph, the quantity of money and the price level are almost parallel.

4. These episodes illustrate Principle #9: Prices rise when the government prints too much money.

H. The Inflation Tax

1. Some countries use money creation to pay for spending instead of using tax revenue.

2. Definition of **inflation tax: the revenue the government raises by creating money**.

3. The inflation tax is like a tax on everyone who holds money.

Point out that an inflation tax is a more subtle form of taxation than the standard forms of taxation (income tax, sales tax, etc.).

4. Almost all hyperinflations follow the same pattern.

a. The government has a high level of spending and inadequate tax revenue to pay for its spending.

b. The government's ability to borrow funds is limited.

c. As a result, it turns to printing money to pay for its spending.

d. The large increases in the money supply lead to large amounts of inflation.

e. The hyperinflation ends when the government cuts its spending and eliminates the need to create new money.

5. *FYI: Hyperinflation in Zimbabwe*

    a. In the 2000s, Zimbabwe faced one of history's most extreme examples of hyperinflation.

    b. Before the period of hyperinflation, one Zimbabwe dollar was worth a bit more than one U.S. dollar.

    c. By 2009, the Zimbabwe government was issuing noted with denominations as large as 10 trillion Zimbabwe dollars (which was worth less than three U.S. dollars).

I. The Fisher Effect

    1. Recall that the real interest rate is equal to the nominal interest rate minus the inflation rate.

    2. This, of course, means that:

nominal interest rate = real interest rate + inflation rate

    a. The supply and demand for loanable funds determines the real interest rate.

    b. Growth in the money supply determines the inflation rate.

ALTERNATIVE CLASSROOM EXAMPLE:
Real interest rate = 5%
Inflation rate = 2%

This means that the nominal interest rate will be 5% + 2% = 7%.

If the inflation rate rises to 3%, the nominal interest rate will rise to 5% + 3% = 8%.

---

    3. When the Fed increases the rate of growth of the money supply, the inflation rate increases. This in turn will lead to an increase in the nominal interest rate.

    4. Definition of **Fisher effect: the one-for-one adjustment of the nominal interest rate to the inflation rate**.

    a. The Fisher effect does not hold in the short run to the extent that inflation is unanticipated.

    b. If inflation catches borrowers and lenders by surprise, the nominal interest rate will fail to reflect the rise in prices.

Figure 5

    5. Figure 5 shows the nominal interest rate and the inflation rate in the U.S. economy since 1960.

III. The Costs of Inflation

    A. A Fall in Purchasing Power? The Inflation Fallacy

1. Most individuals believe that the major problem caused by inflation is that inflation lowers the purchasing power of a person's income.

2. However, as prices rise, so do incomes. Thus, inflation does not in itself reduce the purchasing power of incomes.

> Point out to students that prices involve both buyers and sellers. This implies that the higher prices paid by consumers are exactly offset by the higher incomes received by the sellers. Also remind students that workers often get pay increases over time to compensate for increases in the cost of living.

B. Shoeleather Costs

1. Because inflation erodes the value of money that you carry in your pocket, you can avoid this drop in value by holding less money.

2. However, holding less money generally means more trips to the bank.

3. Definition of **shoeleather costs: the resources wasted when inflation encourages people to reduce their money holdings**.

4. This cost can be considerable in countries experiencing hyperinflation.

C. Menu Costs

1. Definition of **menu costs: the costs of changing prices**.

2. During periods of inflation, firms must change their prices more often.

D. Relative-Price Variability and the Misallocation of Resources

1. Because prices of most goods change only once in a while (instead of constantly), inflation causes relative prices to vary more than they would otherwise.

2. When inflation distorts relative prices, consumer decisions are distorted and markets are less able to allocate resources to their best use.

E. Inflation-Induced Tax Distortions

1. Lawmakers fail to take inflation into account when they write tax laws.

2. The nominal values of interest income and capital gains are taxed (not the real values).

> Students find this section intriguing. Most have not considered the fact that tax laws do not differentiate between nominal and real interest income and capital gains, and they soon realize that this can lead to effects on rates of saving. Work through an example of the after-tax real interest rate under different inflation scenarios as is done in the text.

Table 1

a. Table 1 shows a hypothetical example of two individuals, living in two countries earning the same real interest rate, and paying the same tax rate, but one individual lives in a country without inflation and the other lives in a country with 8% inflation.

b. The person living in the country with inflation ends up with a smaller after-tax real interest rate.

3. This implies that higher inflation will tend to discourage saving.

4. A possible solution to this problem would be to index the tax system.

ALTERNATIVE CLASSROOM EXAMPLE:

Hannah and Miley each earn a real interest rate on their savings account of 3%. However, Hannah lives in a country with a 1% inflation rate, while Miley lives in a country with a 10% inflation rate. Both countries have a 20% tax on income.

	Hannah	Miley
Real interest rate	3%	3%
Inflation rate	1	10
Nominal interest rate	4	13
Reduced interest due to 20% tax	0.8	2.6
After-tax nominal interest rate	3.2	11.4
After-tax real interest rate	2.2	1.4

Note that the after-tax return on saving is lower in Miley's country than in Hannah's. This means that individuals in Miley's country will be less likely to save.

F. Confusion and Inconvenience

1. Money is the yardstick that we use to measure economic transactions.

2. When inflation occurs, the value of money falls. This alters the yardstick that we use to measure important variables like incomes and profit.

G. A Special Cost of Unexpected Inflation: Arbitrary Redistributions of Wealth

1. Example: Sam Student takes out a $20,000 loan at 7% interest (nominal). In 10 years, the loan will come due. After his debt has compounded for 10 years at 7%, Sam will owe the bank $40,000.

2. The real value of this debt will depend on inflation.

a. If the economy has a hyperinflation, wages and prices will rise so much that Sam may be able to pay the $40,000 out of pocket change.

b. If the economy has deflation, Sam will find the $40,000 a greater burden than he imagined.

3. Because inflation is often hard to predict, it imposes risk on both Sam and the bank that the real value of the debt will differ from that expected when the loan is made.

4. Inflation is especially volatile and uncertain when the average rate of inflation is high.

H. Inflation Is Bad, but Deflation May Be Worse

1. Although inflation has been the norm in recent U.S. history, Japan has been experiencing deflation in recent years.

2. Deflation leads to lower shoeleather costs, but still creates menu costs and relative-price variability.

3. Deflation also results in the redistribution of wealth toward creditors and away from debtors.

I. *Case Study:* The Wizard of Oz *and the Free Silver Debate*

1. Most people do not know that the book *The Wizard of Oz* was written about U.S. monetary policy in the late 19th century.

2. From 1880 to 1896, the United States experienced deflation, redistributing wealth from farmers (with outstanding loans) to banks.

3. Because the United States followed the gold standard at this time, one possible solution to the problem was to start to use silver as well. This would increase the supply of money, raising the price level, and reduce the real value of the farmers' debts.

4. There has been some debate over the interpretation assigned to each character, but it is clear that the story revolves around the monetary policy debate at that time in history.

5. Even though those who wanted to use silver were defeated, the money supply in the United States increased in 1898 when gold was discovered in Alaska and supplies of gold were shipped in from Canada and South Africa.

6. Within 15 years, prices were back up and the farmers were better able to handle their debts.

 The Wizard of Oz, Chapter 12 (45:04-47:50) and Chapter 34 (57:17-1:01:14). These scenes demonstrate how the Wizard of Oz related to the gold/silver standard debate in the late 1800s.

J. *In the News: Inflationary Threats*

1. During the recession of 2008 and 2009, some individuals began worrying about the possibility of inflation in the U.S.

2. This is an article written by Professor Mankiw in *The New York Times* detailing these concerns.

Activity 1—The Inflation Fairy

Type:	In-class demonstration
Topics:	Inflation
Materials needed:	None
Time:	10 minutes
Class limitations:	Works in any size class

Purpose
This activity demonstrates the effects of inflation.

Instructions
Ask the class to consider the effect of an overnight doubling of prices.

Tell them everything doubled in price while they slept. A soft drink that sold for a dollar, now sells for two dollars; a car that sold for $20,000 now sells for $40,000.

The price of labor doubled as well, so a job paying $6 an hour now pays $12; a $30,000 annual salary becomes a $60,000 annual salary.

The value of all assets doubled as well. Stock prices are twice what they were at yesterday's closing. A $1,000 bond becomes a $2,000 bond. A $35 balance in a checking account become $70, and so on.

Debts have also doubled. The $5 borrowed from a roommate becomes $10. The $3,000 in student loans becomes $6,000. A $75,000 home mortgage becomes a $150,000 mortgage.

And even cash balances double. The inflation fairy sneaks in at night and replaces the $10 bill in their wallet with a new $20 bill. The inflation fairy even doubles the coins in their piggy banks.

If the prices of everything doubled overnight, what would happen?

POINTS FOR DISCUSSION
If the prices of everything doubled overnight, what would happen: NOTHING.

If all prices adjusted perfectly there would be no real effect. Everyone would have exactly the same purchasing power. They have twice as much money but everything costs twice as much. There have been no relative changes in price.

This is a fantastic rate of inflation: 100% daily. Prices would increase more than a billion-fold in a month at this rate of price change. Yet, if everything adjusts perfectly there will be no real effect on the economy.

The problem, of course, is there is no inflation fairy ensuring that everything adjusts smoothly. Some prices adjust quickly and others do not.

Cash balances would not double without the inflation fairy, so people would not be willing to hold cash or accept cash in payment. This would increase transaction costs considerably.

If prices do not change at the same rate, there will be winners and losers from inflation. For example, if everything doubled in price overnight except debt, then borrowers would see the real value of their loan payments halved. Borrowers would win and lenders would lose. If the overnight inflation is an ongoing process, everyone would try to borrow, but no one would be willing to lend. Credit markets would collapse.

More generally, anyone whose income does not keep up with inflation will lose. Anyone whose costs rise less than inflation will come out ahead.

Other problems can be introduced here: bracket creep, increased uncertainty, weakening of price signals, shoeleather costs, menu costs, etc.

Much of the problem with inflation is distributional, but there are real consequences as well. Time spent worrying about inflation, or profiting from inflation, is a diversion of resources away from productive activity.

SOLUTIONS TO TEXT PROBLEMS:

Quick Quizzes

1. When the government of a country increases the growth rate of the money supply from 5 percent per year to 50 percent per year, the average level of prices will start rising very quickly, as predicted by the quantity theory of money. Nominal interest rates will increase dramatically as well, as predicted by the Fisher effect. The government may be increasing the money supply to finance its expenditures.

2. Six costs of inflation are: (1) shoeleather costs; (2) menu costs; (3) relative-price variability and the misallocation of resources; (4) inflation-induced tax distortions; (5) confusion and inconvenience; and (6) arbitrary redistributions of wealth. Shoeleather costs arise because inflation causes people to spend resources going to the bank more often. Menu costs occur when people spend resources changing their posted prices. Relative-price variability occurs because as general prices rise, a fixed dollar price translates into a declining relative price, so the relative prices of goods are constantly changing, causing a misallocation of resources. The combination of inflation and taxation causes distortions in incentives because people are taxed on their nominal capital gains and interest income instead of their real income from these sources. Inflation causes confusion and inconvenience because it reduces money's ability to function as a unit of account. Unexpected inflation redistributes wealth between borrowers and lenders.

Questions for Review

1. An increase in the price level reduces the real value of money because each dollar in your wallet now buys a smaller quantity of goods and services.

2. According to the quantity theory of money, an increase in the quantity of money causes a proportional increase in the price level.

3. Nominal variables are those measured in monetary units, while real variables are those measured in physical units. Examples of nominal variables include the prices of goods, wages, and nominal GDP. Examples of real variables include relative prices (the price of one good in terms of another), real wages, and real GDP. According to the principle of monetary neutrality, only nominal variables are affected by changes in the quantity of money.

4. Inflation is like a tax because everyone who holds money loses purchasing power. In a hyperinflation, the government increases the money supply rapidly, which leads to a high rate of inflation. Thus the government uses the inflation tax, instead of taxes, to finance its spending.

5. According to the Fisher effect, an increase in the inflation rate raises the nominal interest rate by the same amount that the inflation rate increases, with no effect on the real interest rate.

6. The costs of inflation include shoeleather costs associated with reduced money holdings, menu costs associated with more frequent adjustment of prices, increased variability of relative prices, unintended changes in tax liabilities due to nonindexation of the tax code, confusion and inconvenience resulting from a changing unit of account, and arbitrary redistributions of wealth between debtors and creditors. With a low and stable rate of inflation like that in the United States, none of these costs are very high. Perhaps the most important one is the interaction between inflation and the tax code, which may reduce saving and investment even though the inflation rate is low.

7. If inflation is less than expected, creditors benefit and debtors lose. Creditors receive dollar payments from debtors that have a higher real value than was expected.

Problems and Applications

1. In this problem, all amounts are shown in billions.

   a. Nominal GDP = $P \times Y$ = $10,000 and Y = real GDP = $5,000, so $P = (P \times Y)/Y$ = $10,000/$5,000 = 2.

      Because $M \times V = P \times Y$, then $V = (P \times Y)/M$ = $10,000/$500 = 20.

   b. If M and V are unchanged and Y rises by 5%, then because $M \times V = P \times Y$, P must fall by 5%. As a result, nominal GDP is unchanged.

   c. To keep the price level stable, the Fed must increase the money supply by 5%, matching the increase in real GDP. Then, because velocity is unchanged, the price level will be stable.

   d. If the Fed wants inflation to be 10%, it will need to increase the money supply 15%. Thus $M \times V$ will rise 15%, causing $P \times Y$ to rise 15%, with a 10% increase in prices and a 5% rise in real GDP.

2. a. If people need to hold less cash, the demand for money shifts to the left, because there will be less money demanded at any price level.

   b. If the Fed does not respond to this event, the shift to the left of the demand for money combined with no change in the supply of money leads to a decline in the value of money (1/P), which means the price level rises, as shown in Figure 1.

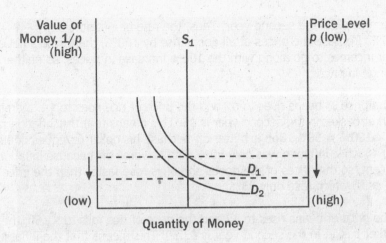

Figure 1

c. If the Fed wants to keep the price level stable, it should reduce the money supply from S_1 to S_2 in Figure 2. This would cause the supply of money to shift to the left by the same amount that the demand for money shifted, resulting in no change in the value of money and the price level.

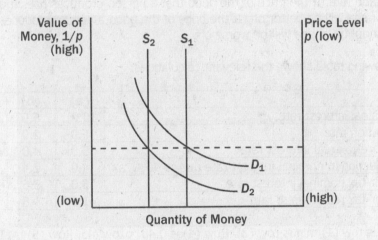

Figure 2

3. With constant velocity, reducing the inflation rate to zero would require the money growth rate to equal the growth rate of output, according to the quantity theory of money ($M \times V = P \times Y$).

4. If a country's inflation rate increases sharply, the inflation tax on holders of money increases significantly. Wealth in savings accounts is not subject to a change in the inflation tax because the nominal interest rate will increase with the rise in inflation. But holders of savings accounts are hurt by the increase in the inflation rate because they are taxed on their nominal interest income, so their real returns are lower.

5. Hyperinflations usually arise when governments try to finance much of their expenditures by printing money. This is unlikely to occur if the central bank (which is responsible for controlling the level of the money supply) is independent of the government.

6. a. When the price of both goods doubles in a year, inflation is 100%. Let's set the market basket equal to one unit of each good. The cost of the market basket is initially $4 and

becomes $8 in the second year. Thus, the rate of inflation is ($8 − $4)/$4 × 100% = 100%. Because the prices of all goods rise by 100%, the farmers get a 100% increase in their incomes to go along with the 100% increase in prices, so neither is affected by the change in prices.

b. If the price of beans rises to $2 and the price of rice rises to $4, then the cost of the market basket in the second year is $6. This means that the inflation rate is ($6 − $4) / $4 × 100% = 50%. Bob is better off because his dollar revenues doubled (increased 100%) while inflation was only 50%. Rita is worse off because inflation was 50% percent, so the prices of the goods she buys rose faster than the price of the goods (rice) she sells, which rose only 33%.

c. If the price of beans rises to $2 and the price of rice falls to $1.50, then the cost of the market basket in the second year is $3.50. This means that the inflation rate is ($3.5 − $4) / $4 × 100% = -12.5%. Bob is better off because his dollar revenues doubled (increased 100%) while prices overall fell 12.5%. Rita is worse off because inflation was -12.5%, so the prices of the goods she buys didn't fall as fast as the price of the goods (rice) she sells, which fell 50%.

d. The relative price of rice and beans matters more to Bob and Rita than the overall inflation rate. If the price of the good that a person produces rises more than inflation, he or she will be better off. If the price of the good a person produces rises less than inflation, he or she will be worse off.

7. The following table shows the relevant calculations:

	(a)	(b)	(c)
(1) Nominal interest rate	10.0	6.0	4.0
(2) Inflation rate	5.0	2.0	1.0
(3) Before-tax real interest rate	5.0	4.0	3.0
(4) Reduction in nominal interest rate due to 40% tax	4.0	2.4	1.6
(5) After-tax nominal interest rate	6.0	3.6	2.4
(6) After-tax real interest rate	1.0	1.6	1.4

Row (3) is row (1) minus row (2). Row (4) is 0.40 × row (1). Row (5) is (1 − .40) × row (1), which equals row (1) minus row (4). Row (6) is row (5) minus row (2). Note that even though part (a) has the highest before-tax real interest rate, it has the lowest after-tax real interest rate. Note also that the after-tax real interest rate is much lower than the before-tax real interest rate.

8. The shoeleather costs of going to the bank include the value of your time, gas for your car that is used as you drive to the bank, and the inconvenience of not having more money on hand. These costs could be measured by valuing your time at your wage rate and valuing the gas for your car at its cost. Valuing the inconvenience of being short of cash is harder to measure, but might depend on the value of the shopping opportunities you give up by not having enough money to buy things you want. Your college president differs from you mainly in having a higher wage, thus having a higher cost of time.

9. The functions of money are to serve as a medium of exchange, a unit of account, and a store of value. Inflation mainly affects the ability of money to serve as a store of value, because inflation erodes money's purchasing power, making it less attractive as a store of value. Money also is not as useful as a unit of account when there is inflation, because stores have to change prices more often and because people are confused and inconvenienced by the

changes in the value of money. In some countries with hyperinflation, stores post prices in terms of a more stable currency, such as the U.S. dollar, even when the local currency is still used as the medium of exchange. Sometimes countries even stop using their local currency altogether and use a foreign currency as the medium of exchange as well.

10. a. Unexpectedly high inflation helps the government by providing higher tax revenue and reducing the real value of outstanding government debt.

   b. Unexpectedly high inflation helps a homeowner with a fixed-rate mortgage because he pays a fixed nominal interest rate that was based on expected inflation, and thus pays a lower real interest rate than was expected.

   c. Unexpectedly high inflation hurts a union worker in the second year of a labor contract because the contract probably based the worker's nominal wage on the expected inflation rate. As a result, the worker receives a lower-than-expected real wage.

   d. Unexpectedly high inflation hurts a college that has invested some of its endowment in government bonds because the higher inflation rate means the college is receiving a lower real interest rate than it had planned. (This assumes that the college did not purchase indexed Treasury bonds.)

11. The redistribution from creditors to debtors is something that happens when inflation is unexpected, not when it is expected. The problems that occur with both expected and unexpected inflation include shoeleather costs associated with reduced money holdings, menu costs associated with more frequent adjustment of prices, increased variability of relative prices, unintended changes in tax liabilities due to nonindexation of the tax code, and the confusion and inconvenience resulting from a changing unit of account.

12. a. The statement that "Inflation hurts borrowers and helps lenders, because borrowers must pay a higher rate of interest," is false. Higher expected inflation means borrowers pay a higher nominal rate of interest, but it is the same real rate of interest, so borrowers are not worse off and lenders are not better off. Higher unexpected inflation, on the other hand, makes borrowers better off and lenders worse off.

   b. The statement, "If prices change in a way that leaves the overall price level unchanged, then no one is made better or worse off," is false. Changes in relative prices can make some people better off and others worse off, even though the overall price level does not change. See problem 7 for an illustration of this.

   c. The statement, "Inflation does not reduce the purchasing power of most workers," is true. Most workers' incomes keep up with inflation reasonably well.

18 OPEN-ECONOMY MACROECONOMICS: BASIC CONCEPTS

WHAT'S NEW IN THE SIXTH EDITION:

There are no major changes in this chapter.

LEARNING OBJECTIVES:

By the end of this chapter, students should understand:

➢ how net exports measure the international flow of goods and services.

➢ how net capital outflow measures the international flow of capital.

➢ why net exports must always equal net foreign investment.

➢ how saving, domestic investment, and net capital outflow are related.

➢ the meaning of the nominal exchange rate and the real exchange rate.

➢ purchasing-power parity as a theory of how exchange rates are determined.

CONTEXT AND PURPOSE:

Chapter 18 is the first chapter in a two-chapter sequence dealing with open-economy macroeconomics. Chapter 18 develops the basic concepts and vocabulary associated with macroeconomics in an international setting: net exports, net capital outflow, real and nominal exchange rates, and purchasing-power parity. The next chapter, Chapter 19, builds an open-economy macroeconomic model that shows how these variables are determined simultaneously.

The purpose of Chapter 18 is to develop the basic concepts macroeconomists use to study open economies. It addresses why a nation's net exports must equal its net capital outflow. It also addresses the concepts of the real and nominal exchange rate and develops a theory of exchange rate determination known as purchasing-power parity.

KEY POINTS:

- Net exports are the value of domestic goods and services sold abroad (exports) minus the value of foreign goods and services sold domestically (imports). Net capital outflow is the acquisition of foreign assets by domestic residents (capital outflow) minus the acquisition of domestic assets by foreigners (capital inflow). Because every international transaction involves an exchange of an asset for a good or service, an economy's net capital outflow always equals its net exports.

- An economy's saving can be used to finance investment at home or buy assets abroad. Thus, national saving equals domestic investment plus net capital outflow.

- The nominal exchange rate is the relative price of the currency of two countries, and the real exchange rate is the relative price of the goods and services of two countries. When the nominal exchange rate changes so that each dollar buys more foreign currency, the dollar is said to *appreciate* or *strengthen*. When the nominal exchange rate changes so that each dollar buys less foreign currency, the dollar is said to *depreciate* or *weaken*.

- According to the theory of purchasing-power parity, a dollar (or a unit of any other currency) should be able to buy the same quantity of goods in all countries. This theory implies that the nominal exchange rate between the currencies of two countries should reflect the price levels in those two countries. As a result, countries with relatively high inflation should have depreciating currencies, and countries with relatively low inflation should have appreciating currencies.

CHAPTER OUTLINE:

I. We will no longer be assuming that the economy is a closed economy.

   A. Definition of **closed economy: an economy that does not interact with other economies in the world**.

   B. Definition of **open economy: an economy that interacts freely with other economies around the world**.

II. The International Flows of Goods and Capital

   A. The Flow of Goods: Exports, Imports, and Net Exports

      1. Definition of **exports: goods and services that are produced domestically and sold abroad**.

      2. Definition of **imports: goods and services that are produced abroad and sold domestically**.

    Point out foreign products that students are likely to buy.

      3. Definition of **net exports: the value of a nation's exports minus the value of its imports, also called the trade balance**.

$$NX = \text{Exports} - \text{Imports}$$

4. Definition of **trade balance: the value of a nation's exports minus the value of its imports, also called net exports**.

5. Definition of **trade surplus: an excess of exports over imports**.

6. Definition of **trade deficit: an excess of imports over exports**.

7. Definition of **balanced trade: a situation in which exports equal imports**.

> Point out to students that a trade surplus implies a positive level of net exports, a trade deficit means that net exports are negative, and balanced trade occurs when net exports are equal to zero. While this will likely be obvious to most students, some will benefit if you review this.

8. There are several factors that influence a country's exports, imports, and net exports:

   a. The tastes of consumers for domestic and foreign goods.

   b. The prices of goods at home and abroad.

   c. The exchange rates at which people can use domestic currency to buy foreign currencies.

   d. The incomes of consumers at home and abroad.

   e. The cost of transporting goods from country to country.

   f. Government policies toward international trade.

9. *Case Study: The Increasing Openness of the U.S. Economy*

Figure 1

   a. Figure 1 shows the total value of exports and imports (expressed as a percentage of GDP) for the United States since 1950.

   b. Advances in transportation, telecommunications, and technological progress are some of the reasons why international trade has increased over time.

   c. Policymakers around the world have also become more accepting of free trade over time.

10. *In the News: Breaking Up the Chain of Production*

   a. Some goods have parts that are manufactured in many countries.

   b. This is an article from *The New York Times* describing the origin of the 451 parts that make up the Apple iPod.

B. The Flow of Financial Resources: Net Capital Outflow

1. Definition of **net capital outflow (NCO): the purchase of foreign assets by domestic residents minus the purchase of domestic assets by foreigners**.

$$NCO = \begin{array}{c} \text{purchases of foreign assets} \\ \text{by domestic residents} \end{array} - \begin{array}{c} \text{purchases of domestic assets} \\ \text{by foreigners} \end{array}$$

 You will likely have to write this equation several times on the board for students when discussing this chapter and the next. Students can grasp the concept of net exports more easily than they can grasp the concept of net capital outflow.

2. The flow of capital abroad takes two forms.

   a. Foreign direct investment occurs when a capital investment is owned and operated by a foreign entity.

   b. Foreign portfolio investment involves an investment that is financed with foreign money but operated by domestic residents.

3. Net capital outflow can be positive or negative.

   a. When net capital outflow is positive, domestic residents are buying more foreign assets than foreigners are buying domestic assets. Capital is flowing out of the country.

   b. When net capital outflow is negative, domestic residents are buying fewer foreign assets than foreigners are buying domestic assets. The country is experiencing a capital inflow.

4. There are several factors that influence a country's net capital outflow:

   a. The real interest rates being paid on foreign assets.

   b. The real interest rates being paid on domestic assets.

   c. The perceived economic and political risks of holding assets abroad.

   d. The government policies that affect foreign ownership of domestic assets.

C. The Equality of Net Exports and Net Capital Outflow

1. Net exports and net capital outflow each measure a type of imbalance in a world market.

   a. Net exports measure the imbalance between a country's exports and imports in world markets for goods and services.

   b. Net capital outflow measures the imbalance between the amount of foreign assets bought by domestic residents and the amount of domestic assets bought by foreigners in world financial markets.

2. For an economy, net exports must be equal to net capital outflow.

3. Example: You are a computer programmer who sells some software to a Japanese consumer for 10,000 yen.

a. The sale is an export for the United States so net exports increases.

b. There are several things you could do with the 10,000 yen

c. You could hold the yen (which is a Japanese asset) or use it to purchase another Japanese asset. Either way, net capital outflow rises.

d. Alternatively, you could use the yen to purchase a Japanese good. Thus, imports will rise so the net effect on net exports will be zero.

e. One final possibility is that you could exchange the yen for dollars at a bank. This does not change the situation though, because the bank then must use the yen for something.

ALTERNATIVE CLASSROOM EXAMPLE:

Assume that U.S. residents do not want to buy any foreign assets, but foreign residents want to purchase some stock in a U.S. firm (such as Microsoft).

How are the foreigners going to get the dollars to purchase the stock?

They would do it the same way U.S. residents would purchase the stock—they would have to earn more than they spend. In other words, foreigners must sell the United States more goods and services than they purchase from the United States.

This leads to negative net exports for the United States. The extra dollars spent by U.S. residents on foreign-produced goods and services would be used to purchase the stock in Microsoft.

---

4. This example can be generalized to the economy as a whole.

   a. When a nation is running a trade surplus (NX > 0), it must be using the foreign currency to purchase foreign assets. Thus, capital is flowing out of the country (NCO > 0).

   b. When a nation is running a trade deficit (NX < 0), it must be financing the net purchase of these goods by selling assets abroad. Thus, capital is flowing into the country (NCO < 0).

5. Every international transaction involves exchange. When a seller country transfers a good or service to a buyer country, the buyer country gives up some asset to pay for the good or service.

6. Thus, the net value of the goods and services sold by a country (net exports) must equal the net value of the assets acquired (net capital outflow).

D. Saving, Investment, and Their Relationship to the International Flows

1. Recall that GDP (Y) is the sum of four components: consumption (C), investment (I), government purchases (G) and net exports (NX).

$$Y = C + I + G + NX$$

2. Recall that national saving is equal to the income of the nation after paying for current consumption and government purchases.

$$S = Y - C - G$$

3. We can rearrange the equation for GDP to get:

$$Y - C - G = I + NX$$

   Substituting for the left-hand side, we get:

$$S = I + NX$$

4. Because net exports and net capital outflow are equal, we can rewrite this as:

$$S = I + NCO$$

5. This implies that saving is equal to the sum of domestic investment (I) and net capital outflow (NCO).

6. When an American citizen saves $1 of his income, that dollar can be used to finance accumulation of domestic capital or it can be used to finance the purchase of capital abroad.

7. Note that, in a closed economy such as the one we assumed earlier, net capital outflow would equal zero and saving would simply be equal to domestic investment.

E. Summing Up

1. Table 1 describes three possible outcomes for an open economy: a country with a trade deficit, a country with balanced trade, or a country with a trade surplus.

Table 1

2. *Case Study: Is the U.S. Trade Deficit a National Problem?*

Figure 2

   a. Panel (a) of Figure 2 shows national saving and domestic investment for the United States as a percentage of GDP since 1960.

   b. Panel (b) of Figure 2 shows net capital outflow for the United States as a percentage of GDP for the same time period.

   c. Before 1980, domestic investment and national saving were very close, meaning that net capital outflow was small.

   d. National saving fell after 1980 (in part due to large government budget deficits) but domestic investment did not change by as much. This led to a dramatic increase in the size of net capital outflow (in absolute value because it was negative).

e. From 1991 to 2000, the capital flow into the United States also increased as investment went from 13.4% to 17.7% of GDP.

f. From 2000 to 2006, the capital flow into the United States increased further, reaching a record 5.7% of GDP.

g. Since 2006, this trend has reversed with a dramatic drop in investment during the economic downturn.

h. When national saving falls, either investment will have to fall or net capital outflow will have to fall.

i. On the other hand, a trade deficit led by an increase in investment will not pose a large problem for the United States if the increased investment leads to a higher production of goods and services.

III. The Prices for International Transactions: Real and Nominal Exchange Rates

 Students are curious about the currencies of other countries. Bring in a current list of nominal exchange rates between several currencies and the U.S. dollar. Quiz the students to see if they can match up the currencies with the countries where they are used. Encourage students to bring in foreign currencies if they have them.

A. Nominal Exchange Rates

1. Definition of **nominal exchange rate: the rate at which a person can trade the currency of one country for the currency of another**.

2. An exchange rate can be expressed in two ways.

   a. Example: 80 yen per dollar.

   b. This can also be written as 1/80 dollar (or 0.0125 dollar) per yen.

ALTERNATIVE CLASSROOM EXAMPLE:

   $1 = 10 pesos
1 peso = $0.10

3. Definition of **appreciation: an increase in the value of a currency as measured by the amount of foreign currency it can buy**.

4. Definition of **depreciation: a decrease in the value of a currency as measured by the amount of foreign currency it can buy**.

5. When a currency appreciates, it is said to *strengthen;* when a currency depreciates, it is said to *weaken*.

6. When economists study nominal exchange rates, they often use an exchange rate index, which converts the many nominal exchange rates into a single measure.

7. *FYI: The Euro*

a. During the 1990s, many European nations decided to give up their national currencies and use a new common currency called the *euro*.

b. The euro started circulating on January 1, 2002.

c. Monetary policy is now set by the European Central Bank (ECB), which controls the supply of euros in the economy.

d. Benefits of a common currency include easier trading ability and increased unity.

e. However, because there is only one currency, there can be only one monetary policy.

f. In 2010, worries about having a common currency came to the forefront when Greece faced a possible default of its government debt.

Make sure that you emphasize that when the dollar appreciates against a particular currency that currency must depreciate against the dollar. Use an example to illustrate this point.

Seinfeld, "The Checks." **(Season 8, 11:44-12:33).** Kramer ends up hosting a group of Japanese tourists, saying, "Manhattan can be quite pricey, even with 50,000 yen." To which Elaine says, "50,000 yen—isn't that only a few hundred dollars?" "Evidently," Kramer replies. This illustrates the nominal exchange rate (50,000 yen for a few hundred dollars) and points to the idea of the real exchange rate (in terms of purchasing power, 50,000 yen doesn't purchase many visiting days in Manhattan).

B. Real Exchange Rates

1. Definition of **real exchange rate: the rate at which a person can trade the goods and services of one country for the goods and services of another**.

2. Example: A bushel of American rice sells for $100 and a bushel of Japanese rice sells for 16,000 yen. The nominal exchange rate is 80 yen per dollar.

3. The real exchange rate depends on the nominal exchange rate and on the prices of goods in the two countries measured in the local currencies.

$$\text{real exchange rate} = \frac{\text{Nominal exchange rate} \times \text{Domestic price}}{\text{Foreign price}}$$

4. In our example:

$$\text{real exchange rate} = \frac{(80 \text{ yen per dollar})(\$100 \text{ per bushel of American rice})}{16,000 \text{ yen per bushel of Japanese rice}}$$

$$\text{real exchange rate} = \frac{8,000 \text{ yen per bushel of American rice}}{16,000 \text{ yen per bushel of Japanese rice}}$$

real exchange rate =   1/2 bushel of Japanese rice per bushel of American rice

---

ALTERNATIVE CLASSROOM EXAMPLE:

Price of Mexican corn = 50 pesos/bushel
Price of American corn = $10/bushel
Nominal exchange rate: $1 = 12 pesos

real exchange rate = $\dfrac{(12 \text{ pesos per dollar})(\$10 \text{ per bushel of American corn})}{50 \text{ pesos per bushel of Mexican corn}}$

real exchange rate = $\dfrac{120 \text{ pesos per bushel of American corn}}{50 \text{ pesos per bushel of Mexican corn}}$

real exchange rate = 2.4 bushels of Mexican corn per bushel of American corn

---

5. The real exchange rate is a key determinant of how much a country exports and imports.

6. When studying an economy as a whole, macroeconomists focus on overall prices instead of the prices of individual goods and services.

   a. Price indexes are used to measure the level of overall prices.

   b. Assume that P is the price index for the United States, P^* is a price index for prices abroad, and e is the nominal exchange rate between the U.S. dollar and foreign currencies.

$$\text{real exchange rate} = \frac{e \times P}{P^*}$$

7. The real exchange rate measures the price of a basket of goods and services available domestically relative to the price of a basket of goods and services available abroad.

8. A depreciation in the U.S. real exchange rate means that U.S. goods have become cheaper relative to foreign goods. U.S. exports will rise, imports will fall, and net exports will increase.

9. Likewise, an appreciation in the U.S. real exchange rate means that U.S. goods have become more expensive relative to foreign goods. U.S. exports will fall, imports will rise, and net exports will decline.

IV. A First Theory of Exchange-Rate Determination: Purchasing-Power Parity

   A. Definition of **purchasing-power parity**: a theory of exchange rates whereby a unit of any given currency should be able to buy the same quantity of goods in all countries.

   B. The Basic Logic of Purchasing-Power Parity

      1. The law of one price suggests that a good must sell for the same price in all locations.

         a. If a good sold for less in one location than another, a person could make a profit by buying the good in the location where it is cheaper and selling it in the location where it is more expensive.

b. The process of taking advantage of differences in prices for the same item in different markets is called *arbitrage*.

c. Note what will happen as people take advantage of the differences in prices. The price in the location where the good is cheaper will rise (because the demand is now higher) and the price in the location where the good was more expensive will fall (because the supply is greater). This will continue until the two prices are equal.

2. The same logic should apply to currency.

a. A U.S. dollar should buy the same quantity of goods and services in the United States and Japan; a Japanese yen should buy the same quantity of goods and services in the United States and Japan.

b. Purchasing-power parity suggests that a unit of all currencies must have the same real value in every country.

c. If this was not the case, people would take advantage of the profit-making opportunity and this arbitrage would then push the real values of the currencies to equality.

Activity 1—A Profitable Opportunity

Type:	In-class assignment
Topics:	Exchange rates, arbitrage
Materials needed:	None
Time:	20 minutes
Class limitations:	Works in any size class

Purpose
This assignment lets the students practice calculating prices with exchange rates and looking for profit opportunities.

Instructions
Explain the following: Molson's Beer is produced in Canada and sold in many countries. In the province of Ontario, a six-pack of Molson's beer sells for $12.95 Canadian. Across the border in Michigan, a six pack of the same beer sells for $6.99 U.S. Suppose that the exchange rate is $0.90 U.S. = $1.00 Canadian.

Ask the class to make the following calculations:
1. How much would it cost in U.S. currency to buy the beer in Ontario?
2. How much would it cost in Canadian currency to buy the beer in Michigan?
3. Is there an arbitrage opportunity?
4. If there is an arbitrage opportunity, where would you buy and where would you sell? How much profit could you expect on a six-pack?

Common Answers and Points for Discussion
1. How much would it cost in U.S. currency to buy the beer in Ontario?
   $12.95 × 0.90 = $11.66 U.S.
2. How much would it cost in Canadian currency to buy the beer in Michigan?
   $6.99/0.90 = $7.77 Canadian

---

3. Is there an arbitrage opportunity?
    Yes. A price differential exists. The beer is more expensive in Canada, cheaper in the United States.
4. If there is an arbitrage opportunity, where would you buy and where would you sell? How much profit could you expect on a six-pack?
    Buy in Michigan, sell in Ontario. The profit per six-pack would be the difference between the price in Ontario, $11.66, and the price in Michigan, $6.99, which equals $4.67 U.S. (Or, measured in Canadian currency, a profit of $5.19 Canadian.)

C. Implications of Purchasing-Power Parity

1. Purchasing-power parity means that the nominal exchange rate between the currencies of two countries will depend on the price levels in those countries.

2. If a dollar buys the same amount of goods and services in the United States (where prices are measured in dollars) as it does in Japan (where prices are measured in yen), then the nominal exchange rate (the number of yen per dollar) must reflect the prices of goods and services in the two countries.

3. Suppose that P is the price of a basket of goods in the United States (measured in dollars), $P*$ is the price of a basket of goods in Japan (measured in yen), and e is the nominal exchange rate (the number of yen each dollar can buy).

    a. In the United States, the purchasing power of $1 is $1/P$.

    b. In Japan, $1 can be exchanged for e units of yen, which in turn have the purchasing power of $e/P*$.

    c. Purchasing-power parity implies that the two must be equal:

    $$1/P = e/P*$$

    d. Rearranging, we get:

    $$1 = (eP)/P*$$

    Note that the left-hand side is a constant and the right-hand side is the real exchange rate. This implies that if the purchasing power of a dollar is always the same at home and abroad, then the real exchange rate cannot change.

    e. We can rearrange again to see that:

    $$e = {P}/{P*}$$

    This implies that the nominal exchange rate is determined by the ratio of the foreign price level to the domestic price level. Nominal exchange rates will change when price levels change.

4. Because the nominal exchange rate depends on the price levels, it must also depend on the money supply and money demand in each country.

    a. If the central bank increases the supply of money in a country and raises the price level, it also causes the country's currency to depreciate relative to other currencies in the world.

    b. When a central bank prints large quantities of money, that money loses value both in terms of the goods and services it can buy and in terms of the amount of other currencies it can buy.

5. *Case Study: The Nominal Exchange Rate during a Hyperinflation*

Figure 3

    a. Figure 3 shows the German money supply, the German price level, and the nominal exchange rate (measured as U.S. cents per German mark) during Germany's hyperinflation in the early 1920s.

    b. When the supply of money begins growing, the price level also increases and the German mark depreciates.

D. Limitations of Purchasing-Power Parity

1. Exchange rates do not always move to ensure that a dollar has the same real value in all countries all of the time.

2. There are two reasons why the theory of purchasing-power parity does not always hold in practice.

    a. Many goods are not easily traded (haircuts in Paris versus haircuts in New York). Thus, arbitrage would be too limited to eliminate the difference in prices between the locations.

    b. Tradable goods are not always perfect substitutes when they are produced in different countries (American cars versus German cars). There is no opportunity for arbitrage here, because the price difference reflects the different values the consumer places on the two products.

3. *Case Study: The Hamburger Standard*

    a. *The Economist*, an international news magazine, occasionally compares the cost of a Big Mac in various countries all around the world.

    b. Once we have the prices of Big Macs in two countries, we can compute the nominal exchange rate predicted by the theory of purchasing-power parity and compare it with the actual exchange rate.

    c. In an article from July 2009, it was shown that the exchange rates predicted by the theory were not exactly equal to the actual rates. However, the predicted rates were fairly close to the actual rates.

Students who have lived or traveled overseas will often point out that many American products (such as blue jeans) are much more expensive overseas than they are in the United States. Point out to students that this could be the result of trade restrictions or price discrimination. Examine the implications of each.

Point out to students that, even with its flaws, purchasing-power parity does tell us about exchange rates. Large and persistent movements in nominal exchange rates typically reflect changes in price level at home and abroad.

SOLUTIONS TO TEXT PROBLEMS:

Quick Quizzes

1. Net exports are the value of a nation's exports minus the value of its imports, also called the trade balance. Net capital outflow is the purchase of foreign assets by domestic residents minus the purchase of domestic assets by foreigners. Net exports equal net capital outflow.

2. The nominal exchange rate is the rate at which a person can trade the currency of one country for the currency of another. The real exchange rate is the rate at which a person can trade the goods and services of one country for the goods and services of another. They are related through the expression: real exchange rate equals nominal exchange rate times domestic price divided by foreign price.

   If the nominal exchange rate goes from 100 to 120 yen per dollar, the dollar has appreciated because a dollar now buys more yen.

3. Because Mexico has had high inflation and Japan has had low inflation, the number of Mexican pesos a person can buy with Japanese yen has increased.

Questions for Review

1. The net exports of a country are the value of its exports minus the value of its imports. Net capital outflow refers to the purchase of foreign assets by domestic residents minus the purchase of domestic assets by foreigners. Net exports are equal to net capital outflow by an accounting identity, because exports from one country to another are matched by payments of some asset from the second country to the first.

2. Saving equals domestic investment plus net capital outflow, because any dollar saved can be used to finance accumulation of domestic capital or it can be used to finance the purchase of capital abroad.

3. If a dollar can buy 100 yen, the nominal exchange rate is 100 yen per dollar. The real exchange rate equals the nominal exchange rate times the domestic price divided by the foreign price, which equals 100 yen per dollar times $10,000 per American car divided by 500,000 yen per Japanese car, which equals two Japanese cars per American car.

4. The economic logic behind the theory of purchasing-power parity is that a good must sell for the same price in all locations. Otherwise, people would profit by engaging in arbitrage.

5. If the Fed started printing large quantities of U.S. dollars, the U.S. price level would increase, and a dollar would buy fewer Japanese yen.

Problems and Applications

1. a. When an American art professor spends the summer touring museums in Europe, he spends money buying foreign goods and services, so U.S. exports are unchanged, imports increase, and net exports decrease.

   b. When students in Paris flock to see the latest movie from Hollywood, foreigners are buying a U.S. good, so U.S. exports rise, imports are unchanged, and net exports increase.

   c. When your uncle buys a new Volvo, an American is buying a foreign good, so U.S. exports are unchanged, imports rise, and net exports decline.

   d. When the student bookstore at Oxford University sells a pair of Levi's 501 jeans, foreigners are buying U.S. goods, so U.S. exports increase, imports are unchanged, and net exports increase.

   e. When a Canadian citizen shops in northern Vermont to avoid Canadian sales taxes, a foreigner is buying U.S. goods, so U.S. exports increase, imports are unchanged, and net exports increase.

2. a. When an American buys a Sony TV, there is a decrease in net exports.

   b. When an American buys a share of Sony stock, there is an increase in net capital outflow.

   c. When the Sony pension fund buys a U.S. Treasury bond, there is a decrease in net capital outflow.

   d. When a worker at Sony buys some Georgia peaches from an American farmer, there is an increase in net exports.

3. Foreign direct investment requires actively managing an investment, for example, by opening a retail store in a foreign country. Foreign portfolio investment is passive, for example, buying corporate stock in a retail chain in a foreign country. As a result, a corporation is more likely to engage in foreign direct investment, while an individual investor is more likely to engage in foreign portfolio investment.

4. a. When an American cellular phone company establishes an office in the Czech Republic, U.S. net capital outflow increases, because the U.S. company makes a direct investment in capital in the foreign country.

   b. When Harrod's of London sells stock to the General Electric pension fund, U.S. net capital outflow increases, because the U.S. company makes a portfolio investment in the foreign country.

   c. When Honda expands its factory in Marysville, Ohio, U.S. net capital outflow declines, because the foreign company makes a direct investment in capital in the United States.

   d. When a Fidelity mutual fund sells its Volkswagen stock to a French investor, U.S. net capital outflow declines (if the French investor pays in U.S. dollars), because the U.S. company is reducing its portfolio investment in a foreign country.

5. a. The newspaper shows nominal exchange rates, because it shows the number of units of one currency that can be exchanged for another currency.

    b. Many answers are possible. In October 2010, the nominal exchange rate between the U.S. dollar and the Canadian dollar was 1 U.S. dollar = 1.0133 Canadian dollars. The nominal exchange rate between the U.S. dollar and the Japanese yen was 1 U.S. dollar = 82 yen. Therefore, the exchange rate between the Canadian dollar and the Japanese yen should be 1.0133 Canadian dollars = 82 yen. This implies that 1 Canadian dollar = 82/1.10133 yen = 80.92 yen.

    c. If U.S. inflation exceeds Japanese inflation over the next year, you would expect the dollar to depreciate relative to the Japanese yen because a dollar would decline in value (in terms of the goods and services it can buy) more than the yen would.

6. a. Dutch pension funds holding U.S. government bonds would be happy if the U.S. dollar appreciated. They would then get more Dutch guilders for each dollar they earned on their U.S. investment. In general, if you have an investment in a foreign country, you are better off if that country's currency appreciates.

    b. U.S. manufacturing industries would be unhappy if the U.S. dollar appreciated because their prices would be higher in terms of foreign currencies, which will reduce their sales.

    c. Australian tourists planning a trip to the United States would be unhappy if the U.S. dollar appreciated because they would get fewer U.S. dollars for each Australian dollar, so their vacation will be more expensive.

    d. An American firm trying to purchase property overseas would be happy if the U.S. dollar appreciated because it would get more units of the foreign currency and could thus buy more property.

7. All the parts of this question can be answered by keeping in mind the definition of the real exchange rate. The real exchange rate equals the nominal exchange rate times the domestic price level divided by the foreign price level.

    a. If the U.S. nominal exchange rate is unchanged, but prices rise faster in the United States than abroad, the real exchange rate rises.

    b. If the U.S. nominal exchange rate is unchanged, but prices rise faster abroad than in the United States, the real exchange rate declines.

    c. If the U.S. nominal exchange rate declines and prices are unchanged in the United States and abroad, the real exchange rate declines.

    d. If the U.S. nominal exchange rate declines and prices rise faster abroad than in the United States, the real exchange rate declines.

8. If purchasing-power parity holds, then 12 pesos per soda divided by $0.75 per soda equals the exchange rate of 16 pesos per dollar. If prices in Mexico doubled, the exchange rate will double to 32 pesos per dollar.

9. a. To make a profit, you would want to buy rice where it is cheap and sell it where it is expensive. Because American rice costs 100 dollars per bushel, and the exchange rate is 80 yen per dollar, American rice costs 100 × 80 equals 8,000 yen per bushel. So

American rice at 8,000 yen per bushel is cheaper than Japanese rice at 16,000 yen per bushel. So you could take 8,000 yen, exchange them for 100 dollars, buy a bushel of American rice, then sell it in Japan for 16,000 yen, making a profit of 8,000 yen. As people did this, the demand for American rice would rise, increasing the price in America, and the supply of Japanese rice would rise, reducing the price in Japan. The process would continue until the prices in the two countries were the same.

b. If rice were the only commodity in the world, the real exchange rate between the United States and Japan would start out too low, then rise as people bought rice in America and sold it in Japan, until the real exchange became one in long-run equilibrium.

10. If you take X units of foreign currency per Big Mac divided by 3.57 dollars per Big Mac, you get $X/3.57$ units of the foreign currency per dollar; that is the predicted exchange rate.

a. Chile: 1,750 pesos/3.57 = 490 pesos/$
Hungary: 720 forints/3.57 = 202 forints/$
Czech Republic: 67.9 korunas/3.57 = 19 korunas/$
Brazil: 8.03 reales/3.57 = 2.25 reales/$
Canada: 3.89C$/3.57 = 1.09C$/$

b. Under purchasing-power parity, the exchange rate of the Hungarian forint to the Canadian dollar is 720 forints per Big Mac divided by 3.89 Canadian dollars per Big Mac equals 185 forints per Canadian dollar. The actual exchange rate is 199 forints per dollar divided by 1.16 Canadian dollars per dollar equals 172 forints per Canadian dollar.

c. The exchange rate predicted by the Big Mac index (185 forints per Canadian dollar) is somewhat close to the actual exchange rate of 172 forints per Canadian dollar.

11. a. The exchange rate is 1 Ecterian dollar is equal to 3 Wiknamian pesos.

b. In Ecteria, the price of Spam would double. The price level will quadruple in Wiknam. The exchange rate between the two countries' currencies would double because of the differences in inflation rates.

c. Wiknam will have a higher nominal interest rate because of the Fisher effect.

d. The get-rich scheme would only work if there were a difference in real interest rates, not nominal interest rates. The nominal exchange rate between the two countries will adjust for the effects of inflation.

19 A MACROECONOMIC THEORY OF THE OPEN ECONOMY

WHAT'S NEW IN THE SIXTH EDITION:

A new *In the News* box on "Alternative Exchange Rate Regimes" has been added.

LEARNING OBJECTIVES:

By the end of this chapter, students should understand:

➢ how to build a model to explain an open economy's trade balance and exchange rate.

➢ how to use the model to analyze the effects of government budget deficits.

➢ how to use the model to analyze the macroeconomic effects of trade policies.

➢ how to use the model to analyze political instability and capital flight.

CONTEXT AND PURPOSE:

The purpose of Chapter 19 is to establish the interdependence of a number of economic variables in an open economy. In particular, Chapter 19 demonstrates the relationships between the prices and quantities in the market for loanable funds and the prices and quantities in the market for foreign-currency exchange. Using these markets, we can analyze the impact of a variety of government policies on an economy's exchange rate and trade balance.

KEY POINTS:

• Two markets are central to the macroeconomics of open economies: the market for loanable funds and the market for foreign-currency exchange. In the market for loanable funds, the real interest rate adjusts to balance the supply of loanable funds (from national saving) and the demand for loanable funds (from domestic investment and net capital outflow). In the market for foreign-currency exchange, the real exchange rate adjusts to balance the supply of dollars (from net capital outflow) and the demand for dollars (for net exports). Because net capital outflow is part of the demand for loanable funds and because it provides the supply of dollars for foreign-currency exchange, it is the variable that connects these two markets.

- A policy that reduces national saving, such as a government budget deficit, reduces the supply of loanable funds and drives up the interest rate. The higher interest rate reduces net capital outflow, which reduces the supply of dollars in the market for foreign-currency exchange. The dollar appreciates, and net exports fall.

- Although restrictive trade policies, such as tariffs or quotas on imports, are sometimes advocated as a way to alter the trade balance, they do not necessarily have that effect. A trade restriction increases net exports for a given exchange rate and, therefore, increases the demand for dollars in the market for foreign-currency exchange. As a result, the dollar appreciates in value, making domestic goods more expensive relative to foreign goods. This appreciation offsets the initial impact of the trade restriction on net exports.

- When investors change their attitudes about holding assets of a country, the ramifications for the country's economy can be profound. In particular, political instability can lead to capital flight, which tends to increase interest rates and cause the currency to depreciate.

CHAPTER OUTLINE:

I. Supply and Demand for Loanable Funds and for Foreign-Currency Exchange

A. The Market for Loanable Funds

1. Whenever a nation saves a dollar of income, it can use that dollar to finance the purchase of domestic capital or to finance the purchase of an asset abroad.

2. The supply of loanable funds comes from national saving.

3. The demand for loanable funds comes from domestic investment and net capital outflow.

a. Because net capital outflow can be positive or negative, it can either add to or subtract from the demand for loanable funds that arises from domestic investment.

b. When $NCO > 0$, the country is experiencing a net outflow of capital. When $NCO < 0$, the country is experiencing a net inflow of capital.

4. The quantity of loanable funds demanded and the quantity of loanable funds supplied depend on the real interest rate.

a. A higher real interest rate encourages people to save and thus raises the quantity of loanable funds supplied.

b. A higher interest rate makes borrowing to finance capital projects more costly, discouraging investment and reducing the quantity of loanable funds demanded.

c. A higher real interest rate in a country will also lower net capital outflow. All else being equal, a higher domestic interest rate implies that purchases of foreign assets by domestic residents will fall and purchases of domestic assets by foreigners will rise.

You may need to write the equation for net capital outflow on the board to explain its relationship with the real interest rate. Point out that when the U.S. real interest rate rises, purchases of foreign assets by domestic residents fall and purchases of U.S. assets by foreigners rise. Thus, net capital outflow is inversely related to the real interest rate.

5. The supply and demand for loanable funds can be shown graphically.

    a. The real interest rate is the price of borrowing funds and is therefore on the vertical axis; the quantity of loanable funds is on the horizontal axis.

    b. The supply of loanable funds is upward sloping because of the positive relationship between the real interest rate and the quantity of loanable funds supplied.

    c. The demand for loanable funds is downward sloping because of the inverse relationship between the real interest rate and the quantity of loanable funds demanded.

Figure 1

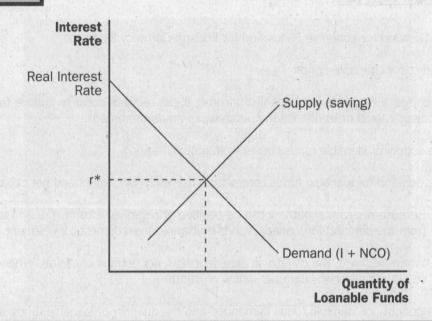

Put "saving" in parentheses next to the supply of loanable funds and "$I + NCO$" next to the demand for loanable funds. Encourage students to do the same. These will serve as reminders of from where the supply and demand for loanable funds are derived.

6. The interest rate adjusts to bring the supply and demand for loanable funds into balance.

    a. If the interest rate was below r^*, the quantity of loanable funds demanded would be greater than the quantity of loanable funds supplied. This would lead to upward pressure on the interest rate.

b. If the interest rate was above r^*, the quantity of loanable funds demanded would be less than the quantity of loanable funds supplied. This would lead to downward pressure on the interest rate.

7. At the equilibrium interest rate, the amount that people want to save is exactly equal to the desired quantities of domestic investment and net capital outflow.

B. The Market for Foreign-Currency Exchange

1. The imbalance between the purchase and sale of capital assets abroad must be equal to the imbalance between exports and imports of goods and services.

2. Net capital outflow represents the quantity of dollars supplied for the purpose of buying assets abroad.

3. Net exports represent the quantity of dollars demanded for the purpose of buying U.S. net exports of goods and services.

4. The real exchange rate is the price that balances the supply and demand in the market for foreign-currency exchange.

a. When the U.S. real exchange rate appreciates, U.S. goods become more expensive relative to foreign goods, lowering U.S. exports and raising imports. Thus, an increase in the real exchange rate will reduce the quantity of dollars demanded.

b. The key determinant of net capital outflow is the real interest rate. Thus, as the real exchange rate changes, there will be no change in net capital outflow.

> Go back to the list of factors that influence net capital outflow (from the previous chapter). Show students that the exchange rate is not there.

5. We can show the market for foreign-currency exchange graphically.

a. The real exchange rate is on the vertical axis; the quantity of dollars exchanged is on the horizontal axis.

b. The demand for dollars will be downward sloping because of the inverse relationship between the real exchange rate and the quantity of dollars demanded.

c. The supply of dollars will be a vertical line because of the fact that changes in the real exchange rate have no influence on the quantity of dollars supplied.

Figure 2

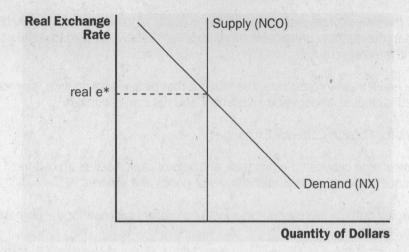

 Remind students that net exports determine the demand for dollars by placing "*NX*" in parentheses next to the demand curve. Show that net capital outflow determines the supply of dollars by placing "*NCO*" in parentheses next to the supply curve.

6. The real exchange rate adjusts to balance the supply and demand for dollars.

   a. If the real exchange rate was lower than real *e**, the quantity of dollars demanded would be greater than the quantity of dollars supplied and there would be upward pressure on the real exchange rate.

   b. If the real exchange rate was higher than real *e**, the quantity of dollars demanded would be less than the quantity of dollars supplied and there would be downward pressure on the real exchange rate.

7. At the equilibrium real exchange rate, the demand for dollars to buy net exports exactly balances the supply of dollars to be exchanged into foreign currency to buy assets abroad.

C. *FYI: Purchasing-Power Parity as a Special Case*

   1. Purchasing-power parity suggests that a dollar must buy the same quantity of goods and services in every country. As a result, the real exchange rate is fixed and the nominal exchange rate is determined by the price levels in the two countries.

   2. Purchasing-power parity assumes that international trade responds quickly to international price differences.

      a. If goods were cheaper in one country than another, they would be exported from the country where they are cheaper and imported into the second country where the prices are higher until the price differential disappears.

      b. Because net exports are so responsive to small changes in the real exchange rate, purchasing-power parity implies that the demand for dollars would be horizontal. Thus, purchasing-power parity is simply a special case of the model of the foreign-currency exchange market.

      c. However, it is more realistic to draw the demand curve downward sloping.

II. Equilibrium in the Open Economy

   A. Net Capital Outflow: The Link between the Two Markets

      1. In the market for loanable funds, net capital outflow is one of the sources of demand.

Figure 3

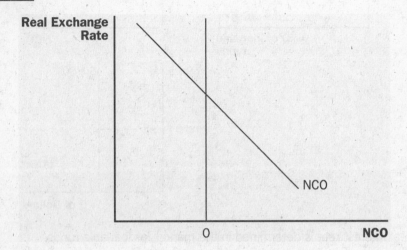

      2. In the foreign-currency exchange market, net capital outflow is the source of the supply of dollars.

      3. This means that net capital outflow is the variable that links the two markets.

      4. The key determinant of net capital outflow is the real interest rate.

      5. We can show the relationship between net capital outflow and the real interest rate graphically.

         a. When the real interest rate is high, owning domestic assets is more attractive and thus, net capital outflow is low.

 Again, you may need to write the equation for net capital outflow on the board to demonstrate the inverse relationship between the real interest rate and net capital outflow.

         b. This inverse relationship implies that net capital outflow will be downward sloping.

         c. Note that net capital outflow can be positive or negative.

   B. Simultaneous Equilibrium in Two Markets

 Students will be frightened by the next diagram showing the market for loanable funds and the market for foreign-currency exchange, with the diagram of net capital outflow linking the two. Go through it <u>very</u> slowly. You will likely have to repeat the equilibrium process several times before students understand it.

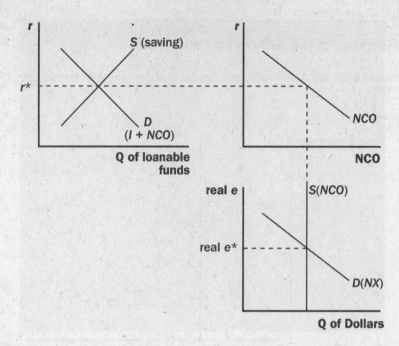

1. The real interest rate is determined in the market for loanable funds.

Figure 4

2. This real interest rate determines the level of net capital outflow.

3. Because net capital outflow must be paid for with foreign currency, the quantity of net capital outflow determines the supply of dollars.

4. The equilibrium real exchange rate brings into balance the quantity of dollars supplied and the quantity of dollars demanded.

5. Thus, the real interest rate and the real exchange rate adjust simultaneously to balance supply and demand in the two markets. As they do so, they determine the levels of national saving, domestic investment, net capital outflow, and net exports.

C. *FYI: Disentangling Supply and Demand*

1. Sometimes it is a bit arbitrary how we divide things between supply and demand.

2. In the market for loanable funds, our model treats net capital outflow as part of the demand for loanable funds.

   a. Investment plus net capital outflow must equal saving ($I + NCO = S$).

   b. Thus, we could say instead that investment is equal to saving minus net capital outflow ($I = S - NCO$).

3. In the market for foreign-currency exchange, net exports are the source of the demand for dollars and net capital outflow is the source of the supply of dollars.

a. When a U.S. citizen buys an imported good, we treat it as a decrease in the demand for dollars rather than an increase in the supply of dollars.

b. When a Japanese citizen buys a U.S. government bond, we treat the transaction as a decline in the supply of dollars rather than an increase in the demand for dollars.

III. How Policies and Events Affect an Open Economy

For the next three applications, use the three-step process developed in Chapter 4. First, determine which of the curves have been affected. Second, determine in which direction the curves shift, and finally, use the diagrams to examine how these shifts alter equilibrium in the two markets.

A. Government Budget Deficits

Figure 5

1. A government budget deficit occurs when the government spending exceeds government revenue.

2. Because a government deficit represents negative public saving, it lowers national saving. This leads to a decline in the supply of loanable funds.

3. The real interest rate rises, leading to a decline in both domestic investment and net capital outflow.

4. Because net capital outflow falls, people need less foreign currency to buy foreign assets, and therefore supply fewer dollars in the market for foreign-currency exchange.

5. The real exchange rate rises, making U.S. goods more expensive relative to foreign goods. Exports will fall, imports will rise, and net exports will fall.

6. In an open economy, government budget deficits raise real interest rates, crowd out domestic investment, cause the dollar to appreciate, and push the trade balance toward deficit.

7. Because they are so closely related, the budget deficit and the trade deficit are often called the *twin deficits*. Note that because many other factors affect the trade deficit, these "twins" are not identical.

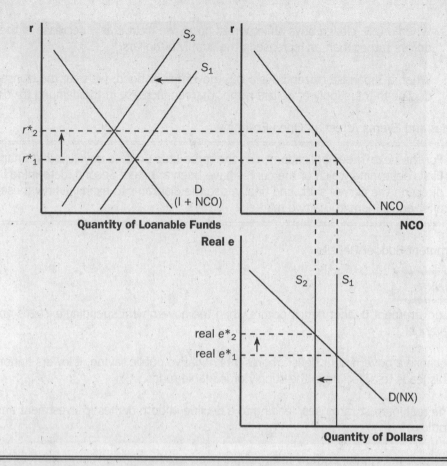

Now would be a good time to discuss the debate in Chapter 23 concerning whether the federal government should balance the budget.

B. Trade Policy

Figure 6

1. Definition of **trade policy: a government policy that directly influences the quantity of goods and services that a country imports or exports**.

2. Two common types of trade policies are tariffs (taxes on imported goods) and quotas (limits on the quantity of imported goods).

3. Example: The U.S. government imposes a quota on the number of cars imported from Japan.

4. Note that the quota will have no effect on the market for loanable funds. Thus, the real interest rate will be unaffected.

5. The quota will lower imports and thus increase net exports. Because net exports are the source of demand for dollars in the market for foreign-currency exchange, the demand for dollars will increase.

6. The real exchange rate will rise, making U.S. goods relatively more expensive than foreign goods. Exports will fall, imports will rise, and net exports will fall.

7. In the end, the quota reduces both imports and exports but net exports remain the same.

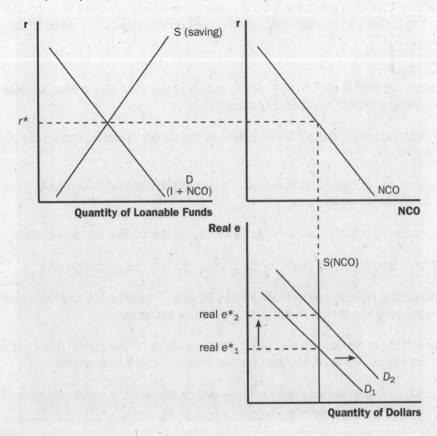

8. Trade policies do not affect the trade balance.

9. Recall that $NX = NCO$. Also remember that $S = I + NCO$.

    Rewriting, we get:

    $NCO = S - I$.

    Substituting for NCO, we get:

    $NX = S - I$.

10. Because trade policies do not affect national saving or domestic investment, they cannot affect net exports.

11. Trade policies do have effects on specific firms, industries, and countries. But these effects are more microeconomic than macroeconomic.

C. Political Instability and Capital Flight

1. Definition of **capital flight: a large and sudden reduction in the demand for assets located in a country**.

2. Capital flight often occurs because investors feel that the country is unstable, due to either economic or political problems.

3. Example: Investors around the world observe political problems in Mexico and begin selling Mexican assets and buying assets from other countries that are viewed as safe.

Figure 7

4. Mexican net capital outflow will rise because investors are selling Mexican assets and purchasing assets from other countries.

   a. Because net capital outflow determines the supply of pesos, the supply of pesos increases.

   b. Because net capital outflow is also a part of the demand for loanable funds, the demand for loanable funds rises.

5. The increased demand for loanable funds causes the equilibrium real interest rate to rise.

6. The increased supply of pesos lowers the equilibrium real exchange rate.

7. Thus, capital flight from Mexico increases Mexican interest rates and lowers the value of the Mexican peso in the market for foreign-currency exchange.

8. Capital flight in Mexico will also affect other countries. If the capital flows out of Mexico and into the United States, it has the opposite effect on the U.S. economy.

9. In 1997, several Asian countries experienced capital flight. A similar experience occurred in Russia in 1998 and Argentina in 2002.

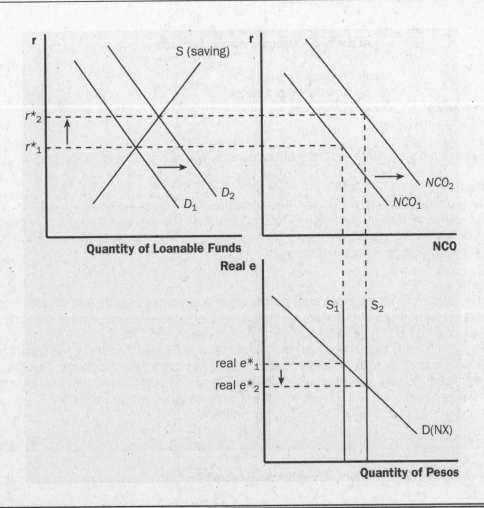

Quantity of Loanable Funds

NCO

Quantity of Pesos

ALTERNATIVE CLASSROOM EXAMPLE:

Suppose that investors feel very confident about the prospects for investment in Brazilian assets.

In this case (from the perspective of Brazil):

1. The demand for loanable funds will shift left because *NCO* decreases.
2. The *NCO* curve will also shift left.
3. The real interest rate in Brazil will fall.
4. The supply of reals (the "real" is the currency of Brazil) will shift left.
5. The real exchange rate will rise.
6. Brazilian net exports will fall.

---

10. *Case Study: Capital Flows from China*

   a.   What happens if a country's government encourages capital to flow to other countries?

   b.   It leads to a weaker currency and a trade surplus.

   c.   In recent years, this has been the case with China as its government has tried to depress its currency.

Activity 1—Open Economy Article

Type: Take-home assignment
Topics: Open-economy macroeconomics
Class limitations: Works in any class

Purpose
This assignment helps students apply the open-economy macro model to world events.

Instructions
This model is often confusing to students. This assignment has them work through an example of real-world events that relate to international macroeconomics. Students may need some direction in finding appropriate topics such as interest rate changes, changes in net capital outflow, or changes in net exports.

Assignment
1. Find an article in a recent newspaper or magazine illustrating a change that will affect net capital outflow or net exports.
2. Explain how and why net capital outflow or net exports would shift.
3. Use the three market open-economy model (the market for loanable funds, net capital outflow, and the market for foreign-currency exchange) to analyze this change.
4. Graph the equilibrium real interest rate, level of net capital outflow, and real exchange rate before the change. Then show how the change will affect these variables.
5. Turn in a copy of the article along with your explanation.

---

11. *In the News: Alternative Exchange-Rate Regimes*

   a. Countries face a trilemma when it comes to developing exchange rate policies.

   b. This is an article by Professor Mankiw detailing these issues.

SOLUTIONS TO TEXT PROBLEMS:

Quick Quizzes

1. The supply of loanable funds comes from national saving. The demand for loanable funds comes from domestic investment and net capital outflow. The supply in the market for foreign-currency exchange comes from net capital outflow. The demand in the market for foreign-currency exchange comes from net exports.

2. The two markets in the model of the open economy are the market for loanable funds and the market for foreign-currency exchange. These markets determine two relative prices: (1) the market for loanable funds determines the real interest rate and (2) the market for foreign-currency exchange determines the real exchange rate.

3. If Americans decided to spend a smaller fraction of their incomes, the increase in saving would shift the supply curve for loanable funds to the right, as shown in Figure 1. The decline in the real interest rate increases net capital outflow and shifts the supply of dollars to the right in the market for foreign-currency exchange. The result is a decline in the real

exchange rate. Since the real interest rate is lower, domestic investment increases. Since the real exchange rate declines, net exports increase and the trade balance moves toward surplus. Overall, saving and domestic investment increase, the real interest rate and real exchange rate decrease, and the trade balance moves toward surplus.

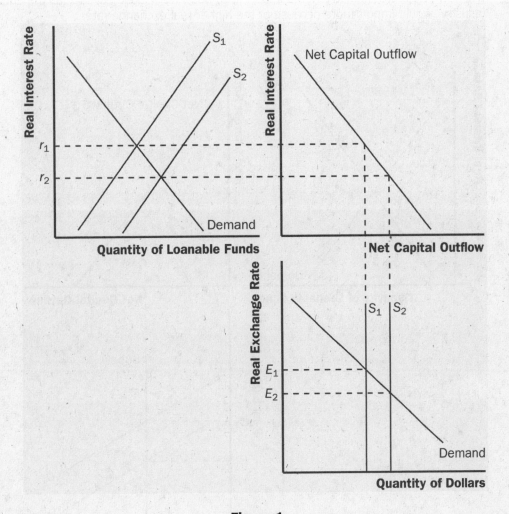

Figure 1

Questions for Review

1. The supply of loanable funds comes from national saving; the demand for loanable funds comes from domestic investment and net capital outflow. The supply of dollars in the market for foreign exchange comes from net capital outflow; the demand for dollars in the market for foreign exchange comes from net exports. The link between the two markets is net capital outflow.

2. Government budget deficits and trade deficits are sometimes called the twin deficits because a government budget deficit often leads to a trade deficit. The government budget deficit leads to reduced national saving, causing the interest rate to increase, and reducing net capital outflow. The decline in net capital outflow reduces the supply of dollars, raising the real exchange rate. Thus, the trade balance will move toward deficit.

3. If a union of textile workers encourages people to buy only American-made clothes, imports would be reduced, so net exports would increase for any given real exchange rate. This would cause the demand curve in the market for foreign exchange to shift to the right, as shown in Figure 2. The result is a rise in the real exchange rate, but no effect on the trade balance. The textile industry would import less, but other industries, such as the auto industry, would import more because of the higher real exchange rate.

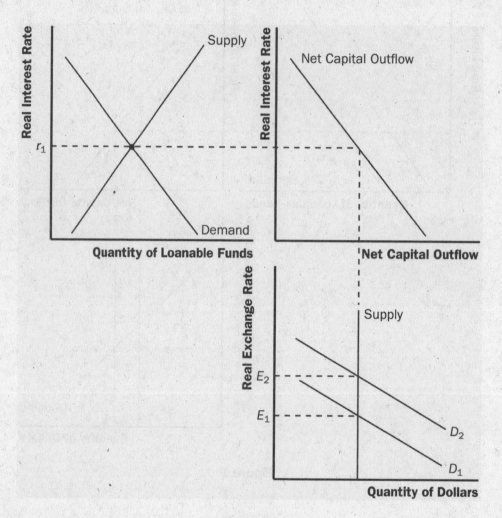

Figure 2

4. Capital flight is a large and sudden movement of funds out of a country. Capital flight causes the interest rate to increase and the exchange rate to depreciate.

Problems and Applications

1. Japan generally runs a trade surplus because the Japanese savings rate is high relative to Japanese domestic investment. The result is high net capital outflow, which is matched by high net exports, resulting in a trade surplus. The other possibilities (high foreign demand for Japanese goods, low Japanese demand for foreign goods, and structural barriers against imports into Japan) would affect the real exchange rate, but not the trade surplus.

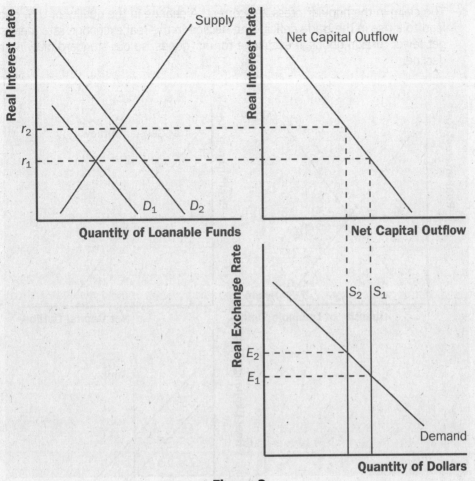

Figure 3

2. a. If Congress passes an investment tax credit, it subsidizes domestic investment. The desire to increase domestic investment leads firms to borrow more, increasing the demand for loanable funds, as shown in Figure 3. This raises the real interest rate, thus reducing net capital outflow. The decline in net capital outflow reduces the supply of dollars in the market for foreign exchange, raising the real exchange rate. The trade balance also moves toward deficit, because net capital outflow, hence net exports, is lower. The higher real interest rate also increases the quantity of national saving. In summary, saving increases, domestic investment increases, net capital outflow declines, the real interest rate increases, the real exchange rate increases, and the trade balance moves toward deficit.

   b. A rise in the real exchange rate reduces exports.

3. a. A decline in the quality of U.S. goods at a given real exchange rate would reduce net exports, reducing the demand for dollars, thus shifting the demand curve for dollars to the left in the market for foreign exchange, as shown in Figure 4.

   b. The shift to the left of the demand curve for dollars leads to a decline in the real exchange rate. Because net capital outflow is unchanged, and net exports equals net capital outflow, there is no change in equilibrium in net exports or the trade balance.

c. The claim in the popular press is incorrect. A change in the quality of U.S. goods cannot lead to a rise in the trade deficit. The decline in the real exchange rate means that we get fewer foreign goods in exchange for our goods, so our standard of living may decline.

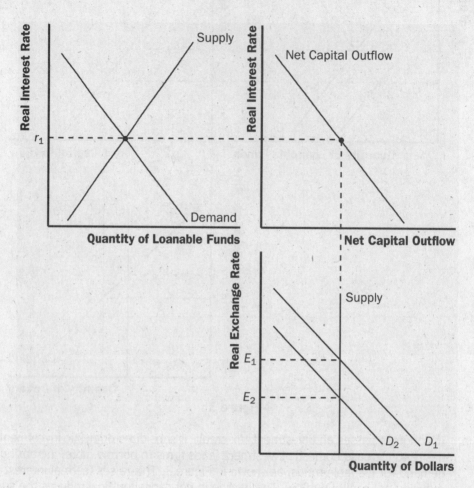

Figure 4

4. A reduction in restrictions of imports would reduce net exports at any given real exchange rate, thus shifting the demand curve for dollars to the left. The shift of the demand curve for dollars leads to a decline in the real exchange rate, which increases net exports. Because net capital outflow is unchanged, and net exports equals net capital outflow, there is no change in equilibrium in net exports or the trade balance. But both imports and exports rise, so export industries benefit.

5. a. When the French develop a strong taste for California wines, the demand for dollars in the foreign-currency market increases at any given real exchange rate, as shown in Figure 5.

   b. The result of the increased demand for dollars is a rise in the real exchange rate.

   c. The quantity of net exports is unchanged.

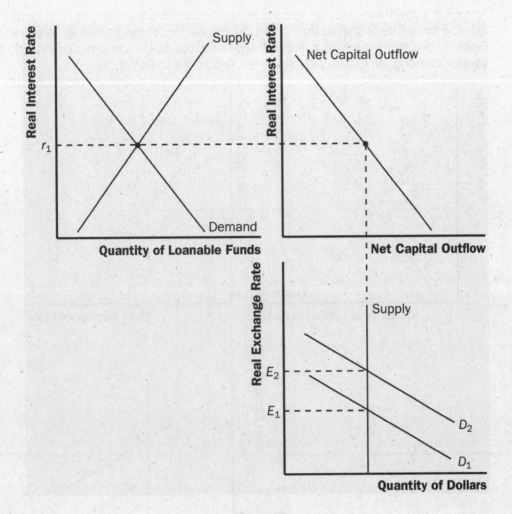

Figure 5

6. An export subsidy increases net exports at any given real exchange rate. This causes the demand for dollars to shift to the right in the market for foreign exchange, as shown in Figure 6. The effect is a higher real exchange rate, but no change in net exports. So the senator is wrong; an export subsidy will not reduce the trade deficit.

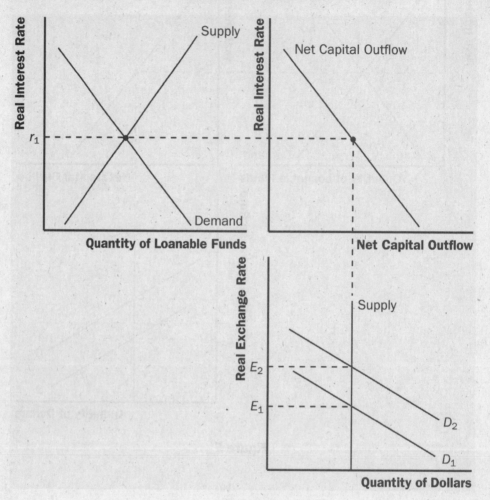

Figure 6

7. If the government increases its spending without increasing taxes, public saving will fall (as will national saving). As Figure 7 shows, this will raise the real interest rate, reducing investment. Net capital outflow will fall. The real exchange rate will rise, causing exports to fall and imports to rise, moving the trade balance toward deficit.

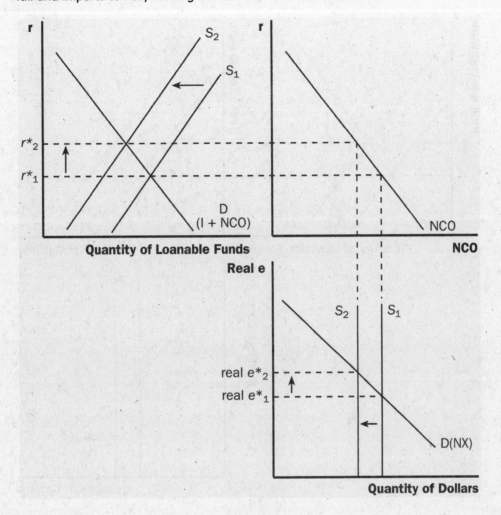

Figure 7

8. Higher real interest rates in Europe lead to increased U.S. net capital outflow. Higher net capital outflow leads to higher net exports, because in equilibrium net exports equal net capital outflow ($NX = NCO$). Figure 8 shows that the increase in net capital outflow leads to a lower real exchange rate, higher real interest rate, and increased net exports.

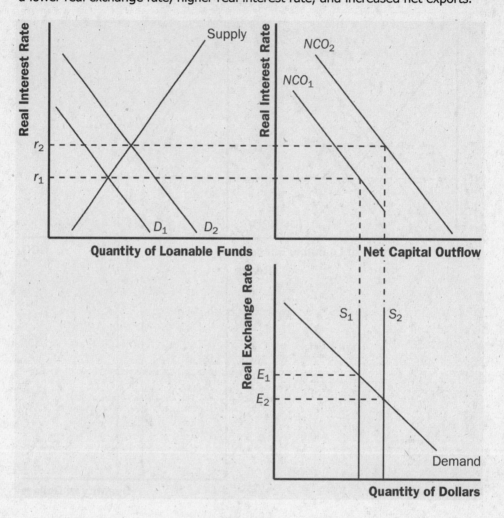

Figure 8

9. a. If the elasticity of U.S. net capital outflow with respect to the real interest rate is very high, the lower real interest rate that occurs because of the increase in private saving will increase net capital outflow a great deal, so U.S. domestic investment will not increase much.

    b. Because an increase in private saving reduces the real interest rate, inducing an increase in net capital outflow, the real exchange rate will decline. If the elasticity of U.S. exports with respect to the real exchange rate is very low, it will take a large decline in the real exchange rate to increase U.S. net exports by enough to match the increase in net capital outflow.

10. a. If the Chinese decided they no longer wanted to buy U.S. assets, U.S. net capital outflow would increase, increasing the demand for loanable funds, as shown in Figure 9. The result is a rise in U.S. interest rates, an increase in the quantity of U.S. saving (because of the higher interest rate), and lower U.S. domestic investment.

b. In the market for foreign exchange, the real exchange rate declines and the balance of trade moves toward surplus.

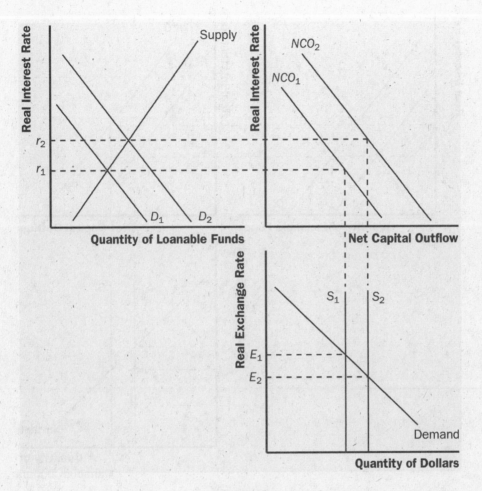

Figure 9

11. a. When U.S. mutual funds become more interested in investing in Canada, Canadian net capital outflow declines as the U.S. mutual funds make portfolio investments in Canadian stocks and bonds. The demand for loanable funds shifts to the left and the net capital outflow curve shifts to the left, as shown in Figure 10. As the figure shows, the real interest rate declines, thus reducing Canada's private saving, but increasing Canada's domestic investment. In equilibrium, Canadian net capital outflow declines.

  b. Because Canada's domestic investment increases, in the long run, Canada's capital stock will increase.

  c. With a higher capital stock, Canadian workers will be more productive (the value of their marginal product will increase) so wages will rise. Thus, Canadian workers will be better off.

  d. The shift of investment into Canada means increased U.S. net capital outflow. As a result, the U.S. real interest rises, leading to less domestic investment, which in the long run reduces the U.S. capital stock, lowers the value of marginal product of U.S. workers, and therefore decreases the wages of U.S. workers. The impact on U.S. citizens would be different from the impact on U.S. workers because some U.S. citizens own capital that now earns a higher real interest rate.

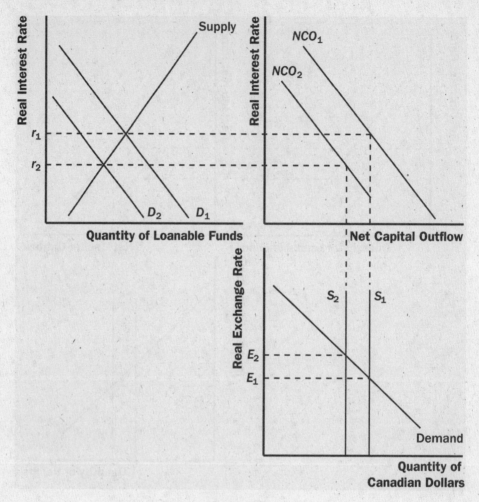

Figure 10

20 AGGREGATE DEMAND AND AGGREGATE SUPPLY

WHAT'S NEW IN THE SIXTH EDITION:

There are two new *In the News* boxes on "The Social Influences of Economic Downturns" and "Modern Parallels to the Great Depression." A new *Case Study* on "The Recession of 2008–2009" has also been added.

LEARNING OBJECTIVES:

By the end of this chapter, students should understand:

➤ three key facts about short-run economic fluctuations.

➤ how the economy in the short run differs from the economy in the long run.

➤ how to use the model of aggregate demand and aggregate supply to explain economic fluctuations.

➤ how shifts in either aggregate demand or aggregate supply can cause booms and recessions.

CONTEXT AND PURPOSE:

To this point, our study of macroeconomic theory has concentrated on the behavior of the economy in the long run. Chapters 20 through 22 now focus on short-run fluctuations in the economy around its long-term trend. Chapter 20 introduces aggregate demand and aggregate supply and shows how shifts in these curves can cause recessions. Chapter 21 focuses on how policymakers use the tools of monetary and fiscal policy to influence aggregate demand. Chapter 22 addresses the relationship between inflation and unemployment.

The purpose of Chapter 20 is to develop the model economists use to analyze the economy's short-run fluctuations—the model of aggregate demand and aggregate supply. Students will learn about some of the sources for shifts in the aggregate-demand curve and the aggregate-supply curve and how these shifts can cause recessions. This chapter also introduces actions policymakers might undertake to offset recessions.

337

KEY POINTS:

- All societies experience short-run economic fluctuations around long-run trends. These fluctuations are irregular and largely unpredictable. When recessions do occur, real GDP and other measures of income, spending, and production fall, and unemployment rises.

- Classical economic theory is based on the assumption that nominal variables such as the money supply and the price level do not influence real variables such as output and employment. Most economists believe that this assumption is accurate in the long run but not in the short run. Economists analyze short-run economic fluctuations using the model of aggregate demand and aggregate supply. According to this model, the output of goods and services and the overall level of prices adjust to balance aggregate demand and aggregate supply.

- The aggregate-demand curve slopes downward for three reasons. The first is the wealth effect: A lower price level raises the real value of households' money holdings, which stimulates consumer spending. The second is the interest-rate effect: A lower price level reduces the quantity of money households demand; as households try to convert money into interest-bearing assets, interest rates fall, which stimulates investment spending. The third is the exchange-rate effect: As a lower price level reduces interest rates, the dollar depreciates in the market for foreign-currency exchange, which stimulates net exports.

- Any event or policy that raises consumption, investment, government purchases, or net exports at a given price level increases aggregate demand. Any event or policy that reduces consumption, investment, government purchases, or net exports at a given price level decreases aggregate demand.

- The long-run aggregate-supply curve is vertical. In the long run, the quantity of goods and services supplied depends on the economy's labor, capital, natural resources, and technology, but not on the overall level of prices.

- Three theories have been proposed to explain the upward slope of the short-run aggregate-supply curve. According to the sticky-wage theory, an unexpected fall in the price level temporarily raises real wages, which induces firms to reduce employment and production. According to the sticky-price theory, an unexpected fall in the price level leaves some firms with prices that are temporarily too high, which reduces their sales and causes them to cut back production. According to the misperceptions theory, an unexpected fall in the price level leads suppliers to mistakenly believe that their relative prices have fallen, which induces them to reduce production. All three theories imply that output deviates from its natural rate when the actual price level deviates from the price level that people expected.

- Events that alter the economy's ability to produce output, such as changes in labor, capital, natural resources, or technology, shift the short-run aggregate-supply curve (and may shift the long-run aggregate-supply curve as well). In addition, the position of the short-run aggregate-supply curve depends on the expected price level.

- One possible cause of economic fluctuations is a shift in aggregate demand. When the aggregate-demand curve shifts to the left, output and prices fall in the short run. Over time, as a change in the expected price level causes perceptions, wages, and prices to adjust, the short-run aggregate-supply curve shifts to the right. This shift returns the economy to its natural rate of output at a new, lower price level.

- A second possible cause of economic fluctuations is a shift in aggregate supply. When the short-run aggregate-supply curve shifts to the left, the short-run effect is falling output and rising prices—a combination called stagflation. Over time, as perceptions, wages, and prices adjust, the short-run aggregate-supply curve shifts back to the right, returning the price level and output back to their original levels.

CHAPTER OUTLINE:

I. Economic activity fluctuates from year to year.

   A. Definition of **recession: a period of declining real incomes and rising unemployment**.

   B. Definition of **depression: a severe recession**.

II. Three Key Facts about Economic Fluctuations

> **Figure 1**

   A. Fact 1: Economic Fluctuations Are Irregular and Unpredictable

      1. Fluctuations in the economy are often called the business cycle.

      2. Economic fluctuations correspond to changes in business conditions.

      3. These fluctuations are not at all regular and are almost impossible to predict.

      4. Panel (a) of Figure 1 shows real GDP since 1965. The shaded areas represent recessions.

   B. Fact 2: Most Macroeconomic Quantities Fluctuate Together

      1. Real GDP is the variable that is most often used to examine short-run changes in the economy.

      2. However, most macroeconomic variables that measure some type of income, spending, or production fluctuate closely together.

      3. Panel (b) of Figure 1 shows how investment spending changes over the business cycle. Note that investment spending falls during recessions just as real GDP does.

   C. Fact 3: As Output Falls, Unemployment Rises

      1. Changes in the economy's output level will have an effect on the economy's utilization of its labor force.

      2. When firms choose to produce a smaller amount of goods and services, they lay off workers, which increases the unemployment rate.

      3. Panel (c) of Figure 1 shows how the unemployment rate changes over the business cycle. Note that during recessions, unemployment generally rises. Note also that the unemployment rate never approaches zero but instead fluctuates around its natural rate of about 5% or 6%.

D. *In The News: The Social Influences of Economic Downturns*

1. The U.S. economy suffered a severe economic downturn in 2008 and 2009.

2. This is an article from *The New York Times* examining how an event like this affects society as a whole.

III. Explaining Short-Run Economic Fluctuations

A. The Assumptions of Classical Economics
1. The classical dichotomy is the separation of variables into real variables and nominal variables.

2. According to classical theory, changes in the money supply only affect nominal variables.

B. The Reality of Short-Run Fluctuations

1. Most economists believe that the classical theory describes the world in the long run but not in the short run.

2. Beyond a period of several years, changes in the money supply affect prices and other nominal variables, but do not affect real GDP, unemployment, or other real variables.

3. However, when studying year-to-year fluctuations in the economy, the assumption of monetary neutrality is not appropriate. In the short run, most real and nominal variables are intertwined.

C. The Model of Aggregate Demand and Aggregate Supply

Begin by reviewing demand, supply, and equilibrium. Make it clear that the microeconomic variables of price and quantity can be aggregated into a price level (measured by either the GDP deflator or the Consumer Price Index) and total output (real GDP).

1. Definition of **model of aggregate demand and aggregate supply: the model that most economists use to explain short-run fluctuations in economic activity around its long-run trend**.

2. We can show this model using a graph.

Figure 2

a. The variable on the vertical axis is the average level of prices in the economy, as measured by the CPI or the GDP deflator.

b. The variable on the horizontal axis is the economy's output of goods and services, as measured by real GDP.

c. Definition of **aggregate-demand curve: a curve that shows the quantity of goods and services that households, firms, and the government want to buy at each price level**.

d. Definition of **aggregate-supply curve: a curve that shows the quantity of goods and services that firms choose to produce and sell at each price level**.

3. In this model, the price level and the quantity of output adjust to bring aggregate demand and aggregate supply into balance.

IV. The Aggregate-Demand Curve

A. Why the Aggregate-Demand Curve Slopes Downward

Figure 3

1. Recall that GDP (Y) is made up of four components: consumption (C), investment (I), government purchases (G), and net exports (NX).

$$Y = C + I + G + NX$$

2. Each of the four components is a part of aggregate demand.

a. Government purchases are assumed to be fixed by policy.

b. This means that to understand why the aggregate-demand curve slopes downward, we must understand how changes in the price level affect consumption, investment, and net exports.

You will likely need to remind students of the difference between changes in quantity demanded (movements along the demand curve) and changes in demand (shifts in the demand curve).

Highlight the fact that all three of these effects begin with a decrease (or increase) in the price level and end with an increase (decrease) in aggregate quantity demanded.

Table 1

3. The Price Level and Consumption: The Wealth Effect

a. A decrease in the price level raises the real value of money and makes consumers feel wealthier, which in turn encourages them to spend more.

b. The increase in consumer spending means a larger quantity of goods and services demanded.

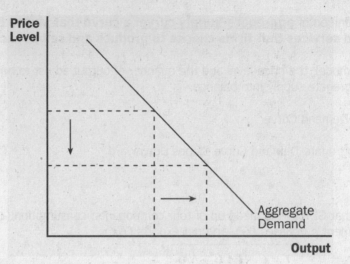

4. The Price Level and Investment: The Interest-Rate Effect

    a. The lower the price level, the less money households need to buy goods and services.

    b. When the price level falls, households try to reduce their holdings of money by lending some out (either in financial markets or through financial intermediaries).

    c. As households try to convert some of their money into interest-bearing assets, the interest rate will drop.

    d. Lower interest rates encourage borrowing firms to borrow more to invest in new plants and equipment and it encourages households to borrow more to invest in new housing.

    e. Thus, a lower price level reduces the interest rate, encourages greater spending on investment goods, and therefore increases the quantity of goods and services demanded.

5. The Price Level and Net Exports: The Exchange-Rate Effect

    a. A lower price level in the United States lowers the U.S. interest rate.

    b. American investors will seek higher returns by investing abroad, increasing U.S. net capital outflow.

    c. The increase in net capital outflow raises the supply of dollars, lowering the real exchange rate.

    d. U.S. goods become relatively cheaper to foreign goods. Exports rise, imports fall, and net exports increase.

    e. Therefore, when a fall in the U.S. price level causes U.S. interest rates to fall, the real exchange rate depreciates, and U.S. net exports rise, thereby increasing the quantity of goods and services demanded.

6. All three of these effects imply that, all else being equal, there is an inverse relationship between the price level and the quantity of goods and services demanded.

 Remind students that the aggregate-demand curve (like all demand curves) is drawn assuming that everything else is held constant.

B. Why the Aggregate-Demand Curve Might Shift

> Get the students involved in suggesting factors that might shift the aggregate-demand curve. Relate changes in aggregate demand to changes in consumption, investment, government purchases, and net exports. Show students that, if any of these four components of GDP change (for reasons other than a change in the price level), the aggregate-demand curve will shift.

1. Shifts Arising from Changes in Consumption

   a. If Americans become more concerned with saving for retirement and reduce current consumption, aggregate demand will decline.

   b. If the government cuts taxes, it encourages people to spend more, resulting in an increase in aggregate demand.

2. Shifts Arising from Changes in Investment

   a. Suppose that the computer industry introduces a faster line of computers and many firms decide to invest in new computer systems. This will lead to an increase in aggregate demand.

   b. If firms become pessimistic about future business conditions, they may cut back on investment spending, shifting aggregate demand to the left.

   c. An investment tax credit increases the quantity of investment goods that firms demand, which results in an increase in aggregate demand.

   d. An increase in the supply of money lowers the interest rate in the short run. This leads to more investment spending, which causes an increase in aggregate demand.

3. Shifts Arising from Changes in Government Purchases

   a. If Congress decides to reduce purchases of new weapon systems, aggregate demand will fall.

   b. If state governments decide to build more highways, aggregate demand will shift to the right.

4. Shifts Arising from Changes in Net Exports

   a. When Europe experiences a recession, it buys fewer American goods, which lowers net exports at every price level. Aggregate demand will shift to the left.

   b. If the exchange rate of the U.S. dollar increases, U.S. goods become more expensive to foreigners. Net exports fall and aggregate demand shifts to the left.

V. The Aggregate-Supply Curve

A. The relationship between the price level and the quantity of goods and services supplied depends on the time horizon being examined.

> **Figure 4**

B. Why the Aggregate-Supply Curve Is Vertical in the Long Run

1. In the long run, an economy's production of goods and services depends on its supplies of resources along with the available production technology.

2. Because the price level does not affect these determinants of output in the long run, the long-run aggregate-supply curve is vertical.

3. The vertical long-run aggregate-supply curve is a graphical representation of the classical theory.

C. Why the Long-Run Aggregate-Supply Curve Might Shift

1. The position of the aggregate-supply curve occurs at an output level sometimes referred to as *potential output* or *full-employment output*.

2. Definition of **natural rate of output: the production of goods and services that an economy achieves in the long run when employment is at its natural level.**

3. This is the level of output that the economy produces when unemployment is at its natural rate.

4. Any change in the economy that alters the natural rate of output shifts the long-run aggregate-supply curve.

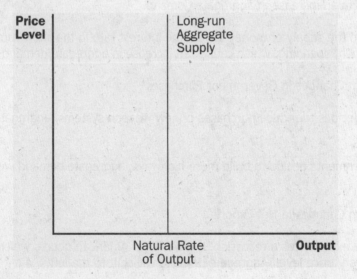

5. Shifts Arising from Changes in Labor

   a. Increases in immigration increase the number of workers available. The long-run aggregate-supply curve would shift to the right.

   b. Any change in the natural rate of unemployment will alter long-run aggregate supply as well.

5. Shifts Arising from Changes in Capital

   a. An increase in the economy's capital stock raises productivity and thus shifts long-run aggregate supply to the right.

   b. This would also be true if the increase occurred in human capital rather than physical capital.

6. Shifts Arising from Changes in Natural Resources

   a. A discovery of a new mineral deposit increases long-run aggregate supply.

   b. A change in weather patterns that makes farming more difficult shifts long-run aggregate supply to the left.

   c. A change in the availability of imported resources (such as oil) can also affect long-run aggregate supply.

7. Shifts Arising from Changes in Technological Knowledge

   a. The invention of the computer has allowed us to produce more goods and services from any given level of resources. As a result, it has shifted the long-run aggregate-supply curve to the right.

   b. Opening up international trade has similar effects to inventing new production processes. Therefore, it also shifts the long-run aggregate-supply curve to the right.

D. Using Aggregate Demand and Aggregate Supply to Depict Long-Run Growth and Inflation

Figure 5

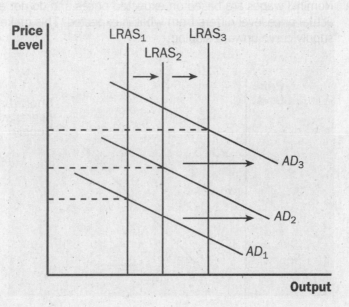

1. Two important forces that govern the economy in the long run are technological progress and monetary policy.

   a. Technological progress shifts long-run aggregate supply to the right.

b. The Fed increases the money supply over time, which raises aggregate demand.

2. The result is growth in output and continuing inflation (increases in the price level).

3. Although the purpose of developing the model of aggregate demand and aggregate supply is to describe short-run fluctuations, these short-run fluctuations should be considered deviations from the continuing long-run trends developed here.

E. Why the Aggregate-Supply Curve Slopes Upward in the Short Run

1. The Sticky-Wage Theory

Table 2

Figure 6

a. Nominal wages are often slow to adjust to changing economic conditions due to long-term contracts between workers and firms along with social norms and notions of fairness that influence wage setting and are slow to change over time.

b. Example: Suppose a firm has agreed in advance to pay workers an hourly wage of $20 based on the expectation that the price level will be 100. If the price level is actually 95, the firm receives 5% less for its output than it expected and its labor costs are fixed at $20 per hour.

c. Production is now less profitable, so the firm hires fewer workers and reduces the quantity of output supplied.

d. Nominal wages are based on expected prices and do not adjust immediately when the actual price level differs from what is expected. This makes the short-run aggregate-supply curve upward sloping.

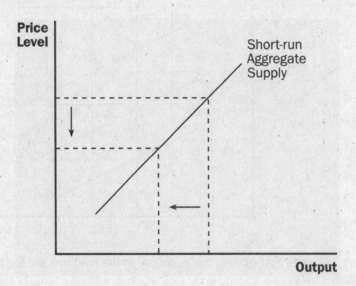

e. This is the theory of short-run aggregate supply that is emphasized in the text.

2. The Sticky-Price Theory

   a. The prices of some goods and services are also sometimes slow to respond to changing economic conditions. This is often blamed on menu costs.

   b. If the price level falls unexpectedly, and a firm does not change the price of its product quickly, its relative price will rise and this will lead to a loss in sales.

   c. Thus, when sales decline, firms will produce a lower quantity of goods and services.

   d. Because not all prices adjust instantly to changing conditions, an unexpected fall in the price level leaves some firms with higher-than-desired prices, which depress sales and cause firms to lower the quantity of goods and services supplied.

3. The Misperceptions Theory

   a. Changes in the overall price level can temporarily mislead suppliers about what is happening in the markets in which they sell their output.

   b. As a result of these misperceptions, suppliers respond to changes in the level of prices and thus, the short-run aggregate-supply curve is upward sloping.

   c. Example: The price level falls unexpectedly. Suppliers mistakenly believe that as the price of their product falls, it is a drop in the relative price of their product. Suppliers may then believe that the reward of supplying their product has fallen, and thus they decrease the quantity that they supply. The same misperception may happen if workers see a decline in their nominal wage (caused by a fall in the price level).

   d. Thus, a lower price level causes misperceptions about relative prices, and these misperceptions lead suppliers to respond to the lower price level by decreasing the quantity of goods and services supplied.

4. Note that each of these theories suggest that output deviates from its natural rate when the price level deviates from the price level that people expected.

5. Note also that the effects of the change in the price level will be temporary. Eventually people will adjust their price level expectations and output will return to its natural level; thus, the aggregate-supply curve will be vertical in the long run.

6. Because the sticky-wage theory is the simplest of the three theories, it is the one that is emphasized in the text.

F. Summing Up

   1. Economists debate which of these theories is correct and it is possible that each contains an element of truth.

   2. All three theories suggest that output deviates in the short run from its long-run level when the actual price level deviates from the expected price level.

$$\frac{\text{Quantity of}}{\text{output}} = \frac{\text{Natural rate}}{\text{of output}} + a\left(\text{Actual price level} - \text{Expected price level}\right)$$

3. Each of the three theories emphasizes a problem that is likely to be temporary.

   a. Over time, nominal wages will become unstuck, prices will become unstuck, and misperceptions about relative prices will be corrected.

   b. In the long run, it is reasonable to assume that wages and prices are flexible and that people are not confused about relative prices.

G. Why the Short-Run Aggregate-Supply Curve Might Shift

   1. Events that shift the long-run aggregate-supply curve will shift the short-run aggregate-supply curve as well.

   2. However, expectations of the price level will affect the position of the short-run aggregate-supply curve even though it has no effect on the long-run aggregate-supply curve.

   3. A higher expected price level decreases the quantity of goods and services supplied and shifts the short-run aggregate-supply curve to the left. A lower expected price level increases the quantity of goods and services supplied and shifts the short-run aggregate-supply curve to the right.

VI. Two Causes of Economic Fluctuations

A. Long-Run Equilibrium

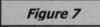

Figure 7

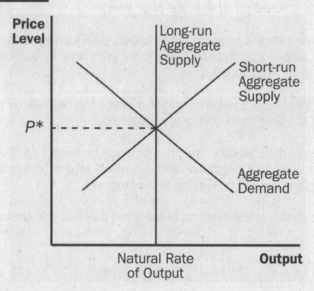

1. Long-run equilibrium is found where the aggregate-demand curve intersects with the long-run aggregate-supply curve.

2. Output is at its natural rate.

3. Also at this point, perceptions, wages, and prices have all adjusted so that the short-run aggregate-supply curve intersects at this point as well.

B. The Effects of a Shift in Aggregate Demand

> **Figure 8**

> **Table 3**

 Students will be confused by the graphs showing the adjustment process that occurs when aggregate demand shifts. Take the time to walk them through step by step several times, summarizing what moves the economy from one point to the next.

1. Example: Pessimism causes household spending and investment to decline.

2. This will cause the aggregate-demand curve to shift to the left.

3. In the short run, both output and the price level fall. This drop in output means that the economy is in a recession.

4. In the long run, the economy will move back to the natural rate of output.

    a. People will correct the misperceptions, sticky wages, and sticky prices that cause the aggregate-supply curve to be upward sloping in the short run.

    b. The expected price level will fall, shifting the short-run aggregate-supply curve to the right.

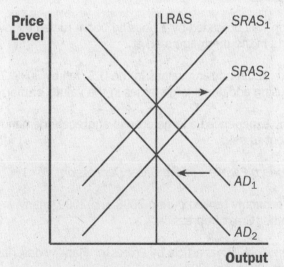

5. In the long run, the decrease in aggregate demand can be seen solely by the drop in the equilibrium price level. Thus, the long-run effect of a change in aggregate demand is a nominal change (in the price level) but not a real change (output is the same).

6. Instead of waiting for the economy to adjust on its own, policymakers may want to eliminate the recession by boosting government spending or increasing the money supply. Either way, these policies could shift the aggregate demand curve back to the right.

7. *FYI: Monetary Neutrality Revisited*

   a. According to classical theory, changes in the quantity of money affect nominal variables such as the price level, but not real variables such as output.

   b. If the Fed decreases the money supply, aggregate demand shifts to the left. In the short run, output and the price level decline. After expectations, prices, and wages have adjusted, the economy finds itself back on the long-run aggregate-supply curve at the natural rate of output.

   c. Thus, changes in the money supply have effects on real output in the short run only.

8. *Case Study: Two Big Shifts in Aggregate Demand: The Great Depression and World War II*

   a. Figure 9 shows real GDP for the United States since 1900.

Figure 9

   b. Two time periods of economic fluctuations can be seen dramatically in the picture. These are the early 1930s (the Great Depression) and the early 1940s (World War II).

   c. From 1929 to 1933, GDP fell by 27%. From 1939 to 1944, the economy's production of goods and services almost doubled.

9. *Case Study: The Recession of 2008–2009*

   a. The United States experienced a financial crisis and severe economic downturn in 2008 and 2009.

   b. The recession was preceded by a housing boom fueled by low interest rates and various developments in the mortgage market.

   c. From 2006 to 2009, housing values in the U.S. fell by 30%. This led to substantial defaults, causing additional large losses in the values of mortgage-backed securities.

   d. The economy experienced a large drop in aggregate demand causing real GDP to fall and unemployment to rise.

10. *In the News: Modern Parallels to the Great Depression*

   a. As the U.S. economy tanked during 2008 and 2009, many wondered if we were on the brink of another Great Depression.

   b. This is a *New York Times* article by Professor Mankiw describing how the economy looked midway through 2008.

C. The Effects of a Shift in Aggregate Supply

Figure 10

   1. Example: Firms experience a sudden increase in their costs of production.

2. This will cause the short-run aggregate-supply curve to shift to the left. (Depending on the event, long-run aggregate supply may also shift. We will assume that it does not.)

3. In the short run, output will fall and the price level will rise. The economy is experiencing stagflation.

4. Definition of **stagflation: a period of falling output and rising prices**.

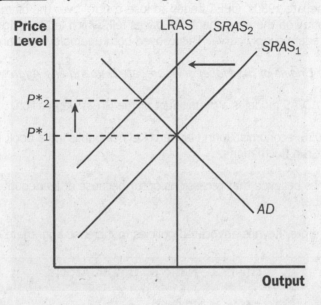

Figure 11

5. The result over time may be a wage-price spiral.

6. Eventually, the low level of output will put downward pressure on wages.

   a. Producing goods and services becomes more profitable.

   b. Short-run aggregate supply shifts to the right until the economy is again producing at the natural rate of output.

7. If policymakers want to end the stagflation, they can shift the aggregate-demand curve. Note that they cannot simultaneously offset the drop in output and the rise in the price level. If they increase aggregate demand, the recession will end, but the price level will be permanently higher.

8. *Case Study: Oil and the Economy*

   a. Crude oil is a key input in the production of many goods and services.

   b. When some event (often political) leads to a rise in the price of crude oil, firms must endure higher costs of production and the short-run aggregate-supply curve shifts to the left.

  c. In the mid-1970s, OPEC lowered production of oil and the price of crude oil rose substantially. The inflation rate in the United States was pushed to over 10%. Unemployment also grew from 4.9% in 1973 to 8.5% in 1975.

  d. This occurred again in the late 1970s. Oil prices rose, output fell, and the rate of inflation increased.

  e. In the late 1980s, OPEC began to lose control over the oil market as members began cheating on the agreement. Oil prices fell, which led to a rightward shift of the short-run aggregate-supply curve. This caused both unemployment and inflation to decline.

9. *FYI: The Origins of the Model of Aggregate Demand and Aggregate Supply*

  a. The AD/AS model is a by-product of the Great Depression.

  b. In 1936, economist John Maynard Keynes published a book that attempted to explain short-run fluctuations.

  c. Keynes believed that recessions occur because of inadequate demand for goods and services.

  d. Therefore, Keynes advocated policies to increase aggregate demand.

Activity 1—National Output Article

Type: Take-home assignment
Topics: Fluctuations in output and the price level
Class limitations: Works in any class

Purpose
This assignment is a good way for students to connect economic theory to actual events.

Assignment
1. Find an article in a recent newspaper or magazine illustrating a change that will affect national output.
2. Analyze the situation using economic reasoning.
3. Draw an aggregate demand and aggregate supply graph to explain this change. Be sure to label your graph and clearly indicate which curve shifts. Explain what happens to national income and to the price level in the short run.
4. Turn in a copy of the article along with your explanation.

Points for Discussion
This can be a nice way to review the elements of aggregate demand (consumption, investment, government spending, and net exports) and the elements of aggregate supply (productive resources, technology).

Most changes will only shift one curve.

Discussing the long-run impact of these changes can emphasize the differences between AS and AD shifts.

Activity 2—The Economics of War

Type: In-class assignment
Topics: National income, price levels, total spending, resources
Materials needed: None
Time: 20 minutes
Class limitations: Works in any size class

Purpose
This assignment asks students to examine their beliefs about the impact of war on the economy. It can be used to examine aggregate demand shifts and aggregate supply shifts. This assignment can generate lively discussion.

Instructions
Ask the class to answer the following questions. Give them time to write an answer to a question, then discuss their answers before moving to the next question.
1.   Is war good or bad for the economy?
2.   What are the opportunity costs of using resources in wars?
3.   How would a war affect aggregate supply?
4.   Graph the shift in aggregate supply. What happens to output and the price level?
5.   How would a war affect aggregate demand?
6.   Graph the shift in aggregate demand. What happens to output and the price level?
7.   Is peace good or bad for the economy?

SOLUTIONS TO TEXT PROBLEMS:

Quick Quizzes

1.   Three key facts about economic fluctuations are: (1) economic fluctuations are irregular and unpredictable; (2) most macroeconomic quantities fluctuate together; and (3) as output falls, unemployment rises.

     Economic fluctuations are irregular and unpredictable, as you can see by looking at a graph of real GDP over time. Some recessions are close together and others are far apart. There appears to be no recurring pattern.

     Most macroeconomic quantities fluctuate together. In recessions, real GDP, consumer spending, investment spending, corporate profits, and other macroeconomic variables decline or grow much more slowly than during economic expansions. However, the variables fluctuate by different amounts over the business cycle, with investment varying much more than other variables.

     As output falls, unemployment rises, because when firms want to produce less, they lay off workers, thus causing a rise in unemployment.

2.   The economy's behavior in the short run differs from its behavior in the long run because the assumption of monetary neutrality applies only to the long run, not the short run. In the short run, real and nominal variables are highly intertwined. Figure 1 shows the model of

aggregate demand and aggregate supply. The horizontal axis shows the quantity of output, and the vertical axis shows the price level.

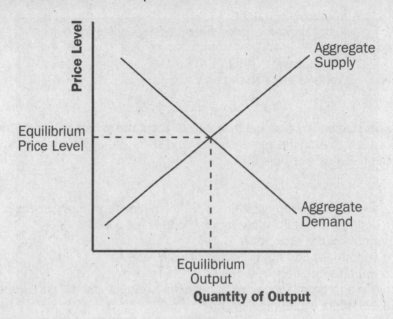

Figure 1

3. The aggregate-demand curve slopes downward for three reasons. First, when prices fall, the value of dollars in people's wallets and bank accounts rises, so they are wealthier. As a result, they spend more, thereby increasing the quantity of goods and services demanded. Second, when prices fall, people need less money to make their purchases, so they lend more out, which reduces the interest rate. The lower interest rate encourages businesses to invest more, increasing the quantity of goods and services demanded. Third, since lower prices lead to a lower interest rate, some U.S. investors will invest abroad, supplying dollars to the foreign-exchange market, thus causing the dollar to depreciate. The decline in the real exchange rate causes net exports to increase, which increases the quantity of goods and services demanded.

   Any event that alters the level of consumption, investment, government purchases, or net exports at a given price level will lead to a shift in aggregate demand. An increase in expenditure will shift the aggregate-demand curve to the right, while a decline in expenditure will shift the aggregate-demand curve to the left.

4. The long-run aggregate-supply curve is vertical because the price level does not affect the long-run determinants of real GDP, which include supplies of labor, capital, natural resources, and the level of available technology. This is just an application of the classical dichotomy and monetary neutrality.

   There are three reasons the short-run aggregate-supply curve slopes upward. First, the sticky-wage theory suggests that because nominal wages are slow to adjust, a decline in the price level means real wages are higher, so firms hire fewer workers and produce less, causing the quantity of goods and services supplied to decline. Second, the sticky-price theory suggests that the prices of some goods and services are slow to change. If some economic event causes the overall price level to decline, the relative prices of goods whose prices are sticky will rise and the quantity of those goods sold will decline, leading firms to cut back on production. Thus, a lower price level reduces the quantity of goods and services supplied. Third, the misperceptions theory suggests that changes in the overall price level can temporarily mislead suppliers. When the price level falls below the level that was expected, suppliers think that the relative prices of their products have declined, so they produce less. Thus, a lower price level reduces the quantity of goods and services supplied.

The long-run and short-run aggregate-supply curves will both shift if the supplies of labor, capital, or natural resources change or if technology changes. A change in the expected price level will shift the short-run aggregate-supply curve but will have no effect on the long-run aggregate-supply curve.

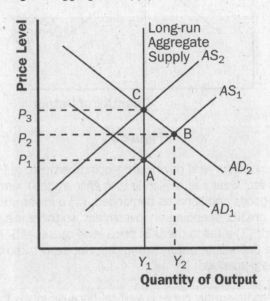

Figure 2

5. When a popular presidential candidate is elected, causing people to be more confident about the future, they will spend more, causing the aggregate-demand curve to shift to the right, as shown in Figure 2. The economy begins at point A with aggregate-demand curve AD_1 and short-run aggregate-supply curve AS_1. The equilibrium has price level P_1 and output level Y_1. Increased confidence about the future causes the aggregate-demand curve to shift to AD_2. The economy moves to point B, with price level P_2 and output level Y_2. Over time, price expectations adjust and the short-run aggregate-supply curve shifts up to AS_2 and the economy moves to equilibrium at point C, with price level P_3 and output level Y_1.

Questions for Review

1. Two macroeconomic variables that decline when the economy goes into a recession are real GDP and investment spending (many other answers are possible). A macroeconomic variable that rises during a recession is the unemployment rate.

2. Figure 3 shows aggregate demand, short-run aggregate supply, and long-run aggregate supply.

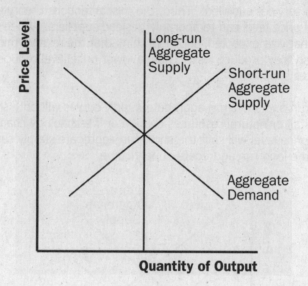

Figure 3

3. The aggregate-demand curve is downward sloping because: (1) a decrease in the price level makes consumers feel wealthier, which in turn encourages them to spend more, so there is a larger quantity of goods and services demanded; (2) a lower price level reduces the interest rate, encouraging greater spending on investment, so there is a larger quantity of goods and services demanded; (3) a fall in the U.S. price level causes U.S. interest rates to fall, so the real exchange rate depreciates, stimulating U.S. net exports, so there is a larger quantity of goods and services demanded.

4. The long-run aggregate supply curve is vertical because in the long run, an economy's supply of goods and services depends on its supplies of capital, labor, and natural resources and on the available production technology used to turn these resources into goods and services. The price level does not affect these long-run determinants of real GDP.

5. Three theories explain why the short-run aggregate-supply curve is upward sloping: (1) the sticky-wage theory, in which a lower price level makes employment and production less profitable because wages do not adjust immediately to the price level, so firms reduce the quantity of goods and services supplied; (2) the sticky-price theory, in which an unexpected fall in the price level leaves some firms with higher-than-desired prices because not all prices adjust instantly to changing conditions, which depresses sales and induces firms to reduce the quantity of goods and services they produce; and (3) the misperceptions theory, in which a lower price level causes misperceptions about relative prices, and these misperceptions induce suppliers to respond to the lower price level by decreasing the quantity of goods and services supplied.

6. The aggregate-demand curve might shift to the left when something (other than a rise in the price level) causes a reduction in consumption spending (such as a desire for increased saving), a reduction in investment spending (such as increased taxes on the returns to investment), decreased government spending (such as a cutback in defense spending), or reduced net exports (such as when foreign economies go into recession).

Figure 4 traces through the steps of such a shift in aggregate demand. The economy begins in equilibrium, with short-run aggregate supply, AS_1, intersecting aggregate demand, AD_1, at point A. When the aggregate-demand curve shifts to the left to AD_2, the economy moves from point A to point B, reducing the price level and the quantity of output. Over time, people adjust their perceptions, wages, and prices, shifting the short-run aggregate-supply curve down to AS_2, and moving the economy from point B to point C, which is back on the long-run aggregate-supply curve and has a lower price level.

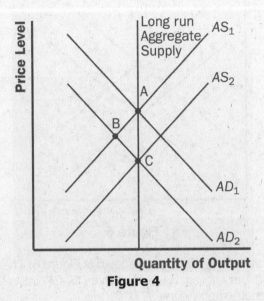

Figure 4

7. The aggregate-supply curve might shift to the left because of a decline in the economy's capital stock, labor supply, or productivity, or an increase in the natural rate of unemployment, all of which shift both the long-run and short-run aggregate-supply curves to the left. An increase in the expected price level shifts just the short-run aggregate-supply curve (not the long-run aggregate-supply curve) to the left.

   Figure 5 traces through the effects of a shift in short-run aggregate supply. The economy starts in equilibrium at point A. The aggregate-supply curve shifts to the left from AS_1 to AS_2. The new equilibrium is at point B, the intersection of the aggregate-demand curve and AS_2. As time goes on, perceptions and expectations adjust and the economy returns to long-run equilibrium at point A, because the short-run aggregate-supply curve shifts back to its original position.

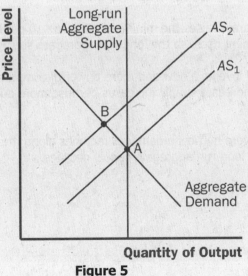

Figure 5

Problems and Applications

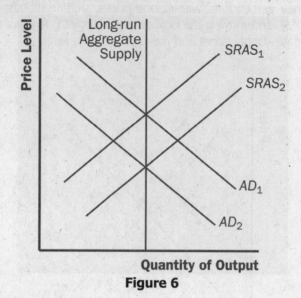

Figure 6

1. a. The current state of the economy is shown in Figure 6. The aggregate-demand curve (*AD₁*) and short-run aggregate-supply curve (*SRAS₁*) intersect at the same point on the long-run aggregate-supply curve.

   b. A stock market crash leads to a leftward shift of aggregate demand (to *AD₂*). The equilibrium level of output and the price level will fall. Because the quantity of output is less than the natural rate of output, the unemployment rate will rise above the natural rate of unemployment.

   c. If nominal wages are unchanged as the price level falls, firms will be forced to cut back on employment and production. Over time as expectations adjust, the short-run aggregate-supply curve will shift to the right (to *SRAS₂*), moving the economy back to the natural rate of output.

2. a. When the United States experiences a wave of immigration, the labor force increases, so long-run aggregate supply shifts to the right.

   b. When Congress raises the minimum wage to $10 per hour, the natural rate of unemployment rises, so the long-run aggregate-supply curve shifts to the left.

   c. When Intel invents a new and more powerful computer chip, productivity increases, so long-run aggregate supply increases because more output can be produced with the same inputs.

   d. When a severe hurricane damages factories along the East Coast, the capital stock is smaller, so long-run aggregate supply declines.

3. a. The current state of the economy is shown in Figure 7. The aggregate-demand curve and short-run aggregate-supply curve intersect at the same point on the long-run aggregate-supply curve.

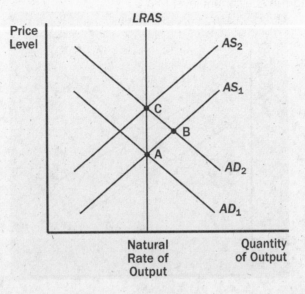

Figure 7

b. If the central bank increases the money supply, aggregate demand shifts to the right (to point B). In the short run, there is an increase in output and the price level.

c. Over time, nominal wages, prices, and perceptions will adjust to this new price level. As a result, the short-run aggregate-supply curve will shift to the left. The economy will return to its natural rate of output (point C).

d. According to the sticky-wage theory, nominal wages at points A and B are equal. However, nominal wages at point C are higher.

e. According to the sticky-wage theory, real wages at point B are lower than real wages at point A. However, real wages at points A and C are equal.

f. Yes, this analysis is consistent with long-run monetary neutrality. In the long run, an increase in the money supply causes an increase in the nominal wage, but leaves the real wage unchanged.

4. During the Great Depression, equilibrium output (Y_1) was lower than the natural rate of output (Y_2). The idea of lengthening the shopping period between Thanksgiving and Christmas was to increase aggregate demand. As Figure 8 shows, this could increase output back to its long-run equilibrium level (Y_2).

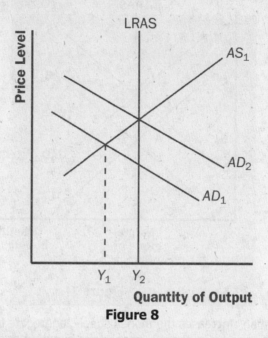

Figure 8

5. a. The statement that "the aggregate-demand curve slopes downward because it is the horizontal sum of the demand curves for individual goods" is false. The aggregate-demand curve slopes downward because a fall in the price level raises the overall quantity of goods and services demanded through the wealth effect, the interest-rate effect, and the exchange-rate effect.

   b. The statement that "the long-run aggregate-supply curve is vertical because economic forces do not affect long-run aggregate supply" is false. Economic forces of various kinds (such as population and productivity) do affect long-run aggregate supply. The long-run aggregate-supply curve is vertical because the price level does not affect long-run aggregate supply.

   c. The statement that "if firms adjusted their prices every day, then the short-run aggregate-supply curve would be horizontal" is false. If firms adjusted prices quickly and if sticky prices were the only possible cause for the upward slope of the short-run aggregate-supply curve, then the short-run aggregate-supply curve would be vertical, not horizontal. The short-run aggregate supply curve would be horizontal only if prices were completely fixed.

   d. The statement that "whenever the economy enters a recession, its long-run aggregate-supply curve shifts to the left" is false. An economy could enter a recession if either the aggregate-demand curve or the short-run aggregate-supply curve shifts to the left.

6. a. According to the sticky-wage theory, the economy is in a recession because the price level has declined so that real wages are too high, thus labor demand is too low. Over time, as nominal wages are adjusted so that real wages decline, the economy returns to full employment.

According to the sticky-price theory, the economy is in a recession because not all prices adjust quickly. Over time, firms are able to adjust their prices more fully, and the economy returns to the long-run aggregate-supply curve.

According to the misperceptions theory, the economy is in a recession when the price level is below what was expected. Over time, as people observe the lower price level, their expectations adjust, and the economy returns to the long-run aggregate-supply curve.

b. The speed of the recovery in each theory depends on how quickly price expectations, wages, and prices adjust.

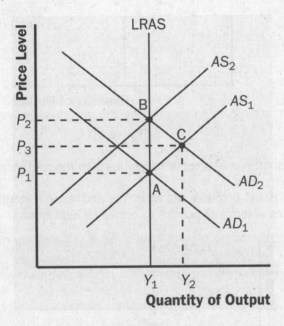

Figure 9

7. If the Fed increases the money supply and people expect a higher price level, the aggregate-demand curve shifts to the right and the short-run aggregate-supply curve shifts to the left, as shown in Figure 9. The economy moves from point A to point B, with no change in output and a rise in the price level (to P_2). If the public does not change its expectation of the price level, the short-run aggregate-supply curve does not shift, the economy ends up at point C, and output increases along with the price level (to P_3).

8. a. People will likely expect that the new chairman will not actively fight inflation so they will expect the price level to rise.

    b. If people believe that the price level will be higher over the next year, workers will want higher nominal wages.

    c. At any given price level, higher labor costs lead to reduced profitability.

d. The short-run aggregate-supply curve will shift to the left as shown in Figure 10.

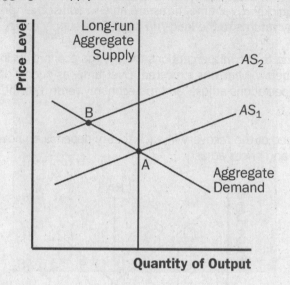

Figure 10

e. A decline in short-run aggregate supply leads to reduced output and a higher price level.

f. No, this choice was probably not wise. The end result is stagflation, which provides limited choices in terms of policies to remedy the situation.

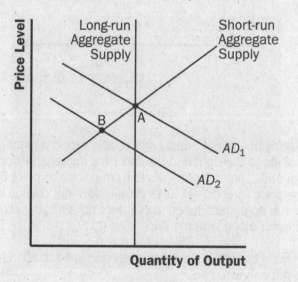

Figure 11

9. a. If households decide to save a larger share of their income, they must spend less on consumer goods, so the aggregate-demand curve shifts to the left, as shown in Figure 11. The equilibrium changes from point A to point B, so the price level declines and output declines.

b. If Florida orange groves suffer a prolonged period of below-freezing temperatures, the orange harvest will be reduced. This decline in the natural rate of output is represented in Figure 12 by a shift to the left in both the short-run and long-run aggregate-supply curves. The equilibrium changes from point A to point B, so the price level rises and output declines.

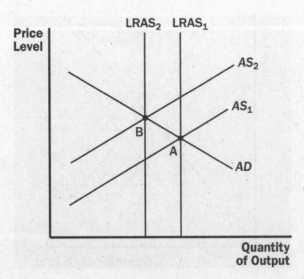

Figure 12

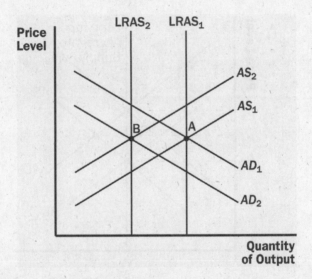

Figure 13

c. If increased job opportunities cause people to leave the country, the long-run and short-run aggregate-supply curves will shift to the left because there are fewer people producing output. The aggregate-demand curve will also shift to the left because there are fewer people consuming goods and services. The result is a decline in the quantity of output, as Figure 13 shows. Whether the price level rises or declines depends on the relative sizes of the shifts in the aggregate-demand curve and the aggregate-supply curves.

10. a. When the stock market declines sharply, wealth declines, so the aggregate-demand curve shifts to the left, as shown in Figure 14. In the short run, the economy moves from point A to point B, as output declines and the price level declines. In the long run, the

short-run aggregate-supply curve shifts to the right to restore equilibrium at point C, with unchanged output and a lower price level compared to point A.

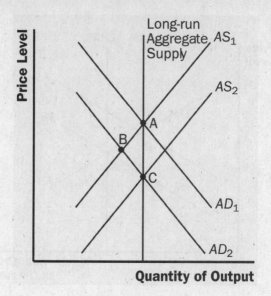

Figure 14

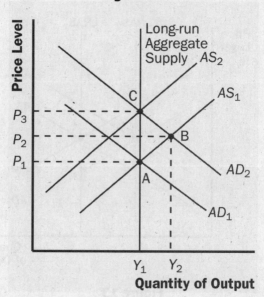

Figure 15

b. When the federal government increases spending on national defense, the rise in government purchases shifts the aggregate-demand curve to the right, as shown in Figure 15. In the short run, the economy moves from point A to point B, as output and the price level rise. In the long run, the short-run aggregate-supply curve shifts to the left to restore equilibrium at point C, with unchanged output and a higher price level compared to point A.

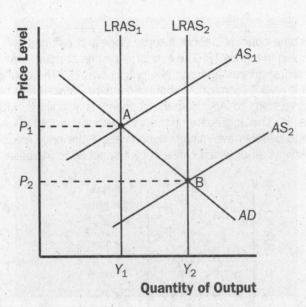

Figure 16

c. When a technological improvement raises productivity, the long-run and short-run aggregate-supply curves shift to the right, as shown in Figure 16. The economy moves from point A to point B, as output rises and the price level declines.

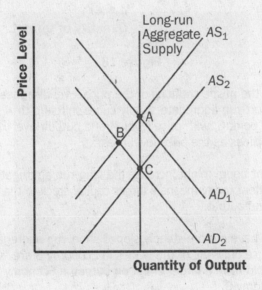

Figure 17

d. When a recession overseas causes foreigners to buy fewer U.S. goods, net exports decline, so the aggregate-demand curve shifts to the left, as shown in Figure 17. In the short run, the economy moves from point A to point B, as output declines and the price level declines. In the long run, the short-run aggregate-supply curve shifts to the right to restore equilibrium at point C, with unchanged output and a lower price level compared to point A.

11. a. If firms become optimistic about future business conditions and increase investment, the result is shown in Figure 18. The economy begins at point A with aggregate-demand curve AD_1 and short-run aggregate-supply curve AS_1. The equilibrium has price level P_1 and output level Y_1. Increased optimism leads to greater investment, so the aggregate-demand curve shifts to AD_2. Now the economy is at point B, with price level P_2 and output level Y_2. The aggregate quantity of output supplied rises because the price level has risen and people have misperceptions about the price level, wages are sticky, or prices are sticky, all of which cause output supplied to increase.

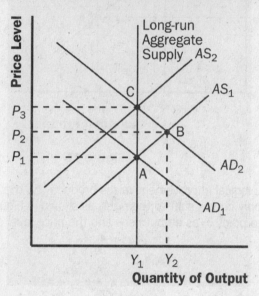

Figure 18

   b. Over time, as the misperceptions of the price level disappear, wages adjust, or prices adjust, the short-run aggregate-supply curve shifts up to AS_2 and the economy gets to equilibrium at point C, with price level P_3 and output level Y_1. The quantity of output demanded declines as the price level rises.

   c. The investment boom might increase the long-run aggregate-supply curve because higher investment today means a larger capital stock in the future, thus higher productivity and output.

12. Economy B would have a more steeply sloped short-run aggregate-supply curve than would Economy A, because only half of the wages in Economy B are "sticky." A 5% increase in the money supply would have a larger effect on output in Economy A and a larger effect on the price level in Economy B.

21 THE INFLUENCE OF MONETARY AND FISCAL POLICY ON AGGREGATE DEMAND

WHAT'S NEW IN THE SIXTH EDITION:

There is a new *In the News* feature on "How Large is the Fiscal Policy Multiplier?" A new *FYI* on "The Zero Lower Bound" has also been added.

LEARNING OBJECTIVES:

By the end of this chapter, students should understand:

➤ the theory of liquidity preference as a short-run theory of the interest rate.

➤ how monetary policy affects interest rates and aggregate demand.

➤ how fiscal policy affects interest rates and aggregate demand.

➤ the debate over whether policymakers should try to stabilize the economy.

CONTEXT AND PURPOSE:

Chapter 21 is the second chapter in a three-chapter sequence that concentrates on short-run fluctuations in the economy around its long-term trend. In Chapter 20, the model of aggregate supply and aggregate demand is introduced. In Chapter 21, we see how the government's monetary and fiscal policies affect aggregate demand. In Chapter 22, we will see some of the trade-offs between short-run and long-run objectives when we address the relationship between inflation and unemployment.

The purpose of Chapter 21 is to address the short-run effects of monetary and fiscal policies. In Chapter 20, we found that when aggregate demand or short-run aggregate supply shifts, it causes fluctuations in output. As a result, policymakers sometimes try to offset these shifts by shifting aggregate demand with monetary and fiscal policy. Chapter 21 addresses the theory behind these policies and some of the shortcomings of stabilization policy.

KEY POINTS:

• In developing a theory of short-run economic fluctuations, Keynes proposed the theory of liquidity preference to explain the determinants of the interest rate. According to this theory, the interest rate adjusts to balance the supply and demand for money.

367

- An increase in the price level raises money demand and increases the interest rate that brings the money market into equilibrium. Because the interest rate represents the cost of borrowing, a higher interest rate reduces investment and, thereby, the quantity of goods and services demanded. The downward-sloping aggregate-demand curve expresses this negative relationship between the price level and the quantity demanded.

- Policymakers can influence aggregate demand with monetary policy. An increase in the money supply reduces the equilibrium interest rate for any given price level. Because a lower interest rate stimulates investment spending, the aggregate-demand curve shifts to the right. Conversely, a decrease in the money supply raises the equilibrium interest rate for any given price level and shifts the aggregate-demand curve to the left.

- Policymakers can also influence aggregate demand with fiscal policy. An increase in government purchases or a cut in taxes shifts the aggregate-demand curve to the right. A decrease in government purchases or an increase in taxes shifts the aggregate-demand curve to the left.

- When the government alters spending or taxes, the resulting shift in aggregate demand can be larger or smaller than the fiscal change. The multiplier effect tends to amplify the effects of fiscal policy on aggregate demand. The crowding-out effect tends to dampen the effects of fiscal policy on aggregate demand.

- Because monetary and fiscal policy can influence aggregate demand, the government sometimes uses these policy instruments in an attempt to stabilize the economy. Economists disagree about how active the government should be in this effort. According to the advocates of active stabilization policy, changes in attitudes by households and firms shift aggregate demand; if the government does not respond, the result is undesirable and unnecessary fluctuations occur in output and employment. According to critics of active stabilization policy, monetary and fiscal policy work with such long lags that attempts at stabilizing the economy often end up being destabilizing.

CHAPTER OUTLINE:

I.   How Monetary Policy Influences Aggregate Demand

> Students are very interested in the way in which the Fed changes interest rates. Review what they learned about the Fed and its tools to change the money supply.

> The effects of monetary policy are easy to show graphically. Begin with money supply, money demand, and an equilibrium interest rate. Show how both an increase and a decrease in the money supply affect interest rates.

A.   The aggregate-demand curve is downward sloping for three reasons.

1.   The wealth effect.

2.   The interest-rate effect.

3.   The exchange-rate effect.

B. All three effects occur simultaneously, but are not of equal importance.

   1. Because a household's money holdings are a small part of total wealth, the wealth effect is relatively small.

   2. Because imports and exports are a small fraction of U.S. GDP, the exchange-rate effect is also fairly small for the U.S. economy.

   3. Thus, the most important reason for the downward-sloping aggregate-demand curve is the interest-rate effect.

C. Definition of **theory of liquidity preference**: **Keynes's theory that the interest rate adjusts to bring money supply and money demand into balance**.

D. The Theory of Liquidity Preference

   1. This theory is an explanation of the supply and demand for money and how they relate to the interest rate.

   > Point out that when we discuss the "interest rate" we are discussing both the nominal interest rate and the real interest rate because we are assuming that they will move together. Remind the students of the Fisher equation.

   2. Money Supply

Figure 1

      a. The money supply in the economy is controlled by the Federal Reserve.

      b. The Fed can alter the supply of money using open market operations, changes in the discount rate, and changes in reserve requirements.

      c. Because the Fed can control the size of the money supply directly, the quantity of money supplied does not depend on any other economic variables, including the interest rate. Thus, the supply of money is represented by a vertical supply curve.

   3. Money Demand

      a. Any asset's liquidity refers to the ease with which that asset can be converted into a medium of exchange. Thus, money is the most liquid asset in the economy.

      b. The liquidity of money explains why people choose to hold it instead of other assets that could earn them a higher return.

      c. However, the return on other assets (the interest rate) is the opportunity cost of holding money. All else being equal, as the interest rate rises, the quantity of money demanded will fall. Therefore, the demand for money will be downward sloping.

   4. Equilibrium in the Money Market

      a. The interest rate adjusts to bring money demand and money supply into balance.

b. If the interest rate is higher than the equilibrium interest rate, the quantity of money that people want to hold is less than the quantity that the Fed has supplied. Thus, people will try to buy bonds or deposit funds in an interest-bearing account. This increases the funds available for lending, pushing interest rates down.

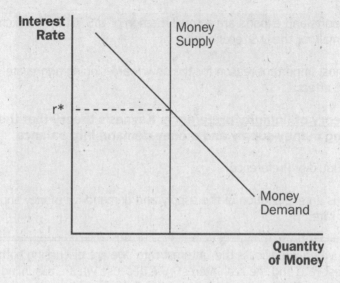

c. If the interest rate is lower than the equilibrium interest rate, the quantity of money that people want to hold is greater than the quantity that the Fed has supplied. Thus, people will try to sell bonds or withdraw funds from an interest-bearing account. This decreases the funds available for lending, pulling interest rates up.

E. *FYI: Interest Rates in the Long Run and the Short Run*

1. In an earlier chapter, we said that the interest rate adjusts to balance the supply and demand for loanable funds.

2. In this chapter, we proposed that the interest rate adjusts to balance the supply and demand for money.

3. To understand how these two statements can both be true, we must discuss the difference between the short run and the long run.

4. In the long run, the economy's level of output, the interest rate, and the price level are determined by the following manner:

   a. *Output* is determined by the levels of resources and technology available.

   b. For any given level of output, the *interest rate* adjusts to balance the supply and demand for loanable funds.

   c. Given output and the interest rate, the *price level* adjusts to balance the supply and demand for money. Changes in the supply of money lead to proportionate changes in the price level.

5. In the short run, the economy's level of output, the interest rate, and the price level are determined by the following manner:

a. The *price level* is stuck at some level (based on previously formed expectations) and is unresponsive to changes in economic conditions.

b. For any given price level, the *interest rate* adjusts to balance the supply and demand for money.

c. The interest rate that balances the money market influences the quantity of goods and services demanded and thus the level of *output*.

F. The Downward Slope of the Aggregate-Demand Curve

Figure 2

1. When the price level increases, the quantity of money that people need to hold becomes larger. Thus, an increase in the price level leads to an increase in the demand for money, shifting the money demand curve to the right.

2. For a fixed money supply, the interest rate must rise to balance the supply and demand for money.

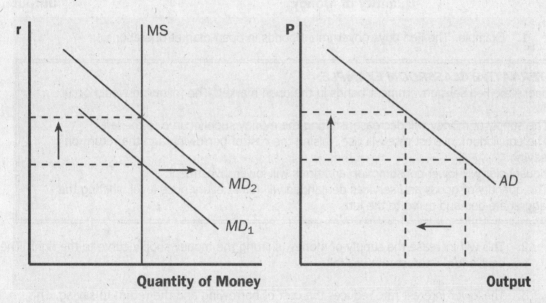

3. At a higher interest rate, the cost of borrowing and the return on saving both increase. Thus, consumers will choose to spend less and will be less likely to invest in new housing. Firms will be less likely to borrow funds for new equipment or structures. In short, the quantity of goods and services purchased in the economy will fall.

4. This implies that as the price level increases, the quantity of goods and services demanded falls. This is Keynes's interest-rate effect.

 Go through the example above in reverse as well. Make sure that students understand that a decline in the price level will lead to a drop in money demand and the interest rate and that this will cause a rise in aggregate quantity demanded.

G. Changes in the Money Supply

Figure 3

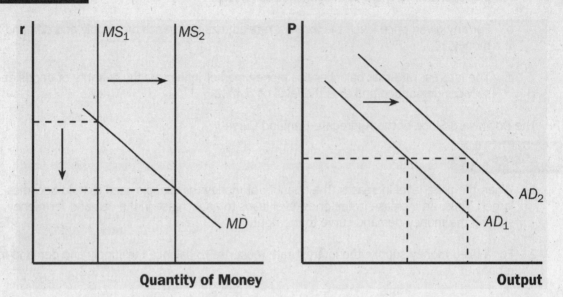

Quantity of Money   **Output**

1. Example: The Fed buys government bonds in open-market operations.

ALTERNATIVE CLASSROOM EXAMPLE:
Suppose the Fed sells government bonds in the open market. The following would occur:

1. The supply of money will decrease, shifting the money supply curve to the left.
2. The equilibrium interest rate will rise, raising the cost of borrowing and the return on saving.
3. Households will lower consumption and firms will lower investment.
4. The quantity of goods and services demanded will fall at every price level, shifting the aggregate-demand curve to the left.

---

2. This will increase the supply of money, shifting the money supply curve to the right. The equilibrium interest rate will fall.

3. The lower interest rate reduces the cost of borrowing and the return to saving. This encourages households to increase their consumption and desire to invest in new housing. Firms will also increase investment, building new factories and purchasing new equipment.

4. The quantity of goods and services demanded will rise at every price level, shifting the aggregate-demand curve to the right.

5. Thus, a monetary injection by the Fed increases the money supply, leading to a lower interest rate, and a larger quantity of goods and services demanded.

 Point out the circumstances under which the Fed is likely to increase the money supply. Then, discuss the circumstances under which the Fed is likely to decrease the money supply. Discuss the short- and long-run effects of each.

H. The Role of Interest-Rate Targets in Fed Policy

 Show students that the Fed can target either the money supply or the interest rate, but not both.

1. In recent years, the Fed has conducted policy by setting a target for the federal funds rate (the interest rate that banks charge one another for short-term loans).

    a. The target is reevaluated every six weeks when the Federal Open Market Committee meets.

    b. The Fed has chosen to use this interest rate as a target in part because the money supply is difficult to measure with sufficient precision.

2. Because changes in the money supply lead to changes in interest rates, monetary policy can be described either in terms of the money supply or in terms of the interest rate.

 Make sure that you point out to students that, while the media describes the actions of the Federal Reserve as "changing interest rates," they instead could be described as "changing the money supply."

I. *FYI: The Zero Lower Bound*

1. What if the Fed's target interest rate is already close to zero?

2. Some economists describe this situation as a liquidity trap.

    a. Nominal interest rates cannot fall below zero.

    b. Expansionary monetary policy cannot work.

3. Other economists are less concerned with this situation.

    a. The central bank could alter inflationary expectations.

    b. The Fed could also use other financial instruments in open market operations.

J. *Case Study: Why the Fed Watches the Stock Market (and Vice Versa)*

1. A booming stock market expands the aggregate demand for goods and services.

    a. When the stock market booms, households become wealthier, and this increased wealth stimulates consumer spending.

    b. Increases in stock prices make it attractive for firms to issue new shares of stock and this increases investment spending.

2. Because one of the Fed's goals is to stabilize aggregate demand, the Fed may respond to a booming stock market by keeping the supply of money lower and raising interest rates. The opposite would hold true if the stock market would fall.

3. Stock market participants also keep an eye on the Fed's policy plans. When the Fed lowers the money supply, it makes stocks less attractive because alternative assets (such as bonds) pay higher interest rates. Also, higher interest rates may lower the expected profitability of firms.

II. How Fiscal Policy Influences Aggregate Demand

A. Definition of **fiscal policy: the setting of the level of government spending and taxation by government policymakers**.

B. Changes in Government Purchases

1. When the government changes the level of its purchases, it influences aggregate demand directly. An increase in government purchases shifts the aggregate-demand curve to the right, while a decrease in government purchases shifts the aggregate-demand curve to the left.

2. There are two macroeconomic effects that cause the size of the shift in the aggregate-demand curve to be different from the change in the level of government purchases. They are called the multiplier effect and the crowding-out effect.

C. The Multiplier Effect

Figure 4

1. Suppose that the government buys a product from a company.

   a. The immediate impact of the purchase is to raise profits and employment at that firm.

   b. As a result, owners and workers at this firm will see an increase in income, and will therefore likely increase their own consumption.

   c. Thus, total spending rises by more than the increase in government purchases.

Pay It Forward, Chapter 10. This movie suggests that if each person could help three others do something they were not able to do alone, the world would be a much greater place. This scene provides a nice parallel to the multiplier in the economy as the benefits of each step are magnified as these good deeds are paid forward.

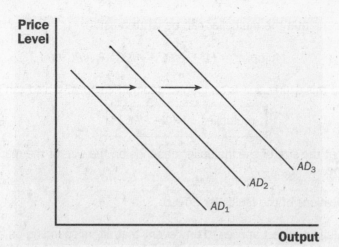

2. Definition of **multiplier effect**: **the additional shifts in aggregate demand that result when expansionary fiscal policy increases income and thereby increases consumer spending**.

3. The multiplier effect continues even after the first round.

   a. When consumers spend part of their additional income, it provides additional income for other consumers.

   b. These consumers then spend some of this additional income, raising the incomes of yet another group of consumers.

4. A Formula for the Spending Multiplier

   a. The *marginal propensity to consume* (*MPC*) is the fraction of extra income that a household consumes rather than saves.

   b. Example: The government spends $20 billion on new planes. Assume that $MPC = 3/4$.

   c. Incomes will increase by $20 billion, so consumption will rise by $MPC \times$ $20 billion. The second increase in consumption will be equal to $MPC \times (MPC \times$ $20 billion) or $MPC^2 \times$ $20 billion.

   d. To find the total impact on the demand for goods and services, we add up all of these effects:

Change in government purchases	= $20 billion
First change in consumption	= $MPC \times$ $20 billion
Second change in consumption	= $MPC^2 \times$ $20 billion
Third change in consumption	= $MPC^3 \times$ $20 billion

   $$\text{Total Change} = (1 + MPC + MPC^2 + MPC^3 + \ldots) \times \$20 \text{ billion}$$

e. This means that the multiplier can be written as:

$$\text{Multiplier} = (1 + MPC + MPC^2 + MPC^3 + \ldots).$$

f. Because this expression is an infinite geometric series, it also can be written as:

$$\boxed{\text{multiplier} = 1/(1 - MPC)}$$

g. Note that the size of the multiplier depends on the size of the marginal propensity to consume.

5. Other Applications of the Multiplier Effect

a. The multiplier effect applies to any event that alters spending on any component of GDP (consumption, investment, government purchases, or net exports).

b. Examples include a reduction in net exports due to a recession in another country or a stock market boom that raises consumption.

D. The Crowding-Out Effect

Figure 5

1. The crowding-out effect works in the opposite direction.

2. Definition of **crowding-out effect: the offset in aggregate demand that results when expansionary fiscal policy raises the interest rate and thereby reduces investment spending**.

3. As we discussed earlier, when the government buys a product from a company, the immediate impact of the purchase is to raise profits and employment at that firm. As a result, owners and workers at this firm will see an increase in income, and will therefore likely increase their own consumption.

4. If consumers want to purchase more goods and services, they will need to increase their holdings of money. This shifts the demand for money to the right, pushing up the interest rate.

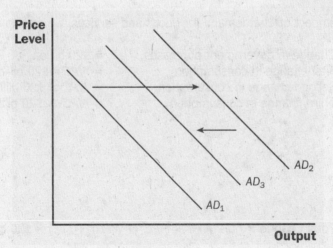

5. The higher interest rate raises the cost of borrowing and the return to saving. This discourages households from spending their incomes for new consumption or investing in new housing. Firms will also decrease investment, choosing not to build new factories or purchase new equipment.

6. Thus, even though the increase in government purchases shifts the aggregate-demand curve to the right, this fall in consumption and investment will pull aggregate demand back toward the left. Thus, aggregate demand increases by less than the increase in government purchases.

7. Therefore, when the government increases its purchases by $X, the aggregate demand for goods and services could rise by more or less than $X, depending on whether the multiplier effect or the crowding-out effect is larger.

    a. If the multiplier effect is greater than the crowding-out effect, aggregate demand will rise by more than $X.

    b. If the multiplier effect is less than the crowding-out effect, aggregate demand will rise by less than $X.

E. Changes in Taxes

1. Changes in taxes affect a household's take-home pay.

    a. If the government reduces taxes, households will likely spend some of this extra income, shifting the aggregate-demand curve to the right.

    b. If the government raises taxes, household spending will fall, shifting the aggregate-demand curve to the left.

2. The size of the shift in the aggregate-demand curve will also depend on the sizes of the multiplier and crowding-out effects.

    a. When the government lowers taxes and consumption increases, earnings and profits rise, which further stimulate consumer spending. This is the multiplier effect.

    b. Higher incomes lead to greater spending, which means a higher demand for money. Interest rates rise and investment spending falls. This is the crowding-out effect.

3. Another important determinant of the size of the shift in aggregate demand due to a change in taxes is whether people believe that the tax change is permanent or temporary. A permanent tax change will have a larger effect on aggregate demand than a temporary one.

F. *FYI: How Fiscal Policy Might Affect Aggregate Supply*

1. Because people respond to incentives, a decrease in tax rates may cause individuals to work more, because they get to keep more of what they earn. If this occurs, the aggregate-supply curve would increase (shift to the right).

2. Changes in government purchases may also affect supply. If the government increases spending on capital projects or education, the productive ability of the economy is enhanced, shifting aggregate supply to the right.

III. Using Policy to Stabilize the Economy

 If you would like, now would be a good time to cover the debate in Chapter 23 concerning whether or not policymakers should actively attempt to stabilize the economy.

A. The Case for Active Stabilization Policy

1. Example: The government reduces its spending to cut the budget deficit, lowering aggregate demand (shifting the curve to the left).

    a. The Fed can offset this government action by increasing the money supply.

    b. This would lower interest rates and boost spending, shifting the aggregate-demand curve back to the right.

2. Policy instruments are often used in this manner to stabilize demand. Economic stabilization has been an explicit goal of U.S. policy since the Employment Act of 1946.

    a. One implication of the Employment Act is that the government should avoid being the cause of economic fluctuations.

    b. The second implication of the Employment Act is that the government should respond to changes in the private economy in order to stabilize aggregate demand.

3. The Employment Act occurred in response to a book by John Maynard Keynes, an economist who emphasized the important role of aggregate demand in explaining short-run fluctuations in the economy.

4. Keynes also felt strongly that the government should stimulate aggregate demand whenever necessary to keep the economy at full employment.

    a. Keynes felt that aggregate demand responds strongly to pessimism and optimism. When consumers are pessimistic, aggregate demand is low, output is low, and unemployment is increased. When consumers are optimistic, aggregate demand is high, output is high, and unemployment is lowered.

    b. It is possible for the government to adjust monetary and fiscal policy in response to optimistic or pessimistic views. This helps stabilize aggregate demand, keeping output stable at full employment.

5. *Case Study: Keynesians in the White House*

    a. In 1961, President Kennedy pushed for a tax cut to stimulate aggregate demand. Several of his economic advisers were followers of Keynes.

    b. In 2009, President Obama pushed for a stimulus bill that included several increases in government spending.

6. *In the News: How Large is the Fiscal Policy Multiplier?*

    a. During the large economic recession of 2008–2009, many governments tried using expansionary fiscal policy to stimulate aggregate demand.

b. This is an article from *The Economist* describing the debate over the estimated effects of these policies.

B. The Case against Active Stabilization Policy

1. Some economists believe that fiscal and monetary policy tools should only be used to help the economy achieve long-run goals, such as low inflation and rapid economic growth.

2. The primary argument against active policy is that these policy tools may affect the economy with a long lag.

   a. With monetary policy, the change in money supply leads to a change in interest rates. This change in interest rates affects investment spending. However, investment decisions are usually made well in advance, so the effects from changes in investment will not likely be felt in the economy very quickly.

   b. The lag in fiscal policy is generally due to the political process. Changes in spending and taxes must be approved by both the House and the Senate (after going through committees in both houses).

3. By the time these policies take effect, the condition of the economy may have changed. This could lead to even larger problems.

C. Automatic Stabilizers

1. Definition of **automatic stabilizers: changes in fiscal policy that stimulate aggregate demand when the economy goes into a recession without policymakers having to take any deliberate action**.

2. The most important automatic stabilizer is the tax system.

   a. When the economy falls into a recession, incomes and profits fall.

   b. The personal income tax depends on the level of households' incomes and the corporate income tax depends on the level of firm profits.

   c. This implies that the government's tax revenue falls during a recession. This tax cut stimulates aggregate demand and reduces the magnitude of this economic downturn.

3. Government spending is also an automatic stabilizer.

   a. More individuals become eligible for transfer payments during a recession.

   b. These transfer payments provide additional income to recipients, stimulating spending.

   c. Thus, just like the tax system, our system of transfer payments helps to reduce the size of short-run economic fluctuations.

SOLUTIONS TO TEXT PROBLEMS:

Quick Quizzes

1. According to the theory of liquidity preference, the interest rate adjusts to balance the supply and demand for money. Therefore, a decrease in the money supply will increase the equilibrium interest rate. This decrease in the money supply reduces aggregate demand because the higher interest rate causes households to buy fewer houses, reducing the demand for residential investment, and causes firms to spend less on new factories and new equipment, reducing business investment.

2. If the government reduces spending on highway construction by $10 billion, the aggregate-demand curve shifts to the left because government purchases are lower. The shift to the left of the aggregate-demand curve could be more than $10 billion if the multiplier effect outweighs the crowding-out effect, or it could be less than $10 billion if the crowding-out effect outweighs the multiplier effect.

3. If people become pessimistic about the future, they will spend less, causing the aggregate-demand curve to shift to the left. If the Fed wants to stabilize aggregate demand, it should increase the money supply. The increase in the money supply will cause the interest rate to decline, thus stimulating residential and business investment. The Fed might choose not to do this because by the time the policy action takes effect, the long lag time might mean the economy would have recovered on its own, and the increase in the money supply will cause inflation.

Questions for Review

1. The theory of liquidity preference is Keynes's theory of how the interest rate is determined. According to the theory, the aggregate-demand curve slopes downward because: (1) a higher price level raises money demand; (2) higher money demand leads to a higher interest rate; and (3) a higher interest rate reduces the quantity of goods and services demanded. Thus, the price level has a negative relationship with the quantity of goods and services demanded.

2. A decrease in the money supply shifts the money-supply curve to the left. The equilibrium interest rate will rise. The higher interest rate reduces consumption and investment, so aggregate demand falls. Thus, the aggregate-demand curve shifts to the left.

3. If the government spends $3 billion to buy police cars, aggregate demand might increase by more than $3 billion because of the multiplier effect on aggregate demand. Aggregate demand might increase by less than $3 billion because of the crowding-out effect on aggregate demand.

4. If pessimism sweeps the country, households reduce consumption spending and firms reduce investment, so aggregate demand falls. If the Fed wants to stabilize aggregate demand, it must increase the money supply, reducing the interest rate, which will induce households to save less and spend more and will encourage firms to invest more, both of which will increase aggregate demand. If the Fed does not increase the money supply, Congress could increase government purchases or reduce taxes to increase aggregate demand.

5. Government policies that act as automatic stabilizers include the tax system and government spending through the unemployment-benefit system. The tax system acts as an automatic stabilizer because when incomes are high, people pay more in taxes, so they cannot spend as much. When incomes are low, so are taxes; thus, people can spend more. The result is that spending is partly stabilized. Government spending through the unemployment-benefit system acts as an automatic stabilizer because in recessions the government transfers money to the unemployed so their incomes do not fall as much and thus their spending will not fall as much.

Problems and Applications

1. a. When the Fed's bond traders buy bonds in open-market operations, the money-supply curve shifts to the right from MS_1 to MS_2, as shown in Figure 1. The result is a decline in the interest rate.

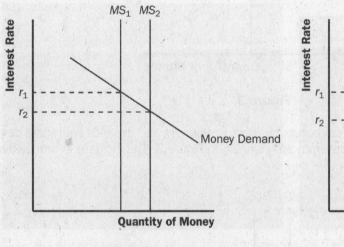

Figure 1

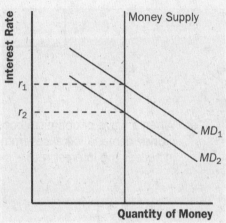

Figure 2

   b. When an increase in credit card availability reduces the cash people hold, the money-demand curve shifts to the left from MD_1 to MD_2, as shown in Figure 2. The result is a decline in the interest rate.

   c. When the Federal Reserve reduces reserve requirements, the money supply increases, so the money-supply curve shifts to the right from MS_1 to MS_2, as shown in Figure 1. The result is a decline in the interest rate.

d.   When households decide to hold more money to use for holiday shopping, the money-demand curve shifts to the right from MD_1 to MD_2, as shown in Figure 3. The result is a rise in the interest rate.

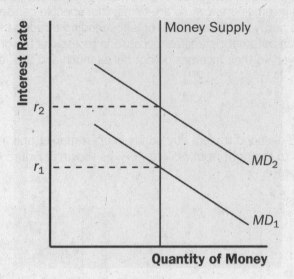

Figure 3

e.   When a wave of optimism boosts business investment and expands aggregate demand, money demand increases from MD_1 to MD_2 in Figure 3. The increase in money demand increases the interest rate.

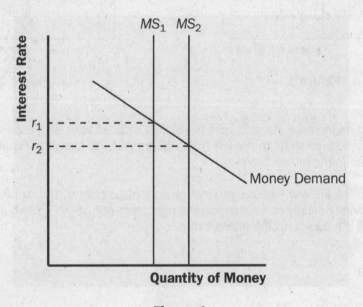

Figure 4

2. a. The increase in the money supply will cause the equilibrium interest rate to decline, as shown in Figure 4. Households will increase spending and will invest in more new housing. Firms too will increase investment spending. This will cause the aggregate demand curve to shift to the right as shown in Figure 5.

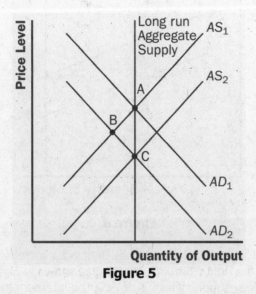

Figure 5

b. As shown in Figure 5, the increase in aggregate demand will cause an increase in both output and the price level in the short run (point B).

c. When the economy makes the transition from its short-run equilibrium to its long-run equilibrium, short-run aggregate supply will decline, causing the price level to rise even further (point C).

d. The increase in the price level will cause an increase in the demand for money, raising the equilibrium interest rate.

e. Yes. While output initially rises because of the increase in aggregate demand, it will fall once short-run aggregate supply declines. Thus, there is no long-run effect of the increase in the money supply on real output.

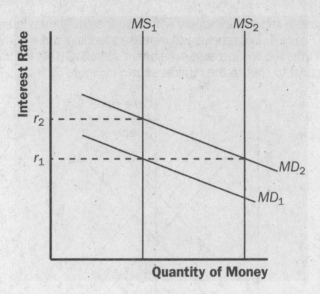

Figure 6

3. a. When fewer ATMs are available, money demand is increased and the money-demand curve shifts to the right from MD_1 to MD_2, as shown in Figure 6. If the Fed does not change the money supply, which is at MS_1, the interest rate will rise from r_1 to r_2. The increase in the interest rate shifts the aggregate-demand curve to the left, as consumption and investment fall.

   b. If the Fed wants to stabilize aggregate demand, it should increase the money supply to MS_2, so the interest rate will remain at r_1 and aggregate demand will not change.

   c. To increase the money supply using open market operations, the Fed should buy government bonds.

4. A tax cut that is permanent will have a bigger impact on consumer spending and aggregate demand. If the tax cut is permanent, consumers will view it as adding substantially to their financial resources, and they will increase their spending substantially. If the tax cut is temporary, consumers will view it as adding just a little to their financial resources, so they will not increase spending as much.

5. a. The current situation is shown in Figure 7.

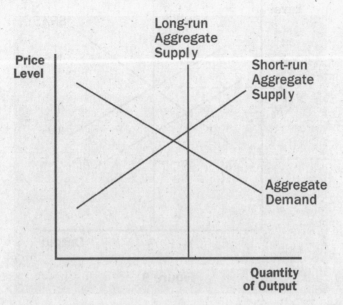

Figure 7

b. The Fed will want to stimulate aggregate demand. Thus, it will need to lower the interest rate by increasing the money supply. This could be achieved if the Fed purchases government bonds from the public.

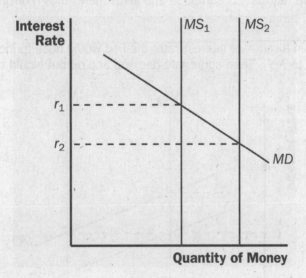

Figure 8

c. As shown in Figure 8, the Fed's purchase of government bonds shifts the supply of money to the right, lowering the interest rate.

d. The Fed's purchase of government bonds will increase aggregate demand as consumers and firms respond to lower interest rates. Output and the price level will rise as shown in Figure 9.

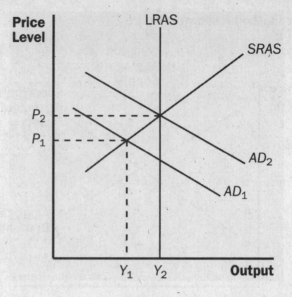

Figure 9

6. a. Legislation allowing banks to pay interest on checking deposits increases the return to money relative to other financial assets, thus increasing money demand.

   b. If the money supply remained constant (at MS_1), the increase in the demand for money would have raised the interest rate, as shown in Figure 10. The rise in the interest rate would have reduced consumption and investment, thus reducing aggregate demand and output.

   c. To maintain a constant interest rate, the Fed would need to increase the money supply from MS_1 to MS_2. Then aggregate demand and output would be unaffected.

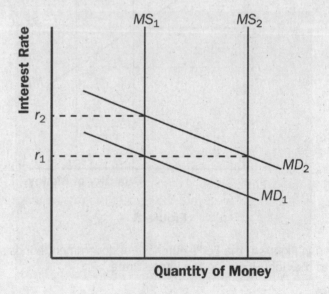

Figure 10

7. a. If there is no crowding out, then the multiplier equals $1/(1 - MPC)$. Because the multiplier is 3, then $MPC = 2/3$.

b. If there is crowding out, then the *MPC* would be larger than 2/3. An *MPC* that is larger than 2/3 would lead to a larger multiplier than 3, which is then reduced down to 3 by the crowding-out effect.

8. a. The initial effect of the tax reduction of $20 billion is to increase aggregate demand by $20 billion × 3/4 (the *MPC*) = $15 billion.

b. Additional effects follow this initial effect as the added incomes are spent. The second round leads to increased consumption spending of $15 billion × 3/4 = $11.25 billion. The third round gives an increase in consumption of $11.25 billion × 3/4 = $8.44 billion. The effects continue indefinitely. Adding them all up gives a total effect that depends on the multiplier. With an *MPC* of 3/4, the multiplier is $1/(1 - 3/4) = 4$. So the total effect is $15 billion × 4 = $60 billion.

c. Government purchases have an initial effect of the full $20 billion, because they increase aggregate demand directly by that amount. The total effect of an increase in government purchases is thus $20 billion × 4 = $80 billion. So government purchases lead to a bigger effect on output than a tax cut does. The difference arises because government purchases affect aggregate demand by the full amount, but a tax cut is partly saved by consumers, and therefore does not lead to as much of an increase in aggregate demand.

d. The government could increase taxes by the same amount it increases its purchases.

9. If the marginal propensity to consume is 0.8, the spending multiplier will be $1/(1 - 0.8) = 5$. Therefore, the government would have to increase spending by $400/5 = $80 billion to close the recessionary gap.

10. If government spending increases, aggregate demand rises, so money demand rises. The increase in money demand leads to a rise in the interest rate and thus a decline in aggregate demand if the Fed keeps the money supply constant. But if the Fed maintains a fixed interest rate, it will increase money supply, so aggregate demand will not decline. Thus, the effect on aggregate demand from an increase in government spending will be larger if the Fed maintains a fixed interest rate.

11. a. Expansionary fiscal policy is more likely to lead to a short-run increase in investment if the investment accelerator is large. A large investment accelerator means that the increase in output caused by expansionary fiscal policy will induce a large increase in investment. Without a large accelerator, investment might decline because the increase in aggregate demand will raise the interest rate.

b. Expansionary fiscal policy is more likely to lead to a short-run increase in investment if the interest sensitivity of investment is small. Because fiscal policy increases aggregate demand, thus increasing money demand and the interest rate, the greater the sensitivity of investment to the interest rate the greater the decline in investment will be, which will offset the positive accelerator effect.

12. a. Tax revenue declines when the economy goes into a recession because taxes are closely related to economic activity. In a recession, people's incomes and wages fall, as do firms' profits, so taxes on these things decline.

b. Government spending rises when the economy goes into a recession because more people get unemployment-insurance benefits, welfare benefits, and other forms of income support.

c. If the government were to operate under a strict balanced-budget rule, it would have to raise tax rates or cut government spending in a recession. Both would reduce aggregate demand, making the recession more severe.

13. a. If there were a contraction in aggregate demand, the Fed would need to increase the money supply to increase aggregate demand and stabilize the price level, as shown in Figure 11. By increasing the money supply, the Fed is able to shift the aggregate-demand curve back to AD_1 from AD_2. This policy stabilizes output and the price level.

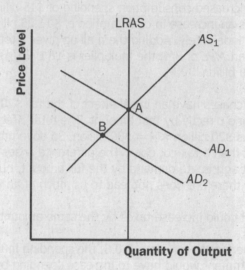

Figure 11

b. If there were an adverse shift in short-run aggregate supply, the Fed would need to decrease the money supply to stabilize the price level, shifting the aggregate-demand curve to the left from AD_1 to AD_2, as shown in Figure 12. This worsens the recession caused by the shift in aggregate supply. To stabilize output, the Fed would need to increase the money supply, shifting the aggregate-demand curve from AD_1 to AD_3. However, this action would raise the price level.

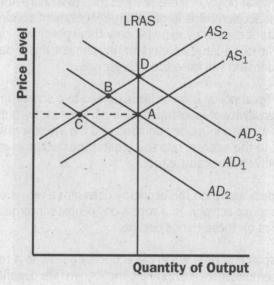

Figure 12

THE SHORT-RUN TRADE-OFF BETWEEN INFLATION AND UNEMPLOYMENT

WHAT'S NEW IN THE SIXTH EDITION:

There is a new section on "The Phillips Curve during the Financial Crisis." A new *In the News* box on "Do We Need More Inflation?" has also been added.

LEARNING OBJECTIVES:

By the end of this chapter, students should understand:

➢ why policymakers face a short-run trade-off between inflation and unemployment.

➢ why the inflation-unemployment trade-off disappears in the long run.

➢ how supply shocks can shift the inflation-unemployment trade-off.

➢ the short-run cost of reducing inflation.

➢ how policymakers' credibility might affect the cost of reducing inflation.

CONTEXT AND PURPOSE:

Chapter 22 is the final chapter in a three-chapter sequence on the economy's short-run fluctuations around its long-term trend. Chapter 20 introduced aggregate supply and aggregate demand. Chapter 21 developed how monetary and fiscal policies affect aggregate demand. Both Chapters 20 and 21 addressed the relationship between the price level and output. Chapter 22 will concentrate on a similar relationship between inflation and unemployment.

The purpose of Chapter 22 is to trace the history of economists' thinking about the relationship between inflation and unemployment. Students will see why there is a temporary trade-off between inflation and unemployment, and why there is no permanent trade-off. This result is an extension of the results produced by the model of aggregate supply and aggregate demand where a change in the price level induced by a change in aggregate demand temporarily alters output but has no permanent impact on output.

KEY POINTS:

- The Phillips curve describes a negative relationship between inflation and unemployment. By expanding aggregate demand, policymakers can choose a point on the Phillips curve with higher inflation and lower unemployment. By contracting aggregate demand, policymakers can choose a point on the Phillips curve with lower inflation and higher unemployment.

- The trade-off between inflation and unemployment described by the Phillips curve holds only in the short run. In the long run, expected inflation adjusts to changes in actual inflation, and the short-run Phillips curve shifts. As a result, the long-run Phillips curve is vertical at the natural rate of unemployment.

- The short-run Phillips curve also shifts because of shocks to aggregate supply. An adverse supply shock, such as an increase in world oil prices, gives policymakers a less favorable trade-off between inflation and unemployment. That is, after an adverse supply shock, policymakers have to accept a higher rate of inflation for any given rate of unemployment, or a higher rate of unemployment for any given rate of inflation.

- When the Fed contracts growth in the money supply to reduce inflation, it moves the economy along the short-run Phillips curve, which results in temporarily high unemployment. The cost of disinflation depends on how quickly expectations of inflation fall. Some economists argue that a credible commitment to low inflation can reduce the cost of disinflation by inducing a quick adjustment of expectations.

CHAPTER OUTLINE:

I. The Phillips Curve

   A. Origins of the Phillips Curve

      1. In 1958, economist A. W. Phillips published an article discussing the negative correlation between inflation rates and unemployment rates in the United Kingdom.

      2. American economists Paul Samuelson and Robert Solow showed a similar relationship between inflation and unemployment for the United States two years later.

      3. The belief was that low unemployment is related to high aggregate demand, and high aggregate demand puts upward pressure on prices. Likewise, high unemployment is related to low aggregate demand, and low aggregate demand pulls price levels down.

      4. Definition of **Phillips curve: a curve that shows the short-run trade-off between inflation and unemployment**.

Figure 1

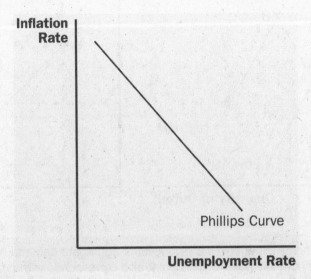

5. Samuelson and Solow believed that the Phillips curve offered policymakers a menu of possible economic outcomes. Policymakers could use monetary and fiscal policy to choose any point on the curve.

B. Aggregate Demand, Aggregate Supply, and the Phillips Curve

Figure 2

 Show how the Phillips curve is derived from the aggregate demand/aggregate supply model step by step. This graph is different from all the other graphs that they have drawn in macroeconomics, because it is not a supply-and-demand diagram.

1. The Phillips curve shows the combinations of inflation and unemployment that arise in the short run due to shifts in the aggregate-demand curve.

2. The greater the aggregate demand for goods and services, the greater the economy's output and the higher the price level. Greater output means lower unemployment. Whatever the previous year's price level happens to be, the higher the price level in the current year, the higher the rate of inflation.

3. Example: The price level is 100 (measured by the Consumer Price Index) in the year 2020. There are two possible changes in the economy for the year 2021: a low level of aggregate demand or a high level of aggregate demand.

    a. If the economy experiences a low level of aggregate demand, we would be at a short-run equilibrium like point A. This point also corresponds with point A on the Phillips curve. Note that when aggregate demand is low, the inflation rate is relatively low and the unemployment rate is relatively high.

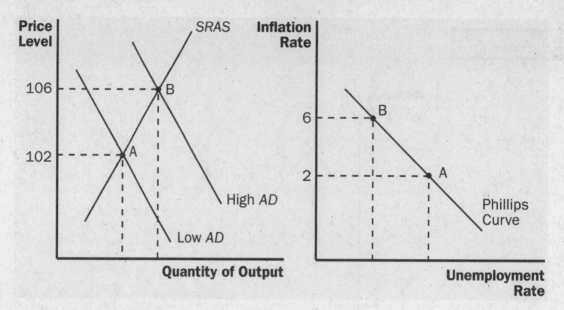

b. If the economy experiences a high level of aggregate demand, we would be at a short-run equilibrium like point B. This point also corresponds with point B on the Phillips curve. Note that when aggregate demand is high, the inflation rate is relatively high and the unemployment rate is relatively low.

4. Because monetary and fiscal policies both shift the aggregate-demand curve, these policies can move the economy along the Phillips curve.

a. Increases in the money supply, increases in government spending, or decreases in taxes all increase aggregate demand and move the economy to a point on the Phillips curve with lower unemployment and higher inflation.

b. Decreases in the money supply, decreases in government spending, or increases in taxes all lower aggregate demand and move the economy to a point on the Phillips curve with higher unemployment and lower inflation.

II. Shifts in the Phillips Curve: The Role of Expectations

A. The Long-Run Phillips Curve

Figure 3

1. In 1968, economist Milton Friedman argued that monetary policy is only able to choose a combination of unemployment and inflation for a short period of time. At the same time, economist Edmund Phelps wrote a paper suggesting the same thing.

2. In the long run, monetary growth has no real effects. This implies that it cannot affect the factors that determine the economy's long-run unemployment rate.

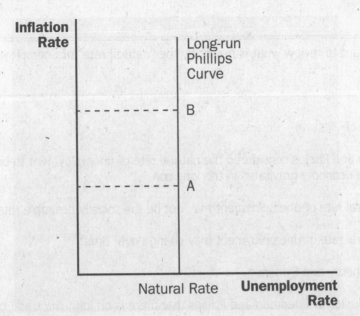

3. Thus, in the long run, we would not expect there to be a relationship between unemployment and inflation. This must mean that, in the long run, the Phillips curve is vertical.

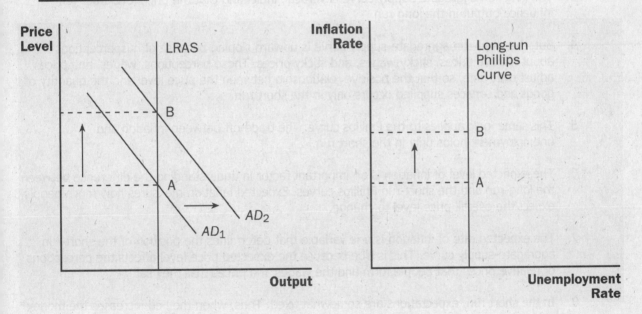

4. The vertical Phillips curve occurs because, in the long run, the aggregate supply curve is vertical as well. Thus, increases in aggregate demand lead only to changes in the price level and have no effect on the economy's level of output. Thus, in the long run, unemployment will not change when aggregate demand changes, but inflation will.

5. The long-run aggregate-supply curve occurs at the economy's natural rate of output. This means that the long-run Phillips curve occurs at the natural rate of unemployment.

> You may want to review what is meant by the "natural rate" of unemployment.

B. The Meaning of "Natural"

1. Friedman and Phelps considered the natural rate of unemployment to be the rate toward which the economy gravitates in the long run.

2. The natural rate of unemployment may not be the socially desirable rate of unemployment.

3. The natural rate of unemployment may change over time.

C. Reconciling Theory and Evidence

1. The conclusion of Friedman and Phelps that there is no long-run trade-off between inflation and unemployment was based on *theory*, while the correlation between inflation and unemployment found by Phillips, Samuelson, and Solow was based on actual *evidence*.

2. Friedman and Phelps believed that an inverse relationship between inflation and unemployment exists in the short run.

3. The long-run aggregate-supply curve is vertical, indicating that the price level does not influence output in the long run.

4. But, the short-run aggregate-supply curve is upward sloping because of misperceptions about relative prices, sticky wages, and sticky prices. These perceptions, wages, and prices adjust over time, so that the positive relationship between the price level and the quantity of goods and services supplied occurs only in the short run.

5. This same logic applies to the Phillips curve. The trade-off between inflation and unemployment holds only in the short run.

6. The expected level of inflation is an important factor in understanding the difference between the long-run and the short-run Phillips curves. Expected inflation measures how much people expect the overall price level to change.

7. The expected rate of inflation is one variable that determines the position of the short-run aggregate-supply curve. This is true because the expected price level affects the perceptions of relative prices that people form and the wages and prices that they set.

8. In the short run, expectations are somewhat fixed. Thus, when the Fed increases the money supply, aggregate demand increases along the upward sloping short-run aggregate-supply curve. Output grows (unemployment falls) and the price level rises (inflation increases).

9. Eventually, however, people will respond by changing their expectations of the price level. Specifically, they will begin expecting a higher rate of inflation.

D. The Short-Run Phillips Curve

1. We can relate the actual unemployment rate to the natural rate of unemployment, the actual inflation rate, and the expected inflation rate using the following equation:

    > unemp. rate = natural rate – a(actual inflation – expected inflation)

    a. Because expected inflation is already given in the short run, higher actual inflation leads to lower unemployment.

    b. How much unemployment changes in response to a change in inflation is determined by the variable a, which is related to the slope of the short-run aggregate-supply curve.

Be sure to discuss why actual inflation always equals expected inflation along the long-run Phillips curve.

Figure 5

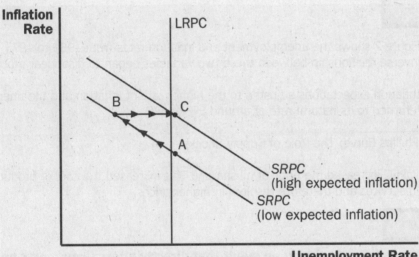

Unemployment Rate

2. If policymakers want to take advantage of the short-run trade-off between unemployment and inflation, it may lead to negative consequences.

    a. Suppose the economy is at point A and policymakers wish to lower the unemployment rate. Expansionary monetary policy or fiscal policy is used to shift aggregate demand to the right. The economy moves to point B, with a lower unemployment rate and a higher rate of inflation.

    b. Over time, people get used to this new level of inflation and raise their expectations of inflation. This leads to an upward shift of the short-run Phillips curve. The economy ends up at point C, with a higher inflation rate than at point A, but the same level of unemployment.

E. The Natural Experiment for the Natural-Rate Hypothesis

1. Definition of the **natural-rate hypothesis: the claim that unemployment eventually returns to its normal, or natural rate, regardless of the rate of inflation**.

Figure 6

2. Figure 6 shows the unemployment and inflation rates from 1961 to 1968. It is easy to see the inverse relationship between these two variables.

3. Beginning in the late 1960s, the government followed policies that increased aggregate demand.

    a. Government spending rose because of the Vietnam War.

    b. The Fed increased the money supply to try to keep interest rates down.

4. As a result of these policies, the inflation rate remained fairly high. However, even though inflation remained high, unemployment did not remain low.

Figure 7

    a. Figure 7 shows the unemployment and inflation rates from 1961 to 1973. The simple inverse relationship between these two variables began to disappear around 1970.

    b. Inflation expectations adjusted to the higher rate of inflation and the unemployment rate returned to its natural rate of around 5% to 6%.

III. Shifts in the Phillips Curve: The Role of Supply Shocks

A. In 1974, OPEC increased the price of oil sharply. This increased the cost of producing many goods and services and therefore resulted in higher prices.

Figure 8

1. Definition of **supply shock: an event that directly alters firms' costs and prices, shifting the economy's aggregate-supply curve and thus the Phillips curve**.

2. Graphically, we could represent this supply shock as a shift in the short-run aggregate-supply curve to the left.

3. The decrease in equilibrium output and the increase in the price level left the economy with stagflation.

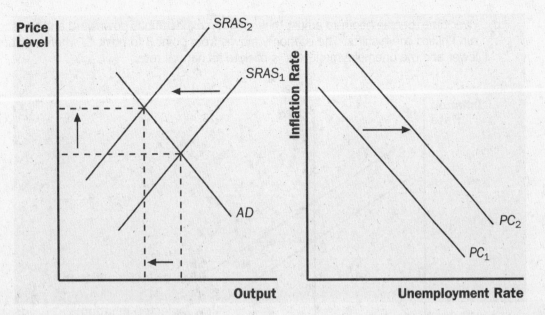

B. Given this turn of events, policymakers are left with a less favorable short-run trade-off between unemployment and inflation.

1. If they increase aggregate demand to fight unemployment, they will raise inflation further.

2. If they lower aggregate demand to fight inflation, they will raise unemployment further.

C. This less favorable trade-off between unemployment and inflation can be shown by a shift of the short-run Phillips curve. The shift may be permanent or temporary, depending on how people adjust their expectations of inflation.

Figure 9

D. During the 1970s, the Fed decided to accommodate the supply shock by increasing the supply of money. This increased the level of expected inflation. Figure 9 shows inflation and unemployment in the United States during the late 1970s and early 1980s.

IV. The Cost of Reducing Inflation

A. The Sacrifice Ratio

Figure 10

1. To reduce the inflation rate, the Fed must follow contractionary monetary policy.

a. When the Fed slows the rate of growth of the money supply, aggregate demand falls.

b. This reduces the level of output in the economy, increasing unemployment.

c. The economy moves from point A along the short-run Phillips curve to point B, which has a lower inflation rate but a higher unemployment rate.

d. Over time, people begin to adjust their inflation expectations downward and the short-run Phillips curve shifts. The economy moves from point B to point C, where inflation is lower and the unemployment rate is back to its natural rate.

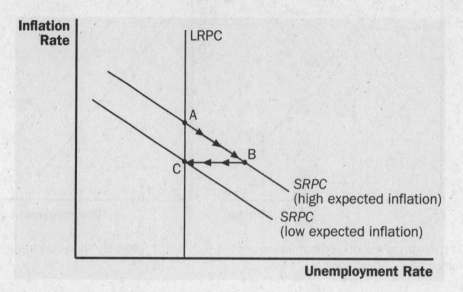

2. Therefore, to reduce inflation, the economy must suffer through a period of high unemployment and low output.

3. Definition of **sacrifice ratio: the number of percentage points of annual output lost in the process of reducing inflation by one percentage point**.

4. A typical estimate of the sacrifice ratio is five. This implies that for each percentage point inflation is decreased, output falls by 5%.

B. Rational Expectations and the Possibility of Costless Disinflation

1. Definition of **rational expectations: the theory according to which people optimally use all the information they have, including information about government policies, when forecasting the future**.

2. Proponents of rational expectations believe that when government policies change, people alter their expectations about inflation.

3. Therefore, if the government makes a credible commitment to a policy of low inflation, people would be rational enough to lower their expectations of inflation immediately. This implies that the short-run Phillips curve would shift quickly without any extended period of high unemployment.

 If you would like, now would be a good time to discuss the debate in Chapter 23 concerning whether the central bank should aim for zero inflation.

C. The Volcker Disinflation

Figure 11

1. Figure 11 shows the inflation and unemployment rates that occurred while Paul Volcker worked at reducing the level of inflation during the 1980s.

2. As inflation fell, unemployment rose. In fact, the United States experienced its deepest recession since the Great Depression.

3. Some economists have offered this as proof that the idea of a costless disinflation suggested by rational-expectations theorists is not possible. However, there are two reasons why we might not want to reject the rational-expectations theory so quickly.

    a. The cost (in terms of lost output) of the Volcker disinflation was not as large as many economists had predicted.

    b. While Volcker promised that he would fight inflation, many people did not believe him. Few people thought that inflation would fall as quickly as it did; this likely kept the short-run Phillips curve from shifting quickly.

D. The Greenspan Era

Figure 12

1. Figure 12 shows the inflation and unemployment rate from 1984 to 1999, called the Greenspan era because Alan Greenspan became the chairman of the Federal Reserve in 1987.

2. In 1986, OPEC's agreement with its members broke down and oil prices fell. The result of this favorable supply shock was a drop in both inflation and unemployment.

3. The rest of the 1990s witnessed a period of economic prosperity. Inflation gradually dropped, approaching zero by the end of the decade. Unemployment also reached a low level, leading many people to believe that the natural rate of unemployment has fallen.

4. The economy ran into problems in 2001 due to the end of the dot-com stock market bubble, the 9-11 terrorist attacks, and corporate accounting scandals that reduced aggregate demand. Unemployment rose as the economy experienced its first recession in a decade.

5. But a combination of expansionary monetary and fiscal policies helped end the downturn, and by early 2005, the unemployment rate was close to the estimated natural rate.

6. In 2005, President Bush nominated Ben Bernanke as the Fed chairman.

E. The Phillips Curve during a Financial Crisis

1. In his first couple of years as Fed chairman, Bernanke faced some significant economic challenges.

a. One challenge arose from problems in the housing and financial markets.

b. The resulting financial crisis led to a large drop in aggregate demand and high rates of unemployment.

c. As the unemployment rate rose, the inflation rate fell.

d. Policymakers used expansionary monetary and fiscal policy to move the economy along the short-term Phillips curve with lower unemployment and somewhat higher inflation.

F. *In The News: Do We Need More Inflation?*

1. In 2010, as the U.S. was trying to climb out of a severe economic downturn, some individuals suggested that a bit more inflation would do the economy some good.

2. This is an article from *The Wall Street Journal* arguing against such a suggestion.

SOLUTIONS TO TEXT PROBLEMS:

Quick Quizzes

1. The Phillips curve is shown in Figure 1.

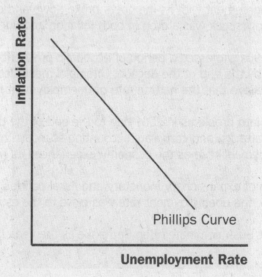

Figure 1

To see how policy can move the economy from a point with high inflation to a point with low inflation, suppose the economy begins at point A in Figure 2. If policy is used to reduce aggregate demand (such as a decrease in the money supply or a decrease in government purchases), the aggregate-demand curve shifts from AD_1 to AD_2, and the economy moves from point A to point B with lower inflation, a reduction in real GDP, and an increase in the unemployment rate.

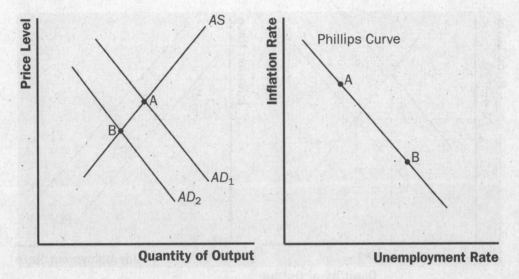

Figure 2

2. Figure 3 shows the short-run Phillips curve and the long-run Phillips curve. The curves are different because in the long run, monetary policy has no effect on unemployment, which tends toward its natural rate. However, in the short run, monetary policy can affect the unemployment rate. An increase in the growth rate of money raises actual inflation above expected inflation, causing firms to produce more since the short-run aggregate supply curve is positively sloped, which reduces unemployment temporarily.

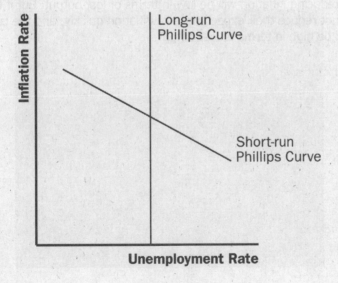

Figure 3

3. Examples of favorable shocks to aggregate supply include improved productivity and a decline in oil prices. Either shock shifts the aggregate-supply curve to the right, increasing output and reducing the price level, moving the economy from point A to point B in Figure 4. As a result, the Phillips curve shifts to the left, as the figure shows.

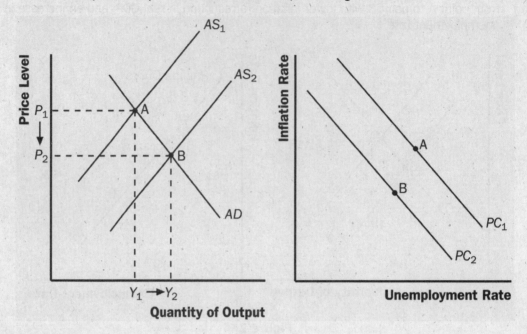

Figure 4

4. The sacrifice ratio is the number of percentage points of annual output lost in the process of reducing inflation by 1 percentage point. The credibility of the Fed's commitment to reduce inflation might affect the sacrifice ratio because it affects the speed at which expectations of inflation adjust. If the Fed's commitment to reduce inflation is credible, people will reduce their expectations of inflation quickly, the short-run Phillips curve will shift downward, and the cost of reducing inflation will be low in terms of lost output. But if the Fed is not credible, people will not reduce their expectations of inflation quickly, and the cost of reducing inflation will be high in terms of lost output.

Questions for Review

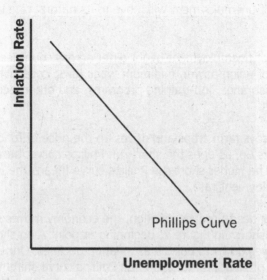

Figure 5

1. Figure 5 shows the short-run trade-off between inflation and unemployment. The Fed can move from one point on this curve to another by changing the money supply. An increase in the money supply reduces the unemployment rate and increases the inflation rate, while a decrease in the money supply increases the unemployment rate and decreases the inflation rate.

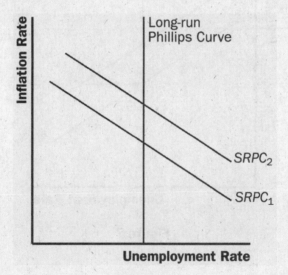

Figure 6

2. Figure 6 shows the long-run trade-off between inflation and unemployment. In the long run, there is no trade-off, as the economy must return to the natural rate of unemployment on the long-run Phillips curve. In the short run, the economy can move along a short-run Phillips curve, like $SRPC_1$ shown in the figure. But over time (as inflation expectations adjust) the short-run Phillips curve will shift to return the economy to the long-run Phillips curve, for example shifting from $SRPC_1$ to $SRPC_2$.

3. The natural rate of unemployment is natural because it is beyond the influence of monetary policy. The rate of unemployment will move to its natural rate in the long run, regardless of the inflation rate.

    The natural rate of unemployment might differ across countries because countries have varying degrees of union power, minimum-wage laws, collective-bargaining laws, unemployment insurance, job-training programs, and other factors that influence labor-market conditions.

4. If a drought destroys farm crops and drives up the price of food, the short-run aggregate-supply curve shifts up, as does the short-run Phillips curve, because the costs of production have increased. The higher short-run Phillips curve means the inflation rate will be higher for any given unemployment rate.

5. When the Fed decides to reduce inflation, the economy moves down along the short-run Phillips curve, as shown in Figure 7. Beginning at point A on short-run Phillips curve $SRPC_1$, the economy moves down to point B as inflation declines. Once people's expectations adjust to the lower rate of inflation, the short-run Phillips curve shifts to $SRPC_2$, and the economy moves to point C. The short-run costs of disinflation, which arise because the unemployment rate is temporarily above its natural rate, could be reduced if the Fed's action was credible, so that expectations would adjust more rapidly.

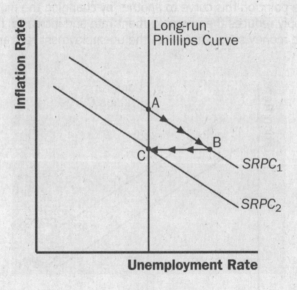

Figure 7

Problems and Applications

1. Figure 8 shows two different short-run Phillips curves depicting these four points. Points A and D are on $SRPC_1$ because both have expected inflation of 3%. Points B and C are on $SRPC_2$ because both have expected inflation of 5%.

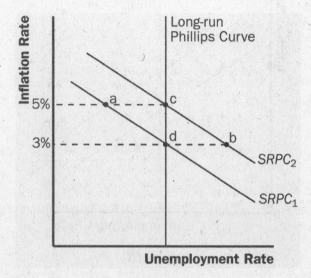

Figure 8

2. a. A rise in the natural rate of unemployment shifts the long-run Phillips curve to the right and the short-run Phillips curve up, as shown in Figure 9. The economy is initially on $LRPC_1$ and $SRPC_1$ at an inflation rate of 3%, which is also the expected rate of inflation. The increase in the natural rate of unemployment shifts the long-run Phillips curve to $LRPC_2$ and the short-run Phillips curve to $SRPC_2$, with the expected rate of inflation remaining equal to 3%.

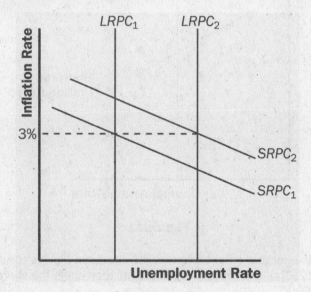

Figure 9

b. A decline in the price of imported oil shifts the short-run Phillips curve down, as shown in Figure 10, from $SRPC_1$ to $SRPC_2$. For any given unemployment rate, the inflation rate is lower, because oil is such a significant aspect of production costs in the economy.

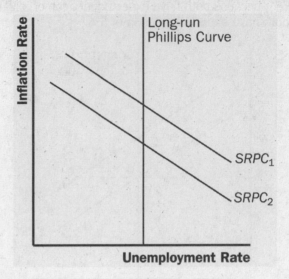

Figure 10

c. A rise in government spending represents an increase in aggregate demand, so it moves the economy along the short-run Phillips curve, as shown in Figure 11. The economy moves from point A to point B, with a decline in the unemployment rate and an increase in the inflation rate.

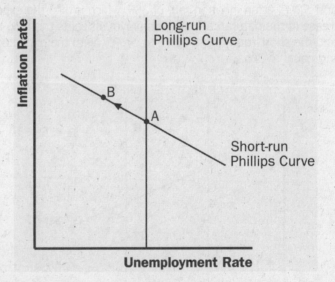

Figure 11

d. A decline in expected inflation causes the short-run Phillips curve to shift down, as shown in Figure 12. The lower rate of expected inflation shifts the short-run Phillips curve from $SRPC_1$ to $SRPC_2$.

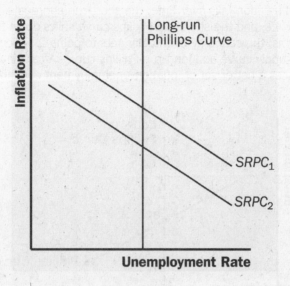

Figure 12

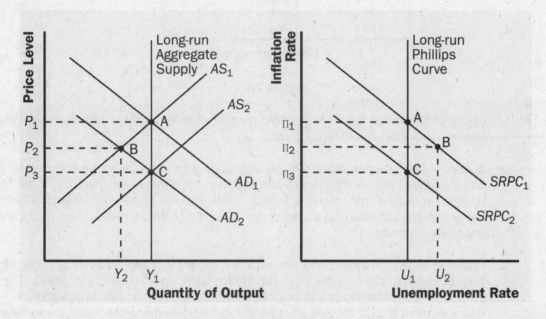

Figure 13

3. a. Figure 13 shows how a reduction in consumer spending causes a recession in both an aggregate-supply/aggregate-demand diagram and a Phillips-curve diagram. In both diagrams, the economy begins at full employment at point A. The decline in consumer spending reduces aggregate demand, shifting the aggregate-demand curve to the left from AD_1 to AD_2. The economy initially remains on the short-run aggregate-supply curve AS_1, so the new equilibrium occurs at point B. The movement of the aggregate-demand curve along the short-run aggregate-supply curve leads to a movement along short-run Phillips curve $SRPC_1$, from point A to point B. The lower price level in the aggregate-supply/aggregate-demand diagram corresponds to the lower inflation rate in the Phillips-curve diagram. The lower level of output in the aggregate-supply/aggregate-demand diagram corresponds to the higher unemployment rate in the Phillips-curve diagram.

b. As expected inflation falls over time, the short-run aggregate-supply curve shifts down from AS_1 to AS_2, and the short-run Phillips curve shifts down from $SRPC_1$ to $SRPC_2$. In both diagrams, the economy eventually gets to point C, which is back on the long-run aggregate-supply curve and long-run Phillips curve. After the recession is over, the economy faces a better set of inflation-unemployment combinations.

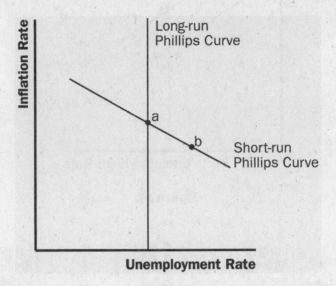

Figure 14

4. a. Figure 14 shows the economy in long-run equilibrium at point A, which is on both the long-run and short-run Phillips curves.

    b. A wave of business pessimism reduces aggregate demand, moving the economy to point B in the figure. The unemployment rate rises and the inflation rate declines. If the Fed undertakes expansionary monetary policy, it can increase aggregate demand, offsetting the pessimism and returning the economy to point A, with the initial inflation rate and unemployment rate.

    c. Figure 15 shows the effects on the economy if the price of imported oil rises. The higher price of imported oil shifts the short-run Phillips curve up from $SRPC_1$ to $SRPC_2$. The economy moves from point A to point C, with a higher inflation rate and higher unemployment rate. If the Fed engages in expansionary monetary policy, it can return the economy to its original unemployment rate at point D, but the inflation rate will be higher. If the Fed engages in contractionary monetary policy, it can return the economy to its original inflation rate at point E, but the unemployment rate will be higher. This situation differs from that in part (b) because in part (b) the economy stayed on the same short-run Phillips curve, but in part (c) the economy moved to a higher short-run Phillips curve, which gives policymakers a less favorable trade-off between inflation and unemployment.

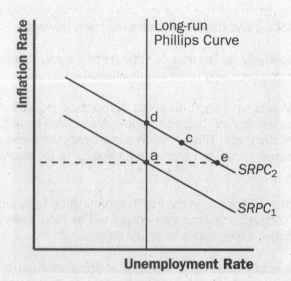

Figure 15

5. Economists who believe that expectations adjust quickly in response to changes in policy would be more likely to favor using contractionary policy to reduce inflation than economists with the opposite views. If expectations adjust quickly, the costs of reducing inflation (in terms of lost output) will be relatively small. Thus, Milton would be more in favor of following a policy to reduce inflation than would James.

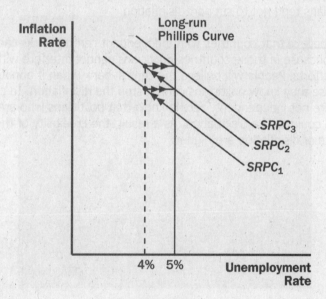

Figure 16

6. If the Fed acts on its belief that the natural rate of unemployment is 4%, when the natural rate is in fact 5%, the result will be a spiraling up of the inflation rate, as shown in Figure 16. Starting from a point on the long-run Phillips curve, with an unemployment rate of 5%, the Fed will believe that the economy is in a recession, because the unemployment rate is greater than its estimate of the natural rate. Therefore, the Fed will increase the money supply, moving the economy along the short-run Phillips curve *SRPC₁*. The inflation rate will rise and the unemployment rate will fall to 4%. As the inflation rate rises over time,

expectations of inflation will rise, and the short-run Phillips curve will shift up to *SRPC₂*. This process will continue, and the inflation rate will spiral upwards.

The Fed may eventually realize that its estimate of the natural rate of unemployment is wrong by examining the rising trend in the inflation rate.

7. a. If wage contracts have short durations, a recession induced by contractionary monetary policy will be less severe, because wage contracts can be adjusted more rapidly to reflect the lower inflation rate. This will allow a more rapid movement of the short-run aggregate-supply curve and short-run Phillips curve to restore the economy to long-run equilibrium.

   b. If there is little confidence in the Fed's determination to reduce inflation, a recession induced by contractionary monetary policy will be more severe. It will take longer for people's inflation expectations to adjust downwards.

   c. If expectations of inflation adjust quickly to actual inflation, a recession induced by contractionary monetary policy will be less severe. In this case, people's expectations adjust quickly, so the short-run Phillips curve shifts quickly to restore the economy to long-run equilibrium at the natural rate of unemployment.

8. Even though inflation is unpopular, elected leaders do not always support efforts to reduce inflation because of the short-run costs associated with disinflation. In particular, as disinflation occurs, the unemployment rate rises, and when unemployment is high people tend not to vote for incumbent politicians, blaming them for the bad state of the economy. Thus, politicians tend not to support disinflation.

Economists believe that countries with independent central banks can reduce the cost of disinflation because in those countries politicians cannot interfere with central banks' disinflation efforts. People will believe the central bank when it announces a disinflation policy because they know politicians cannot stop the disinflation. In countries with central banks that are not independent, people know that politicians who are worried they will not be reelected could stop a disinflation. As a result, the credibility of the central bank is lower and the costs of disinflation are higher.

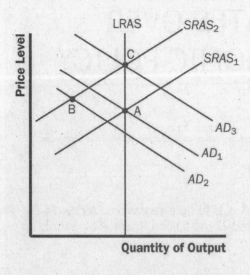

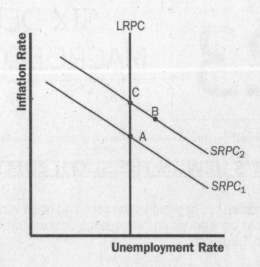

Figure 17

9. a. As shown in the left diagram of Figure 17, equilibrium output and employment will fall. However, the effects on the price level and inflation rate will be ambiguous. The fall in aggregate demand puts downward pressure on prices, while the decline in short-run aggregate supply pushes prices up. The diagram on the right side of Figure 17 assumes that the inflation rate rises.

   b. The Fed would have to use expansionary monetary policy to keep output and employment at their natural rates. Aggregate demand would have to shift to AD_3.

   c. The Fed may not want to pursue this action because it will lead to a rise in the inflation rate as shown by point C.

10. If policymakers are uncertain about the value of the natural rate of unemployment, they need to look at other variables. Because there is a correspondence through the Phillips curve between inflation and unemployment, when unemployment is close to its natural rate, inflation should not change. Thus, policymakers can look at data on the inflation rate to judge how close unemployment is to its natural rate. In addition, they can look at other macroeconomic variables, including the components of GDP and interest rates, to try to disentangle shifts in aggregate supply from shifts in aggregate demand, which (when combined with information about inflation) can help them determine the appropriate stance for monetary policy.

23 SIX DEBATES OVER MACROECONOMIC POLICY

WHAT'S NEW IN THE SIXTH EDITION:

A sixth debate has been added on spending hikes versus tax cuts to fight recessions. A new *In the News* feature has been added on "What is the Optimal Inflation Rate?" In addition, there is a new *FYI* on "Inflation Targeting."

LEARNING OBJECTIVES:

By the end of this chapter, students should understand:

➢ the debate concerning whether policymakers should try to stabilize the economy.

➢ the debate concerning whether the government should fight recessions with spending hikes or tax cuts.

➢ the debate concerning whether monetary policy should be made by rule rather than by discretion.

➢ the debate concerning whether the central bank should aim for zero inflation.

➢ the debate concerning whether the government should balance its budget.

➢ the debate concerning whether the tax laws should be reformed to encourage saving.

CONTEXT AND PURPOSE:

Chapter 23 is the final chapter in the text. It addresses six unresolved issues in macroeconomics, each of which is central to current political debates. The chapter can be studied all at once, or portions of the chapter can be studied in conjunction with prior chapters that deal with the related material.

The purpose of Chapter 23 is to provide both sides of six leading debates over macroeconomic policy. It employs information and tools that students have accumulated in their study of this text. This chapter may help students take a position on the issues addressed or, at least, it may help them understand the reasoning of others who have taken a position.

412

KEY POINTS:

- Advocates of active monetary and fiscal policy view the economy as inherently unstable and believe that policy can manage aggregate demand in order to offset the inherent instability. Critics of active monetary and fiscal policy emphasize that policy affects the economy with a lag and that our ability to forecast future economic conditions is poor. As a result, attempts to stabilize the economy can end up being destabilizing.

- Advocates of increased government spending to fight recessions argue that because tax cuts may be saved rather than spent, direct government spending does more to increase aggregate demand, which is key to promoting production and employment. Critics of spending hikes argue that tax cuts can expand both aggregate demand and aggregate supply and that hasty increases in government spending may lead to wasteful public projects.

- Advocates of rules for monetary policy argue that discretionary policy can suffer from incompetence, abuse of power, and time inconsistency. Critics of rules for monetary policy argue that discretionary policy is more flexible in responding to changing economic circumstances.

- Advocates of a zero-inflation target emphasize that inflation has many costs and few, if any benefits. Moreover, the cost of eliminating inflation—depressed output and employment—is only temporary. Even this cost can be reduced if the central bank announces a credible plan to reduce inflation, thereby directly lowering expectations of inflation. Critics of a zero-inflation target claim that moderate inflation imposes only small costs on society, whereas the recession necessary to reduce the inflation is quite costly. The critics also point out several ways in which moderate inflation may be helpful to an economy.

- Advocates of a balanced government budget argue that budget deficits impose a burden on future generations by raising their taxes and lowering their incomes. Critics of a balanced government budget argue that the deficit is only one small piece of fiscal policy. Single-minded concern about the budget deficit can obscure the many ways in which policy, including various spending programs, affect different generations.

- Advocates of tax incentives for saving point out that our society discourages saving in many ways, such as by heavily taxing capital income and by reducing benefits for those who have accumulated wealth. They endorse reforming the tax laws to encourage saving, perhaps by switching from an income tax to a consumption tax. Critics of tax incentives for saving argue that many proposed changes to stimulate saving would primarily benefit the wealthy, who do not need a tax break. They also argue that such changes might have only a small effect on private saving. Raising public saving by increasing the government's budget surplus would provide a more direct and equitable way to increase national saving.

CHAPTER OUTLINE:

> Provide supporting facts and figures for each side of the debates. Emphasize that there are no clear right or wrong answers. Do not forget to mention the political dimensions involved with these debates. At the heart of these debates is that there is a great deal of wealth and power at stake, and these considerations often are more important than the consensus of economists.

Instead of lecturing, divide the students into groups and have them present the debates discussed in the chapter. Ask them to provide facts and figures to support their positions.

I. Should Monetary and Fiscal Policymakers Try to Stabilize the Economy?

A. Pro: Policymakers Should Try to Stabilize the Economy

1. When households and firms feel pessimistic, aggregate demand falls. This causes output to fall and unemployment to rise.

2. There is no reason for the economy to suffer through a recession when policymakers can reduce the severity of economic fluctuations.

3. Thus, policymakers should take an active role in leading the economy to stability.

4. When aggregate demand is inadequate to ensure full employment, policymakers should act to boost spending in the economy. When aggregate demand is excessive and there is a risk of inflation, policymakers should act to lower spending.

5. Such policy actions put macroeconomic theory to its best use by leading to a more stable economy.

B. Con: Policymakers Should Not Try to Stabilize the Economy

1. There are substantial difficulties associated with running fiscal and monetary policy. One of the most important problems to remember is the time lag that often occurs with policy.

2. Economic conditions change over time. Thus, policy effects that occur with a lag may hit the economy at the wrong time, leading to a more unstable economy.

3. Therefore, policymakers should refrain from intervening and be content with "doing no harm."

II. Should the Government Fight Recessions with Spending Hikes Rather than Tax Cuts?

A. Pro: The Government Should Fight Recessions with Spending Hikes

1. Traditional Keynesian analysis indicates that increases in government spending are a more potent tool than cuts in taxes.

a. Tax cuts can lead to increases in spending and saving.

b. Increases in government spending raise spending directly.

2. Estimates from the Obama administration suggest that $1 of tax cuts raises GDP by $0.99, but a $1 increase in government spending raises GDP by $1.59.

B. Con: The Government Should Fight Recessions with Tax Cuts

   1. Policymakers can target particular types of spending (such as investment) with the right tax incentives.

   2. Tax cuts may also increase aggregate supply.

      a. Reducing marginal tax rates may provide greater incentive to work.

      b. Increases in aggregate supply that accompany an increase in aggregate demand will keep the price level more stable.

III. Should Monetary Policy Be Made by Rule Rather than by Discretion?

   A. Pro: Monetary Policy Should Be Made by Rule

   1. Discretionary monetary policy leads to two problems.

      a. It does not limit incompetence and abuse of power. For example, a central banker may choose to create a *political business cycle* to help out a particular candidate.

      b. It may lead to a greater amount of inflation than is desirable. Policymakers often renege on the actions that they promise. If individuals do not believe that the central bank will follow a low inflation policy, the short-run Phillips curve will shift, resulting in a less favorable trade-off between inflation and unemployment.

   2. One way to avoid these problems is to force the central bank to follow a monetary rule. This rule could be flexible enough to allow for some information on the state of the economy.

   B. Con: Monetary Policy Should Not Be Made by Rule

   1. Discretionary monetary policy allows flexibility. This gives the Fed the ability to react to unforeseen situations quickly.

   2. It is also unclear that Fed central bankers use policy to help political candidates. Often, the policy used is one that actually lowers the candidate's popularity (such as during the Carter administration).

   3. The Fed can gain the confidence of people by following through on its promises. If it promises to fight inflation and then runs policies that keep the growth of the money supply low, there is no reason why inflation expectations would be high. Thus, the economy can achieve low inflation without a policy rule. (This was shown to be the case in the United States in the 1990s.)

   4. It would also be very difficult to specify a precise rule.

   C. *FYI: Inflation Targeting*

   1. Many central banks around the world have adopted explicit targets for inflation.

   2. The Federal Reserve has not adopted a formal policy of inflation targeting.

IV. Should the Central Bank Aim for Zero Inflation?

    A. Pro: The Central Bank Should Aim for Zero Inflation

        1. Inflation confers no benefits on society, but it poses real costs.

            a. Shoeleather costs

            b. Menu costs

            c. Increased variability of relative prices

            d. Tax distortions

            e. Confusion and inconvenience

            f. Arbitrary redistributions of wealth

        2. Reducing inflation usually is associated with higher unemployment in the short run. However, once individuals see that policymakers are trying to lower inflation, inflation expectations will fall, and the short-run Phillips curve will shift down. The economy will move back to the natural rate of unemployment at a lower inflation rate.

        3. Therefore, reducing inflation is a policy with temporary costs and permanent benefits.

        4. It is not clear that a case could be made for any other level of inflation. Price stability only occurs if the inflation rate is zero.

    B. Con: The Central Bank Should Not Aim for Zero Inflation

        1. The benefits of zero inflation are small relative to the costs. Estimates of the sacrifice ratio suggest that lowering inflation by one percentage point lowers output in the economy by 5%. These costs are borne by the workers with the lowest level of skills and experience who lose their jobs.

        2. There is no evidence that the costs of inflation are large. Also, policymakers may be able to lower the costs of inflation (by changing tax laws, for example) without actually lowering the inflation rate.

        3. Although, in the long run, the economy will move back to the natural rate of unemployment, there is no certainty that this will occur quickly. It may take time for the central bank to gain the trust of the people.

        4. Moreover, recessions have permanent effects. Investment falls, lowering the future capital stock. When workers become unemployed, they lose valuable job skills.

        5. A small amount of inflation may actually benefit the economy.

    C. *In the News: What is the Optimal Inflation Rate?*

        1. After the economic downturn of 2008 and 2009, economists began to wonder whether some inflation might be desirable.

2. This is an article from *The Wall Street Journal* describing these considerations.

V. Should the Government Balance Its Budget?

A. Pro: The Government Should Balance Its Budget

1. Future generations of taxpayers will be burdened by the federal government's debt. This will lower the standard of living for these future generations.

2. Budget deficits cause crowding out. Reduced national saving raises interest rates and lowers investment. A lower capital stock reduces productivity and thus leads to a smaller amount of economic growth than would have occurred in the absence of this budget deficit.

3. While it is sometimes justifiable to run budget deficits (such as in times of war or recession), recent budget deficits are not easily justified. It appears that Congress simply found it easier to borrow to pay for its spending instead of raising taxes.

B. Con: The Government Should Not Balance Its Budget

1. The problems caused by the government debt are overstated. The future generation's burden of debt is relatively small when compared with their lifetime incomes.

2. It is important that any change in government spending is examined for external effects. If education spending is cut, for example, this will likely lead to lower economic growth in the future. This will certainly not make future generations better off.

3. To some extent, parents who leave a bequest to their children can offset the effects of the budget deficits on future generations.

C. *In the News: Dealing with Debt and Deficits*

1. Is the federal government's budget situation as bad as that of the state of California?

2. This is an article from *The Wall Street Journal* discussing how the U.S. national debt-to-GDP ratio has changed over time.

VI. Should the Tax Laws Be Reformed to Encourage Saving?

A. Pro: The Tax Laws Should Be Reformed to Encourage Saving

1. The greater the amount of saving in an economy, the more funds there are available for investment. This increases productivity, raising the nation's standard of living.

2. Because people respond to incentives, changing the tax laws to make saving more attractive will raise the amount of funds saved. Current laws tax the return on saving fairly heavily. Some forms of capital income (such as corporate profits) are taxed twice: first at the corporate level and then at the stockholder level. Large bequests are also taxed, limiting the amount of incentive parents have to save for their children.

3. Tax laws are not the only government policy that discourage saving. Transfer programs such as welfare and Medicaid are reduced for those who have saved past income. College financial aid policies also are a function of income and wealth, penalizing those who have saved.

4. There are various ways to change the tax laws to encourage saving.

   a. Expand the ability of households to use tax-advantaged savings accounts such as Individual Retirement Accounts.

   b. Replace the current income tax system with a tax on consumption.

B. Con: The Tax Laws Should Not Be Reformed to Encourage Saving

   1. Increasing saving is not the only goal of tax policy. Policymakers are interested in using tax policy to redistribute income, making sure that the burden of taxation falls on those who can most afford it. Any tax change that encourages saving will favor high-income households as they are more likely to be saving in the first place.

   2. Changes in tax rates have conflicting substitution and income effects.

   3. Saving can be increased in other ways. For example, governments could lower budget deficits (or increase budget surpluses) to raise public saving.

   4. Lowering the tax on capital income lowers the revenue of the government. This may increase the budget deficit, lower public saving, and push national saving down as well.

SOLUTIONS TO TEXT PROBLEMS:

Quick Quizzes

1. Monetary and fiscal policies work with a lag. Monetary policy works with a lag because it affects spending for residential and business investment, but spending plans for such investment are often set in advance. Thus, it takes time for changes in monetary policy, working through interest rates, to affect investment. Fiscal policy works with a lag because of the long political process that governs changes in spending and taxes.

   These lags matter for the choice between active and passive policy because if the lags are long, policy must be set today for conditions far in the future, about which we can only guess. Since economic conditions may change between the time a policy is implemented and when it takes effect, policy changes may be destabilizing. Thus, long lags suggest a policy that is passive rather than active.

2. A dollar of additional government spending has a larger effect on GDP than a dollar of tax cuts. This occurs because, in general, some of the dollar tax cut will end up as saving.

3. There are many possible rules for monetary policy. One example is a rule that sets money growth at 3 percent per year. This rule might be better than discretionary policy because it prevents a political business cycle and the time inconsistency problem. It might be worse than discretionary policy because it would tie the Fed's hands when there are shocks to the economy. For example, in response to a stock-market crash, the rule would prevent the Fed from easing monetary policy, even if it saw the economy slipping into recession.

4. The benefits of reducing inflation to zero include: (1) reducing shoeleather costs; (2) reducing menu costs; (3) reducing the variability of relative prices; (4) preventing unintended

changes in tax liabilities due to nonindexation of the tax code; (5) eliminating the confusion and inconvenience resulting from a changing unit of account; and (6) preventing arbitrary redistribution of wealth associated with dollar-denominated debts. These benefits are all permanent. The costs of reducing inflation to zero are the high unemployment and low output needed to reduce inflation. According to the natural rate hypothesis, these costs are temporary.

5. Reducing the budget deficit makes future generations better off because with lower debt, future taxes will be lower. In addition, lower debt will reduce real interest rates, causing investment to increase, leading to a larger stock of capital in the future, which means higher future labor productivity and higher real wages. A fiscal policy that might improve the lives of future generations even more than reducing the budget deficit is increased spending on education, which will also increase incomes in the future.

6. Our society discourages saving in a number of ways: (1) taxing the return on interest income; (2) taxing some forms of capital twice; (3) taxing bequests; (4) having means tests for welfare and Medicaid; and (5) granting financial aid as a function of wealth. The drawback of eliminating these disincentives is that, in many cases, doing so would reduce the tax burden on wealthy taxpayers. The lost revenue to the government could require raising other taxes, which might increase the tax burden on the poor.

Questions for Review

1. The lags in the effect of monetary and fiscal policy on aggregate demand are caused by the fact that many households and firms set their spending plans in advance, so it takes time for changes in interest rates or taxes to alter the aggregate demand for goods and services. In addition, the effects of fiscal policy are slowed by the political process. As a result, it is more difficult to engage in activist stabilization policy, because the economy will not respond immediately to policy changes.

2. According to traditional Keynesian analysis, a tax cut has a smaller effect than an equal rise in government spending because some of the tax cut may be saved rather than spent. However, a tax cut may also boost aggregate supply leading to a larger impact on output than a rise in government spending.

3. A central banker might be motivated to cause a political business cycle by trying to influence the outcome of elections. A central banker who is sympathetic to the incumbent knows that if the economy is doing well at election time, the incumbent is likely to be reelected. So the central banker could stimulate the economy before the election. To prevent this, it might be desirable to have monetary policy set by rules rather than discretion.

4. Credibility might affect the cost of reducing inflation because it influences how quickly the short-run Phillips curve adjusts. If the Fed announces a credible plan to reduce inflation, the short-run Phillips curve will shift down quickly and the cost of disinflation will be low. But if the plan is not credible, people will not adjust their expectations of inflation, the short-run Phillips curve will not shift down quickly, and the cost of disinflation will be high.

5. Some economists are against a target of zero inflation because they believe the costs of reaching zero inflation are large and the benefits are small.

6. Two ways in which a government budget deficit hurts a future worker are: (1) taxes on future workers are higher to pay off the government debt; and (2) because of crowding out, budget deficits lead to a reduction in the economy's capital stock, so future workers have lower incomes.

7. Two situations in which a budget deficit is justifiable are: (1) in wartime, so tax rates will not have to be increased so much that they lead to large deadweight losses; and (2) during a temporary downturn in economic activity, because balancing the budget would force the government to increase taxes and cut spending, making the downturn even worse.

8. An example of how the government might hurt young generations while reducing the government debt they inherit occurs if the government reduces spending on education. The government debt will be smaller, so future generations will pay less in taxes. But they will also be less educated, so they will have less human capital and thus have lower incomes. Future generations might be worse off in this case.

9. The government can run a budget deficit forever because population and productivity continuously increase. Thus the economy's capacity to pay off its debt grows over time. As long as the government debt grows slower than the economy's income, government deficits can continue forever.

10. Income from capital is taxed twice in the case of dividends on corporate stock. The income is taxed once by the corporate income tax and a second time by the individual income tax on dividend income.

11. Examples, other than tax policy, of how our society discourages saving include: (1) the fact that some government benefits, such as welfare and Medicaid, are means-tested, implying that people who save get reduced benefits; and (2) the fact that colleges and universities grant financial aid inversely to the wealth of students and their families, so people who save get a smaller amount of financial aid.

12. Tax incentives to raise saving may have the adverse effect of raising the government budget deficit, which reduces public saving. Thus, national saving may not increase even though private saving rises.

Problems and Applications

1. a. Figure 1 illustrates the short-run effect of a fall in aggregate demand. The economy starts at point A on aggregate-demand curve AD_1 and short-run aggregate-supply curve $SRAS_1$. The decline in aggregate demand shifts the aggregate-demand curve from AD_1 to AD_2 and the economy moves to point B. Total output falls from Y_1 to Y_2, so income and employment fall as well.

   b. With no policy changes, the economy restores itself gradually over time. The recession induces declines in wages, so the cost of production declines, and the short-run aggregate-supply curve shifts down to $SRAS_2$. The economy ends up at point C, with a lower price level, but with output back at Y_1. However, this process may take years to complete.

   c. If policymakers are passive, the economy restores itself, but very slowly. If policymakers shift aggregate demand to the right, they can get the economy back to long-run equilibrium much more quickly. However, due to lags and imperfect information, a policy to increase aggregate demand may be destabilizing.

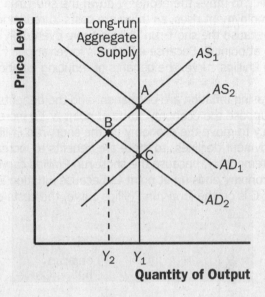

Figure 1

2. It is difficult for policymakers to choose the appropriate strength of their actions because of lags between when policy is changed and when it affects aggregate demand, as well as the difficulty in forecasting the economy's future condition. It is also difficult to anticipate how sensitive consumers and firms will be to the changes in policy.

3. a. If investors believe that capital taxes will remain low, then a reduction in capital taxes leads to increased investment.

    b. After the increase in investment has occurred, the government has an incentive to renege on its policy because it can get more tax revenue by increasing taxes on the higher income from the larger capital stock.

    c. Given the government's obvious incentive to renege on its promise, firms will be reluctant to increase investment when the government reduces tax rates. The government can increase the credibility of its tax change by somehow committing to low future tax rates. For example, it could write a law that guarantees low future tax rates for all capital income from investments made within the next year, or write a law penalizing itself if it raises future taxes.

    d. This situation is similar to the time-inconsistency problem facing monetary policymakers because the government's incentives change over time. In both cases, the policymaker has an incentive to tell people one thing, then to do another once people have made an economic decision. For example, in the case of monetary policy, policymakers could announce an intention to lower inflation (so firms and workers will enter labor contracts with lower nominal wages), and policymakers could increase inflation to reduce real wages and stimulate the economy.

4. Issues about whether the costs of inflation are large or small are positive statements, as is the question about the size of the costs of reducing inflation. But the question of whether the Fed should reduce inflation to zero is a normative question.

5. The benefits of reducing inflation are permanent and the costs are temporary. Figure 2 illustrates this. The economy starts at point A. To reduce inflation, the Fed uses contractionary policy to move the economy down the short-run Phillips curve $SRPC_1$. Inflation declines and unemployment rises, so there are costs to reducing inflation. But the costs are only temporary, because the short-run Phillips curve eventually shifts down to $SRPC_2$, and the economy ends up at point B. Because inflation is lower at point B than at point A, and point B is on the long-run Phillips curve, the benefits of reducing inflation are permanent.

The costs of increasing inflation are permanent and the benefits are temporary for similar reasons. Again, suppose the economy starts at point A. To increase inflation, the Fed uses expansionary policy to move the economy up the short-run Phillips curve $SRPC_1$. Inflation rises and unemployment declines, so there are benefits to increasing inflation. But the benefits are only temporary, because the short-run Phillips curve eventually shifts up to $SRPC_3$, and the economy ends up at point C. Because inflation is higher at point C than at point A, and point C is on the long-run Phillips curve, the costs of increasing inflation are permanent.

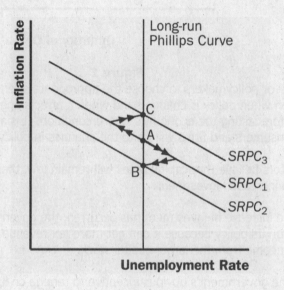

Figure 2

6. If the budget deficit is 12% of GDP and nominal GDP is rising 5% each year, the ratio of government debt to GDP will rise until it hits a fairly high level. (That level turns out to be debt/income = 12/5, because at that point, a deficit that is 12% of GDP with GDP growing 5% maintains the debt/income ratio at exactly 12/5. To be sustainable, debt and GDP must grow at the same rate, 5% each year. If the deficit is 12% of GDP, which is growing 5% each year, the ratio of debt to GDP must be 12/5, so that the deficit can be both 12% of GDP and maintain a constant ratio of debt to GDP.) Such a high debt level is likely to require a big tax increase on future generations. To keep future generations from having to pay such high taxes, you could increase your savings today and leave a bequest to them.

7. a. An increase in the budget deficit redistributes income from young to old, because future generations will have to pay higher taxes and will have a lower capital stock.

   b. More generous subsidies for education loans redistribute income from old to young, because future generations benefit from having higher human capital.

c. Greater investments in highways and bridges redistribute income from old to young, because future generations benefit from having a higher level of public capital than otherwise.

d. An increase in Social Security benefits redistributes income from young to old, because current workers fund the benefits of those retired.

8. In a recession, the government can use a budget deficit to increase aggregate demand, thus boosting income and output. But in the long run, budget deficits raise interest rates, reducing investment, thus leading to a lower capital stock and reduced future income. An ideal fiscal policy would be one that allows budget deficits in the short run to combat recessions, but requires that the budget be balanced over time so that it does not have a detrimental effect on future income.

9. The fundamental trade-off that society faces if it chooses to save more is that it will have to reduce its consumption. Thus, society can consume less today and save more if it wants higher future income and consumption. The choice is really one of consumption today versus consumption in the future. The government can increase national saving by revising tax laws or by reducing its budget deficit.

10. a. A reduction in the tax rate on income from saving would most directly benefit wealthy people who have a greater amount of capital income. The rise in the tax rate on workers would harm individuals whose incomes come mainly from labor earnings.

b. The increased incentive to save would reduce the interest rate, thus increasing investment, so the capital stock would be larger. As capital per worker rises, productivity would increase, as well as the real wage paid to workers.

c. Thus, in the long run, everyone, not just the wealthy, can benefit from reducing the tax rate on income from savings. However, these benefits would be reduced by the level of taxes paid on earnings.

www.cengage.com/economics/mankiw

SOUTH-WESTERN
CENGAGE Learning™

For your course and learning solutions, visit **www.cengage.com**
Purchase any of our products at your local college store or at our
preferred online store **www.cengagebrain.com**

ISBN-13: 978-0-538-46832-9
ISBN-10: 0-538-46832-7

90000

9 780538 468329

www.cengage.com/economics/mankiw

ISBN-13: 978-0-538-46832-9
ISBN-10: 0-538-46832-7

90000

9 780538 468329